THE SOUND OF WINGS

Amelia's favorite photograph of herself, c. 1930-31.

the SOUND of WINGS

THE LIFE OF AMELIA EARHART

MARY S. LOVELL

St. Martin's Press New York

Cover photo: Amelia as she appeared on her 1923 pilot's license issued by the Federation Aeronautique Internationale and National Aeronautics Association of U.S.A., Inc.

First published in Great Britain by Century Hutchinson Ltd.

Endpaper map by Hadel Line Art
Internal maps by Rodney Paul
Design by Guenet Abraham

Library of Congress Cataloging-in-Publication Data

Lovell, Mary S.
    The sound of wings : the biography of Amelia Earhart / Mary S. Lovell.
        p. cm.
    ISBN 0-312-03431-8
    1. Earhart, Amelia, 1897–1937. 2. Air pilots—United States—Biography. I. Title.
TL540.E3L68 1989
629.13′092—dc20   89-34935
[B]   CIP

First Edition
10 9 8 7 6 5 4 3 2 1

Note to the Reader

The author has chosen to retain the original spellings of words in the extracted material. Often "[sic]" will appear after these apparent errors in grammar or spelling; other times they are left as is without "[sic]," to convey intentional humor or the flavor of the writer's style.

This book is dedicated to the memory of
John A. Belcher

"He was a verray parfit gentil knight"
—*Chaucer's* Canterbury Tales

By the same author:

A Hunting Pageant
Straight On Till Morning: The Biography of Beryl Markham

Courage

Courage is the price that Life exacts for granting peace,
The soul that knows it not, knows no release
From little things;
Knows not the livid loneliness of fear,
Nor mountain heights where bitter joy can hear
The sound of wings.

How can Life grant us boon of living, compensate
For dull grey ugliness and pregnant hate
Unless we dare
The soul's dominion? Each time we make a choice, we pay
With courage to behold the restless day,
And count it fair.

—*Amelia Earhart, 1927. "Courage" appeared in
Marion Perkins's "Who Is Amelia Earhart?"
Survey magazine, July 1, 1928, p. 60*

Contents

Acknowledgments

Many organizations provided me with access to collections of documents, materials, and facilities with unfailing patience:

American Heritage Center, University of Wyoming (Emmett D. Chisum). Collection: Papers of Eugene Vidal.

Atchison County Library, Atchison, Kansas. Collection: Amelia Earhart.

Atchison Museum, Atchison, Kansas (Father Angelus and his team). Collection: Amelia Earhart.

British Library, Newspaper Collection, Colindale, London, England.

British Library, Reading Room, London, England.

Butler Library, and Oral History Research Office, Columbia University, New York, New York. Aviation tapes.

The Carnegie Library, Pittsburgh, Pennsylvania (Mrs. Ann Lloyd). Phipps family records.

Amelia Earhart's Home and Museum, Atchison, Kansas.

International Women's Air and Space Museum, Centerville, Ohio. (Ms. Steadman). Amelia Earhart files.

Library of Congress, Map Room, Madison Building, Washington, D.C. (Tom De Claire). Charts of Howland Island and Pacific Ocean, before and after *Itasca* survey of 1936.

National Archives and Record Service, Washington, D.C. (Richard Van Dernhoff, Military Records): Record Group 80 (file A21–5) and M1067 (roll 48) room 400.

Ninety-Nines Resource Center, Oklahoma (Loretta Gragg and Virginia Oualline). Collection: Amelia Earhart.

Public Record Office, Kew, England. File: AVIA2–1082 Amelia Earhart.

Purdue University, Lafayette, Indiana, Special Collections Library (Ms. Helen Q. Schroyer), Publishing Department (Mr. Bob Topping).

Franklin D. Roosevelt Library (Raymond Teichman), Hyde Park, New York.

Royal Geographical Society, London, England (Mr. Jeremy Smith—Map Room).

Salisbury Library, Salisbury, Wiltshire, England.

Arthur and Elizabeth Schlesinger Library, Radcliffe College, Cambridge, Massachusetts. Collections: Amy Otis Earhart; Muriel Morrissey; Amelia Earhart. Refs: 83–M69; A129; 78/M147.

Seaver Center for Western History Research, Natural History Museum of Los Angeles County, Los Angeles, California (Janet Evenden). Amelia Earhart Collection 1061.

Smithsonian Institution, National Air and Space Museum Library, Washington, D.C. File: F0171300.

University of California at Los Angeles, Library and Special Collections. Collection: Elizabeth Hyatt Gregory.

University of California at Santa Barbara, Library and Special Collections.

University of California at Berkeley, Library and Special Collections.

U.S. Naval Archives, Navy Yard, Bldg. 210, Washington, D.C. (Janice Beatty, Paula Murphy; reference staff in the Naval history department). Records held on seven reels of microfilm: NRS246 A–G.

Wellesley College, Wellesley, Massachusetts (Ms. Jean Berry). Women's Union and student records; Dorothy Binney Putnam.

I would like to make it very clear that at no time did I meet any resistance to my researches, and everyone with whom I met or spoke, in what might be called "official" circles in the United States, was most helpful.

The amount of research material available on the subject of Amelia's disappearance is enormous, amounting to many thousands of original contemporary documents, much of which is on microfilm. In addition, much material of a more personal nature exists in private collections. There is, inevitably, duplication; and where I have attributed a source in the book, it may be that I have accessed that particular document in other collections elsewhere as well.

It would be impossible to produce a work of this scope without the assistance and cooperation of a great number of people, and so I wish to

Acknowledgments

thank the following: Richard Sanders Allen; Jean-Marie Asp; Russell E. Belous; Albert Bresnik; Montgomery R. Budd; Sally Putnam Chapman; James LeRoy Crowell; Vera Dunrud; Peggy Erasmus; Jill Fitzhugh; Les George; Lester E. Hopper; Elspeth Huxley; Shirley Johansen; Jerome Lawrence; Robert E. Lee; Margaret Lewis; Elgen and Marie Long; Cliff Lovell; Graeme and Shari Lovell; Dorice McKelvy; Sandy MacKenzie; Greg Mantz; Muriel Earhart Morrissey; Claudia Oakes; Helen Ogston; Carol Osborne; David Putnam; George Palmer and Marie Putnam; Helen B. Schleman; Helen Q. Schroyer; Marion Sharpe; Doris Smart; Mrs. Kit Smith; Richard K. Smith; Laura Stickney; Peter Stevenson; R. B. Stewart; Elinor Smith Sullivan; Ann Cain Tibbets; Robert W. Topping; Cynthia Putnam Trefelner; Bobbi Trout; Gore Vidal; John Underwood.

Although I have mentioned the various members of the Putnam family by name, I should like to thank them collectively for their kindness to me, their marvelous cooperation in allowing me to see documents that for so long had been considered very personal, and last—but not least—for their hospitality. George Putnam's fourth wife—his widow, Peg—was an unfailing source of information, and for a while it seemed that every mail brought some new anecdote, photograph, or document.

While most of Amelia and George's story lies in the United States, both in archives and in the minds of their many connections, there is also a British connection, due to Amelia's two record-breaking flights across the Atlantic. One of my last research tasks was a visit to Burry Port in South Wales, where Amelia and her two male companions landed in June 1928. There I met Les George, a restaurateur, who has made a point of keeping Amelia's name alive in the small town with The Amelia Dining Room and The Friendship Bar. On the walls are newspaper cuttings, photographs, and paintings of the *Friendship*'s landing; menu cards and coasters are also dedicated to the story. Mr. George kindly provided audiotapes of townspeople who actually witnessed the landing over sixty years ago, and he has also provided other memorabilia that have proved helpful.

I wish to thank Katy Belcher, who undertook two lengthy research trips with me to the United States, and in so doing halved the time required to delve through the masses of documentation held in various collections there; and Susan Rabiner, who was responsible for reawakening my interest in the subject.

My editors, Tony Whittome and Barbara Anderson, have been a source of enormous help, especially during the final stages of the book, and I am most grateful for their interest and always constructive advice.

Finally, a very special thanks to G.A.H.W., without whose help and encouragement this book would probably have been finished in half the time.

PHOTOGRAPHIC ACKNOWLEDGMENTS

I also wish to thank all those who kindly provided photographs during the course of my research. I regret that only a small number of them can be reproduced here. As with original documents, many photographs are duplicated in various collections and in some cases several people have provided me with the same picture. Those that are featured in this book are used with appropriate permission from the following:

Purdue University: plates 2, 3, 4, 8, 10, 32, 34, 36, 40, 42, 43, 45, 50, 51, 53, 61, 62, 65, 66, 68

Mrs. Margaret Lewis: frontispiece, plates 6, 9, 15, 16, 17, 18, 19, 28, 31, 35, 37, 41, 71, 72, 73

Mrs. Margaret Lewis (courtesy Seaver Center for Western History Research): plates 7, 22, 23, 24, 25, 26, 27, 29, 30, 33, 38, 39, 44, 46, 48, 49, 54, 63, 64, 67

James Crowell: plates 11, 12, 13, 14

Albert Bresnik: plates 57, 60, 70

Albert Bresnik (courtesy Mrs. Margaret Lewis): plates 55, 56, 59

BBC Hulton Picture Library: plate 20

Cap Palmer: plate 47

Laura Stickney: plate 52

Geoffrey A. H. Watts: plate 21

Introduction

It is now more than fifty years since Amelia Earhart disappeared while attempting to be the first woman to fly around the world. In 1928, she had been the first woman to fly across the Atlantic; four years later, she became the first woman to fly it solo at a time when only one other person—Charles Lindbergh—had done so. Subsequently, she performed any number of aviation "firsts," many of which were also "first woman" records.

What is it about Amelia Earhart that has kept her name alive? Charles Lindbergh achieved a similar lasting fame, but most of the other early aviators have—for the most part—been forgotten by all except aviation enthusiasts.

Amelia's achievements were remarkable, but some of her reputation rests on the outstanding management skills of her husband, George Palmer Putnam. Putnam was a publicist of such ability that during Amelia's life her name received almost constant media exposure. Indeed, my research indicates that it was mainly due to Putnam's brilliant management of the name Amelia Earhart that she is still remembered.

Much has already been written about Amelia Earhart. She wrote three books herself, mainly about her flying exploits. Her husband followed these with a biography shortly after her presumed death in 1937, and any number of books have been written since, theorizing on what might have happened to Amelia when her plane failed to arrive at its destination on a small island in the Pacific Ocean. Why the abiding interest?

I began to research Amelia's story in 1962, not for a book but out of personal curiosity. I was then (honorary) secretary to the Los Angeles Chapter of the Antique Airplane Association, and in this connection I met the famous Hollywood stunt pilot Paul Mantz. It was common knowledge that Paul had been closely involved with Amelia in her later record-breaking flights. The aviation expert on Amelia's team, Mantz had been her copilot when she took part in the National Air Races, and was also a business partner in a California flying school. What Paul told me about the circumstances surrounding Amelia's departure on her world-circling final flight precipitated my initial interest in her.

Amelia had been very much on Paul's mind at that time, for he had recently been interviewed by CBS journalist Fred Goerner. Goerner believed that she had been on a spy mission for the United States government, using the round-the-world flight as a cover. Further, he believed that she had made a forced landing near a Japanese-mandated island in the Pacific, had been captured, and died in captivity.

Paul did not believe that Amelia had been a spy, but what he told me—and others—seemed equally interesting: that Amelia's plane was not ready when she took off on that fatal flight; that Paul anticipated at least another two days' work. He was shocked, he said, to hear that she had gone without even saying goodbye to him. Later, his inquiries led him to believe that George Putnam had pressured Amelia into leaving early because he had organized a huge civic welcome for her return to Los Angeles, timed for July 4. If she delayed any longer, then, allowing for contingency delays for weather conditions, spare parts, or engineering faults, she could not make it back in time.

Paul also claimed that Putnam used Amelia and her reputation, implying that she was driven to exhaustion because of George's manipulative methods.

This seemed an interesting and plausible story from a man I admired and respected, and it never occurred to me to doubt it or consider that it was simply one side of the story. I had no reason, either, to suspect that after Amelia's disappearance, Paul Mantz and George Putnam had become enemies over a matter concerning her estate. So when, in early 1987, I started researching Amelia Earhart full-time for a biography under contract with a publisher, I was content to accept the story that George Putnam had used Amelia for his own ends. This has been written about by so many Earhart researchers that I had no cause to question its authenticity.

As my research progressed, however, I realized that not only was George Putnam a fascinating person in his own right but also that if it had not been for him, Amelia would undoubtedly have dropped out of public awareness. Women fliers such as Ruth Law, Louise Thaden, Ruth Elder, Elinor Smith, Ruth Nichols, Katherine Stinson, Bobbi Trout, and

Introduction

Phoebe Omlie are remembered with respect by those interested in American civil aviation, but I suspect few others would recognize their names. Yet all these women were contemporaries of Amelia and all had to their credit great "firsts" in aviation that at the time made headline news. Without George, Amelia probably never would have performed many of her record-breaking feats, and even if she had, it is doubtful that this alone would have been sufficient to keep her name alive for fifty years.

What George did for Amelia's career was threefold. Firstly, he inspired and encouraged her; secondly, he worked on her behalf to publicize her name and reputation, creating openings for a financially viable career in aviation; thirdly, he introduced her to a wide circle of powerful people and obtained the necessary financial backing for her record attempts. Arguably, without this help, Amelia would never have made that final flight with its tragic outcome (for the sponsorship would not have been available to support the venture except to someone of public stature beyond the ordinary); and so Amelia might have lived to a ripe old age.

George himself said of Amelia after her death that "if there had been no George Putnam to lend a hand here and there, some way would have appeared by which the individuality which was A.E. would have secured its freedom to flower, and the wings with which to soar to fame." However, my opinion is that without George Putnam, my generation would have not heard of the name Amelia Earhart outside of aviation circles.

Then, too, there was the accusation that George "used" Amelia and that she recognized and resented George's manipulations of her time and reputation. I found no evidence to support this; indeed, quite the reverse was true. There was love between George and Amelia. Those closest to them were aware of it and spoke about it. Surviving correspondence contains loving endearments, and it is necessary only to watch the couple together on old newsreel footage to see the warmth and comfortable rapport that existed between them. If the couple had disagreements, they were no more than the normal everyday ones that exist in any healthy relationship, particularly when the two people involved also work together and have strong personalities.

So this story, which began as a biography of Amelia, has become the story of Amelia and George, and their relationship is the real core of the book. I have also covered the early part of their lives, before they met, so that their characters could be seen developing.

In Amelia's case, it has been necessary to cover ground that has already been broken, some of it many times. I have tried to weed out the myths and highlight what I consider to be the essential parts of her story. This book does not include all my research—one could fill two volumes with anecdotes and stories, but there is not always evidence to prove that they are anything more than the perpetuation of legend.

Fortunately, I have uncovered new information that may illustrate some previously unknown facts of Amelia's character and throughout my work, I have been aware of Amelia's calm, efficient, and, above all, humorous spirit. It is extremely difficult not to like Amelia.

I do not subscribe, however, to the "Saint Amelia" concept that I often encountered. Amelia, I feel, would have hooted derisively at this canonization. She could be waspish, intolerant, and ill-humored, just like any of us. Stress often lay at the root of this.

As for George Putnam, very little has been previously published about him, except what he chose to tell in his memoir, *Wide Margins*. This is a most frustrating book because it consists largely of portraits of the interesting people he met in his career. As a close friend summed up, "I told him it was the only autobiography I'd ever read that was about *other* people!" And this is the man who has been accused of gross self-aggrandizement. People either loved or loathed George Putnam, and there is still no middle ground. I find him altogether fascinating, with an agile mind and a tremendous drive that also drove and inspired others. However, he could not tolerate fools, bores, or laziness and he did not bother to hide his intolerance.

A great injustice has been done to George, though it is fair to say that he was not always entirely blameless. He had an explosive temper and those who suffered the effects of his anger found it hard to forgive him. He had the killer instinct in business; he was savage to anyone who stood between him and success and this earned him many enemies.

Jim Crowell was a student in Bend, Oregon, in 1965, when he came across part of George's story while searching for the subject for a thesis. George had been editor of the local Bend paper before the First World War, as well as being an all-round colorful character in Bend folklore. I had nearly finished my research when I was put in touch with Mr. Crowell by members of the Putnam family, and his thesis material, including photographs, which he has kindly allowed me to include here, has been enormously helpful.

Work on this book has brought me into contact with notable people in the world of aviation whom I had greatly admired for many years but never expected to meet. Elinor Smith and Bobbi Trout, for example, both still live life to the full and are fascinating personalities. In addition, there was a visit to Muriel Morrissey, Amelia's sister, which really made me feel close to my subject.

Over eighty when I met her in 1987, Muriel was fine-boned and stooped slightly. On the walls of her West Medford, Massachusetts, apartment are photographs and paintings of Amelia, and there are other memorabilia dotted around on tables and in cupboards. When Muriel serves tea, it is always done formally from an antique tea service of paper-thin china. She does not allow the arthritis in her hands to prevent her pouring the tea with careful precision, handing over the milk jug and sugar bowl in the way most easy for her guest to take.

Apart from the pleasure of meeting Mrs. Morrissey and interviewing her about Amelia, I gained a good impression of the upbringing the two Earhart girls had received; for here was a lady in the true sense. Muriel's life has not always been an easy one, but she has retained an innate grace and soft-spoken charm; and I suppose had Amelia lived, she would have been similar in many ways.

Many of my informants still have sharp memories of George and Amelia. Others have only the haziest of recollections: "You know, all this was a *very* long time ago, my dear. . . ." The memories and recollections, the evidence (one might say), differ enormously and so I have tried to bring all shades of opinion into this book in an attempt to paint my portraits of Amelia and George as faithfully as possible.

This book is a biography. It does not set out to add yet another theory to the enduring mystery of "Whatever happened to Amelia Earhart?" All the known facts are covered in the appropriate chapters and I hope readers will use them to draw their own conclusions about the most likely explanation. For those not familiar with the various theories, knowledge of which might explain why I have sometimes overstressed certain pieces of information, I have included the best-known ones in Appendix C, beginning on page 354. Some theories rely on outright sensationalism, others on detailed detective work based on a snippet of information that caught the attention of the researcher. In some, one can see the author almost unconsciously manipulating what is known to match and prove a theory. And undoubtedly, there will be yet more theories to come, even if Amelia's plane is eventually located.

My editors feel that I should explain the technical terms of aviation such as *ground loop* and *stall speed.* Since to explain these within the text would be tedious to the reader and patronizing to anyone involved in aviation, I have included a glossary at the end of the book (page 364).

Finally, there are several teams of people still working avidly to discover what happened to Amelia's plane on that July day in 1937—most notably Marie and Elgen Long of California. I visited this charming couple in 1988—purely coincidentally on the anniversary of the day Amelia disappeared—and since then we have been in contact by telephone and letters. Their research, conducted over nearly twenty years, is staggeringly detailed and their objective is to locate Amelia's airplane, which they believe lies some thirty-five miles west of Howland Island in the Pacific Ocean. If it is *possible* for Amelia's plane to be found by research and deduction, I believe they will find it.

Mary S. Lovell
Lyndhurst, Hampshire
April 1989

Prologue

It was June 19, 1928. In the city of Southampton, England, a crowd of several thousand people had gathered on the banks of the River Itchen at its broad mouth into Southampton Water. Despite the unseasonable chill in the damp, gray day, there was an expectant gaiety in the air.

Shortly after 1 P.M., the sound of aircraft engines was heard overhead. Nothing could be seen at first because a squall obscured everything above a few hundred feet. All eyes searched the sky and at last the misty shape of an orange airplane with floats was spotted, escorted by one of the huge Imperial Airways flying boats. There was spasmodic cheering as the float-plane settled on the choppy surface of the water. On the plane's side was the name *Friendship*, in large black letters.

Almost as soon as the engines were switched off, a door in the side of the plane opened and a young woman and two men appeared. One of the men dropped down onto a pontoon and casually lit a cigarette while he waited for a boat to provide a tow. Within minutes, two ropes had been attached to the airplane and the *Friendship* was on its way to the Imperial Airways landing stage, while its former occupants, seated in a launch, were headed toward the waiting crowd on shore. Crew and workmen lining the decks of ships in the busy port cheered, clapped, and whistled as the launch passed by. Ship's sirens and hooters provided a cacophony of noise.[1]

The aviators had not come far that day—only from Burry Port in South Wales, a flight of some two hours. Once on land, the young woman was hugged with proprietary enthusiasm by a plump matron, although it was their first meeting. "Well done, my girl!" Mrs. Amy Guest said roundly. The crowd cheered wildly and some of the men flung their hats into the air.

It was cold for June, a favorite trick of English weather. Southampton's mayor, Mrs. Louise M. Foster-Welsh, headed the welcoming committee, and she wisely wore a warm suit with a fur collar under her impressive chain of office.[2] The young woman wore an odd-looking fur-lined flying suit that was too large by several sizes. Her hair was covered by a leather helmet. Her face was thin, her expression one of eager intelligence, and she had a ready boyish grin, but her eyes were ringed with dark smudges defining obvious physical fatigue.

The two men accompanying the young woman seemed uncertain of their part in the reception and hung about awkwardly on the fringe of the handshaking and speech-making center of the crowd. Reporters and cameramen ignored them. It was clearly the young woman that the crowd had come to see, for, as the mayor was shortly to announce, this young woman had done something no other woman had yet done. "She is the first woman who can say 'I have crossed the Ocean by air. . . . ' "[3]

The two men were Wilmer "Bill" Stultz, the pilot of the plane, and Louis "Slim" Gordon, mechanic. The young woman was Amelia Earhart. She was merely a passenger, but she had been the sole reason for the flight of the *Friendship* on June 17–18, 1928, from the United States of America to Britain. As a stand-in for Amy Guest (who had wanted to make the flight herself but had yielded to shocked opposition from her family), Amelia had jumped onto the front page of every newspaper in the world and instantly achieved the status of heroine.

Southampton had been the original destination for the transatlantic flight, but after the long crossing, the fliers had been uncertain of their exact destination and had landed in Burry Port, thinking they were in Ireland. There was not enough fuel left in the plane for them to take off again. After an overnight rest and refueling, they had flown to Southampton to enable the planned reception to take place.

Amelia was showered with flowers and tributes. She tried hard to ensure that the two men appeared in the hundreds of photographs taken of her. She insisted that all technical credit for the flight be directed at Stultz and Gordon. In this alone, she was largely ignored. These were the days when heroism came in a masculine form. Only a year earlier, Charles Lindbergh had stormed to international fame by virtue of his solo flight across the Atlantic. To have a *woman* transatlantic flier was a treat for the press and a gift for copywriters, and they made the most of it.

Over the next few days, reporters examined Amelia's history and wrote thousands of yards of column inches about her. If fact was not available, invention took over. Legends, some of them completely untrue, that were to follow her for the rest of her life—and long after—were spun.

Prologue

Back in the United States, the manager of the project, George Putnam, who had recruited Amelia for the great adventure, was busily drafting the early chapters of an "autobiographical" version of Amelia's story so that it could be ready for publication shortly after her return to the States. Despite the fact that Amelia was already engaged to be married, and despite his own married state, Putnam had already made advances to the young woman whom he saw as a potential celebrity. Amelia, in turn, was intrigued by Putnam. She had not liked him at first but thought him such an intelligent man that she was soon fascinated.

Putnam exuded confidence, power, and success. Although his background was a cultured one, he was an entrepreneur and a wheeler-dealer by nature so that the aura he unintentionally created around himself was one of excitement. Well over six feet in height and with matinee-idol looks, he was forty years of age, looked younger, and was at the peak of his career in publishing. Behind him lay enough adventure to fill two lifetimes.

"When I first met Mr. Putnam," Amelia Earhart was fond of saying, "I just didn't like him . . . [he] seemed brusque."[4] George Putnam would explain, "When she called at my office [and] I was busy, she had to cool her heels—and didn't like it much."[5]

Notwithstanding this uneasy start to their relationship, the two developed a respect and liking for each other that eventually deepened into love. More unusually for the times, they shared a working relationship that was fulfilling and exciting to them both. Many people, writing about Amelia Earhart, have denigrated George Putnam's role in her life, claiming that he "used" her fame and drove her too hard. In fact, Amelia was lucky that she had met the one man who could hold her respect and to whom she could be married without feeling she was caged by her marital vows.

At their first meeting, Amelia was thirty years old, tall and slim, with her fair, curly hair cut short—not in a fashionable bob but in a style more suited to today than to 1928. "Unruly," said some; "windswept" said others. Her face reflected a natural intelligence and quiet humor lurked in her gray eyes. She was attractive and poised, but there was a hint of anxiety about her demeanor, for she knew that if she could persuade George Putnam she was the woman for his project she would be embarking upon the greatest adventure of her life so far.

BOOK ONE:

AMELIA MARY EARHART

Women must try to do things as men have tried.
When they fail, their failure must be but a challenge
to others.

— *Amelia Earhart to George Putnam,
January 8, 1935, Seaver Center for Western
History Research, Natural History Museum of
Los Angeles County, California*

C h a p t e r   O n e

1 8 9 7

The small town of Atchison, Kansas, seems an unlikely birthplace for a woman whose name, more than fifty years after her death, remains synonymous with adventure, heroism, and posthumous mystery. Atchison is a typical midwestern town, built in the 1860s literally in the heart of America and situated on the Missouri River. The town owed its survival to the fact that for the huge wagon trains on the trek westward, it was a good place to cross the great river, and for a while Atchison was the last outpost of civilization before the Wild West.

And yet is it so unlikely? Is there a more American heroine than Amelia Earhart? Amelia had that particular brand of questing courage that typi-fied American settlers in the century in which she was born. Although her early years were spent in the safe and sheltered communities of Atchison and nearby Kansas City, almost every adult with whom she came in contact was, to some degree, a pioneer. Perhaps the drive to succeed that she displayed as an adult germinated in these early relationships, fostered by the town itself.

Her distant ancestors were European and although Amelia grew up to be more appreciative of her maternal connections, the Earhart family's lineage was impressive, too, with one strand stretching back to Mariah Josephs, a Frenchwoman thought to be a niece of King Louis XV. Mariah is said to have fallen in love with a German officer, Anthony Altman. The pair were married against the wishes of the king and both subsequently were disinherited by their respective families. To avoid magisterial wrath, the newlyweds fled to America and settled in Pennsylvania.[1]

The Altmans had one son, Philip, who with his wife, Louisa, moved to Indiana County, Pennsylvania, in 1789.

. . . when the country was very new and before the Indians had all left the county . . . at one time provisions became so scarce that . . . the family had to cook greens for their daily food for some time, and to insure getting safe plants for their greens, they followed the cows to learn of them the kind of plants that could be used safely. Besides the fear of Indians [who were encamped on the Altman's 102-acre farm] venomous snakes were very numerous, as were the copperhead and rattlesnake.[2]

It must have been very different from life in the French court. Along with the other women, Louisa made all the clothing for their family of nine children—from clipping the sheep, to spinning and weaving the wool, to making up the clothes. Indeed, the lot of women was so hard that in 1897, on reading about their daily life, a descendant inquired of the author of the account, "What did the men do?"[3] The men did plenty, for the country was rolling and hilly, overgrown with brush and timber. Clearing the land was a backbreaking and endless task and besides that, homes had to be built, families kept fed, and farms established.

It was Philip Altman's daughter Catherine who married into the Earhart family in 1813, when she took David Earhart as her husband. The third son of this union (there were nine sons and two daughters) was David Earhart, "a modest and happy man" who became a preacher in the Evangelical Lutheran Church. In 1841, the Reverend David Earhart married Mary Wells Patton, whose family was of English descent through Colonel James Wells of Revolutionary War fame. The Earharts had twelve children, three of whom died of scarlet fever and one who was killed in her cradle when a bolt of lightning shot through an open window. It was their son Edwin Stanton Earhart who was to become the father of Amelia.[4]

In an autobiographical memoir, the Reverend David Earhart recalled:

Kansas was opened for settlement in 1854. But owing to a border ruffian conflict [and] the proslavery and antislavery parties, settlement and improvements in the country were much retarded till 1857. In 1860, the year I moved to Kansas, there was such a severe drought [there] that the farmers' crops almost entirely failed. The people of Kansas had to be assisted by other States to secure the means of a livelihood. The following year, the civil war broke out. . . .

The country being new and largely settled by poor people, and having had [for] two or three years a border war, a year's drought, and then the civil war, it was a hard time to gather and organize churches. Not twenty members were in organized Lutheran churches in Kansas

when I moved there in 1860. A few years thereafter several plagues
of grasshoppers ravaged the country. During the drought in 1860 I
received about $100 . . . and during 1861 and 1862 $150 a year, from
the Home Missionary Society. By teaching school and other secular
labors I managed to live and rear a large family. . . .⁵

For thirteen years, Reverend Earhart preached twice "nearly every Sunday in churches that were anything up to sixty miles from his home." One,
"though fifty miles from the place I lived, I visited and preached [in] for
several years, riding mostly on horseback or sulky every four weeks, summer and winter, never failing for heat or cold."⁶ As regent of the state
agricultural college for six years, Reverend Earhart frequently had to make
the one-hundred-mile journey to that establishment before the Kansas
Pacific Railroad was built.

Such was the stuff of the Earharts, Amelia's paternal relations.

On the maternal side, the family history has been traced back to
England in 1581, when John Otis was born in Barnstaple, Devon. He
sailed for America in 1635 with his fifteen-year-old son, also named John,
and drew house lots in the first division of land at Hingham, Massachusetts. The Otis descendants produced leading scholars, politicians, law-
yers, and physicians. One married into the family from which Abraham
Lincoln descended. Various family members served with distinction in
the Revolutionary and Civil wars.

Amelia's grandfather, Alfred Gideon Otis, was a noted lawyer and,
later, judge. Born in 1827, after the age of nine he stayed with his
grandparents in New York, while his young parents traveled west to the
new state of Michigan and settled there. Alfred was succeeded by ten
more children, but it was not until he was fourteen that he joined his
parents. Then, as the eldest son, he threw in his lot as a farmer, pursuing
classical studies in Greek and Latin each evening after the day's work was
done. At the age of twenty-two, he decided upon a more cerebral career
and, financially unaided by his family, put himself through college, graduating from the University of Michigan in 1852. He then went south to
Mississippi, where he taught school and studied law at the same time,
graduating in 1854 from a Louisville law school.⁷

In October 1855, with "some other young bloods,"⁸ Alfred Otis moved
to Leavenworth, Kansas. Shortly afterward, he transferred to the township
of Atchison, then no more than a few timber buildings at a convenient
crossing of the vast Missouri River, where he worked for a law practice.
He was kept busy with land litigation cases that proliferated in the new
territory, and over the next few years he worked hard and prospered.⁹

Prior to 1854, Kansas was part of Indian Territory. The Kickapoo Indians were relocated from the east and occupied the land in 1832. Only white men holding the rare and necessary permits were allowed to enter this area until the Kansas-Nebraska Act was passed by Congress in spring 1854, opening the land to settlement. The site that would become Atchison was selected by a resourceful early settler who built a small log cabin at a suitable place on the river, from which he operated a ferryboat across the river during the 1848 and 1849 California Gold Rush, supplementing this income by supplying wood to the steamboats that plied the great river.[10]

The town was named after the famous Missouri senator David Atchison, who was pro tem President of the United States for one day. Just about the same time as Alfred Otis arrived there, the great Mormon wagon train was encamped some three miles to the west, equipping for the trek to Salt Lake. These were exciting days for the young lawyer as the town grew along with his practice. By 1858, the town was served by a steamship and by the daily arrival of the four-horse stage. Then it took "only four days" for a copy of an address by the President to reach Atchison from Washington, its impressive speed aided by the Hannibal and St. Joseph Railroad. The progress of the railroad and the advantageous location of the town for equipping the wagon trains that constantly streamed west made Atchison's future secure. For two building lots in the business section of the town, a member of Congress from Pennsylvania paid three thousand dollars. On the hills surrounding the town, desirable residential plots fetched up to $350.[11]

> The merchants of Atchison [did] a great trade with the Indians. For several weeks a great number had been in Atchison nearly every day to get their winter supplies. They never left until all the money paid to them by the government disappeared. The Indian men, women and children came to Atchison on beautiful ponies and usually brought along a few to sell. They generally wore nothing on their heads . . . moccasins ornamented with beads and . . . winter or summer . . . a coarse blanket was thrown over their shoulders. Around their waists, tied in their hair and hanging from their ears were pieces of ornamental tin. Sometimes the Indian men would come to Atchison with painted faces and with Eagle feathers in their hair.[12]

The town's great new asset, the Massasoit House Hotel, opened in September 1858 and was headquarters for the Overland Stage line. It had many famous visitors such as Abraham Lincoln, Kit Carson, Mark Twain,

Horace Greeley, and even Jesse James! By 1860, there were forty-six freighting firms doing business out of Atchison, and in June of that year, the town heartily celebrated the completion of the Atchison and St. Joseph Railroad.[13]

The gestation of the town was not without its problems, however. Neighboring Missouri was fiercely proslavery, and Kansas settlers tended initially to adopt this policy, but there were a few abolitionists. There were some unpleasant incidents of tarring and feathering, scuffles and gun-fights. Alfred, a lifelong Democrat, was known to be an active abolitionist, smuggling runaway slaves—covered in grain—to safety in his wagon. Small children were carried in trunks as part of his luggage.[14]

At the age of thirty-five, with his future looking ever more secure despite the great drought of 1860, Alfred Otis, now a full partner in law practice, decided to set down his roots in the booming little town.[15]

Almost certainly, Alfred met his future wife, Amelia Josephine Harres, when she visited her elder sister Mary in Atchison. Mary had recently married Mr. W. L. Challiss ("he wore the smallest shoes ever seen on a man").[16] Amelia Josephine was a fine young lady from Philadelphia, handsome and of prosperous Germanic stock. Alfred's attraction must have been great indeed to entice her to Atchison, though the nearness of her sister undoubtedly played some part in her decision to move to the little frontier town. True, she did not find it necessary to travel by covered wagon, for she "traveled as far as St. Louis by train and then came down the river on the steamboat."[17] Nevertheless, Atchison, Kansas, was far different from the civilized society of Philadelphia. At this point, it could not even boast a paved sidewalk.

Alfred and Amelia Josephine were married in the Harres home in 1862, after which they returned to Atchison and moved into the fine new house built by the industrious bridegroom on the high bluffs behind the town, which looked down on the fast-flowing Missouri River and the rich, flat farmlands beyond. This pleasant, brick- and timber-clad home, with its large, high-ceilinged, cool rooms was later to become the birthplace of Amelia Earhart.[18]

A period of service in a Kansas regiment during the Civil War hardly interrupted Alfred's career and he was soon regarded as one of the town's leading citizens. In retrospect, the couple's lives appear to have been idyllic. They had eight children, six of whom survived childhood. Life was busy, but Alfred's success had made him a wealthy man, so the traumas of life in the midwest were inevitably cushioned. In 1876, Alfred was elected to the bench and served with distinction.[19]

Amelia Earhart's mother, Amy, the couple's oldest surviving daughter, was born in 1869. Hers was a privileged existence. The home on Quality Hill was not a typical midwestern homestead. Its amenities included crystal chandeliers, a piano in the drawing room, Irish maids and cooks, and men to keep the riding and carriage horses in the large barn and to tend the extensive gardens. Little Amy's grandmother had come from Philadelphia to live with the family, and the child was petted and loved by everyone. She and her siblings were all good riders. Amy rode her own pony "sidesaddle and with long skirts," and the whole family "loved the smell of a book." The house had a well-stocked library and books formed a great part of the family's life, as did travel. At least once a year, the family took a trip:

> . . . father took the whole family. He went with a sense of responsibility, and mother just went because she loved it. We all had to know all of our own country first, before we went to Europe and of course that was very unusual . . . because the first thing you [usually] did upon graduation . . . was to take a trip to Europe. Father and I loved California. . . . [He] would often have the coachman stop when we got to the top of the hills and have him turn the carriage around so that we could see the rivers and hills and valleys, and fields of grain waving. . . . He wanted us to have seeing eyes, and said, "Your eyes were given to you to see things and I want you to see and remember."[20]

There were other trips to Utah, Oklahoma, and Colorado, and Amelia's mother thus saw much of the great continent of America when it was still unsettled and grazed by herds of buffalo.

Amy was not physically strong and her health often caused concern. Despite a number of absences from her studies at prep school, her natural intelligence enabled her to fulfill her college-entrance requirements, but she was unable to capitalize on her success due to a bout of diphtheria.[21] In any case, she said, "Mother didn't want me to go so far away," so she stayed in Atchison.[22]

Her physical delicacy was, however, no impediment to her adventurous spirit, for on a trip with her father to Colorado in the summer of 1890, Amy became the first woman to climb Pikes Peak. For the first ten thousand feet, donkeys were used, but then the party had to proceed on foot; some of the men who were affected by nosebleeds had to turn back. Amy was the only woman to attempt the last hazardous quarter-mile climb.

That same summer, when Amy was twenty-one, her parents threw a coming-out ball for her in the garden of their home. It was a warm June night and the syringa and heliotrope made the whole bluff fragrant. Amy's parents had a timber dance floor built over the grass; they couldn't move an old wrought-iron Stag-at-Eve, so they built flooring around him and Amy put a garland of scarlet roses around his neck and hung a lantern on one of his horns. Wires were strung between the trees and every few feet or so, Japanese lanterns were hooked on, to be lighted at nine o'clock, just as it began to get dark.

> It was a beautiful evening with very little breeze, which was fortunate as [Amy's father] would not have let us have the lanterns lighted, for fear of the candles tipping and causing fire. . . . Seven musicians came down from St. Joseph and played music for the Virginia Reel and the Lancers, as well as for waltzing.[23]

One of the guests introduced to Amy by her brother Mark was Edwin Stanton Earhart, a young lawyer. The young couple were soon deeply in love, but when Edwin subsequently petitioned the judge for his daughter's hand, he was told, not unreasonably, that he would have to be earning at least fifty dollars a month. It was fully five years before Edwin's earnings reached the required sum, but eventually he was able to re-present his suit and win Amy's hand. The pair were married on October 16, 1895, whereupon they moved to their own home in nearby Kansas City. The house, fully furnished down to its library of books, was a wedding gift from the bride's parents.[24]

The railroad company was one of Edwin's clients in his legal work, but even so, his means were vastly different from those of Judge Otis. Nevertheless, the marriage was, by all accounts, a happy one despite some initial tears on Amy's part. She was unused to housework and was made further miserable by the miscarriage of a baby girl within a year of their marriage (caused when she was thrown against the brake lever of a cable car). When Amy found she was pregnant again, it was quite natural for her to return to her parents' home in Atchison for the confinement, where she would be pampered and well cared for.[25]

The baby was born on July 24, 1897, at 11:30 P.M., and was named Amelia Mary, after her two grandmothers.[26]

Who could have guessed that the well-behaved and contented baby would blaze a name across the world's headlines? Amy's grandmother died only a year before Amelia's birth and her proudest boast was that she had watched George Washington pass by on his way to meet President Adams.[27] How could parents who had traveled the continent of America in horses and carts possibly imagine that this longed-for child would one day cross the oceans of the world in an airplane?

Chapter Two

1897-1914

A melia Earhart was in her early teens when it became obvious to her that her father was a drunkard. This fact was made all the more painful to her, and to her entire family, by the fact that her father's disgraceful behavior was equally obvious to everyone in their neighborhood, and that his job was in jeopardy.[1]

Life in the midwest in the first decade of this century was parochial in the extreme. Although we may look back on the security of those days with fondness, seeing freedom from the problems of life today (there were few crimes of rape, mugging, or burglary), life then carried its own problems. For example, it was almost impossible to maintain one's privacy. In one way, this was a good thing. Moral behavior was exemplary, by today's standards, because, apart from any other consideration, "What would folks say?" On the other hand, the lack of personal privacy could be very tedious. Amelia's childhood in this tight-knit world may explain much of her seeming "closeness" about her personal life as an adult. "What folks said" about Edwin was deeply shaming to Amy and her two daughters, but Amelia, because of her pubescent sensitivity, undoubtedly felt the shame to a greater degree.

Some two and a half years after Amelia's birth, Amy gave birth to another child, Muriel. The two little girls—Amelia was known as "Millie" and Muriel was called "Pidge"—were very close, as was the entire family. Although there was never much money, domestic problems began to occur only after Edwin attempted to make the family's fortune. There is little doubt that his eagerness to obtain success stemmed from Judge Otis's opinion that his son-in-law was a ne'er-do-well and would never amount to anything. Determined to prove himself, and in the best traditions of the nineteenth-century entrepreneur, Edwin invented a device to hold signal flags on trains, and spent long hours perfecting it. Unfortunately, when he traveled to Washington to patent it, he found that a similar item already had been accepted. Worse, he had used money that Amy had set aside to pay their taxes to pay for his trip and the application fee.[2] Edwin's disappointment was touchingly expressed in a letter to his wife:

> *My dearest wife,*
>
> For two days I did nothing except tramp from one office to another . . . to establish the classification of my poor little flag holder as mechanical, semi-mechanical or non-mechanical and then as to the area of its usefulness: household, farm, factory and so on. . . . When I returned to the main office by appointment about an hour ago, the clerk handed me back my two models with the information that a man from Colorado had filed a patent on an identical holder two years ago. . . . This news is a terrible blow, because I had been counting on receiving several hundred dollars from the railroad for my flag holder. . . . Give love to our small daughters, and as much to your sweet self. Ever thine, Edwin[3]

When the tax bill was presented, there were no savings and Edwin had to raise the money quickly to avoid default and quell Amy's panicky fear of prosecution. He called in some outstanding debts and sold a collection of valuable law books that Judge Otis had given him. The immediate problem was resolved, but it was not long before the judge heard through the grapevine that his gift had been disposed of in a manner that he thought shameful. It was the beginning of an irreparable rift between Edwin and his father-in-law. From that time on, Judge Otis regarded Edwin as totally unable to provide for his family.

In fact, the young Earhart family lived in reasonable comfort, even though not to the high standards considered by the judge to be those required for his family. Amelia and Muriel, unaware of any financial constraints whatever, felt secure and happy. Amy may well have had to lower her former living standards, but Edwin was a good and faithful husband, a man of great humor and patience. Long afterward, the two girls recalled the trip the family took to the 1904 World's Fair in St. Louis. It was a happy holiday, which the family enjoyed to the hilt. Edwin paid for the trip from a hundred-dollar fee he had received from the railroad for defending an obscure right-of-way dispute. The judge thought it an appalling waste of money considering the state of the family finances.

On their return from the fair, the seven-year-old Amelia designed and built a roller coaster in the yard, with long planks propped against the toolshed's roof. An uncle helped in the construction and the children sawed and hammered away with much enthusiasm. Amelia declared it a huge success and her contemporaries thought it great fun, but Amy said it was dangerous, so it was demolished after only a few short runs. Such tomboyish games were very much to Amelia's taste, and Amy, while perhaps despairing of this unladylike behavior, was a practical person. She had two gym suits with bloomers, gathered at the knees, made for the girls. "This was unusual," Muriel recalled, "because in those days nice little girls wore long, fullskirted dresses, with ruffled pinafores over them."[4] The neighbors may have raised eyebrows at this unconventional attire, but Amy realized that the girls were happier in their new freedom.[5]

Because Edwin's work often required him to travel away from home and Amy liked to accompany him, the two girls frequently spent time at the home of their doting, wealthy grandparents. In Atchison, the two girls were "the judge's granddaughters" and as such enjoyed a certain social cachet. Poor Edwin could never hope to provide his daughters with the advantages that Amy had grown up to take for granted and he felt the Otis patronage deeply. He provided his daughters with a great deal besides wealth, however. He took them fishing and played ball games with them. Despite her grandparents' protests, Edwin presented the nine-year-old Amelia with a .22 rifle so that she could "clear the barn of rats." "Oh now, don't worry, Mother Otis," he said. "This is really a very small rifle." He imbued them with a sense of humor and sang and played the piano with them.[6] Small wonder that they adored him. "Loving, generous, impractical" was how Muriel summed him up years later.[7]

Over a period of several years, Edwin had acted for the Rock Island Line. During that time, he had obviously impressed the company's management, for in 1905, he was offered a permanent post in the claims department. The opportunity of a regular salary meant freedom from waiting for settlement of small fees by often penurious clients. The job meant that the family would have to move to Des Moines, of course, leaving their happy Kansas City home, but the promotion was too good an opportunity to miss. While Amy and Edwin went to Iowa to look for a new house, the two little girls were left with their grandparents for what was intended to be a few weeks. It took longer than Edwin and Amy anticipated to find a suitable home and settle in, and the weeks ran to nearly a year. Although the girls missed their parents, the Otis home was happy and secure and the proximity of their two Challiss cousins meant that they never lacked for companionship.

When the Kansas sunshine became too hot for the children to play outside, they stayed in the cool interior of the large house and read books.[8] Books too large to hold had to be read lying flat on one's stomach on the floor.[9] Classics by Victor Hugo and Alexandre Dumas, housed in grandfather Otis's comprehensive library, were read and loved, and these were backed up by boys' adventure stories in periodical magazines.

A contemporary recalled how Amy encouraged her daughters' love of literature: "My earliest memories of Amelia and her family are of her mother reading to us as we sat on the floor at the Otis home."[10] The Earhart family had joined a neighborhood scheme whereby a large number of magazines were subscribed to and passed from household to household. Amelia's young, open, and impressionable mind fed on stories from *Harper's Weekly* or *The Youth's Companion. The Tale of Peter Rabbit* and *Black Beauty* were favorites from the girls' earliest days, while among Amelia's own collection was a much-thumbed copy of *Insect Life.*[11]

Amy also encouraged inquisitiveness into things that might normally make little girls squeamish: Her small daughters kept worms, moths, katydids, and a tree toad—all collected on nature outings organized by Amy, and the outings were often shared by orphans from a nearby children's home. Once, when Amy prepared a freshly killed chicken, she called her daughters' attention to its biophysics. "See, girls, how neatly this hen's little lungs fit here, just above her tiny heart."[12]

There were horses to ride, and there were imaginary horses on which Amelia and her sister and cousins escaped from all sorts of invented perils. Amelia was an excellent horsewoman all her life and many childhood incidents surrounded this love of horses. A friend recalled how she would adjust the tack on horses tied up outside houses to make them "more comfortable."[13] Cars were beginning to be seen in Kansas, but they were very much a rarity.

Amelia and Muriel attended the small private College Preparatory School during 1906 and early 1907 while their parents settled in Des Moines. Amelia's report cards, headed MILLIE EARHART, gave her a gratifying number of *E*'s (excellent) and *VG*'s (very good) covering the curriculum of reading, spelling, writing, arithmetic, English, French, geography, and sewing.[14]

In 1908 the girls moved to Des Moines to rejoin their parents. In her biography of her sister, *Courage Is the Price,* written in 1963, Muriel recalled the radical change in the girls' lives. Here they had no orchard or private park; no barn to play in; no cousins with similar background and interests; and no private school. Altogether, they felt the drop in their social status from that of "members of the aristocracy of a small town" most keenly. Amy considered the public school inadequate when it was suggested that the girls' hair should be cut to discourage the inevitable lice they would pick up. One of the teachers from Atchison's College Preparatory School was sent for and she became the girls' private governess. Geography was now omitted from their studies and the former curriculum was enhanced by more poetry and music lessons.

Before a year had passed, the governess returned to Kansas and the girls had to attend the dreaded public school. No lice were contracted, however, and they settled in well despite a certain amount of superiority in their approach to the other children.

Amelia was eleven years old when she saw her first airplane in 1908. She was taken to the Iowa State Fair in Des Moines, but when told to look at the contraption because it could fly, she was dismissive: "It was a thing of rusty wire and wood and not at all interesting," she recalled. She was much more interested in a paper hat shaped like a peach basket, which she had purchased for a few cents. This was only five years after the Wright Brothers had made their epic flight and it would be more than that again before Amelia's interest in aviation was awakened.

Edwin worked hard at his job and in 1909 was promoted to claims agent, heading a department of five loss adjusters and a small clerical staff. His salary was doubled, his name displayed prominently on the company letterhead, and as a perquisite, he received the use of a private rail car for business and personal use.[15] The sudden change in their circumstances enabled the Earharts to move to a larger house in a better part of town, and Amy was not slow to advise her parents of Edwin's success.

The happiness of the little family during this period is reflected in Edwin's charming reply on official Rock Island Line stationery to his younger daughter's formal claim for compensation after having received an insect bite while en route to visit her grandparents.

AUGUST 2 1909

Miss Muriel Earhart,
Atchison, Kansas

I have your claim for $5.00 for having been bitten by a misquito on our train. Before we can pay the same, we would, at least, like to know how big a bite the misquito took and we would like to see the misquito. Of course, we admit that we owe you something and are willing to pay it but you will have to produce the misquito before you could expect us to pay you.

This case will probably have to be referred to the Chicago office
as it is so serious a case and I hardly feel like handling it.

Very truly yours,
E.S. Earhart. [16]

There were two or three years of real contentment: There were happy
family holidays at Lake Worthington, Minnesota (many years later a
resident wrote to Amelia to tell her she especially remembered her visits;
she had thought Amelia a remarkable child because of her preference for
celery instead of candy and other sweets);[17] their first, somewhat frightening ride in an automobile; games of cowboys and Indians when Edwin
came home from the office early to play the part of Big Chief Geronimo;
concerts attended by the entire family dressed in their best clothes and
rounded off by Millie and Edwin giving a "by ear" rendering of the arias
they'd heard. Amelia liked the opera but criticized the Italian ones: "The
words are so silly!"[18]

"This happy time," Muriel was to write (Amelia never wrote of these
years), "was unfortunately a prelude to a period which saw the loss of our
material prosperity and the beginning of the disintegration of the family
... when the shadows began to fall on our gifted father, and the amenities
of life had to be sacrificed for the necessities of existence ... the hardship
and mental suffering that Amelia and I endured as adolescents made an
indelible impression upon us and help to explain some of Amelia's actions
and attitudes in her later life." Edwin had begun to drink.[19]

Characteristically, it was nothing at first—the odd drink with his colleagues after work, which he couldn't refuse without seeming rude. This
extended to lunchtime drinking, so that his stenographer often had to
confiscate letters by Edwin until he was in a "less belligerent state of
intoxication." Edwin began to lurch home more often than not, and his
sunny nature gave way to bad temper when his family remonstrated in
anxious concern. His condition became known as "Dad's sickness," but
this subterfuge did not fool his employers when his work inevitably suffered.

He overpaid claims and made massive errors that were not picked up
by his loyal staff. The head office warned him about his drop in efficiency,
and this was followed by a visit from the claims attorney, Mr. George
McCaughan. McCaughan found Edwin drunk at his desk and sent him
home. A month in a sanatorium to dry out restored Edwin to his anxious
family as their "old dad back again," but to the despair of Amy and the

two girls, the cure lasted only days and Edwin began to drink heavily again.[20]

Amy's mother had died in 1911, leaving an estate reputedly valued at a million dollars, to be divided equally between the four surviving children. The judge had long ago foreseen Edwin's inadequacy as a provider, and in the last year of Mrs. Otis's life, she had seen that her late husband's assessment of Edwin had been accurate. She was at least able to make some kind of provision for her daughter and two grandchildren to mitigate Edwin's profligate ways and protect against the possibility of his drinking away Amy's fortune. Amy's share of the inheritance was locked into a trust for twenty years, or until Edwin's death.[21]

This only served to worsen the situation, for Edwin used what he considered to be a studied insult as an excuse to increase his drinking. After he failed to gain reinstatement in his old job in Des Moines, he began a fruitless search for work with other railroad companies, but it was many months before he was offered an alternative post.[22] It was a considerable drop in status, a minor clerkship with the Great Northern Railroad in St. Paul, Minnesota, but it was work. Meanwhile, Edwin's status within his family dropped steadily. Whereas before he had been a hero to his daughters, now he was the source of every disappointment.

In St. Paul, the family rented a large house that had stood empty for two years. Edwin's salary hardly covered the rent let alone the heating, so in the depth of winter, the family was confined to the two rooms they could afford to heat. Here, Amelia entered Central High School as a junior. Her mother recalled that Amelia's favorite subjects were Latin and mathematics, and that she preferred geometry to algebra because she had to work at geometry, while she could do algebra in her head. She was "miles above" the other students in her class and regarded the reading matter of her fellow students as "childish."[23]

Amelia played on the basketball team and was a good all-round student. To some extent, she resented the fact that boys were favored above girls, a complaint her mother thought was justified. She was, from all accounts, a perfectly normal student apart from her above-average grades. She went to high school dances and summer camps and debated with her parents how late she should be allowed to stay up. "But she wasn't a rebellious child . . . once in a while she would say 'I don't agree with you at all, Mother. This is the way I look at it.' "[24]

There was a particularly unpleasant incident when Amelia discovered a bottle of whiskey in her father's suitcase as he was packing for a trip. She tipped the bottle out in the sink, but her father caught her and in his fury would have struck her had Amy not intervened. Edwin apologized, but the significance of his behavior, which minutes earlier had been sunny and tolerant, was not lost on the sensitive Amelia.[25]

Amelia maintained an outward confidence in her future and contentment with her lot and relayed this to old friends. In truth, however, she must have felt far from happy about both. Writing to her friend Virginia Parks in Atchison, she discusses in a jocular tone their mutual plans for attending college:

MARCH 6TH 1914

Blessings on thee little Ginger,

How goes everything mit Ihnen (mit governs the dative)? Of course I'm going to Bryn Mawr if I have to drive a grocery wagon to accumulate the cash. . . . You miss a lot by not having a Gym. Last Friday we had a circus. We played basketball, just like you and I did once (remember). No boys tho. I don't know when I've been so tired.

All the girls are so nice it's a joy to be with them don't you know. I am doing my best to get some of them to go to Bryn Mawr with Ginger and Millie. Your letter was scrummy, so long and joysome. . . .

Love, Mill[26]

Some wealthy family connections, living in a better part of town, studiously ignored Amy once Edwin's condition became known. The girls took time to become friends with their contemporaries and it was a long and cheerless winter, for they were not invited to any of the Christmas parties. There was, however, to be a Twelfth Night party organized by the church, and as they had been invited by some boys, the girls especially looked forward to going and dressed early.

Dating, as such, did not yet exist and convention decreed that a girl's father should escort her to a dance and collect her at an appointed time. Edwin promised to be home by six. The two girls sat dressed in their finery, desolation growing as the clock ticked on through six, seven, and eight o'clock. Edwin came home about nine, drunk and full of bonhomie. Muriel, "Pidge" to the family, burst into tears and retired to bed. Millie, steely-eyed and square-jawed, removed the Christmas decorations and pointedly cleared away the preparations she had made to entertain the boys whom they had intended to ask home for hot cocoa and toasted marshmallows.[27] For her, the disillusionment of a broken trust was more hurtful than the disappointment of missing the dance.

Throughout the winter, the girls helped Amy as much as they could, often walking for miles in the snow to get a bargain that would help the family finances. Amelia even made Easter Parade outfits out of some old curtains. In the summer, after they had at last been accepted by fellow students and had just started receiving invitations, Edwin announced they were moving on because he had been offered a job with the railroad in Springfield, Missouri. It was 1914 and in Europe war had been declared, but this all seemed a long way away from their immediate problems.

The family headed for Springfield with packing cases and hand luggage. After a tedious seven-hour journey, they arrived to find that the man whom Edwin was to replace had decided not to retire, after all. The company, in an attempt to compensate Edwin, gave him a month's work and the price of the family's train fare back to St. Paul. Edwin was righteously indignant and angrily demanded the job he'd been promised, but Amy had had enough. She and the girls left Edwin and went to stay with friends, the Shedds, in Chicago. The Shedds were friends from the happy Des Moines period, when Edwin had helped Mr. Shedd to get a good job in the days when he had influence. Edwin returned to Kansas.

Chapter Three

1914 - 1920

A melia was seventeen when the trio arrived in Chicago. Muriel has written that the Shedds never made them feel as if they were a broken family, but, rather, treated them as honored guests. Nevertheless, it is not difficult to imagine Amelia's feelings at this time.

She had grown up in a happy home where the four family members were close and particularly loving. Until Amelia reached the age of twelve or thirteen, home conditions may have veered between genteel poverty and relative affluence, but the stable background of love, support, and humor could be taken for granted. In those early days, too, the little family had always been confident that Edwin's natural gifts would inevitably be recognized and making do was merely part of the progression of his career. Then, when he was promoted and things were going well, they had begun to enjoy the long-anticipated better standard of living and the respect that success can bring. In addition, there was the wealth and position of Amelia's doting grandparents. The social superiority that she had enjoyed as the judge's granddaughter when she lived in Atchison and whenever she visited it could not but help set her slightly apart from many of her contemporaries and make her feel that she had a position to live up to.

Until this point, Amelia must have felt reasonably happy. She knew exactly what her place in society was and she had the respect of her peers for her own intelligence and qualities of natural leadership. She was confident in herself, her family, her friends, her future. However, when her father's drinking had put an end to all their expectations, her age alone ensured that she felt, far more than Muriel, the humiliation and even shame of the previous two years. The family's social and financial security had been eroded, and from occupying a leading position in society, they had become the butt of hushed, pitying gossip. In those days, couples stayed together more often than not. Periods of unhappiness were expected to be worked out. Divorce was a stigma in provincial circles, sufficient to create sidelong glances, and so this separation was always regarded as a breathing space to enable Edwin to regain his self-esteem and for Amy to gather the shreds of reputation and provide a future for her daughters.

That Amy had some income of her own was the purest luck. She could hardly have taken such a course of action without that small security. It was only a modest income earned on the capital of the trust fund, but it was enough. This created in Edwin great bitterness and helped him to assuage any feeling of guilt that his drinking had been the essential cause of the family's downfall. He was more full of self-pity than remorse and even years later, when Amelia achieved great success, his bitterness over the terms of the Otis bequest showed through his natural parental pride.[1] While Amy and the girls made a temporary home in Chicago, Edwin went to stay with his family in Kansas City, where, having realized that he would never again obtain a position with a railroad company, he opened his own law practice and started all over again.

Their arrival in Chicago was a watershed in Amelia's life. The worst had happened. The trust and respect she had in abundance for her father had been destroyed and disillusionment had taken their place. Her love for him remained, but sometimes it was as though she was the parent and he the child. She hid her distress behind a facade of bravado and quiet determination.

Amy found cheap accommodations in a furnished apartment near the University of Chicago campus and enrolled the girls at Hyde Park High School. The living accommodations left much to be desired. Amy, particular to a fault, was disgusted to find that the landladies draped their bedclothes over the sitting room furniture during the day.

At school, Amelia's newly found determination and an understandable intolerance of failure quickly fell afoul of the system. She was scathing about the equipment, declaring the school laboratory consisted of "no more than a sink!" The level of teaching also fell short of her personal high standards. Her ire became directed at an elderly relative of the mayor who worked as an English teacher at Hyde Park High. The woman was not only deaf but also totally inadequately equipped to teach high school students. Within days, Amelia was caught between indignation at the teaching standards and resentment that her fellow pupils were happy to taunt the unfortunate English teacher behind her back.

She also was accustomed to stimulating discussions on the works of standard authors and was bored by the clowning in the classroom. Amelia spoke to two others in the class who agreed that the situation was terrible. They prepared a petition asking that their teacher be replaced by "someone who can teach us something." The morning the petition was ready, one of the girls who had helped prepare it said her parents had forbidden her to sign it. This frightened the second girl so that Amelia's signature stood alone. . . . Sitting sideways at her desk near the front of the room Amelia began to speak above the laughing and talking which characterized the silent reading period. She told her classmates that it was a shame the way they were treating their teacher. . . .[2]

Her opinion was that the teacher could not help her deafness, but even so, they needed a teacher to teach them, and her subsequent requests to fellow students to back her petition created only noisy opposition. The petition was snatched away from her and torn up. As Muriel points out in her memoir, "Perhaps she went about her reform campaign in the wrong way. But it is revealing that she dared to undertake it."[3]

From this point onward, Amelia found ways of continuing her studies by her own exacting standards, alone in the school library, and she never attended another English class. Inevitably, she became regarded as odd, different, and a loner. When she graduated from high school in 1916, she deliberately missed the ceremony and the celebrations. Her graduating-class photograph was suitably captioned "the girl in brown who walks alone," and that one line sums up the solitariness of Amelia's adolescent life.

Amelia must have needed some outlet from her depression over her parents, the disintegration of their family life, and the general uncertainty over their future. To Amelia's credit, her outlet became a driving determination to work her way out of the mess. Despite her unhappiness, she set her sights firmly on attending college, at a time when women did not automatically think of furthering their education.

Muriel records that they hated leaving their friends in Chicago, but it is difficult to feel that Amelia had any such qualms when, in the summer of 1916, Amy decided to return to Edwin in Kansas City. He had managed to stop drinking and persuaded Amy that it was a permanent cessation. For Amelia, it was intended to be a short stay before she went off to college. In many ways, she considered that she had already made the emotional break from the family.

Amelia's stay in Kansas City, where the family were reunited in a small house on Charlotte Street, was to last a year, however. Pictures of this period show a tall, slim, thoughtful young woman dressed in the confining "cover all" long-skirted fashion of the day, with long hair dressed up, while Edwin is gaunt and hollow-cheeked, looking older than his actual years. In an attempt to make the reunion work, Amy complied with Edwin's exhortations to break the terms of her mother's will.

The trust had been badly administered by Amy's brother Mark, who had made some foolish investments. The capital was greatly depleted— probably to a far greater degree than if Edwin had been allowed to drink some of it away. Despite her reluctance to air family differences in court, Amy now saw a chance to assuage some of Edwin's bitterness and to ensure that something was left out of the fast-dwindling inheritance. After a court case based on both the incompetence of the administrator and the evidence that Amy's mother was not fully *compos mentis* and did not realize that she was placing her daughter in the same category as her mentally retarded brother, Theodore, when she put her signature to the trust, the will was broken. Amy's share of the capital, which ought to have been around $250,000, was found to be only $60,000; Edwin's bad feeling over the will seems, in retrospect, to have had some foundation.[4]

Now that she had capital on which to draw, Amy was able to send her two daughters to private intermediate schools to prepare them for college. Muriel, who had already decided that she wished to become a teacher, went to St. Margaret's in Toronto. Amelia, with her eyes still on Bryn Mawr, went to The Ogontz School in Philadelphia.

Although Amelia now felt that she was again moving in her own social milieu, and the range of subjects across the sciences, arts, and humanities was intellectually stimulating, her peripatetic existence and the emotional hurts of the past few years had made her too independent in her thinking to fit neatly into school society with ease. She clashed with fellow students again when she was invited to join a sorority. This time over the cliquey rules, which left some unfortunate girls (but not Amelia) "beyond the pale."[5]

Further, Amelia chafed against the confines of subjects then considered to be suitable for young ladies, and caused a schoolwide debate regarding religious philosophy. Still, she was happy enough, and her letters home told of concerts and dormitory feasts.

> We had a lovely feast the other night. There were about fifteen of
> us and several teachers were away so that it was a lovely opportunity.
> We played the ukuleles at twelve o'clock and sang. Some of the girls
> had been away and brought back chicken sandwiches and cakes and

pastry and we made hot chocolate and put marshmallow on it and
had a beautiful time. . . .

But in the same letter, she strikes a more serious note.

> What do you think of the railroad strike and the abdication of the
> Tsar? There seems to be no public sentiment back of the unions as
> there was in the beginning, which will make their demands harder
> of attainment. They have gone too far. . . .[6]

In the summer of 1917, Amelia spent some time with her parents in
Kansas before joining a group of friends at Camp Gray on the eastern
shore of Lake Michigan. She hated leaving her father, who had traveled
part of the way with her, and wrote home, "Poppy was such a lamb last
night I came near coming back with him."[7] While this indicates an
improvement on the domestic front, it was only shortly afterward that
Amelia was addressing her letters to her mother care of the Hotel Sutherland, rather than the little house on Charlotte Street. Edwin had started
drinking again.

A series of letters from Amelia to her mother reveals a naïveté surprising
in a twenty-year-old. Amelia was still very much the girl rather than the
woman. She was critical of the primitive conditions at Camp Gray—oil
lamps instead of electricity, lack of hot water, rather simple food, and
margarine instead of butter—and she agonized over the fact that her
menstrual period obliged her to refrain from swimming in the first week:
"I am in mental torture at not going in swimming and imagine I am
thought of as somewhat of a piker. . . ."[8] But she thoroughly enjoyed the
company of a group of young friends of both sexes—Sarah, Kenneth, and
Harry—chiefly, one suspects from her letters, Kenneth (Merrill), who was
to remain a friend long afterward. Perhaps Ken was the real reason why
Amelia opposed a suggestion that her younger sister Muriel join her at the
camp, for she insisted that there were no vacant rooms and it was useless
for her mother to inquire. "Under no circumstances could . . . Muriel
come up without you. There is not a place and it is impossible to be alone.
Sarah and I would be lost without the Merrills . . . and Ken has toted me
around considerably."[9] Her letters indicate that she had a schoolgirl crush
on Ken, for after two weeks of intense enjoyment, the camp quickly lost
all its charms for Amelia when he returned home. "I can't stand it any
longer," she wrote to her mother, ". . . and leave tomorrow. . . . Kenneth
and Harry left day before yesterday. Kenneth has done so much for me.
He is very nice and sensitive and almost brilliant."[10]

In the fall of 1917, Amelia returned to Ogontz as a senior, and her letters home show a new maturity. She no longer chattered ingenuously and there is a more serious tone in her writing. According to the headmistress, Miss Sutherland, Amelia "sought out the challenging authors: Shaw, Dreiser, Dostoevski, since for her, reading was an adventure."[11]

The marks awarded to Amelia on her report cards were enviable, ranging from good to excellent in a wide range of subjects. Among more conventional items, however, the bill sent to Amelia's parents for "extras" included some articles that reflected the sinister overtones of war. Books by such authors as Wordsworth, Byron, Burns, and Shakespeare were interspersed with *What's Wrong with the World?*, *War Poetry*, and *Red Cross Hygiene*. Charges for the supply of surgical dressings and a nursing cap and gown indicate that Amelia was taking some form of first-aid training, which would later stand her in good stead. As yet, though, Amelia remained largely untouched by the Great War. Occasional notes in her letters home indicate she helped where she could, knitting khaki garments for the boys in the trenches, and she noted in passing that Ken had joined up.[12]

She was delighted when, shortly after school term started, she learned that Miss Sutherland had swept away the secret sorority system against which Amelia had spoken out, and instituted an honor system for personal conduct. But she was deeply aware of the ever-widening gulf between her parents, and she wrote to her mother: "I have deep twinges of conscience about leaving you to your silent severity (your description). I knew exactly what you were going to have to endure and feel as tho I could have alleviated some of the loneliness had I remained faithful to my intentions." Later she begged, "Dear hen, don't write Miss S. letters of advice and warning. They go through the whole faculty and come to me and I just shrivel. I am not overdoing [things] and all that is needed to [bring me] to bouncing health is plenty to eat and happiness." Amy clearly did not heed this note and Amelia, obviously suffering some embarrassment, had to write again stressing her plea: "You won't write any more about me to school dearest Mummy will you?"[13]

Amelia's leadership qualities were evidently recognized by her peers, for she was voted vice-president of the class and secretary to the local Red Cross chapter. She also held office in several other organizations. She stood out strongly against some of the girls who were agitating for the reinstatement of sororities, and campaigned fiercely against "a useless costly [class] ring which is valuable only for the metal in it as there is no artistic and lasting value in a class ring. We others are only asking [that] we turn our money to Red Cross and have only a little gold band for a trifle, about four or five dollars instead of the expensive ones—in order to keep its precedent and to have a remembrance of our senior days. Much sweeter to me than a gorgeous one to pass on." Despite her strongly held opinions, she seemed to be respected, if not popular, and was known by the sobriquet "Millie" (occasionally "Meelie") or, perhaps as a cynical comment on her overslim physique, "Butterball." ". . . Butter for short!" she wrote home.[14]

Occasionally, when she wanted to visit someone outside the school or go to a ball game with friends, Amelia wrote to her mother for permission; and on the "extras" bill—quaint when one considers the age of the student—is a charge for "chaperonage."[15]

For the 1917 Christmas holidays, Amelia took the train to Toronto, where Muriel was at a college preparatory school working toward her entry requirements for Smith College. Here, for the first time, Amelia came face to face with the grisly effects of war. Although the United States had joined the conflict, its entry was too recent to cause the sights that shocked and saddened Amelia in Toronto.

As a senior member of the Commonwealth of Great Britain, Canada had sent its youth to fight in the trenches from the earliest stages of the Great War. Toronto, with its Spadina Military Convalescent Hospital, saw many of the returned wounded. In her book *The Fun of It*, Amelia noted her reactions.

> There for the first time I realized what the World War meant. Instead of new uniforms and brass bands, I saw only the results of four years' desperate struggle; men without arms and legs, men who were paralyzed and men who were blind. One day I saw four one-legged men at once, walking as best they could down the street together.[16]

After the holidays, she returned as planned to Ogontz, but now all ambitions to graduate had disintegrated and her one goal was to aid the wounded men she had seen and to serve in some useful capacity. Overriding any parental opposition, she left Ogontz within weeks and returned to Toronto, where she took steps to become a nurse's aide. Though she endeavored to join the American Red Cross in some formal capacity, she never quite managed it. Instead, she spent the long months as a V.A.D (Voluntary Aid Detachment) nurse—until the Armistice in November 1918—at the Spadina Hospital.[17]

The work of a nursing aide was varied, from "scrubbing floors to playing tennis with convalescing patients." Later, Amelia was to recall ladling out medicine from buckets, serving meals, and massaging cramps. Because she "knew a little chemistry," she was able to spend some time in the dispensary. In the laboratory, she prepared slides, and she fought successfully to improve the general diet of the patients.[18]

Throughout the summer of 1918, Amelia worked long hours six days a week, generally taking only Sunday off. When her free day coincided with her sister's, they rode out together on borrowed horses. Both were extremely good horsewomen and fond of riding. Amelia made a great pet of a notably difficult thoroughbred, aptly called Dynamite. As summer gave way to the Canadian winter, she used one of her precious days off to visit former patients at the local airfield and there she experienced the first stirring of what was to become an all-encompassing interest in airplanes.

> Though I had seen one or two at county fairs before, I now saw many of them, as the officers were trained at the various fields around the city. Of course no civilian had a chance of going up. But I hung around in spare time and absorbed all I could. I remember the sting of the snow on my face when it was blown back from the propellers when the training plane took off on skis.[19]

When the great influenza epidemic struck, Amelia worked night duty on the pneumonia ward, as the virus attacked patient and staff alike. It is hardly surprising that before long she, too, fell victim. Amelia was still recovering when the armistice was signed on November 11, but, in any case, she was scathing about the peace celebrations.

DECEMBER 1918

> *Kenneth dear,*
>
> ... I am just out of the hospital where the effects of the flu [epidemic] ... put me. I think working twelve to fourteen hours at a stretch added to the strain of having carried on all summer—made me a more than normally easy prey for influenza, and an infection in my nose at the same time which later necessitated an operation after which flu symptoms reappeared. Altogether I have had more than a two months siege and face the awful prospect of doing nothing for two more.[20]

Amelia took grave offense at the peace celebrations, standing back and observing:

What a day! All day long whistles kept up a continuous blowing. No means of transport was available . . . private cars ran the risk of being stalled in the littered streets and the traction company just gave up. . . . Young men ran round with huge dusters of flour and blew it on young women. . . . Supposedly dignified citizens snake-danced and knocked each others' hats off. I didn't hear one serious word of thanksgiving in all the ballyhoo.[21]

Shortly after this letter was written, Amelia went to Northampton, Massachusetts, to convalesce with her sister. Replying to Ken, who had obviously expressed a "wish you were here" in his letter to her, she told him:

If only I *were* over there instead of gravitating in enforced idleness in the confines of this bally little New England village. My sister is here preparing for Smith and as the Pater is in California on an extended business trip, mother and I have taken an apartment for a few months with Muriel. . . .

Europe certainly could not have gone madder than this continent on Peace Day. Toronto was simply a riot and the day was an excuse for every possible license.

. . . What do you think of the President's little flight to France? This country is terribly distrustful of his policies but the other nations don't grasp that and [I] feel objections are to his breaking precedent. Wouldn't it be great to sit at the conference and see people's fate decided for we don't know how long?

I wish after all we could have marched into Berlin as a victorious army and not as the army of occupation. Couldn't the Germans have felt defeat more universally than now, and realized more their inability to trust in arms alone? They are not at all changed as yet. I wonder whether they *will* ever change.[22]

Amelia soon tired of the enforced idleness and though not able to work officially, she found temporary employment working for charity. Her work consisted mainly of stuffing appeal letters into envelopes and addressing them. ". . . The Committee is driving for thirty million and with so large an objective (for now) there must be a correspondingly large amount of work. It is easy to get people to lend the weight of name to a worthy cause but to obtain workers is very different," she wrote to Ken, adding "I was sorry to hear of the flu attack. I hate and fear it somehow, more than a little. Having seen so much of it I suppose has prejudiced me—with the uncertainty of the treatment adding to the prejudice."[23] In an attempt to pass the time and rid herself of depression, Amelia enrolled in an all-girl class on a course in automobile-engine repair.

Together with her mother and sister, Amelia summered at Lake George, where she continued her convalescence. She was still notably low in spirits and her recovery was not helped by news that her father wanted to move permanently to California. Edwin reported that he had ceased drinking by this time, but the marriage was held together only painfully. Amy (as well as her daughters) had lost respect for Edwin and though she continued to persevere at keeping the marriage intact, it was all a great struggle.

In the fall of 1919, Muriel went to Smith College as a freshman. Amy and Amelia traveled to New York, where Amelia had enrolled as a premed student at Columbia University. "I had acquired a yen for medicine and I planned to fit myself for such a career . . . as usual I had a good time, though I studied hard and didn't have any too much money. But students in New York can get so much with so little if they really wish."[24] Quirkily, it was from this date onward that Amelia persisted in knocking a year off her age, always giving her date of birth as 1898 instead of 1897.[25]

Amy's role was again one of chaperone, for, having seen her daughter safely bestowed in a respectable hotel on Morningside Drive, she returned to Muriel in Northampton. Clearly, mother and daughter had some discussion about religion, or at least Amelia's attitude toward it. Amy was also worried about Amelia being alone in New York and whether she would eat properly. In a letter to her mother after her first day at college, Amelia told her about the domestic arrangements. "Whittier Hall is some dump and I'm glad I'm not [living] here," she said, outlining her hotel accommodation. "Don't worry about the meals or mentality. . . . Don't think for an instant I would ever become an atheist or even a doubter nor lose faith in the church's teachings as a whole. That is impossible. But you must admit there is [a] great deal radically wrong in methods and teaching and results today. . . ."[26]

At Columbia, Amelia took various courses in chemistry and the biological sciences. She enjoyed her spare time, too. In now-well-known feats of daring, she climbed to the top of the great dome of the university library and was photographed there in confining bulky clothing complete with ankle-length skirt, buttoned shoes, and enveloping black straw hat. She remembered her time at Columbia and the friendships she made there with great affection, but it took her only a few months to conclude that she would not make an ideal physician.[27]

In the spring of 1920, Amelia wrote to her mother regarding Edwin's pressing suggestion that the family join him in California and the girls continue their studies there. "I believe it will be best to all go together out west under the circumstances . . . however, do as you think best." Amy, recovering from a minor operation, finally joined her husband in California and undoubtedly pressed Amelia to join her in order to ease the tension between husband and wife, for at the end of the semester, Amelia succumbed to the pleas of both her parents to join them.

Ostensibly, Amelia was to continue her studies, but, in fact, she appears to have made no attempt to enroll for further education, and she really acted as a buffer between husband and wife. Muriel, who stayed at Smith College and saw her sister off to California, recalls Amelia's slightly bitter parting shot: "I'll see what I can do to keep Mother and Dad together, Pidge, but after that I'm going to come back here and live my own life."[28]

When Amelia set off for California, she was twenty-three years old. She had no definite ideas about what shape her life should take. As far as is known, she had never indulged in a serious romance—hedged as she was, in the main, by the mores of the period and the need for chaperonage for girls of her social class. At Columbia, she was regarded as a serious student who, when not working, spent her time at concerts, poetry readings, picnicking with her best friend (Louise de Schweinitz) at the top of the Palisades on the New Jersey side of the Hudson River, and joining in naïve, slightly dangerous pranks. She rode hired horses in Central Park and she read a lot.[29] She had sought and rejected several possible avenues. College graduation: to what end? Medical degree? Although she had not given up on medicine, she could not see herself as a doctor, though when she left New York, she still had ambitions to follow a career of some sort in the field of medical research. In short, she was still looking for a life of her own.

Neither Amelia's books nor her letters indicate that she was troubled by this lack of direction (or that she even recognized it as such). Although her parents were not wealthy by any means, she certainly did not appear to be overly troubled by any requirement to contribute financially toward her own upkeep.

Amelia was always starting and abandoning new projects. She was self-confident in her own social milieu and somewhat reserved outside it. Her humor was still childish but not unpleasantly so, perhaps in the fashion of the time. Though her writing had become more mature than that of the schoolgirl, in reality she had tasted little of real life—outside of the time she had spent at Spadina.

C h a p t e r   F o u r

1 9 2 0 - 1 9 2 1

During the time he had been alone in California, Edwin had not only set up a legal practice but also had been befriended by a Christian Scientist neighbor who helped him to overcome his addiction to alcohol. The new start gave hope to the entire family and when Amy joined him it seemed that the family might regain its former happy unity.

The couple rented a house at 1334 West Fourth Street in Los Angeles, not far from Edwin's office. It was a gracious, two-story timber house with a covered porch, but even after reserving rooms for Amelia and Muriel's use, the house was too large, so Amy took in three young male boarders to supplement the family's income. As Edwin recovered his business acumen and his practice grew, Amy tried hard to find again the respect and love she once had had for her husband. This was not an easy task given the suffering and hardships the family had undergone because of Edwin's weakness, and her feelings consisted of a mixture of duty, guilt, and pity for the man that Edwin had become.

Amy obviously felt that the marriage would have a better chance of successful reconciliation if the union was leavened by the presence of the girls, so both Amelia and Muriel were asked to go to California to continue their education. Muriel wished to remain at Smith College and, obliged to operate on a stringent budget, she was not even inclined to go to the expense of spending the summer in California, so it was left to Amelia to give up her place at Columbia. This did not seem to have caused Amelia undue pain, though there was her bitter parting remark to her sister in New York.

By now Amelia was twenty-three years old. Tall, slim, and serious, with fair waist-length hair, she dressed almost exclusively in her favorite color, brown. She was not pretty in the sense that she turned heads, but her expressive eyes, coupled with a ready boyish grin, gave her an appealing and slightly unusual gamine beauty. When she arrived in Los Angeles, she met Sam Chapman, one of her parent's boarders.

Sam was a good-looking man of Amelia's age. Tall and tanned, with thick dark hair, he had grown up in Massachusetts and was graduated as a chemistry engineer from Tufts University before traveling west to carve a career for himself. The two had much in common. Both were well read and serious-minded. According to Amelia's letters to her sister, the two spent more and more time together enjoying tennis, swimming, and the theater. A social conscience had long been apparent in Amelia but Sam kindled it into action. Together, dressed in what Amelia called "slumming clothes," they attended illegal meetings of the socialist organization Industrial Workers of the World (its initials, IWW, were said by its critics to stand for I Won't Work).

On at least one occasion, a meeting was broken up by the police. The subject under discussion had been pensions for everyone over sixty, in anticipation of the Social Security laws proposed by Herbert Hoover.[1] A disgruntled Amelia told her family, idealistically, "Pensions are surely better than poorhouse at sixty. I think the government ought to make people save some of their wages and give it back to them when they are old . . . [and] I think we should have had the right to talk it out tonight instead of being sent home like naughty children."[2]

One day, shortly after her arrival in California, Amelia drove with her father to an aerial meet at Daugherty Field in Long Beach. "The interest aroused in me in Toronto led me to all the air circuses in the vicinity," she wrote, and on this occasion she thought she might like to fly.[3] She asked Edwin to inquire about the cost of flying lessons. Her father made the necessary contacts and told her it cost about a thousand dollars to learn to fly. "Why do you want to know?" he asked her, but he booked a flight for her on the following day.[4] "I am sure he thought that one ride would be enough for me," Amelia wrote.[5] Next morning, he accompanied her to the small dirt strip known as Rogers Field, "no more than an open space on Wilshire Boulevard" and paid ten dollars for his daughter to be taken up as a passenger for a ten-minute flight.[6] Her pilot was Frank Hawks, who was destined to become a high-speed flying record-breaker.[7]

What must that first flight have been like to hint to Amelia that here was the thing she had been seeking; that here was a pursuit to inspire her as she suspected she was capable of being inspired?

Amelia would have been given a helmet and goggles and helped into the deep forward cockpit of the huge open-cockpit biplane (the pilot flew from the rear cockpit). Most airplanes used for this purpose were war surplus Canucks or Jennys, and with Hawks as pilot, it would have been a smooth and uneventful takeoff, followed by a climb to a thousand feet or so. A flight over downtown Los Angeles, then isolated from the outlying suburbs by citrus groves, was almost de rigueur; Amelia would have been able to gauge their speed by glancing down at the occasional automobile on the highways leading in and out of the city. Perhaps this was followed by a sweep out over the Pacific Ocean to enable the passenger to glimpse Catalina Island in the distance, and the beaches and the few big houses in the idyllic setting of the Santa Monica hills. In the month of December, the air in the Los Angeles basin can be as clean and clear as crystal, and silky smooth, with none of the turbulence of the hot summer months. Amelia could hardly have chosen a better pilot with whom to take her first flight. A landing amid clouds of dust would have coated her face, leaving two white circles when she took off her goggles, but from her later writings it is clear that Amelia simply loved the sensation of flying from the first moment.

"As soon as we left the ground I knew I myself had to fly."[8] Here, then, was the thing for which she had been looking. Amelia was lucky indeed that she was able to recognize her destiny in this moment.

> "I think I'd like to fly," I told the family casually that evening, knowing full well I'd die if I didn't. "Not a bad idea," said my father equally casually. "When do you start?"[9]

Her mother raised no opposition, either, so Amelia said she'd make the necessary inquiries and let them know the outcome. Unfortunately, her father's reaction had been an attempt at wry humor rather than a casual acceptance. He was astonished when a short time later Amelia advised him that she had not only completed her preliminary investigations but had also signed up for lessons for which she expected him to pay. The cost was five hundred dollars for about twelve hours of instruction.

Edwin told her he couldn't afford the lessons, and it was not difficult to see his sudden dislike of the entire idea. Amelia would not be put off and said she would get a job in order to pay for the lessons herself. In the meantime, she worked at her father's office to repay him. Eventually, her determination wore down Edwin's opposition and he agreed to allow her to start learning to fly, but the impropriety of his daughter spending all her time with a male instructor was a real concern.

Fortunately, Amelia had heard of a woman pilot who gave flying instruction and shortly afterward Edwin accompanied his daughter when she went to seek out Miss Anita Snook.

It was unusual in December 1920 to find a woman flying instructor. "Neta" Snook was based at Kinner Field, a small dirt strip in the South Gate area of Los Angeles. Although only a year older than Amelia, Neta had been fascinated by aviation since childhood and had set out to become a pilot as soon as she left school. When she needed money to pay for lessons, she took any job that would provide a wage. Training at the Curtiss School of Aviation, she was just about to achieve her ambition—a solo flight—when America entered the war and all civilian flying was prohibited. She caused a stir by her aggressive attempts to get into the United States Air Force but was thwarted because of her sex. Instead, she spent the war working as an expeditor for the British War Mission, checking out Curtiss's OX5 engines that were being assembled in Canada.

A few months after the war ended, Neta purchased a wrecked Canuck, a Canadian training plane that was a contemporary of the ubiquitous American JN4 Jenny. It took her a year to rebuild it and in the spring of 1920, she loaded it onto a truck, drove to a nearby pasture, assembled it, and took off for her first solo flight. During that summer, she barn-stormed her way across the midwest, taking fare-paying passengers up for fifteen-minute flights at fifteen dollars a ride. Photographed for publicity posters in the typical flying togs—riding breeches and boots, with a leather jacket and white silk scarf—she drew huge crowds. At one point, she was earning a thousand dollars a day to make two flights on each of three days, a huge fee at that time. In the autumn, she moved to Los Angeles and started her own business at Kinner Field, flying passengers, doing aerial advertising, and giving instruction to would-be pilots.[10]

Kinner Field was located on the west side of Long Beach Boulevard and Tweedy Road, below Huntington Park.[11] It was a fifty-acre, bumpy, barren, weed-grown piece of ground on which a small hangar and a wind sock had been erected by Bert Kinner a few weeks before Neta's arrival. Here, Kinner was in the process of building a small biplane of his own design—the "Kinner Airster," which he confidently anticipated would one day be owned by every family. It was a two-seat biplane powered by a three-cylinder Lawrence model L2 60hp engine, giving a maximum speed of 85 mph and a designed range of five hundred miles. In return for the commercial flying rights on the field, Neta agreed to test-fly all Kinner's airplanes.[12]

Neta was only a little over five feet in height, and her personality matched her bright red hair. One contemporary wrote, "We were not quite sure as to whether Snooky was a man or a woman, as few of us ever saw her except in a pair of dirty coveralls. . . ."[13] One hot afternoon in

December 1920, as Neta leaned against her biplane between passengers, she noticed:

> . . . a tall, slender young lady and an elderly man approaching. She was wearing a brown suit, plain but of good cut. Her hair was braided and neatly coiled around her head; there was a light scarf around her neck and she carried gloves. She would have stood out in any crowd and she reminded me of the well-groomed and cultured young ladies at the . . . Academy in . . . my childhood home. The gentleman with her was slightly gray at the temples and wore a blue serge business suit. He walked erect with a firm step.
> "I'm Amelia Earhart and this is my father . . . I want to learn to fly and I understand you teach students. . . . Will you teach me?"[14]

Amelia and Neta took to each other on sight. Both were midwesterners from a similar middle-class family background. Both were intelligent women, but while Neta had already taken destiny into her own hands, Amelia was still very much the daughter of the family, still asking permission before she did things or went anywhere. Whether she actually needed this permission or not is open to doubt, but she allowed herself to be bound by conventions. Muriel has said that Amelia decided to leave Ogontz and go to Toronto to nurse without waiting for permission to do so; nevertheless, she certainly asked parental permission on lesser occasions long after this incident.[15] Neta's influence on Amelia's life was to extend beyond her aviation instruction.

From this point, Amelia's life changed. There was no sudden dramatic change, but one detects a new sense of awareness of herself and a new determination in her actions. She had found a direction and unlike previous interests, this one was to last.

Neta advised Amelia that her charges were one dollar a minute in the air and that she expected to be paid each day. Amelia agreed and arranged to pay with Liberty Bonds—presumably part of Amy's inheritance. The next day, January 3, 1921, after work in Edwin's office, Amelia turned up for her first lesson. She wore her old brown riding breeches and boots and "a beautifully tailored brown jacket," riding clothes being considered the most suitable dress for the aviator, and spent half an hour learning to taxi the Canuck. From the library, Amelia had acquired a book on aerodynamics. "I soon became accustomed to seeing her with a book," Neta recalled. "She always carried one." Amelia's literary interests were extremely varied and ranged through technical books on aviation to Rossetti's poems, Omar Khayyám's *Rubáiyát,* and Carl Sandburg. On one occasion, she brought a history of Islam and tried, unsuccessfully, to persuade Neta to read it.[16]

For a few weeks, all the instruction was ground-based while Amelia learned about the principles of flight, and over the next two months she logged four hours in the air. By now, she had taken her first real job, working in the mailroom of the telephone company offices. In addition, she continued to work a half day every Saturday for her father.[17]

Neta recalled those days and the primitive conditions in the hangar, where the fastidious Amelia and the other students spent most of their spare time:

> We had a few cooking utensils, knives and forks. When we cooked Amelia always washed the dishes *before* we ate. When we bought ice-creams she never ate the part that the handler had touched . . . however she never minded if her hands got dirty helping with plane maintenance . . . [and] she never wanted to dally long at what she called "frivolous doings," such as eating and joking, if air conditions were right for flying.[18]

Despite her continuing close friendship with Sam Chapman, Amelia was happy to date other boys in company with Neta, who recalled that Amelia "preferred older men" and was disdainful when a picnic in the mountains with two young men was ruined by torrential rains. The boys suggested they find overnight accommodation in a nearby settlement, but Amelia insisted that her parents would not allow it and made them drive the two hundred miles back to Los Angeles in the rain. She told Neta, "You see why I don't care for these thoughtless, irresponsible young boys. Mature men wouldn't have put us through such an experience." It was daylight when they reached the outskirts of Los Angeles. Neta privately didn't think much of Amelia's opinion, but she held her tongue, even when Amelia later developed a bizarre friendship with "a slight, emaciated old man" who wore a small shawl across his shoulders and a light rug across his knees. He used to collect Amelia in his chauffeur-driven car. He sat ramrod straight in the backseat, his hands resting on a gold-topped cane. Once Neta invited Amelia and her unusual man friend in for a drink, but Amelia's companion declined—it was past his bedtime.[19]

There were other male friends, however, notably Lloyd Royer, a young airplane engineer. Amelia and Neta often double-dated, going to theaters and shows in downtown Los Angeles, and enjoying dinners at ethnic restaurants. Neta recalled that "Amelia had strict scruples. She didn't feel it was right for a boy to spend time and money on her if she, in turn, had no interest in him. To her it was a form of stealing." Neta sometimes dined at the Earhart home after a day at the airstrip and noted that Amy had become hard of hearing and quietly disapproved of the two girls being constantly dressed in "masculine attire."

> She ran her household in a disciplined manner and the food was served formally and in courses. Everyone had his napkin in a ring placed at at the top of the plate, and the serving was done from the left. . . . After dinner everyone read or played a few hands of cards—flinch or whist. [But] when Amelia and I would retire to the privacy of her bedroom we would giggle and exchange confidences.[20]

One such shared confidence was the fact that Amelia had secretly started to cut her hair, an inch or so at a time. Impressed, Neta asked if her mother had noticed. "No, I'm keeping it pinned up when I'm home. I only cut off a little every few weeks."[21] Another and more serious confidence was her request to Neta to help her "work on" her mother.

> Amelia was trying to persuade her mother to buy [Bert Kinner's first airplane, the Airster] for her. Her father was not financially able to do so, nor so inclined. . . . All her pilot friends, including myself, advised her against it. I had had the little plane in the air a few times. There weren't many bugs—only the engine gave us trouble. It was powered by a three-cylinder Lawrence—60 horsepower, radial and air cooled [and] the oil system was so designed that the third cylinder periodically became clogged.[22]

By now, Amelia had received some six months' instruction in Neta's Canuck. Her natural intelligence made her a reasonably competent pilot, but she lacked the inherent ability that makes a great pilot. Sometimes she made silly mistakes, which provoked Neta into castigating her student. "Why do you persist in leveling off so high above the ground? Didn't you notice how I had to shove the nose down several times . . . you know the Airster, or any aircraft for that matter can't stand a 'pancake.' " Amelia would answer ruefully that she "guessed" she "was just daydreaming."

Years later, Neta was to recall Amelia's daydreaming with distress, but at this earlier time she was merely concerned about her friend's insistence on buying the Airster. Her assessment was that it was not a forgiving airplane and lacked the stability of the old Canuck. It was underpowered, landed faster, and tended to ground loop at the merest suggestion of a crosswind. "It was not a plane for a beginner," she said, and in Neta's opinion Amelia was very much a beginner.[23]

This was underlined when one day on a dual instruction flight, Amelia headed for Long Beach without telling Neta of her intention to make what was then regarded as a reasonably long flight. Neta soon suspected Amelia's destination and doubted the plane's ability to make the flight in the head winds unless the tank was full of fuel. Cutting the throttle and yelling to Amelia, she queried the fuel situation. "Did you check it personally?" Amelia shook her head. "Mr. Kinner always keeps it full," she shouted back. Neta grimly opened the throttle, turned the plane, and headed for home. On their return, they were met by a worried Bert Kinner, who informed them that he had not filled the Kinner the night before because he'd been waiting for the fuel tanker to arrive the next day. Not for the first time, Neta angrily wondered whether she hadn't misjudged her friend's ability.[24]

At this point, Muriel went west to join the family. Obviously impressed with her sister's flying activities, she was a regular visitor to the airfield, traveling on the electric streetcar from Los Angeles, through Vernon and Huntington Park to the end of the line. From there to Kinner Field was a walk of about a mile, but the occasional passing motorist could easily tell the girls' destination from Amelia and Neta's flying clothes and so they seldom had to walk the entire distance.

There was always something to do at Kinner even when not flying. Small tears in the fabric of an airplane had to be patched and doped, wooden struts had to be bound and repaired, and flying wires needed to be cleaned and checked for tension. It was a whole new world and though it was populated mainly by men, there seemed to be no restriction on women joining in the fun, too, if they desired. So on weekends, the two sisters would spend their days there, carrying a picnic lunch of sandwiches and chocolate cake. When there were no fare-paying passengers for Neta or Frank Hawks, there was little flying. No one could afford the fuel to fly too often for pleasure alone. As the temperature soared above a hundred degrees, pilots, students, and mechanics would sit in the shade of a tin-roofed shack, to "talk airplanes" and watch the occasional plane land, causing clouds of dust on the unpaved runway.

At that time, almost the dawn of civil aviation, the possibilities ahead of them were seemingly limitless. They happily forecast larger airplanes that would carry tens of passengers and sport planes with cabins designed so that the pilot was not subjected to the extreme effects of the elements. These things were technically possible already, but technical development had not caught up with practical requirements, and all eyes were fixed on what was happening at the Curtiss and Wright companies. There were also the solo operators such as Bert Kinner. The industry would remain fragmented for a long time.

Despite Neta's largely unspoken misgivings, Amelia remained confident in her flying ability and was determined to own the Kinner. Neta was not the only person at the field to advise her against this, mainly because the plane was underpowered and the engine was unreliable. However, Amelia had made her decision based on her own quiet research. The engine was air-cooled, which meant a simplified system and a resultant decrease in weight. Also, because the Kinner was far lighter in weight than the reliable old Canucks or Jennys, Amelia was able to pick the plane up by the tail and move it without help from a man or the use of a dolly.[25]

Shortly before her twenty-fourth birthday in July 1921, Amelia purchased for two thousand dollars the prototype Kinner, which she promptly named *The Canary* because it was finished in bright chromium yellow. Initially, she had asked her father for the money to buy the plane and finally "he agreed that I needed the plane and that I should have it, and promised to help out in paying for it. But I'm afraid my salesmanship was faulty for he did not stay sold . . . ," Amelia recorded. She had saved a little money from her job at the telephone exchange.

> Perhaps this . . . doesn't seem very convincing, for obviously my salary as playmate of office boys would have to run on a long time before it would wipe out the balance of $2,000. But it did help my credit immensely! I think it made my flying companions believe I was in earnest.[26]

Amelia had already paid her small capital to Bert Kinner before learning that her father had changed his mind. Having exhausted her slender funds, she came to an arrangement with Bert Kinner whereby the plane remained available for sales demonstration work, in return for hangarage and mechanical repairs.[27] Meanwhile, in order to pay the balance of the purchase price, she borrowed all of her sister's savings and her mother provided the remainder on condition that she give up the job in the back room at the telephone exchange "and stay at home a little." She resigned as back-room girl but stayed with the company as a telephone operator.

Neta continued to instruct Amelia for a while—free of charge—in the Kinner, because Amelia could not afford to pay and she was still not ready to go solo.[28] On July 23, Amelia and Neta flew to the Goodyear Field to look at the huge Cloudster, Donald Douglas's first aircraft.[29]

A grove of Eucalyptus trees grew at the far end of the runway. On takeoff, the Kinner Airster didn't gain altitude fast enough to quite clear those trees—that pesky oil-clogged third cylinder. There was nothing to do. To nose down for more flying speed meant slamming into the trees. To pull up meant a stall. Amelia pulled up—I would have done the same—the plane stalled [and] on ground contact the propeller was broken and the landing gear damaged. That was Amelia's first crash. She [had bitten] her tongue but had the presence of mind to cut the switch. When I looked back, she was powdering her nose. "We have to look nice when the reporters come," she reminded me.[30]

There were other occasions when Amelia made stupid mistakes that Neta simply couldn't understand. "You have to learn to fly by feel," she told Amelia, who merely replied that she thought Neta was referring to "flying by the seat of your pants" and that one day there'd be instruments to tell you when you were flying level or to show the angle of climb.[31]

More advanced instruction followed but not by Neta. Edwin and Amy, by now obviously reconciled to Amelia's ambitions, raised no objections when their daughter turned to a former World War I pilot, John "Monte" Montijo, who sometimes demonstrated the Airster and flew it in air races for publicity purposes.

According to Neta's records, she gave Amelia four or five hours in the Canuck and some fifteen hours in the Kinner.[32] Amelia still felt she needed some "strenuous" further instruction from Monte before making her first solo flight. While in retrospect this seems an unusually high number of hours to solo, Amelia was later to write that she "refused to fly alone until I knew some stunting. It seemed foolish to try to go up alone without the ability to recognize and recover quickly from any position the plane might assume, a reaction possible with practice."[33]

On Amelia's first solo flight, as she was taking off, one of the shock absorbers broke, causing the port wing to sag; having faced and overcome the mental agony of preparing to take off, she had to abort for on-the-spot repairs. Unlike the average student who is content to fly a circuit or two at low level, when Amelia got off the ground, she went up to five thousand feet and stooged about for a while to the alarm of Monte and Neta,[34] returning to make, in her own words, "a thoroughly rotten landing."[35] She celebrated by purchasing a leather flying coat. The obvious newness of this shiny garment caused a certain amount of good-natured teasing by the crowd at the airfield, so Amelia "aged" it by sleeping in it and staining it appropriately. At least now Amelia looked the part. However, there is serious doubt about her skill as a pilot.

It has been recognized for some time by the air forces of the world that some people have inherent ability in the air. Today, prospective jet-fighter pilots can be recognized long before they set foot in an airplane, for this ability is apparent even in flight simulators. For these people, the air is simply their element and this skill appears to be built in; it cannot be learned.

Any reasonably intelligent person can become a pilot, but it takes that indefinable ingredient to become a good or brilliant pilot. Those who possess it are never at a loss in any aerial situation, even though the pilot concerned may never have been given appropriate instruction, whereas the ordinary pilot who has absorbed teaching may fly well until coming up against a situation not covered by training. Then—unlike the fortunate few—there is no instinctive reaction.

Some people, then, are natural pilots. Unfortunately, though highly intelligent, a quick learner, and possessed of great enthusiasm, Amelia did not, it seems, possess natural ability as a pilot. This is no disparagement of Amelia; it is simply the view of many of her contemporaries in the flying world. Indeed, given this apparently important drawback, it is to her great credit that she was subsequently able to achieve so much.

Chapter Five

1921-1927

With characteristic enthusiasm, Amelia now became more and more obsessed with flying. From earliest childhood days, she had been capable of bringing spirited exuberance to anything that struck her as adventurous.

> Whether it was considered the thing to do or not was irrelevant. As a little girl I had ridden my buggy in the stable; I had once climbed up on a delivery horse; I had explored the fearsome caves in the cliffs overlooking the Missouri; I had invented a trap and caught a chicken; I had jumped over a fence that no boy my age had dared to jump; and I knew there was more fun and excitement in life than I would have time to enjoy.[1]

In time aviation became not only a raison d'être but also a means of escape from an increasingly troubled home life and the place where she could be herself.[2]

Despite the financial difficulties involved, Amelia kept up her flying instruction, and whenever she could earn enough to pay for fuel, she flew solo in her Kinner *Canary*. There was no easy way for Amelia to earn money, but she was not afraid of work. She was still working at the telephone exchange, even though this meant she was "ostracized by right thinking girls" of her class.[3] She also continued to work for her father part-time and, according to her friend Lloyd Royer, she "had several other part-time jobs, too." Some five years later, Amelia wrote that she had had "twenty-eight jobs" among which were "driving a truck, selling sausages and working in a photographic laboratory."[4] Starting with her nursing career and the jobs mentioned above, and three jobs that are known about after she left California, this still leaves some twenty jobs to be accounted for, about which nothing is known. But "like the rest of us," her friend Royer summed up, "she never had any money to buy gasoline."[5]

Neta Snook had sold her airplane and left Los Angeles in the fall of 1921 to visit her parents before getting married.[6] Amelia was thus the sole female representative at the Kinner airstrip. Her careful upbringing enabled her to tread the fine line between friendship and overfamiliarity. She was always happy to be shown how to strip down an engine or to learn some new mechanical skill, "to muck in with the boys" and to laugh with them, so to speak, but at the same time she maintained a reserved dignity so that her male contacts treated her with immense respect.

In the summer of 1922, Amelia was pictured in the Los Angeles *Examiner* with her Kinner airplane, above an interview in which she explained that she hoped to fly across the continent the following year, with the intention of "dropping in at Vassar College," where she hoped to take a postgraduate course. "I don't crave publicity," she told the reporter, "but it seems to me it would be the greatest fun. . . ."[7] The article went on to advise readers that Miss Earhart was popular in society circles in Los Angeles, being the daughter of attorney Edwin Earhart.

By October, despite not being able to fly as often as she wished due to financial constraints, Amelia's flying skills must have improved considerably, for she startled her family by participating in a record-breaking attempt. Her sister tells the story of how she and her father had gone along to a fly-in at Rogers Field, having been handed tickets by Amelia, who told them mysteriously that she wouldn't be able to sit with them. They soon learned why. Amelia took off and was gone for an hour, during which time she set a women's altitude record by reaching fourteen thousand feet. Although her record stood for only a few weeks before being broken by Ruth Nichols, it provided Amelia with greater confidence in herself and in the role of airplanes. Indeed, had she not encountered engine trouble at twelve thousand feet (a fact verified by indications of vibrations recorded by the sealed barograph), she was confident that she could have achieved a much higher altitude.[8]

Some weeks later, Amelia decided to try for the record again. This time, weather conditions were not perfect, which they had been on the first occasion, and at just over ten thousand feet, she flew into thick clouds, encountering snow, sleet, and zero visibility. With all her flying having been carried out in the Los Angeles basin, it is extremely unlikely that she would have been prepared to cope with such conditions and she certainly wrote about becoming disoriented and frightened. She also wrote that she deliberately put the plane into a spin "as the quickest way down my experience would suggest . . . seconds seemed very long, until I saw the clear weather several thousand feet above the world I knew."[9]

Her friends on the ground were appalled at this course of action and after she had landed safely, they told her so in no uncertain terms. This was with good reason; had conditions deteriorated further—according to her own chronicle of events, the ceiling deteriorated from ten thousand feet to "several thousand feet" in the short time since she had entered the clouds—the base could have easily dropped so that she might have emerged from the murk too low to pull out of the spin.

At this distance, one is tempted to wonder whether Amelia really had spun deliberately or whether the more likely explanation is that she became disoriented and the plane fell into an involuntary spin, which she was hesitant to admit to her peers.

There were more incidents; several times, her airplane nosed over when the wheels stuck in thick mud or landed in overlong grass. Once the Kinner stopped so suddenly in high weeds that it turned over on its back with sufficient force to break the safety belt and eject Amelia. Despite this seemingly haphazard flying, however, Amelia was no different from the average pilot of the day. Planes were slow and engines unreliable. The occasional crash or bump was nothing about which to get excited, although it provided good fodder for the newspapers.

On May 16, 1923, Amelia applied for and was granted a flying certificate (number 6017) by the Fédération Aeronautique Internationale. Quaintly, it announced that the holder had fulfilled all the conditions required by the organization for an "Aviator Pilot" and "is hereby brevetted as such." Although it was not, at that time, necessary to have a license in order to fly, and the FAI certificate was not officially recognized by the federal agency that controlled aviation licenses, it was necessary to hold such a certificate in order to make attempts on FAI records.[10]

A further newspaper article appeared in October—in *The New York Times*—with Amelia in flying dress. Certain older family members were not pleased with this publicity and one uncle in particular wrote to Amy to complain that it was simply not done. "The only time a lady's name should appear in print is at her birth, her marriage and her funeral."[11] What must they have thought in later years?

By this time, Amy's inheritance, having put the girls through various private schools and college courses and, of course, having helped Amelia to purchase the Kinner airplane, had shrunk to twenty thousand dollars. Clearly, at the prevailing rate of expenditure, it was not going to last long unless it was lucratively invested. After much discussion, the Earhart family decided to invest most of it in a small gypsum mining business owned by a young friend of Amelia's, Peter Barnes.

The exact circumstances of what happened to the project are not clear and there are several conflicting versions, but the final outcome was the same no matter who told the story. A flash flood wiped out the mine workings and destroyed most of the plant. Shortly afterward, the firm's remaining truck was hit by a train at a crossing. Very little of Amy's savings could be recovered. Lloyd Royer, one of Amelia's closest male friends at the time, and who worked in the venture, recalled:

> We were involved in this business that Amelia had invested in. At that time Boulder Dam was just being built and there was a gypsum mine up there, we used to ship the mineral in big Mack dumper trucks.
>
> Anyway, even before that there was a lot of building going on in the Los Angeles area and there was a big demand for sand and gravel. We used to pick up the material in the hills and come down via Tahuenga, Washington, and Cahuenga, to Los Feliz, to what was then Lankersham across the railroad track just by the San Fernando Road. This was . . . 1923.
>
> The truck got stuck on the railway line and was hit by a train. There had been some floods previously but that wasn't the reason. . . . After that Amelia bought a Moreland Truck for $7,200—that was a lot of money in those days—you had to [break a truck in gently]. I drove it round carefully for three months. . . .[12]

In the archives at the Schlesinger Library is a photograph of Lloyd Royer with a truck. On the photo he has inscribed, "1923. While I was breaking in the Moreland truck for Amelia that summer, after Pete Barnes wrecked the Mac and was laid up."

This can be dated to the early summer months of 1923, for in March 1923, Amelia was one of the advertised attractions at an "Air Rodeo" that took place at Glendale Airport. The advertisement listed the item as " 'Ladies Sportplane Special': Miss Amelia Earhart flying Kinner Airster and Miss Andree Pyre flying a Sport Farman."[13] Since, according to Lloyd Royer, it was at this time that Amelia sold her airplane, it would appear that she may have done so to help pay for the truck. Sam Chapman was said to be pleased at the sale of the airplane but Amelia recorded only that she

> decided to sell it much as I disliked the parting. A young man who had done some flying during the war . . . eventually purchased it.

After the new owner took possession the first thing he did was ask
a friend to go up with him.[14]

At a few hundred feet, the pilot began stunting as Amelia and her friends
stood "rooted to the spot." Bert Kinner was so concerned that he, practical
man that he was, telephoned for an ambulance. It wasn't needed. The
plane slipped off a low-level vertical bank and the occupants were killed
instantly.

In the following months, life at home deteriorated. Edwin suffered
from increasingly poor health, while Amelia suffered from extreme guilt
about the loss of her mother's money; for according to Lloyd Royer, it was
she—acting on advice from Sam Chapman—who originally persuaded
Edwin and Amy to invest in the trucking venture. The sale of the Kinner
was the only thing she had been able to do, personally, to help matters.

The purchase of the Moreland truck was an attempt to keep the
original business going, albeit in a reduced form, with a view to recovering
some of the losses sustained by the family. Life at home became intolerable,
however. Amy, her financial stability removed, became quarrelsome
and bitter. Edwin could do nothing right. Amelia, unable to fly, suffering
guilt and having to work even harder (she was trying to run the trucking
business in addition to her other jobs) without the same rewards, became
tired of it all and moved to a rooming house in Hollywood. Her mother
disapproved. She also "disapproved of the trucking business," just as she
had "disapproved of the airplane, but Amelia went ahead anyway."[15] On
occasions Amelia drove the truck.

At about this time, Amelia allegedly became engaged to Sam Chapman.
However, she also had several other male friends and at least one
of them, Lloyd Royer, was in love with her and proposed marriage. "But,"
he said, "she wasn't interested in marriage."[16] From June to October, she
worked for Peter Barnes's brother, Ralph, who owned a commercial photography
studio at Ninth and Figueroa streets in Los Angeles. Here, she
did the back-room work such as printing and developing. When one of
the partners sold his shares in the business, it nearly went bankrupt and
Amelia had to leave.[17] She then set up her own photographic business and
although this never prospered, she was once in the right place at the right
time. She never traveled anywhere without her camera and one day while
driving along Wilshire Boulevard, an oil well "came in" just as she was
passing. She took a photograph and was immediately accosted by the real
estate agent who was selling nearby plots for development. He purchased
the picture to show prospective buyers what they might expect![18]

To add to Amelia's existing problems—and perhaps exacerbate them—

the condition (an abscess in the nasal passages that had created a deep-seated sinus infection causing a great deal of pain) that had first occurred during her time at Spadina now flared up again. An operation was advised, which she undertook somewhat nervously.[19] The aftermath was months of further physical discomfort and the ignominy of being harried by a debt-collection agency for payment of the five-hundred-dollar medical fees. It took a year for Amelia to pay off this sum, but by then she had left California.

The year 1924 found Amelia frustrated and restless, the victim of self-confessed inertia.[20] Her attempts to revive the family fortunes proved fruitless. Although she somehow managed to purchase another Kinner plane—piecemeal (she said, "I found I could not buy it altogether")—and eventually she flew it, she never achieved the affection for it that she had for the *Canary*. It was a single seater with a three-cylinder Lawrence engine.[21] Amelia wrote little about it except to record that on one occasion, as she flew it between the mainland and Santa Catalina Island, she witnessed the weird darkness of an eclipse of the sun.[22]

By the late spring of 1924, Amelia was thoroughly depressed by family squabbles, lack of money, and her mother's continuous disapproval. At this point, the Earhart marriage broke down irrevocably. Despite all that had happened in the past, it was Edwin who sued for an uncontested divorce.

Under the circumstances, Amelia, Muriel, and Amy decided that they would return to Massachusetts. For at least a year, Amelia had nursed the idea of flying across the continent and returning to further her education. Maps, data, and charts were already prepared and she asked Amy to accompany her, but she found that the recurring pain in her head whenever she flew made the plan impossible. Muriel, who had been teaching fourth grade classes at Huntington Beach, resigned her post and traveled back east immediately—by train—in time for summer classes at Harvard, and lived near Boston.[23]

No matter how difficult her mother had become, Amelia loved her and was extremely supportive of both her parents during this difficult period. She sold her second Kinner airplane and bought a car—a Kissel—which she referred to as "The Kizzle" but which later acquired the nickname "The Yellow Peril" because of its bright paint job. She decided that if she couldn't fly, she would at least drive herself and her mother across America rather than travel ignominiously by train.

Since the divorce, Amy had moved into Amelia's Hollywood apartment and in mid-June 1924, they left there to drive to Boston via Sequoia, Yosemite, and the Canadian towns of Banff and Lake Louise. It was an enterprising scheme given the stage of development that autos had reached, but Amelia thought it an ideal opportunity to see some of the wonderful scenery of the great northwest.

Lloyd Royer was still driving the Moreland truck and keeping the trucking business going, and he wondered what his position was. He wrote to Amelia and received the following reply several weeks later.

CALGARY, ALBERTA
6/26/24

Dear Lloyd,

Our letters crossed. I was glad to hear from you at Seattle.

If you want to cut taitors, little O'Malley, do so. There are no outstanding debts other than those I sent check for, but some I owe the Moreland Company. I am repaying them as fast as I can. We never did agree about some of the items.

I suppose I have a lot of mail waiting for me in Los Angeles but I haven't known where to have it sent. . . . We have only had one hint of trouble with the motor, the head gasket blew out and every little town has a mechanic who strips all the [unreadable] for me and then they all have to be topped and larger ones put in. I carry two extra gaskets and treat Kizzle like a Ford—shift into low on any little incline.

Can you make expenses? If not let me know by wire at Yellowstone, Montana, or later at Chicago, in a week or ten days. Hope your ship was a success. We didn't intend to come into Calgary but found some of the roads better than our awful ones and anyway the scenery is just too grand for words. Heading for Glacier Park in a few minutes. . . . Thank you for your care of my affairs.[24]

By the time the two women reached Boston, they had traveled seven thousand miles and the car was covered in tourist stickers; whenever Amelia stopped, little groups of people gathered to ask how she'd come, what the roads were like, and other questions. Cross-continental travel by automobile was still a novelty and Amelia thought also "the fact that my roadster was a cheerful canary color may have caused some of the excitement. It had been modest enough in California, but was a little outspoken for Boston, I found."[25]

The pain in her head was, by the end of the journey, insupportable. Within days of her arrival in Boston, Amelia entered Massachusetts Memorial Hospital for an operation in which a small piece of bone was removed to allow drainage of the sinuses. It was completely successful and after a short convalescence, she was free of pain for the first time in four years. She then returned to Columbia University for the winter of 1924–25. The direction she had found for herself in California had dissipated and she recalled, "Like a great many other girls at this age I had no special plan for myself."[26] She was then twenty-seven years old and, clearly, from this remark, still thought of herself as a girl!

In May 1925, Amelia returned to the Boston area (Amy and Muriel had an apartment in nearby West Medford)[27] and for a few weeks taught English to foreign students at a Harvard University summer extension program. From June to October, she worked as a companion in a hospital for mental diseases, but she found the work "too confining" and the pay (seventy dollars a month) insufficient.[28]

Amelia still yearned to fly, but with no regular income, her only aviation contact was limited to visits to local fields and correspondence with Bert Kinner and Lloyd Royer, who now wrote to say he was starting his own business in aviation in partnership with John Montijo (Amelia's flying instructor).[29] It was agreed that Royer should sell the Moreland truck and send Amelia her share of the proceeds. She replied on a New York *Evening Journal* letterhead:

> *Dear Lloyd,*
>
> . . . Is there any dope on the truck yet? Is that cash supposed to come in a check to you or me or how? I'd just like to know. The letterhead on this paper is deceptive. I have not joined the staff of the Journal (tho' I wish I had as I find the newspaper interesting). I am just waiting for a lovely reporter . . . and in the meantime using some of Mr. Hearst's paper. . . . I have a friend who is a newspaper woman who-knows-the-man-who-owns the *Aeronautic Airway.* She has sworn to lead him to me but as he takes her flying etc., she may prefer to keep him to herself. I would(!) . . . please give me the details on all that happens out there aeronautically.
>
> *Amelia*[30]

In the autumn of 1925, Amelia answered a newspaper advertisement for the position of "novice" social worker at Denison House, Boston's second oldest settlement house. The principal, Miss Marion Perkins, liked what she saw in the applicant ". . . a strikingly interesting girl—very unusual vocabulary; is a photographer and wants to write . . ."; and she scrawled across the application form, "holds a sky pilots license!" Miss Perkins checked two of Amelia's references and received a reply from Amelia's previous employer, Dr. Torney, attesting "Pleasing personality, active, very willing, obliging, an excellent worker, very capable . . . will do well in anything in which she has training and sufficient self-knowledge not to undertake work in which she has no ability."[31] Sam Chapman, Amelia's fiancé and second reference, wrote quaintly that she was "all right." He had known her for four years, he said, and paid tribute to her scholarship and general ability.

Sam had followed Amelia back to Massachusetts and was now employed at the Edison Electric Company as an industrial heating engineer. Marriage seemed inevitable, at least to Sam, Amy, and Muriel, but one senses there was always a hesitation in Amelia. She obviously cared for Sam a great deal; but was there still a questing in her approach to life that she felt would be quashed by marriage? As a couple, Sam and Amelia joined Muriel and her boyfriend, Albert Morrissey, for outings to the beaches at Marblehead. Sam obviously sensed a withdrawal in Amelia and put it down to his unsocial hours (he worked a night shift), which he tried to change in order to spend more time with his fiancée. This merely annoyed Amelia, who told her sister, "He should do whatever makes him happiest. . . . I know what I want to do and I expect to do it married or single. . . ."[32]

Despite Amelia's lack of experience in social work, Miss Perkins was so impressed with the "tall, slender, boyish-looking woman who walked into my office" that Amelia got the job at Denison, and had she never done anything else in her life, it is likely that she would have been perfectly happy with her lot. In the first year, she had general direction of the evening classes for foreign-born men and women, but as time went on, her workload expanded. Socially responsible, she enthusiastically tackled the work of educating the poor, mainly immigrant families that proliferated in the lower corner of older Boston. She taught them English and was always eager to learn something of the languages of those she taught. She ferried sick patients to the hospital in her car, "The Yellow Peril." She explained Western customs; organized outings, games, and plays for children; ran classes on various subjects including citizenship; and found the work totally fulfilling.

Once again Amelia began to look outward. She had little spare time and even less spare money, but the situation improved as she received a regular salary of thirty-five dollars a week. She made contact with local pilots, joined the Boston chapter of the National Aeronautic Association, and was able to fly occasionally. In the autumn of 1927, she became a full-time resident staff member at Denison House and was also voted into the position of secretary to the board of directors.

She had kept in touch with Bert Kinner and tried to find a potential sales agent in the Boston area for the Kinner Special. Kinner, however, found one himself. A young architect from Boston named Harold T. Dennison (no connection with Denison House) met Kinner while on a trip in California. Their discussions sent Dennison back to Boston determined to build an airport and market Kinner airplanes. On Kinner's recommendation, Dennison contacted Amelia to ask whether she would like to be involved. Amelia hadn't much money but what she had, she willingly invested, becoming a director of the company that shortly afterward built Dennison Airport on the Quincy Shore Reservation Boulevard.[33]

The flying school was equipped with six Waco and Kinner airplanes and the original field (known as Harvard Aviation Field) was, in 1910, the site of the first fly-in in the United States.[34] As well as a flying school and good runways, Dennison operated an air taxi service between Boston, Chicago, and New York, with stops at Hyannis and Boston.[35]

Probably to the distress of her more stuffy relatives, Amelia's name started to appear in the newspapers with a regularity that indicates Amelia not only recognized the value of publicity but also was not averse to it. WOMAN TO FLY FOR CEDAR HILL FETE proclaimed one. MISS AMELIA EARHART FLIES IN A PLANE OVER BOSTON said another when Amelia "bombed" the area with leaflets advertising a fund-raising event. The Boston *Globe* interviewed her a few weeks later in June 1927 and she took full advantage of the occasion to promote flying, especially for women. Thereafter, she was often in the columns of the *Globe*, where she was usually described as "one of the best women pilots in the United States."

Feeling that she had a definite role to play in the development of aviation, Amelia contacted other women pilots (there were few) to see whether they could encourage more women to fly. She wrote a table-thumping, three-page letter to the Boston Chamber of Commerce about the lack of publicity in the area for aviation.

> . . . Why aren't we doing something notable here? You know there are two ways to accomplishment—one, through doing exceptional things, and another by sweeping to it by force of numbers. Boston Chapter of NAA has exceptional men in it but not numbers. Aviation needs widespread support.
>
> . . . The Los Angeles Chamber of Commerce expands all over the map, simply by getting so much publicity that it is considered quite the thing to belong to so well known an organization. So with the California Automobile Club.

There should be advertising. . . . A social worker always thinks of ways to raise money so I propose a benefit of some sort. There are various ways from scalping tickets at a popular performance to putting on one's own. I'd ask Will Rogers to come on, and pay him a thousand to fill Symphony Hall, for a good profit. . . .[36]

Quite what part Sam Chapman played in this busy and fulfilled life is difficult to assess. Amelia hardly mentioned him in any of her writing, and he never spoke of her publicly, though the two were to remain the closest of friends for many years. That they were formally engaged became apparent only when Amelia admitted at a later date to reporters that "I am no longer engaged."

It was in April 1927 that Amelia's life changed forever. She was helping to organize a class play when the telephone rang and she was sent for. "I'm too busy to answer just now," she said. "Ask whoever it is calling to try again later." Pressed, she went to the phone "very unwillingly and heard a masculine voice introduce himself. 'Hello. You don't know me but my name is Railey . . . Captain H. H. Railey.' " Later that day, Captain Railey asked Amelia Earhart if she would like to be the first woman to fly across the Atlantic.[37]

BOOK TWO :

GEORGE PALMER PUTNAM

My father was a publisher, and his father before
him. My earliest recollections are of books; and of
authors, whom I have never held in proper awe
since.

— *George Palmer Putnam,*
Wide Margins *(New York:
Harcourt, Brace and
Company, 1942), p. 3*

Chapter Six

1 8 8 7 - 1 9 0 9

George Palmer Putnam was born in Rye, New York, on September 7, 1887, into a comfortably well-off, if not wealthy, publishing family. His very earliest recollections were of books and his childhood appears to have been singularly happy.[1] The warm and loving family home created by his parents allowed the extraordinary talents of their son to burgeon unfettered, and he grew with an intelligent grasp of what was happening around him, developing a writer's knack of observation.[2]

The atmosphere of the Putnam home was bookish, and it was generally assumed that George Palmer Putnam would grow up to be a publisher or, "at worst, a writer."[3] George's father often took the small boy to New York to "the office" on Fifth Avenue, and they would lunch at the Union League Club or the Fifth Avenue Hotel. The small boy enjoyed these trips, but what fascinated him more was a visit to the family's printing press (The Knickerbocker Press) in New Rochelle. George grew up loving the smells of ink in the press room, of glue and paper in the bindery, and the special fragrance of leather from the rolls of Levant, calfskin, and buckram. But, he said, "the best smells of all, perhaps, were in the foundry . . . where mysterious electrical processes created plates for the presses."[4]

Despite this dedicated nurturing, George had reached the advanced age of eleven before he entered the world of publishing. At this time, he wrote, edited, and sold a "newspaper" under the title *The Will o' the Wisp*—"to be published semi-occasionally," it proclaimed. The Spanish-American War had just begun and the already prescient George made it clear from the start that all profits from his paper were to be donated to the Red Cross. By this device, he was easily able to sell advertising space to local tradesmen (with the exception of the butcher, who would have none of such nonsense), and after the first and only edition, he was able to deliver "a net profit of eighty-six dollars to the Red Cross." Even more satisfying to the youngster, though, was the fact that his name had been "at an editorial masthead."[5]

However, George was even younger when he first started to exploit his formidable entrepreneurial skills. He had been used to visiting a neighbor, a retired mounted policeman from New York who had a beautiful horse trained to do tricks. The neighbor also kept ducks. "My [older] brother, just then, for reasons not clear, wanted ducks. . . . Our neighbor agreed to sell me three ducks for fifty cents each. I told him it was a deal. Then I broached the matter to Brother. I told him I had three particularly fine ducks that I could let him have for $2.50. After bargaining he agreed to pay $2.25 if the ducks suited him." Scampering over to the neighbor, George collected the ducks "on approval," sold them to his brother and, after paying costs, found himself with a clear profit of seventy-five cents. "When Brother found out the facts, he both thrashed me and told Father. . . . Father suspended sentence. Possibly he was pleased."[6]

In his mid-teens, George attended the Gunnery School in Washington, Connecticut. A "fair" scholar, he spent his spare time trout fishing (much fishing and few trout, he said), climbing alone in the hills, and rabbit and partridge hunting. Although well built, he was poor at athletics and sensitive; "a group of sturdy football players who headed up school life regarded me with no warmth. . . . I was not popular." It was his own fault, he claimed, recognizing in retrospect that because of his lonely preoccupations, he probably appeared priggish.[7]

The few friends he had during these years were unusual people themselves, "daffy," George was to reflect in his autobiography, written forty years later. There were Gerald and Gladys Thayer, the children of an artist who lived an unconventional life (thus shocking the neighbors, but of whom George was totally uncritical), whom he had met while on vacation in New Hampshire. Artist and writer Rockwell Kent, some five years older than George, was another friend and seems to have been a sort of ringleader. Theodore Roosevelt, also friends with the Thayers, came into this small milieu as someone at "bitter loggerheads" with Abbott Thayer and his notions of art. "They had a splendid time firing broadsides at each other," George commented, but the young Putnam was content to accept Thayer's theories on coloring and the portrayal of fauna, for the artist was a noted naturalist. Although George never elaborated on this youthful friendship with Roosevelt, it marked the start of a relationship that would play a larger part in George's life in later years.

When he was seventeen years old, George fell in love with Gladys Thayer, "Galla" as he called her, "a fragrant girl with a special beauty all her own." The young couple contemplated marriage but George's parents intercepted the romantic plans and sent him to Scandinavia for the summer. There he had "an experience" with a girl named Helga, who "had eyes the color of cornflowers and fair hair more the shade of honey than buttercups," and who helped him reach the conclusion that he was not yet ready to be tied down in wedlock.[8]

The winter months seemed to hold the promise of fun when George returned from Scandinavia, for he was invited to join Gerald Thayer and Rockwell Kent in what turned out to be a winter-long bachelor party. George was not disappointed. The natives of the hamlet of Dublin, New Hampshire, hastily lowered their blinds when on one occasion Rockwell and Gerald skied naked (except for shoes and socks), pulled along by galloping horses. One typical Rockwell Kent prank involved laying the tracks of a "wildcat" in the snow with the aid of some paws filched from a museum. This, abetted by some realistic wildcat yowling at night, together with the normal countryside predations on chickens and small livestock, created a full-scale "wildcat scare" and terrorized the countryside. Before the joke was through, it had even reached the columns of a Boston newspaper.[9] The ease with which the newspapers took this story on trust made a deep impression on George.

The three young men slept, cooked, ate, and argued, and "on occasion worked." The outside temperature seldom rose above zero, but there was Schopenhauer, Walt Whitman, Milton, Landor, Swinburne, and Coventry Patmore to read and endlessly discuss. George said in his memoir:

> With the way of youth, we discoursed interminably about life and love and death, economics, politics and the welfare of man . . . there was socialism of course, single tax and vegetarianism, and a dash of free love. Communism was not yet in vogue.[10]

Doubtless, the afterthought referred to Rockwell Kent's subsequent political affiliations.

Later, George spent some time at Kent's house on Monhegan Island off the coast of Maine, the subject of many of the artist's best paintings.[11] It was locally held that any young man who had gone to the trouble of building a home must be in search of a wife, and so Kent and George decided it would be uncivil to disappoint the locals. A plot was concocted and on the next occasion that Rockwell Kent visited the mainland on business, George "happened" to look in at the Dublin post office, where he received a letter from his friend, which he opened and partially read aloud in apparent astonishment. He later recalled:

I dare say by evening there was not a person on the island unacquainted with the letter's contents. In that letter Kent (pledging me to secrecy) had unfolded his intimate plans. He was bringing back his bride.

A couple of days later I disappeared, ostensibly to go on a fishing trip, which I often did. Instead I met Kent . . . he had brought from Boston a costume to delight a peripatetic bride, complete with fittings that included a picture hat with veil, a frilly dress, gay shoes and stockings. Also the wherewithal to change my figure so that it would swell at those places where, under the circumstances, it should. Also Kent had with him a gorgeous auburn wig and a make-up box. . . . I was a couple of hands taller than my groom and doubt if I appeared ravishing. But I was rigged out like nobody's business.[12]

The happy couple were transported to the island in traditional fashion—in a boat with an evergreen tree lashed to the masthead. At the landing wharf, "an impromptu orchestra of white-clad summer folks played the wedding march on combs, horns and sundry other instruments." A girl friend and her mother, who had been let in on the secret, shielded the helpless bride from the gaze of the overcurious and helped "her" into the decorated wedding chariot. Back at Kent's home, "eager hands had cleaned [the house] as it had never been cleaned before. They positively polished it and filled it with flowers. I remember that even the pins were arranged in heart-shaped designs in the pine wall over an improvised dressing table. There were too, the usual pranks about the bed."[13]

However, there were doubts voiced about the bride's authenticity and the couple had barely reached home when a crowd, angry at what they suspected was a gross deception, approached the house. George quickly donned a pink nightdress, hopped into bed, and, turning his face to the wall, sobbed softly. Kent arranged the bride's hair appealingly across the sheets and when he opened the door, he was a desperate man. Indicating the piteous figure on the bed, he whispered:

"She's collapsed. . . . It's been too much. I don't know what to do. Won't you . . . won't you *please*, Tom, get me some liquor . . . a little stimulant may revive her."

Tom Spinney's anger melted away and so did he, pellmell for the village to do his good deed. Shortly he was back with a pint bottle.[14]

This prep-school brand of humor stayed with George all his life. He had a well-developed sense of fun and was always ready for a practical joke.

Sometimes, though, it must be said that the subject upon whom the joke was perpetrated found it hard to laugh.

George spent the winter of 1906–07 at Harvard studying German, English, Greek, fine arts, and politics, but left in February "on account of illness."[15] College records show that his work until that time was satisfactory and on the strength of his good record the administrative board voted to allow him to return and take up the courses he had dropped, should he wish to do so. He apparently did not wish to do so, for on recovering his health, he worked for several months in the educational department of G. P. Putnam's Sons, before traveling to California in the spring of 1908. There he spent the summer "on the fringes of the desert south of Los Angeles (now Palm Springs)," where he acquired a few gold-mine claims and with the aid of a favorable letter from the assistant dean of Harvard, enrolled at the University of California at Berkeley for the fall semester, studying French, literature, and economics.[16] His time at Berkeley was as undistinguished as his previous educational career, but by now he had met Dorothy Binney.

Dorothy was the daughter of a wealthy industrialist who (among his other interests) was head of the Binney & Smith Crayola crayon company. She was a socialite but a strong-minded, gifted, and attractive young woman. Fair-haired, tall, and with an outgoing personality, she had a ready sense of humor that George found particularly attractive. Dorothy was spending a holiday in California prior to the new college term at Wellesley and met George "on a Sierra Club outing."[17] "Six feet two inches, dark and *very* handsome, and a confirmed woman hater," she mischievously described him to her classmates.[18] He was not so much a misogynist as all that, apparently, for within a matter of weeks George had fallen in love and proposed. Shortly afterward, Dorothy returned to her parents' home in Old Greenwich, Connecticut, to finish her education. The courtship continued by mail and with at least two visits by George to Connecticut.

Having obtained Dorothy's acceptance of his proposal of marriage, George realized that he needed to make enough money to support a wife, and in time-honored fashion, he set out to make his fortune. At the beginning of 1909, having left college and reached the age of twenty-one, he traveled north from California to Oregon.

It would be as well, at this point, to reflect that, although George was a member of the Putnam family, he was a younger son. George may well have had all the attributes of a publisher bred in him, but his elder brother, Robert, was destined to inherit the role of publisher. George's father had three brothers (Haven, Herbert, and Irving), and among them they owned the publishing firm G. P. Putnam's Sons. Each brother had several sons and probably there was no room for two sons of each partner in the firm.

George, therefore, had to make his own way in life, and his own destiny. As a child, George had been an avid reader of adventure books, particularly those about the wild northwestern United States. Indeed, the first book he discovered for himself, and to which he was very attached, was *The Canoe and the Saddle* by Theodore John Winthrop, which fired the boy's imagination about the adventures to be had in the great unsettled tracts of country.[19]

In 1909, the sage advice "Go west, young man" was still relevant to anyone wishing to make a fortune from nothing but enthusiasm and hard work. George decided to look for adventure and success, and the best place to do this, he concluded, "was Bend . . . geographically at the center of Oregon . . . it was one hundred miles from a railroad . . . [in] what the come-hither literature of the Northwest euphemistically called virgin territory."[20]

"There I was, an easterner in the far reaches of the roaring west," he wrote. "I wanted to hear it roar."[21]

C h a p t e r   S e v e n

1 9 0 9 - 1 9 1 5

George spent the next six years of his life in Bend, Oregon. They marked the beginning of a lifelong love affair with mountains and wilderness, for he was never happier than when living in rugged isolation, although he was adaptable enough to translate, with great élan, to a Fifth Avenue office, a New England drawing room, or even the White House. For the moment, though, George's chosen land—the "largest railroadless area in the United States"—was

> a country where a son of the East could dwell on the wonders of both young and old mountains covered with snow almost the whole year; a country where lava flowed, where volcanic cinder cones, once guides for immigrant trains, stood on the lines of future city limits; where centuries before running lava had trapped and made molds of timber stands; where beautiful blue lakes had been created when mountain tops exploded; where a vast desert stretched a hundred miles north, south and east; and where billions of board feet of pine covered thousands of acres of land.[1]

Though George came to love the rugged terrain, his immediate attentions during that first journey to his chosen objective were more probably riveted upon his personal discomfort. From Portland, he traveled by train to Shaniko, the gateway to central Oregon.

> From this dismal jumping off place freighters hauled merchandise to towns as far distant as two hundred miles, and stages radiated to the south. The sheep of a sheepman's empire congregated there. With streets of mud or dust, according to the season, a score of raw frame shacks, warehouses, livery barns, shipping pens, and hotels Shaniko

in its prime was a busy, boisterous town of freighters and sheep herders.[2]

From Shaniko, George continued by stagecoach to Bend, where many vehicles overturned on the villainous grades of Cow Canyon, or bogged down in the adobe mud of Shaniko Flats. He recalled his own journey on

> . . . a January night when two-day rain had turned to snow, when the air was freezing but the mud was soft, and the up-stage met the down-stage where there was no turning out. Drivers and passengers worked and swore in the murk and the mud, until one stage had been shunted out of the way on a handmade shelf so to speak; the clothing and the dispositions of all concerned were ruined. But the passing was effected.
>
> There were one hundred miles of road between Shaniko and Bend, 528,000 feet of dust, mud, chuck holes, hills, rocks, ruts and bumps.[3]

Nor was there any respite for the weary young man when he arrived at his destination, for there was only one hotel in the little frontier town and it was full. George had to spend the night in a room over the saloon and noted before he slept that there was a hole in the floor through which he could look down at the bar if he wished.[4]

Upon waking, George knew that the tiresome journey had been worth the effort, for the clear, clean beauty of the scenery glimpsed through a small grimy window enchanted him. Located in a great curve on the Deschutes River, Bend looked out upon the panorama of the heavily forested Cascade mountain range, with the snow-covered Three Sisters as a focal point. "In those mountains," he decided on the spot, "I knew I would like to live."[5]

Bend's population was 536 persons, although there were as many again in the outlying areas.[6] George's appearance in the town did not go unnoticed, for the Bend *Bulletin* noted on May 12, 1909 that George would be there for several weeks. "Mr. Putnam has spent about a year on the Pacific Coast representing Putnam and Sons, Publishers [*sic*], of which his father is the head."

George was now twenty-one years of age. He dressed well, imparted an air of great confidence, possessed a forceful personal manner, and, according to his autobiography, he stepped off the stagecoach in Bend with three hundred dollars and a considerable curiosity. "His strong, well-formed face was at the same time sensitive and almost delicate, especially the mouth. [His] uncommonly handsome profile was complemented by an abundance of well-kept, black curly hair and dark, intense eyes . . . and while [he] was in some ways the epitome of the reserved, cool New Englander, he nevertheless fed upon companionship and soon set about seeking new friends."[7] Unmarried young ladies casting a hopeful eye in the direction of this promising newcomer were to be disappointed, however, for residents recalled later that he remained faithful to his fiancée, Dorothy, and kept a life-size photograph of her on his closet door.[8]

The early days of George's residence were notable only for his fishing trips up the Deschutes. Within weeks, however, he had acquired a typewriter and by July was acting as a freelance reporter for *The Oregonian* of Portland, his first published article being a full-page report of Independence Day celebrations in Bend.

Greater things were in store for him. It has been said of Putnam that "He was the right man, in the right place, at the right time."[9] The factors that had drawn him to the town—its frontier conditions and lack of railroad—were also the reasons why, without some positive action, it could easily have become a ghost town like so many other hopeful settlements in the northwest. In fact, the residents of Bend had been agitating to bring the railroad to Bend for a decade and more, but success still eluded them in 1909, though the need for a method of transporting goods, materials, and people in and out of central Oregon was obvious. The chief hindrance to the scheme was competition between two railroad magnates, E. H. Harriman and James J. Hill, who were each fighting for control of the state's railroad system.

By late July 1909, rumors flew that after all the years of fighting, not one but two teams of railroad crew were at work in the area. George, acting as freelance correspondent for *The Oregonian,* set off into the country to investigate. It was the first of two nearly one-hundred-mile walks that George would make through the Deschutes gorge.

> For 10 days Putnam walked along the canyon's bottom, talking to the many Porter Brothers crews and receiving nothing but denials that they were working for Hill. Finally he ascended the walls of the canyon, made his way across the plateau to a telephone and called *The Oregonian* to report on his fruitless efforts. He then put up at the farmhouse of a man and his wife.
>
> There the talk soon got around to the railroads, and the couple casually mentioned that the survey party had been through the area just days before, seeking a right-of-way for a water power project. The men had stopped and purchased some buttermilk from the lady of the house and had paid her with a voucher instead of cash. She asked

George Putnam if it was worth anything. One look at the voucher
and George Putnam hightailed it to the nearest telephone 19 miles
away. It was a Great Northern voucher. Here at last was solid proof
of Hill's link with the Porter Brothers crews.[10]

The story, which George recognized as a sizeable scoop, had unfortunately
broken earlier that morning in a rival paper. His work, however, gained
him the reputation of being the local expert on the railways' progress, and
the *Bulletin* readily published his articles on the subject, one of which
ended with the ringing conclusion: "Unless the courts interfere, the
Deschutes canyon will see the greatest railroad war in Northwestern
history."[11] Nor was he far out in his predictions, for eventually the courts
had to step in when physical confrontation between the rival construction
groups led to riots.

Meanwhile, however, George had secured for himself an important job.
With two railroads racing toward Bend, the little town looked set for a
boom. The full-time salaried position of secretary to the Bend Board of
Trade, itself a newly created body, had the stamp of George Putnam all
over it. It is a safe assumption that he suggested the vacancy to the board
and probably wrote his own job description. Today, he would be described
as the town publicity officer, for the job specifically required George to
"attend to the Advertising Features and Correspondence" and to publicize the virtues and possibilities of Bend. Reporting the new appointment,
the *Bulletin* described George as having been involved in publicity work
in California, possibly referring to some job he had undertaken for G. P.
Putnam's Sons, and stated that he was to devote most of his time to
writing articles for newspapers and magazines.

One of George's first moves was the printing and distribution of five
thousand leaflets extolling the brilliant promise and the inevitable prosperity of Bend. He also took pains to ensure that fellow citizens were made
aware that he was succeeding in his task. "Have you noticed the frequency
with which Bend appears in the Portland newspapers lately? This town
and section are receiving a world of good advertising these days. It pays
to boost . . . ," he proclaimed in the *Bulletin* a month after taking office.
He was never modest but he was effective, and over the next months the
Bulletin carried regular stories on exactly what George was doing to
publicize the town. His many articles and features were accompanied by
photographs, taken by himself with his ever-present Kodak.[12] Each
month he published a newsletter that was vigorously distributed to all
northwestern newspapers and this was backed up with advertisements.

George returned home to New England for Christmas, but a family reunion was not the only thing on his mind. There was, of course, his fiancée, Dorothy Binney, whom he had not seen since May and with whom his only point of contact had been a series of letters. He also hoped to gain wider exposure for his articles on Bend in *Putnam's Magazine,* which enjoyed national circulation. More important, he needed to discuss with his father a project that fueled his ambition.

The Bend *Bulletin* was a typical small-town newspaper. Powerful in its monopoly, if not in circulation, it had been established some six years earlier. Perhaps George was faintly irritated by its parochial style and sensed that he could improve its content. Certainly, he must have been aware of its potential when the prosperity he was constantly predicting and publicizing for the town occurred. Probably, in the fall of 1909, it was making a loss for the current owner, Don Steffa, for it seems that he and George had already started negotiations before George left to travel east, and George later indicated that Steffa was anxious to dispose of it.[13]

The trip was obviously successful. The January cover of *Putnam's Magazine* was an engraving of Bend and the lead article was George's "Opening Up Central Oregon."[14] Immediately following his return to Bend, he left for a trip through central Oregon with a representative of the Great Northern Railroad. In February, he impressed the Board of Trade meeting with news of a pamphlet "designed to be distributed by the millions," upon which he was working in tandem with the Great Northern.[15] He then set off on foot for his second journey through the Deschutes Canyon and the railroad construction camps, gathering material that he used for more articles.[16]

In March 1910, the news broke that George had purchased the *Bulletin.*[17] In his autobiography, he stated that he acquired it

> ... for a very modest consideration and mostly on credit ... and while I was editor wrote blistering editorials. . . . A few were published but most of them went into the lower right-hand drawer of my desk. Writing them was almost as satisfactory as seeing them in print. It relieved blood pressure and hurt nobody. There still is a special place where I put certain letters I write, to stay there during a period of incubation. Usually at the end of the probation it seems best not to send them. I'm increasingly inclined to think the things one does not do make less trouble than the things done.[18]

In fact, George became the archetypal battling frontier newspaperman, declaring war on unnecessary bureaucracy, tackling important local issues with gleeful panache, and attacking local corruption with intelligent use of the power his position as editor provided. When he suspected a local judge of dishonesty, he wrote one of his "blistering editorials" under the headline THE COURTHOUSE STENCH. When the judge protested that he could not get a fair hearing in the newspaper, George provided his protagonist with a blank column "to use as he liked." The paper appeared with the column blank for several issues, bearing only a memorandum to Judge Springer: "You said you can get no hearing. . . . In this space we will print anything you want. There is absolutely no restriction; the space is yours gratis."[19] The judge was subsequently ridiculed out of office. It has been said that "The longer George Palmer Putnam remained in the Bend community, the wider the range of his boosting activities became."[20] His campaigns ranged from cleaning up the town saloons to a drive to build an automobile road to Burns, 150 miles to the east. Meanwhile, his publicity campaign for Bend continued and new settlers began to flow in. "Never has the future held more brilliant promise for Bend than it does today," the *Bulletin* proclaimed in April 1911, gloating over the sawmills, flour mills, woolen mills, and distributing houses then looking at Bend as an ideal location because of its double railroad terminus, unlimited water power, and endless stands of timber.

George was twenty-four years old, an obvious success as promoter of his chosen town and editor of its newspaper, full of confidence and ambition. But he had not forgotten Dorothy Binney, and despite all his work to get the railroads into the town, he missed the great moment when the final "golden spike" was hammered into place. While that great event took place, accompanied by "Railroad Day festivities" consisting of log rolling, a canoe war, a grand parade, boxing contests, horse and foot races, a baby show, pillow fights, and bronco busting, and finished off by a dance in Linster Hall, George was in Connecticut making arrangements for his marriage.

Dorothy had been graduated from Wellesley in June 1910. Her fiancé had not been able to escort her at the graduation ceremonies but she had understood that he was busy building his empire in the west. The marriage took place at the bride's parents' house at Sound Beach, Connecticut, on October 26, 1911, and the newlyweds spent four months honeymooning in Panama, Costa Rica, Nicaragua, Honduras, Guatemala, El Salvador, and Mexico.[21] As usual, George's talent for making important connections surfaced, and they were known to have met and dined with Don Pablo Arosemeña, president of Panama; Dr. Belisario Porras (who subsequently became president of Panama); and Don Ricardo Jiminez, president of Costa Rica. It was February 1912 before they returned to "Pinelyn," George's home in Bend, and it was very quickly evident that

George had not been idle on his long vacation.[22] He managed to produce his first book *(In the Southland of North America),* compiled from his notes and photographs of the trip, as well as numerous articles in newspapers and magazines about the engineering miracle of the Panama Canal.[23] The book was dedicated to Dorothy, "the best of travel partners."

The *Bulletin* had run a front-page piece on the Putnams' honeymoon, but this announcement was totally eclipsed by George's two-column headline that he had purchased A MACHINE THAT WILL SET ITS TYPE. "The new Model 10 Merganthaler . . . is the finest typesetting machine made and will be the only one of its kind in Oregon or Washington."[24]

Mr. and Mrs. Putnam arrived in Bend to start their married life in February 1912. Their home, built in the previous year by George, was a large six-bedroom building boasting its own tennis courts (Dorothy was a keen and excellent tennis player).[25]

George's return to work heralded yet more modern equipment and a new building for the *Bulletin.* Soon the newspaper was capable of producing 1,600 pages an hour on its new presses and the enterprising young owner turned the loss-making concern into a very profitable one.[26] George worked hard and long days during this period and in his autobiography he reckoned that he had done the work of three men.

> Seven o'clock saw me in the shop, and by eight everything was cleaned, from floors to ink rollers, and, if it were winter, the fires blazing in the big sheet metal stove beside the foot-power hand press and in the little potbellied firebox in the front office.[27]

George wrote the editorials and articles for the *Bulletin* and, under several different pen names such as Palmer Bend, he acted as stringer for five big-city newspapers. A stringer was paid by space rates, so each month he would paste up (string) his copy and add up the inches before submitting his bill. The best remuneration was from the *Oregonian,* whose rate was eight dollars a column. When the *Bulletin* needed advertisements, George would take stock of local business, decide what they needed to advertise, write and paste up the copy, and set a proof. Then he would take it to the proprietor and sell the space. He did the same with business cards, letterheads, and brochures. He even provided imaginative letters for the correspondence column.

If there were no stories, the enterprising Putnam wrote articles and, once, "for three weeks there was a prosperous sequence of interviews with a mythical character called Know Joles who went into the mountains clad only in his birthday suit, and had preposterous adventures." These satirical pieces were aimed at a series of back-to-nature articles, appearing in the Portland newspapers, written by Joe Knowles, whose "adventures became pitifully tame compared with what befell my hero." In one piece "Joles" delighted city readers with the story of his pet trout, Lucy.

> I kept [her] in a shallow gold pan until she slopped all the water out and developed the knack of getting on comfortably in air. Sometimes I'd take her to town to do tricks for the boys on the bar at Hugh O'Kanes. But once I forgot to shut the door of my cabin when I'd left Lucy there, and halfway across the foot log over the Deschutes River I looked back and there was Lucy scuffling along after me. I ran back, but before I reached her, Lucy lost her balance on the log and fell into the river and was drowned.[28]

As if his editorial duties were not enough, George acquired, through a bad debt, the town movie house. It was converted from a long, narrow shop and seated sixty people. In the winter, moviegoers froze and in the summer, they baked. George and his assistant ran it after they had completed their day's work at the *Bulletin,* and George stood at the door until he had sold thirty-six tickets, enough to cover the evening's costs. At this point, he could leave the job to a high school girl who doubled as a piano player. This lasted only six months, for George could never make it consistently profitable.[29]

Besides, he had other and more important duties to which to attend. In June 1912, at the age of twenty-four, George was elected mayor. Writing about the incident later, he explained how, when the incumbent mayor resigned, and in the absence of a replacement, the solid citizens could only fume impotently, while the saloons, gambling joints, and bawdy houses ran riot. Finally, a bloody gunfight—involving a woman, her ex-lover, and a current lover—that resulted in the death of the lady and the serious injury of one of the men brought matters to a head. The citizens acted, presenting an antigambling, antiprostitution petition to the council and demanding the immediate election of a new mayor, or, they said, they would elect one themselves.[30]

There were initially two candidates—one in favor of a wide-open, free-and-easy frontier town, the other a virtuous citizen who sought the path of righteousness and sobriety—and for a month there was deadlock among the six city councillors over whom to elect. When at last the county sheriff instructed Bend to "get its house in order or else," a compromise candidate was quickly found who seemed to upset neither the "wide-opens" nor the "tight-shuts." George said:

He gambled a bit, drank decently, and was no prude; he was young, and youth is liberal. On the other hand he was married and respectable; being young he'd not had time to be too contaminated by disreputable influences. So one night, all six harried councilmen voted for this paragon.

I was it.[31]

In fact, George had already served for a very short period as mayor pro tem in August 1910 in the absence of the incumbent mayor, so the duties of office were not exactly new to him. Now, he was elected "six votes to nothing" and became the town's "boy mayor."

The little community, for the moment, was in my lap. I tried to do right by it. A reasonably thorough housecleaning was had. We presented a shining face to the outer world, though perhaps the back of the civic neck had not been scrubbed too thoroughly. Mostly, the dubious ladies went. What gambling remained became orderly and unobtrusive. The saloons found wisdom in keeping strict hours and discouraging drunkenness. Rough stuff was frowned upon. Toughs who wanted to fight were beaten up and sent on their way.[32]

George's term of office lasted a year and a half and included several brushes with Oregon's governor, who when he formally complained to George about Bend's unruly reputation was tartly reminded, in print, that there was far more rottenness in Portland, and even under the governor's own nose in Salem, than in Bend.[33]

Another opponent, according to George's autobiography, was Jack Culpepper, a saloon proprietor with wide blue eyes "that were too guileless, and a dashing swagger." When George and Culpepper clashed over the licensing law, Culpepper spread the word that if George were to appear in the main street, he would be shot full of holes. George recognized that he either had "to show up, or be shown up . . . [for] once the town got to laughing at its boy mayor, he'd be through."[34]

George called Culpepper's bluff. Conspicuously unarmed and with both hands in full view (but, he confessed, with knees shaking), he walked along the main street sidewalk. The chief of police, a man with a reputation as an excellent shot, followed a short distance behind with both hands in his pockets. Nothing happened, but the matter did not end there. George somehow discovered that Culpepper had spent a term in a Montana penitentiary due to a "slight case of homicide." Putnam obtained an official mug shot of Culpepper in prison garb and pasted the picture over a two-column typeset article telling the unembroidered story. He then pulled a proof of the layout, locked up the type, and went round to Culpepper to see whether he was interested. From that moment, Culpepper became George's stoutest supporter and "friend." The article never ran.

After six months, George's first term of office expired and he was voted back by a healthy majority, polling 208 votes to his nearest opponent's 96. He assumed this signified approval and continued to run the town with "a middle-of-the-road approach." He limited the saloons to five in number and issued them with licenses at $1,200 a year. He started a civic project for a main sewer and was soon able to report in the *Bulletin* that CITY FINANCES SHOW UP WELL. Among other municipal triumphs reported were the following: "Council Sets Work Record . . . Realty Dealers Licensed . . . $4,500 in Street Improvements . . . Pest House and Hitching Place Authorized."

In all his work, George was supported by Dorothy. Far from feeling neglected when George drove himself to the limit, she encouraged him and even helped at the newspaper office when necessary. When George could be spared from the office, sometimes the two would go off on horseback to camp in the mountains. Dorothy, too, was an organizer. She founded and directed the town's glee club and (less acceptable to some of George's colleagues) a women's suffrage club, which she claimed "materially aided the State of Oregon to become a suffrage state."[35]

On May 20, 1913, a son, David Binney Putnam, was born to George and Dorothy. He was a fine, healthy boy with blue eyes and blond hair; and "it was all done with a couple of pots of hot water and very little fuss in our house that faced the snowy peaks of the Three Sisters. The lad himself was spanked by [the doctor's] huge hand, washed up on the dining table and then, nested in blankets, set to toast before the open fire."[36]

The little boy's birth almost coincided with the *Bulletin*'s tenth birthday, and George was proudly able to reflect on the success he had wrought during his period as editor. In three years, he had taken the paper's circulation from 450 copies to 1,650; every copy was either sold to a subscriber or over the counter in the office or on the street. When he took the paper over, it was a four-page production. By 1913, it contained sixteen pages; he had just cause to feel pleased with himself.[37]

In addition, he served on the fire brigade, and as all the buildings were wooden, fires were frequent. On one occasion, when the opera house was ablaze, George situated himself on the roof of a neighboring building in order to direct the hose at the center of the fire. He later discovered that the building beneath him housed huge drums of gasoline.[38]

In December 1913, George decided not to run for reelection but to concentrate instead on the *Bulletin*. He summed up his term of office with the simple comment that he was "too tough for the virtuous and too virtuous for the tough."[39] Physically tired, George decided to take Dorothy and little David for an extended trip back east. For three months, they visited relations and cruised the inland waterway through Florida before returning to Bend via New Orleans and San Francisco in March 1914.[40] For the next year, George occupied his time running a fierce and, eventually, successful campaign for irrigation, on behalf of settlers. But the pressure was beginning to tell. He was twenty-seven years old, but he was to write in the following spring that "editing a newspaper in a small town is a wearying pursuit, full of petty trials and tribulations, hedged by irritating routine and woefully limited by the tools one has to work with."[41]

By then, though, George's life had already moved on to the next phase, when, in December 1914, he was selected from a field of twenty candidates to become private secretary to Governor Withycombe, who stated of him:

> In many respects, the appointment was one of the most important at my disposal—if not the most important. I looked into the qualifications and desirability of each of the candidates, and while many of them were acceptable, yet I reached the conclusion that Mr. Putnam was perhaps the best equipped from every point of view. . . .[42]

George left Bend in January 1915, after writing an emotional farewell editorial stating that his removal to Salem was merely temporary. His interest in the town, he said, would not lessen and all his personal wealth would still continue to be invested in Bend. He appointed a managing editor for the *Bulletin* and instructed him only "to turn out the best paper" he could and "to work for Bend, first last and all the time." A civic banquet was held in George's honor.

Despite his intentions, George's departure from the little town was far from temporary. Over the years, he paid occasional visits, but his links with Bend were cut on that day he moved to Salem. The years that he was later to describe with such gusto were behind him. He had arrived six years earlier as a wet-behind-the-ears eastern tenderfoot and had matured in the hurly-burly of frontier life. Certainly, George heard the West roar—several times.

What manner of man was George Putnam at twenty-seven years of age? He was a family man whose wife and son were important to him, although they often seemed a mere backdrop to his business schemes. His ability to give his undivided attention to the matter at hand meant that his wife and son felt no neglect. His family readily attest to the fact that he was a loving husband and father. He had always displayed an air of confidence. Earlier, this had merely been a veneer over his self-confessed sensitivity; but with success behind him, he was genuinely self-assured and assertive. Physically attractive and naturally energetic, he was a hard worker and had earned the respect of the citizens of Bend, particularly the farmers on whose behalf he had fought. He was capable of great kindness and, according to Bend tradition, many of his good works on behalf of others never became known at his own request.[43]

George's various campaigns had made him many friends but he was never afraid to make implacable enemies by saying what he felt. His mind was agile and once a train of thought had been started in his mind, George was difficult to stop. He did not suffer fools gladly and though he was a cultured man with great charm and grace, he was capable of exploding into frightening displays of anger as a result of some minor irritation.

Throughout his life, George was an avid reader and never without some current literary potboiler, his own or someone else's. His second book, *Oregon Country,* was published as he left to take up office in Salem. He loved the outdoors extravagantly, enjoying it most when horseback riding or fishing. It was said of him that he possessed "ambition, kindness, intelligence, impatience, [and] of such things leaders are made."[44]

Chapter Eight

1915 - 1922

Oregon had no lieutenant governor, so George's position as private secretary to Governor James Withycombe held the promise of great influence. George looked forward both to making a contribution to the rapidly growing state and to his own self-advancement.[1]

Unfortunately, Withycombe had appointed George against the advice of the GOP state leaders, who would have preferred an appointee with some political influence. This unknown young man came from "east of the mountains, where votes were few . . ." George was later to recall. "The political organization howled, and thenceforward made matters as uncomfortable for me as they could, which was considerable."[2]

The "political bushwhackers" (as George called them) managed to limit his scope to representing the governor at trade fairs and prisons, operating a publicity machine, and roles of a similar nature.[3] George continued to feed articles to western newspapers and did not forget the *Bulletin*. In April 1916, a feature article called "Interesting Westerners" in *Sunset Magazine* noted that George had recently been offered a position in New York at more than twice his present salary. Possibly the offer was from G. P. Putnam's Sons. The article must have upset some of George's political opponents by pronouncing that Secretary Putnam was "largely responsible today for [the] governor's popularity."[4]

This small puff may have salved George's pride but he was still frustrated and restless. A man of action by nature, he was relieved when in 1916, with World War I at its height, President Wilson issued orders for the immediate mobilization of the National Guard, subject to call for service on the Mexican border. Oregon "led the nation with a volunteer enlistment of 92 percent of its manpower."[5] George, who had enlisted in the state militia in March, was ordered into active service in June with only hours' notice.[6]

If George craved action, he was disappointed again. His main activity while serving in Mexico was to provide feature stories for Oregon newspapers. His disillusionment was apparent in an article published in the *Bulletin* in September 1916 in which he describes his activities as "half police work and half training camp."[7]

A few weeks after this was written, George was honorably discharged from the National Guard and was recalled to Salem to continue his duties as secretary to the governor, where he remained for six months. He had enlisted for a three-year period, however, and though unassigned, he was technically still in the army. In late June 1917, he was assigned to "special work with the Department of Justice in Washington, D.C."[8] He remained there for eighteen months prior to entry into the field artillery officers' training school at Camp Taylor, Kentucky, where he received his commission in December 1918.[9] During this time, George suffered the loss of two members of his family. In 1917 his father, John Bishop Putnam, died and George grieved.[10]

> At heart Father was beautifully gentle. Like many really affectionate people, it was difficult for him to let his feelings show. He was deeply fond of me. Only towards the very end of his life did I understand at all and offer a return half-way decent. And then for the most part I was far away and letters were all we had between us.
>
> . . . in his last fishing trip he was with me in Oregon. I can see him resting at the foot of a tawny pine at the edge of the Deschutes River with a meadow of blue lupin all about, weary and happy. Jaunty flies festooned his battered hat, and his beard, white then, was jaunty too. Though I remember with a pang in my heart the trouble he was having, what with his bifocal glasses and hands a trifle unsteady, adjusting a fresh fly to the leader.[11]

Then, while George was in the army in 1918, his elder brother, Robert, died from influenza in the great epidemic that swept North America. This totally unforeseen event changed the course of George's career, for he never returned to Oregon as planned. Instead, after his discharge from the army in December, he went straight into G. P. Putnam's Sons in his brother's place.[12] When he originally enlisted, he stated his occupation as "newspaperman," but when he applied for discharge, he filed as "publisher."[13]

The firm of G. P. Putnam, Broadway, had been formed in New York in 1840 by George's grandfather and namesake. In 1866, it became G. P. Putnam and Son when George's uncle, George Haven Putnam, joined the family firm.[14] John Bishop Putnam (George's father) took up the honorable calling of publisher in 1868 and, on the death of the founder, the company name became G. P. Putnam's Sons.

George Haven Putnam, universally known in the family and publishing world as "the Major," a title dating from his service in the Civil War, became "the dominant figure in the firm as author, executive and internationally known personality" and ran "the office" that was to become George Palmer Putnam's world.[15] George Haven Putnam is chiefly known for his work in helping to secure the law of international copyright (originally proposed by the first G. P. Putnam), for which he was awarded the order of the Legion of Honor by the French government. Another brother, Herbert, who did not enter the publishing world but became librarian emeritus of Congress, also played his part in the writing of this important piece of legislation. George's father spent half his time at the office, but his special interest and creation was the Knickerbocker Press—located in New Rochelle—which had so engaged his young son's attention. There was also the youngest of the four brothers, Irving, who ran the Putnam bookshop in New York City.

Putnam's, the publishing house, had been in existence for almost eighty years when George joined it. Irving's two sons, George's cousins Edmund and Sydney, were already employed there, but George had no intention of taking anything other than the leading role in the company. His two uncles were both reaching seventy years of age and were apparently content to give the ambitious young man his head, so George had carte blanche to improve and extend the company's lists.

After settling his family into a spacious mansion in Rye, New York, one of George's first tasks was a three-month trip to the European capitals of Paris, Prague, and Warsaw in order to secure the memoirs of the great Polish composer, pianist, and statesman Ignace Jan Paderewski. He met and talked with the great man and managed to extract "a contract of sorts," but despite protracted correspondence, nothing ever came of it; Paderewski was too occupied with affairs of state and his primary art to take time to write his autobiography.[16]

George returned to the United States in December 1919. As usual, his travels created a literary reward in the form of a dozen articles about Poland for popular magazines such as *Collier's* and *Ladies' Home Journal.* [17] In his autobiography, he claims to have written them all—eighteen thousand words—between a Friday midnight and the following Monday morning.[18] His observations were astute and he recognized the serious plight of Poland.

On December 27, a few weeks after his return, George delivered a powerful speech at Delmonico's in New York about Poland's plight. His audience, anticipating a lighthearted social gathering, must have been surprised when George predicted that another European war was inevitable within ten years "because Poland was an impediment to Germany's ambitions, which were far from squashed by her defeat." George made it clear that he did not subscribe to the belief that the Great War had ended all wars. Such an unpopular theory, in 1919, was radical enough to receive coverage in *The New York Times*.

It was George's enthusiasm and drive that caused him to commission what he liked to call "fabricated books." That is, he thought up an idea for a book and then found an author to write it. This method of having books written to order was a comparatively unknown phenomenon in the publishing world in the early twenties and it apparently paid off, as G. P. Putnam's Sons produced, printed, and sold more books than ever before.

George had many successes and, inevitably, some failures. For instance, he turned down the first Ripley's *Believe It or Not*—which later sold in excess of half a million copies—with the comment that "it was good newspaper stuff, but it wouldn't do for a book."[19] He also allowed Lowell Thomas to slip through his hands when he offered too small an advance on royalties. On the other hand, in a typical gesture of faith, loyalty, and generosity, he helped his friend Rockwell Kent to produce his beautiful—and best-selling—book *Wilderness*.

The artist desperately wanted to travel to Alaska to paint but could not afford to make the trip. At George's suggestion, a company was set up to employ Rockwell Kent. Everything the artist produced became the property of the corporation. George and a friend purchased the entire stock and the company then paid Kent a salary and expenses to enable him to make the trip.[20] Within a year, the corporation (that is, George) had sold enough of Kent's work to declare a dividend, and on Kent's return with enough material to produce *Wilderness*, the corporation was dissolved, with the two stockholders repaid in full and Kent financially stable.

George did not shirk the sensational. In 1921, G. P. Putnam's Sons published a collection of brilliant essays (originally published by the London office of G. P. Putnam's Sons) entitled *The Mirrors of Downing Street*, which was less than complimentary to leading British politicians. It was "sizzling stuff," exposing the weaknesses of those in power at a time when most biographies were of the devotee variety.[21] George quickly saw that a book based on the inhabitants of Washington, D.C., could be equally, if not more, sensational. The result, *Mirrors of Washington,* was a success, not least because it was written by two authors who remained anonymous for many years, causing public speculation and keeping the book in the public eye.

Another huge success was a spoof, *The Cruise of the Kawa,* an imaginary adventure cruise under the captaincy of one Dr. Traprock, which George described as a "ribald whimsey that sold near to a hundred thousand copies . . . some publishers looked down their noses. There were those, no doubt, who felt that the ancient respectability of the House of Putnam was being outraged. Myself I always thought that a little laughter was good for any business—especially if it sold merchandise."[22] *Publishers Weekly* editorialized:

> An instance of imagination, ingenuity and cleverness beyond the capabilities of most merchandising wizards. . . . With a book which was at the beginning only a brilliant burlesque with an author masquerading under a *nom de plume,* George Palmer Putnam practically overnight made Dr. Traprock a nationally known figure. . . .[23]

Also in 1921, George tried to publish an American edition of Marie Stopes's sensational *Married Love.* Recognizing that it would never pass the censors in its original form, he prepared a revised edition, but its editor, William J. Robinson, was judged to have violated sections of the New York City Penal Code relating to obscene literature. A severely emasculated form was eventually published a year later, leaving George bitterly acrimonious.[24] His response was to publish a collection of essays by leading authors entitled *Nonsensorship* and to speak out publicly in *The New York Times* against the "menace of censorship," notably John S. Sumner, secretary of the New York Society for Suppression of Vice. Censorship as applied, he contended, was "unworkable, unnecessary and unwise. . . . Publishers are, or at least should be, capable of judging the decency of their own output."[25]

The censorship battle rumbled on for some years, with George in the vanguard. In 1923, George (together with Alfred Harcourt of Harcourt, Brace and Company) resigned in protest from the Censorship Committee of the National Association of Book Publishers when the committee refused to oppose the so-called Clean Books Bill. George's work behind the scenes helped to quash the bill.

George's stable of successful authors grew—Louis Bromfield, Sophie Kerr, George Agnew Chamberlain, Alexander Woollcott, Ben Hecht,

Kermit Roosevelt, Frank Craven, Rockwell Kent, Dorothy Parker. George was never too busy to encourage an aspiring author, and he believed that *"everyone* had a book in them." He must have been responsible for inspiring hundreds of books, many of which were never finished, but many of which found publication and success.

George did not limit his efforts to matching ideas with authors. On one notable occasion, he wrote the entire plot for a novel and then found nineteen other well-known authors (ten women and nine men—George was the tenth man) to write the book. It was published as *Bobbed Hair*, by Twenty Authors.

In 1923, George leased an office on Forty-fifth Street in New York. It was a many-storied "rabbit warren" of a place to house his business interests outside Putnam's. Here, he ran a small literary agency and housed clients who were working on various projects. Writers, illustrators, cartoonists—George took them all on and encouraged them.

Corey Ford, one author who was contacted by George, recalled the initial telephone call. Ford, already under contract to Scribner's, had written a short parody of a best-selling book, which had been published in a magazine. George recognized its potential and telephoned Ford, asking bluntly and without preamble whether Ford could expand it into a book. "He had already arranged for my release from Scribner's, he said to my surprise (later I learned not to be surprised at anything). Could I deliver my copy in ten days? That's fine then. Click."

Ford's literary portrait of Putnam at that time is interesting:

> . . . wiry and dynamic with . . . an engaging laugh (he was fond of outrageous puns), and a disconcerting habit of accenting his speech now and then with a hollow *clunk* like a stone dropped down a well, that came from somewhere deep in his nasal passages. His friendly manner was offset by the hard, calculating glance behind his steely spectacles. A phrase . . . once used in a story kept recurring to me: "His eye was as cold as an undertaker's night bell."
>
> . . . he was usually called "GP," which was sometimes corrupted to "Gyp" [and] was the past master of literary legerdemain, a skilled conjurer who could palm an author, pull a best seller out of a hat, flourish his wand and transform a channel swimmer or explorer or aviator into a national sensation. With his knack for showmanship he published the memoirs of page one celebrities who sparkled briefly and then as they began to fizzle, were discarded for the next headline hero . . . his instinct for the spectacular was almost occult. He could sense a newspaper story before it occurred. When another front-page notable popped up his eyes fairly snapped with electricity, his fingers

coiled and writhed like live wires, his voice had the hum of a loaded power line. He was always calculating, always figuring out how to make use of people, always with the commercial end in mind. Everything was for sale . . . I think he was the loneliest man I've ever met.[26]

Ford's description of George as a lonely man is an interesting observation, for George's circle of friends and acquaintances was huge, often impressive. What could have turned the friendly and open young mayor of a frontier town into the calculating entrepreneur of whom Ford speaks? His home life was happy enough. His "charming and vivacious wife," Dorothy, ran the couple's imposing mansion home in Rye with flair and a growing reputation as a hostess.[27] The couple's first child, David, was nearly ten years old by then and Dorothy had given birth to another son, George Palmer Putnam, Jr., in 1921.

George commuted to the city daily, leaving home shortly after dawn and often returning only shortly before midnight, sometimes to find the last vestiges of a dinner party that he had organized and long since forgotten and that Dorothy had hosted in his absence. One can only assume that to accept such cavalier treatment while remaining so supportive, Dorothy was either very much in love with her husband or else extremely long-suffering. Yet although George has sometimes been portrayed as a cold and lonely man by biographers, his family and those closest to him throughout his life insist that the reverse was true, stating that he was a romantic at heart and a very loving person who (when he was not working) gave himself to his family without reservation. Clearly, George had one face for public life and another for his private life, and this is the answer to the conflicting portraits of him.

In September 1922, George and Dorothy made a return visit to Oregon, taking a party of authors with them on the trip. The object of the trip was to visit the Pendleton Round-up Rodeo, where some of the broncos were named after Putnam and his entourage. The *Oregonian* carried a report referring to George as "Lord High Publisher Putnam," and later a book was written about the trip, as well as an eight-page pamphlet written by George and published by the Union Pacific, entitled *The Rough Riders Go West.*[28]

In his autobiography, George stated that it was in these days that he acquired the habit of "always being in a hurry . . . anyway the saddest people I know are those with nothing to do and too much time to do it in." Certainly, he was involved in a multitude of projects, including publicity scams that occasionally backfired. On one occasion, one of his agency clients, a cartoonist, had a comic strip accepted by a leading newspaper in

Boston. George conceived the idea of swamping the newspaper with letters from delighted readers. Consequently, he had many friends of his and of the cartoonist write to the editor in glowing appreciation:

> Tied in a neat package, the feature editor of the paper sent those letters on to us. Through a change in plans the new comic had not started on Monday and had not appeared at all when the letters started to arrive.[29]

Later, George admitted that perhaps he never took his activities as publisher "quite seriously enough." Certainly, he made many nonsensical forays into what he termed "extracurricular" activities. These ranged from practical jokes, aided and abetted by his great friend Rockwell Kent, to large house parties of literati and other celebrities at Rye. He had a knack of knowing anyone worth knowing—musicians, politicians, comedians, actors, explorers—and the guest list at Rye was impressive, with names such as Leopold Stokowski, Franklin D. Roosevelt, Charlie Chaplin, and Admiral Richard Byrd, to name a few.

He had dozens of books ghosted for well-known names and he continued his practice of "thinking up books that needed to be written and finding an author to do it." G. P. Putnam's Sons was turning out more books than ever before, many of them extremely successful. Each year, George made several trips to Europe to look for books and to oversee operations at the company's London offices.

George continued needling and wheedling and skillfully extracting books from the great as well as the unknown. To his chagrin, however, he failed to get the memoirs of Calvin Coolidge. He had a breakfast appointment with Coolidge at the Vanderbilt Hotel in New York and a friend of George's, who also knew Coolidge well, told George, "I'll bet you ten dollars I can predict what Coolidge will say either the second or third time he opens his mouth."

Thinking the boast absurd, George took the bet, asking what Coolidge would say. "First he'll say 'Good morning.' His next speech, or the one after it will be substantially, 'What advance royalty do you offer?'"

George lost the bet. The conversation apparently went like this:[30]

COOLIDGE: "Good morning."
PUTNAM: "Good morning, sir."
COOLIDGE: "Let's get at this book matter."
PUTNAM: "Fine by me."
COOLIDGE: "What royalties and how much in cash?"

Chapter Nine

1 9 2 6 - 1 9 2 8

B y early 1926, George had identified a market need for adventure
books. This he translated to true-life adventure written in the first
person, and his stable of authors included Marten and Osa Johnson, Knud
Rasmussen, and William Beebe. For George, this was hardly enough. A
close friend said of him "If he went to a dogfight, he'd have to be one
of the dogs."[1] Therefore, it was predictable and probably only a matter
of time before he, too, became an adventurer/explorer. "It seemed inap-
propriate to promote books about exploration without doing a bit of
exploration myself. So I did," he said.[2]

It was while George was walking through a bad snowstorm with Bob
Bartlett—Admiral Peary's skipper on his 1909 conquest of the North
Pole—that Bartlett commented how the weather in Westchester was
puny compared with that which he had observed in Greenland.

Bartlett spoke—sirenlike to George—of his time with Peary, and how
he had been nearer to the North Pole on his own two feet than any white
man living. Indeed, he had spent most of his life north of the Arctic
Circle. George was thirty-eight. He had been in harness throughout his
twenties and early thirties, and, suddenly, listening to Bartlett, nothing
would do for him but to experience adventure and hardship for himself.
Given to sudden, violent enthusiasm that swept all opposition aside,
George immediately proposed that he and Bartlett organize an expedition
to Greenland. He was under no false illusions about his motives. Although
he would endeavor to contribute (and would ultimately succeed in doing
so) to the sum of scientific knowledge, he fully recognized that "it was
a swell chance to have a very good time."[3] Besides, he could always write
a book about it. Within days, an article appeared in *The New York Times*
announcing the expedition headed by George and naming a backer.[4]

Bartlett departed for his home in Newfoundland to collect his two-masted schooner, *Morrisey,* which was one hundred feet in length and built of oak in Massachusetts in 1882.[5] George, meanwhile, approached the American Museum of Natural History, which recently had completed a magnificent new Hall of Ocean Life. They were short of specimens, and with prompting from George, the museum's president, Henry Fairfield Osborn, agreed to back the expedition if financial sponsorship could be obtained.[6]

George knew exactly where to look for backing. A year earlier, William Beebe's expedition to the Sargasso Sea and the Galápagos Islands had been backed by Harrison Williams, a wealthy financier and trustee of the museum. Accordingly, George was later able to report that ". . . then, at once, Harrison Williams came forward with a gift that really launched the undertaking."[7]

How George recruited his team is described by Dan Streeter, official historian to the expedition:

> George was a business man—even worse he was a Publisher with a chronic wanderlust. His was a triple personality. One may expect anything in a case like this and rarely be disappointed. His sanctuary successfully combined a deep monastic calm with the brazen atmosphere of a boiler factory. Yet the only bait that had been needed to lure [me] into it was a telephone call. He sat against a desk in an attitude at once expressive of deep abstraction and alert interest. There was no prologue.
>
> "I'm organizing an Expedition to Greenland," he said. "There are to be fourteen of us . . . our object is to collect for the American Museum a few narwhals, white whales . . . local sharks, artifacts, odds and ends—"
>
> The telephone bell rang. He took up the instrument, speaking into it with meticulous accuracy.
>
> "Yes—yes! No!" That concluded the telephone conversation.
>
> "Where was I? . . . The Arctic? Oh! Yes! We'll touch at Sydney, then make for Greenland, follow the coast north to Cape York and Etah, call on the Smith Sound Eskimo—the last of the world's aborigines. We're making the trip on a hundred foot 'Banker' owned by Bob Bartlett and manned by a crew of those silent men from Newfoundland one reads about—six of them.
>
> "Now a word as to the personnel of the Expedition. Besides myself and Captain Bartlett, there will be a Radio Operator, Pathé News representative, Montana Cowboy, Bow and Arrow expert,

Engineer, Cabin Boy, Zoologist, Taxidermist and Famous Danish
Explorer. . . .
   ". . . Now here's the point. I was taking an artist to paint Northern
backgrounds. He's blown up on me. Will you take his place?"
   "Certainly" [I] answered, "but not as a painter because [I] don't
paint and someone might notice."[8]

The cabin boy, incidentally, was George's thirteen-year-old son, David,
who a year earlier had been a member of Beebe's Galápagos expedition.
He was not George's son for nothing; a book, *David Goes Voyaging*, came
out of the trip.[9] It was the first in a series of best-selling adventure books
for boys written by young David.[10]
   In his memoir, George claimed it took him only six weeks to organize
financial backing, men, stores, and logistics before the *Morrisey* set off
from Rye for her six-month voyage.[11] However, in fact, he announced the
project in February and it was June 21, 1926, when they left—a hectic
six months after his conversation with Bartlett. From the lawns of the
American Yacht Club at Milton Point, hundreds of well-wishers waved
the expedition off into Long Island Sound.[12]
   A month before the departure of the *Morrisey*, Richard "Dick" Byrd
had made history by captaining the first flight over the North Pole.
George had become a friend of Byrd's and had negotiated book rights
on his story prior to the record attempt. The two men also had made an
agreement that, should Byrd's flight come to grief, the *Morrisey* would
sail to Cape Columbia, where Byrd and his crew would trek overland
with hand sleds. When news of the successful flight came through,
George was able to pass on his congratulations live to Byrd from *The
New York Times* offices, on a specially installed radio boosted by "the
most powerful short-wave broadcasting plant in the country: 'Dick, I
hope this reaches you. We are hoping to meet you soon. Bob Bartlett
and I are glad that there is no cause to meet up with you at Cape
Columbia. . . .' "[13] What a story George could have written about *that*
rescue!
   The New York Times carried regular reports from George concerning
the progress of the expedition, including the odd mishaps and near misses,
blown up in true journalistic style. On one occasion, the ship ran aground
and listed at a forty-five-degree angle for days until she was finally floated
off. George fired off a story to *The New York Times;* but Streeter, the
official historian, later observed that while some 5,493 gallons had been
pumped out of the schooner,

. . . the only wreck worth talking about was the man who did the pumping. But when one is sensitive to "news value" and intimately connected with the profession, anything may be expected. George would have stopped in the middle of a rotten plank over a chasm a hundred feet deep to broadcast his reaction to a waiting world.[14]

George's story of a "battle" between a walrus and himself and Bartlett made the front page in those far-off days. The two men were in a dory attempting to harpoon a large bull when the animal threw his flippers around the small vessel and drove his two-foot-long tusks up through the bottom, missing Bartlett by inches. The dory sank and the two adventurers had to be rescued from the icy waters.[15]

Readers of the *Times* were fascinated by George's adventures, and letters to the editor flowed in. Congratulatory telegrams from Byrd and Roosevelt winged their way to the *Morrisey* via the paper's columns. On August 25, *The New York Times* played its part in a domestic conspiracy and hauled Dorothy into the editorial office for a two-way radio conversation with her husband. In those days, voice contact was still not possible, but at least it was direct two-way transmission and a considerable thrill for all concerned. George described his surroundings:

> David and I wish you could share with us this unsultry night as we parade up and down Jones Bay in fog. . . . Just now on deck [we are] clearing ice off insulators. Fog freezing icy coating over all. Temperature twenty-seven . . . just then we crashed against ice-pan . . . convey New York *Times* greetings and gratitude for transmitting congratulatory messages . . . we are having bully time involving nothing remotely heroic. Just some healthy discomfort and normal perseverance. . . . I'd like a swim at the American Yacht Club . . . . George

Reportedly "very moved," Dorothy replied:

> Heavenly full moon; hot night. A hug for David. My love to the whole crowd. I share your thrills and hope for you good hunting but long to have you all home again. Dolly.[16]

Everything was going exceptionally well, but it was nothing compared with the story George came up with on September 25. For then, with his newspaperman's instinct for a really big story, despite being in one of the world's most isolated places, George came up with a major newspaper scoop.

The front-page banner headline screamed ESKIMO KILLED PROF. MAR-

VIN, PEARY AIDE; CONFESSES ARCTIC CRIME OF 17 YEARS AGO; VICTIM REPORTED DROWNED, WAS SHOT. "Grim Tragedy of North . . . Kudlooktoo Says Explorer Went Mad and Left Other Eskimo to Die" was subheadlined over George's sensational revelations that the history books were wrong. "The Arctic has given up another secret," George's article began grimly. *The New York Times* gave it three columns on page one, all of page two, and it ran over onto page three.[17] Fred Birchall, the managing editor, was so impressed that he wired back, QUIT PUBLISHING AND BECOME A REAL REPORTER.[18] George had nursed the story for three weeks, for although there was little likelihood of a rival reporter scooping him, given the remoteness of the drama, he was concerned that his radio signals might be intercepted or misinterpreted, so he waited until they reached Nova Scotia on the return journey to wire the story through with just enough time to make the next edition.

The Putnam expedition arrived back in Rye on October 1, 1926, to general acclaim and a page-one welcome by *The New York Times.* Three books immediately resulted from the pens of Knud Rasmussen, Bob Bartlett, and David Binney Putnam, and the expedition was also adjudged successful from a scientific point of view.[19] So when George, with his appetite for adventure truly whetted, decided to form another expedition to Canada's Baffin Island the following spring, he found no shortage of backers.[20]

It was to be a similar saga, with regular page-one reports in the *Times,* near misses, adventures with polar bears, icy swims, and the inevitable "big story" when the expedition discovered that contemporary maps were in error by some five thousand square miles about the area of Baffin Island.[21]

Before he could leave for Baffin, however, George found he had a publishing sensation on his hands, and it says much for his desire to seek physical adventure that he was able to leave in June 1927 to lead this second expedition. Indeed, in the weeks and months that followed, he must have many times queried his self-judgment in doing so.

In May 1927, while George was in the final stages of preparation for the new expedition, Charles Augustus Lindbergh, a young man of twenty-five, was finalizing his plans to attempt to fly the Atlantic, solo. Atlantic fever was in the air. There had been numerous attempts, many fatal, to fly the Atlantic, but only two (discounting airships) had been successful. One was a crossing in stages to Lisbon via the Azores in May 1919;[22] the other was the first nonstop crossing by Alcock and Brown less than a month afterward. Since that time, no crossings of the North Atlantic had been made and a solo nonstop flight between the United States and

France, for which a prize of twenty-five thousand dollars had been offered by French hotelier Raymond Orteig, was still to be accomplished.

In May 1927, there were three significant contenders: Charles Lindbergh with his *Spirit of St. Louis;* Richard Byrd with *America;* and Clarence Chamberlin with *Columbia* (all of whom subsequently made successful crossings). Such was public interest in the contest that reporters swarmed around the airports and each time any of the airmen took off for a test flight, he was reported as having "left secretly."

Even before he left New York, Lindbergh had been inundated with offers for books and films should his attempt be successful.[23] Despite the stress of preflight preparation upon which his life depended, Lindbergh remained cool enough to fend off these distractions. George may even have been introduced to Lindbergh at this time, or more likely, he had marked the event down as something to monitor, for his subsequent shrewdness in approaching Lindbergh indicates either forward planning or a certain knowledge of the flier's character.

On May 20, 1927, in his modified Ryan, the *Spirit of St. Louis,* Lindbergh took off from Roosevelt Field, Long Island, New York. After a flight of thirty-three hours and thirty minutes, he landed at Le Bourget Field outside of Paris, becoming the first person to complete a solo flight across the Atlantic.[24]

Unprecedented hysteria surrounded the young aviator in those hectic days immediately after his arrival in Paris. If he had been pestered by would-be promoters prior to the flight, now he was besieged, but he resolutely refused to see or talk to anyone except representatives of *The New York Times,* who had exclusive rights to his story. The *Times* had retained journalists Carlisle MacDonald and Edwin James, who interviewed the flier and wrote stories over Lindbergh's name that were cabled back to the States. Often Lindbergh did not have time to read or edit them and subsequently he was deeply unhappy about some of the things that appeared.

The *Times,* in fact, treated Lindbergh with uncharacteristic generosity—uncharacteristic of newspapers, that is—for they decided not to make any profit from the young man's heroic feat. They cabled that they would not hold him to the original five-thousand-dollar contract but would turn over all receipts from his stories (mainly deriving from world syndication rights) after direct expenses had been met. Lindbergh eventually received around sixty thousand dollars from the *Times,* so his initial trust in them seems to have been justified.

On May 21, George Putnam was deeply involved in last-minute preparations for his forthcoming expedition; not too deeply involved not to want to secure Lindbergh's story for G. P. Putnam's Sons, however.

George's relationship with *New York Times* editor Fred Birchall was of long standing both personally and professionally. Now, he traded upon it. Recognizing that if he approached Lindbergh directly, he would simply be another of the many publishers attempting to get an audience, and possibly already having knowledge of Lindbergh's intransigence, George went to Birchall, one of the few people Lindbergh felt he could trust.

> "We'd like to get Lindbergh's book," I said.
> The stocky little Englishman's near-sighted eyes crinkled in a grin as he peered at me over his glasses.
> "Indeed," he chuckled, "you—and who else?" . . . I suppose every publisher in America wanted the book.
> Anyway Birchall did what he properly could to help. What I needed was [assistance] in getting word promptly into the hands of the harassed flyer, and the Paris office of the *Times* could help with that.
> So I penciled out a message on a page of copy paper and Birchall edited it. I remember how he lowered his short-sighted eyes to within inches of the paper on his desk, changing some words, inserting others, in that meticulous way he had, vastly improving my handiwork. Then he swung round at me. "At least you ought to know how to spell Lindbergh's name!" he barked. I'd left off the final "h."[25]

Lindbergh "adopted the suggestion" made through Birchall, under the impression that he would tell his story to a journalist who would write it in the third person.[26] He had already developed a rapport with Carlisle MacDonald and so had no objection to working with him on a biography. As George tells it, by the time Lindbergh sailed for the United States aboard the U.S. cruiser *Memphis* on June 5, a verbal contract had been made that "Lindbergh would write the book and we [Putnam's] would publish it." Unfortunately, there was a serious misunderstanding on both sides as to what had actually been agreed.

MacDonald sailed with Lindbergh and used the voyage to interview him in great depth about his background.[27] Almost certainly, George delayed the start of the Putnam Baffin expedition in order to discuss personally with MacDonald the strategy for the rapid production of the book. Lindbergh arrived back in New York on June 11, and as soon as the *Memphis* docked, MacDonald was whisked to George's home in Rye, where a team of secretaries worked to rush the book out while the story was at its height. Using his interview notes and *The New York Times* stories as sources, MacDonald set to work with a deadline of days rather than weeks. The book was announced in a flurry of publicity.

Because of the short Arctic summer, George could not delay his expedition a day longer and the *Morrisey* departed on June 12. Young David, gathering material for another book, was again part of the expedition, and Dorothy joined them for the first leg of the voyage to Brigus, Newfoundland, which they reached on June 20.[28] From there, George was able to communicate by radio with MacDonald, who was already putting the finishing touches to his work. The manuscript was edited, rushed over to The Knickerbocker Press in New Rochelle, and by June 22, only ten days after MacDonald started work, typeset galley proofs were available for Lindbergh's approval.[29] Secure in the knowledge that everything was going according to plan and that G. P. Putnam's Sons had already received orders for 100,000 copies for immediate delivery,[30] George set off on the next stage of his voyage.[31]

The misunderstanding now came to light. MacDonald had ghosted the book in the true sense, having written it in the first person in Lindbergh's name. Lindbergh would not approve it. It is difficult to believe that MacDonald's impressions could have been so far removed from Lindbergh's understanding of the terms of the agreement. More likely, George realized that what the public wanted was Lindbergh's experiences in his own words, and that he had instructed MacDonald to write the book in the first person, assuming Lindbergh would accept it as a fait accompli once he was shown the completed work in print. Quite uncharacteristically, on this occasion, George misread his man.

Lindbergh refused with a simple but definite no. He raised no specific objections to what MacDonald had written, but—as he later stated—at the time he accepted the contract he was under the impression

> . . . that the account would be written in the third person, through interviews, over someone else's name, and that I would confirm its authenticity and contribute a foreword. Instead, a "ghost-written" manuscript, in the first person, was submitted to me for approval, and rejected.[32]

When it was pointed out to Lindbergh that he'd agreed to the contract, that the announcement had been made, and that orders were already flooding in, Lindbergh acknowledged that he was obligated to produce a book. He insisted, however, that if it was to appear over his own name, he would have to write it himself. How much of this was known to George at the time is not clear, though he later wrote that high blood pressure nearly overcame him, so he was obviously being kept informed to some degree by radio. With scarce-concealed impatience on the part of the publishers, Lindbergh was asked when his book would be completed and was told that a month's delay would be annoying but bearable.

At first, Lindbergh predicted delivery in the autumn. It was late June, and with the pressure of the hundreds of demands on his time, he might have been congratulated at attempting to produce a book in such a short time. Instead, George was apoplectic when advised of this; the demand was *now.* Ignoring Lindbergh's daunting schedule of public appearances, George sent messages to remind the flier that Putnam's had a contract based on his verbal agreement with MacDonald, and that on the strength of that contract, Putnam's had promised delivery of the book to their customers. "The MacDonald manuscript was a good job, complete, dignified, well-written . . . we declared [that] we just *had* to have a book. MacDonald's or his own. But promptly."[33]

If George was hoping to force Lindbergh's hand, it didn't work. The pilot, recognizing the validity of George's arguments, canceled all engagements and retired to the home of his friends Harry and Carol Guggenheim on Sands Point, Long Island. Actually, he interrupted his writing to fly to Ottawa, Canada, but an inspection of his diary shows he had only the last week in June and from July 4 to 19 free of commitments, so his claim that he took "about three weeks" to produce the forty-thousand-word manuscript was probably accurate.[34] George recalled irritably:

> He wrote every word in long-hand, on legal size paper. In the upper right-hand corner of each page, as he completed it, he wrote the number of words on that page. One could almost see him counting and saying to himself as he cast up the total, "Well, *that* many are out of the way, praise be!"[35]

Fitzhugh Green, under commission from Putnam's, wrote an introduction and the book, *We,* was rushed out by the end of August. Lindbergh settled privately with MacDonald for ten thousand dollars and his ghost-written manuscript was never published.[36] Sales of the book, however, were all that were hoped for, ". . . more than 635,000 copies," George said, "which is something of a record for a first book. Or a last one!"[37]

Within the restrained twin versions of this story, one can glean the primary characteristics of both men. Lindbergh, calm, precise, and unflappable, was confident that right was on his side and refused to be hustled. That he wrote his manuscript in longhand and annotated each page ensured that no further misunderstanding or misconstruction could occur. Putnam, frustrated by the distances involved, showed impatience and an unerring scent for colossal success, fretting that delay could damage the property. His pushing and most persuasive cajoling failed to impress or move Lindbergh. George was not used to defeat and he was anything but graceful on the few occasions he suffered it, but he was later to write objectively that Lindbergh "was a very dull demigod indeed, but neither a fool nor a knave."[38]

The *Morrisey* arrived back in Rye on October 6, 1927. A flurry of feature articles, backing up the dispatches that had appeared regularly during the expedition, were published in the Sunday *New York Times.* David's second book, *David Goes to Baffin Land,* appeared in due course and George's paper on the voyage was published by the American Geographical Society.[39]

George jumped back into publishing with preparations for another potential best-seller, Commander Richard E. Byrd's first book, *Skyward,* an account of his 1926 historic first flight over the North Pole in a private expedition with Floyd Bennett as his chief pilot.[40]

There was another foray into the world of aviation when an author who had been a pilot instructor during the war came to George with a book entitled *Wings.* It was a romantic epic of men who lived for today because they knew that tomorrow they would probably be dead. George had the brilliant idea to sell the book as a movie, but Jesse Lasky, head of production at Paramount, could not see how a movie could be made "just about flying." At this time, there had never been a feature picture based on aviation. George exerted his customary alternative charm and pressure and at last Lasky agreed to see George and his author.

They talked from 3 P.M. until midnight. Next day, the contract was signed. The film, first of a genre, was shot at Camp Stanley near San Antonio, Texas, where army engineers created a replica of the Western Front at a cost of $300,000—big money in those days. Within the year, *Wings,* starring Clara Bow, Buddy Rogers, and a very youthful Gary Cooper, was aired to record audiences.[41] George, who had "assisted in the production,"[42] was said to have earned a great deal of money from his connection with this enterprise, but almost certainly what he earned was stock in the newly formed company Talking Picture Epics Ltd., of which he became vice-president. The company produced several real-life adventure movies based on books by George's best-selling authors: *Across the World* (Osa and Martin Johnson); *Hunting Tigers in India* (George M. Dymott); and *Bottom of the World* (Robert Cushman Murphy); but none achieved the success of *Wings,* which won the first Academy Award for best picture of the year. It was during the making of *Wings* that George first encountered a colorful young stunt pilot named Paul Mantz. George "collected" people and seven years later he would contact the young pilot again for help in another venture.

Because of his involvement in *Skyward* and *We* and *Wings,* George was moving in the tight circle of aviation during those early months of 1928. He certainly had many social contacts with Lindbergh, though in the light of their earlier misunderstanding, the relationship was almost certainly uneasy. It was not improved when in January 1928 George had the handwritten manuscript of *We* bound in two leather volumes for which a collector offered thirty thousand dollars. George invited Lindbergh to his office to discuss the matter. He explained to the flier that "under the arrangements" made between them, ownership of the manuscript "possibly" lay with Putnam's. However, he continued, he felt that a fair course would be to split the proceeds equally.[43]

It is highly unlikely that the manuscript could have been owned by Putnam's unless a specific clause to that effect had been inserted in the contract, and this episode is a perfect example of George, the hustler and the dealer, at his most devious. He could hardly bear the fact that he could not reach this man, scarcely more than a boy, whose name was quite literally a license to print money. When George decided to charm, the subject, in general, was charmed; but Lindbergh was the exception and George's smile must have had a fixed quality whenever the two came into contact.

On this occasion, as on others, Lindbergh bested George. He considered the matter carefully before answering the publisher's suggestion, fully aware that had Putnam's had any real title to the manuscript, the author never would have been consulted. Finally the young Solomon said, "If it's yours, you do as you wish. If it isn't, I want it."[44] Of course, it was Lindbergh's property and was later presented to the collection of Lindbergh memorabilia housed in the museum in St. Louis.

1 9 2 8: *Amelia Meets George*

I t was probably in early April of 1928 that George's ever-attentive ear picked up the fact that yet another record attempt was going to be made on the Atlantic. It had been crossed nonstop several times at that stage—by crews in single- and multi-engined airplanes and by Lindbergh. No woman had so far flown across, though several women were in advanced preparations, ranging in various degrees of seriousness. One, Ruth Nichols, was a neighbor of George's in Rye; another, Mabel Boll, was making plans amid as much publicity as she could obtain.

According to George's autobiography, his first inkling that an interesting project was afoot occurred when he went with Bernt Balchen to Miller Field on Staten Island. On the ferry, Balchen, former pilot to Dick Byrd on their successful transatlantic crossing, told George that "Byrd had secretly sold the Fokker trimotor airplane to an English woman who wished to fly the Atlantic." This was all George could discover from Balchen, who had not been given any further information concerning the sale; indeed, he discovered this small amount only because he was organizing the logistics for Byrd's South Pole flight and he needed to order skis to replace the landing gear on the replacement airplane—a Ford trimotor. George noted:

> Just then my career as a publisher of exploration and adventure books was in full cry. And here I had stumbled on an adventure-in-the-making which, once completed, certainly should provide a book.[1]

By pure coincidence, later that day, George's old friend Hilton Railey, whom George had talked into traveling to Poland as a war correspondent seven years earlier, called in at Putnam's offices on a trip from Boston.

> I dropped in to see George—as busy as ever and . . . optimistic. I had
> always liked G.P. in a Mellow mood; on this occasion he was particu-
> larly ingratiating. . . .
> "When are you going back?" he inquired with sudden speculation.
> "Five o'clock."
> "Pull that chair over. I heard something today that might be of
> interest to you."[2]

George told Railey what he'd heard that day from Balchen. He explained
that he did not know the name of the woman or anything about the
project except that he believed floats were being fitted to the Fokker at
the East Boston airport. Why didn't Railey take a run over there to
investigate? Railey was initially unimpressed. "What if it's true?" he
asked. "What then?"

"If it's true," said his wily friend, "we'll crash the gate. It would be
amusing to manage a stunt like that, wouldn't it? Find out all you can.
Locate the ship. Pump the pilots. Chances are they know all about it.
Maybe there's nothing to it . . . telephone me if it's hot."[3]

Before midnight that night, Railey had tracked down Wilmer Stultz,
the pilot, and Lou Gordon, the copilot and flight mechanic (airplane
engineers were always called mechanics in that era), at the Copley Plaza
in Boston. Bill Stultz had been drinking hard and Railey found him to
be a talkative companion. Stultz admitted that they were preparing for
a transatlantic flight but said that his only contact was a New York
attorney, Mr. David T. Layman, who represented the principal.

Here the two stories diverge somewhat, both Putnam and Railey claiming that they were responsible for finding Amelia Earhart. George wrote
that, having learned David Layman's name from Railey, he went to see
him:

> I was able to tell him that I knew my way around in the business of
> expeditions and had considerable experience with aviation projects.
> He seemed visibly relieved.[4]

Layman explained that his client, Mrs. Amy Guest, had wanted to be the
first woman to fly the Atlantic. Mrs. Guest's family, however, had discovered the plan and were intent on stopping her from doing anything so
foolhardy:

> The project, they said, was all right, if she sent someone in her place.
> And reluctantly Mrs. Guest had agreed.

Pretty much at the moment that I dropped from the clouds and introduced myself, Layman was wondering what to do next. So, suddenly I found myself entrusted with an odd chore. I was to find a suitable American woman who wanted to fly the Atlantic.[5]

Railey states in his memoir:

In New York some days later, I got in touch with him [Layman] and learned that Mrs. Frederick E. Guest of London and New York . . . was the mysterious sponsor who planned to be the first of her sex to fly the Atlantic. Her family, Mr. Layman said, was much concerned. Soon it was agreed that if I could find "the right sort of girl" to take her place Mrs. Guest would yield.[6]

The stories are so similar that it seems likely that both men went to see Layman in his office. Layman emphasized that by the "right sort of girl," his client meant "a lady." Both George and Railey were slightly amused by this description, George professing that he was hazy as to what the word precisely meant, though had once humorously defined it neatly: "A real lady is the kind you meet with Mr. and Mrs. M. . . . at their home. Those who are not real ladies are the kind you may meet with Mr. M. . . . when he is out on his own."[7]

Mrs. Guest had set out general specifications to be met by the successful candidate. She should be a pilot and well educated; preferably a college graduate. She should be physically attractive and have manners that would be acceptable to members of English society, who would undoubtedly welcome her on her arrival there. There were several women under consideration at that point.

Miss Ruth Nichols of Rye was an obvious contender. A pilot since 1922, dark-haired, attractive, and well spoken, she met the requirements perfectly. But she had been ill and needed time to recover. Six months earlier, in October 1927, Ruth Elder had made her attempt to be the first woman to fly the Atlantic, in a tri-motored Stinson Detroiter named *American Girl*, piloted by George Haldeman. After engine trouble developed, they went down in the Atlantic 360 miles north of the Azores, landing close to a ship, which picked them up. The plane exploded before it could be hoisted aboard. After a trip to Paris, Miss Elder returned to the United States for a career in vaudeville and, in doing so, probably ruled herself out of Mrs. Guest's search for "the right sort of American girl." It is doubtful whether, in any circumstances, Miss Mabel "Mibs" Boll would have been considered by Amy Guest to be the right sort.

Railey told the story:

> On the merest hunch, when I returned to Boston, I telephoned
> my friend, Rear Admiral Reginald K. Belknap, USN (Ret).
> "Why yes," said he, "I know a young social worker who flies. I'm
> not sure how many hours she's had, but I do know that she's deeply
> interested in aviation—and a thoroughly fine person. Call Denison
> House and ask for Amelia Earhart."[8]

George competed with:

> It was the trivial incident of an overheard conversation that started
> me. It was the accident of an Admiral being in the Boston office of
> my friend Hilton Railey when I telephoned him, that brought our
> quest to the door of Amelia Earhart. For Admiral Belknap had heard
> of a girl who worked in a settlement house and also did a bit of flying.[9]

At least both men agree that it was Hilton Railey who first contacted Miss
Earhart. At first, guardedly, he simply asked the young woman whether
she would come to his office for an interview. Amelia replied that she
would not until he stated the nature of the project. Railey reluctantly told
her that he was organizing an exciting but hazardous flying venture and
asked whether she was interested. Amelia replied, equally guardedly, that
she might be. "There was a pause and she asked for references—personal
references. That afternoon, accompanied by Miss Marion Perkins, head
worker at Denison House, she appeared at my office." Railey was convinced on sight that he had found the right woman to make the flight and
asked almost immediately, "How would you like to be the first woman to
fly the Atlantic?"[10]

Amelia betrayed no unseemly excitement, but he detected a flicker in
her cool eyes while she calmly asked for details. He told her all that he
was at liberty to tell, and that he had been asked by George Palmer
Putnam, the New York publisher, to find the woman who would make
the flight.

She gave him details on her background. All acceptable. Railey claims
to have been struck by a strong resemblance in Amelia's appearance to
Lindbergh and he immediately coined the sobriquet "Lady Lindy" in his
mind. At the very moment he thought of it, he instinctively knew Amelia
would loathe it but he was also aware of the effect it would have on the
newspapers! He was deeply impressed by the poise of the young woman,
who was both warm and dignified in her manner.[11]

On May 2, probably about a week after their meeting in Boston, Amelia wrote to Railey:

It is very kind of you to keep me informed, as far as you are able, concerning developments of the contemplated flight. As you may imagine my suspense is very great indeed.

Please do not think that I hold you responsible, in any way, for my own uncertainty. I realize that you are . . . only the medium of communication between me and the person, or persons, who are financing the enterprise. For your own satisfaction may I add, here, that you have done nothing more than present the facts of the case to me. I appreciate your forebearance in not trying to "sell" the idea, and should like you to know that I assume all responsibility for any risks involved.

At our next interview—if there is one—I shall have all the details you asked for.[12]

A week later, Amelia was invited to an interview by Layman and Mr. John S. Phipps in New York. She was very much aware of being sized up at that meeting.

It should have been slightly embarrassing, for if I were found wanting on too many counts I should be deprived of a trip. On the other hand, if I were too fascinating the gallant gentlemen might be loath to drown me. Anyone can see the meeting was a crisis.[13]

The details Amelia was given concerning the flight were that Mrs. Amy Guest, an American by birth and married to the Honorable Frederick Guest of London, had purchased the airplane from Byrd, who had originally commissioned it for his planned expedition to the Antarctic.

The plane, a Fokker F7, delivered new from the factory in February, had been test-flown by Bernt Balchen and Floyd Bennett, both of whom pronounced it satisfactory. Mrs. Guest had already given a name to the airplane; it was to be called the *Friendship,* representing Anglo-American relationships. Fitted as standard with two 95-gallon fuel tanks in the wings, an additional pair of extra 95-gallon tanks had been installed, also in the wings, and two 245-gallon tanks fixed in the fuselage, providing a total capacity of 870 gallons—so she had the range for a transatlantic flight. The power source was three Wright Whirlwind J-5 engines, each of 220 horsepower. The plane had already been fitted with Duralumin floats in Detroit, Michigan, at the time of the sale, but these were found to leak, so a certain amount of welding was needed to make them sound.[14]

Amelia was told that she would be accompanied by Stultz and Gordon, both sound and experienced for their roles as pilot/navigator and flight mechanic. Stultz, in fact, had already made one attempt to fly "the first woman across" the previous autumn in a twin-engined Sikorsky, but had turned back when he thought he sensed (rather than heard) one of the engines "splutter" five hundred miles out. Despite the commands, followed by pleas of his passenger, Mrs. Frances Grayson, he made for the coast and was vindicated when, thirty miles out, the port engine died and he limped in on one engine to make a forced landing on the beach.[15] Lewes Gower, another well-known pilot, was to go along as understudy in case Stultz became ill or had an accident, at least as far as Newfoundland, where he could help in final preparations. The names of these men would have been well known to Amelia and she could not have felt other than confident in their ability and reputation.

In fact, the information given to Amelia was not entirely accurate. Mrs. Guest had not purchased the Fokker. It was purchased by Jell-O millionaire Donald Woodward on April 9, 1928 for the sum of $62,000, and registered to his Mechanical Science Corporation of Le Roy, New York.[16] Woodward had already backed Byrd's forthcoming expedition substantially and when Byrd decided that the Fokker was not ideal for his project due to the fixed one-piece wing—he eventually took a Ford trimotor "donated" by the Ford Corporation, who were his chief backers on the venture—Woodward obviously stepped in on a business footing. Mrs. Guest leased the plane from Woodward for the flight with some offer of insurance should the flight be unsuccessful, and the *Friendship* was flown to Boston. Plans for the transatlantic flight were already well advanced.[17]

It must have been a tremendous disappointment for Amy Phipps Guest that she would not be undertaking the flight herself. Although photographs of the period show her to be a plump society matron, her record reveals that she spent her life looking for adventure. As a young woman, she was a forceful and fearless rider to hounds, earning an enviable reputation by riding sidesaddle over jumps that were eschewed by other members of the fox-hunting field.[18]

A niece remembered being told that

> poor Amy had always been thwarted in her attempts to be of help to mankind. During the Spanish American War she wanted to go to Mexico to nurse the wounded. Grandpa asked her, "Do you really want to help our soldiers or do you just want to go out there person-

ally, because if you really want to help the wounded, your mother and I will pay for two trained nurses to work at the army hospital for the duration of the war." What could she say?[19]

In common with a number of other extremely rich (her fortune was rumored to be $1.9 billion) young American girls, Amy married into the British aristocracy, taking as her husband the Right Honorable Frederick Guest, third son of Lord Wimborne.[20] Frederick was not only a keen aviator but also a first-class shot, and the couple undertook many trips to Kenya, where Amy's cool courage on safari impressed even the great white hunter Baron Bror Von Blixen.[21]

It was when Amy heard that a nightclub hostess was planning—soon after Lindbergh's triumph—to be the first woman to fly the Atlantic that she decided to make her move for personal fame. Her niece explained:

> There are several versions of the story, but the one I heard was that she did not tell the family about the trip, with the exception of her youngest brother, Howard [Phipps], and she swore him to secrecy. As time for the flight neared, Howard became more and more worried and finally he broke down, called [Amy's son] Winston and spilled the beans. Winston then phoned his mother from Yale and said definitely, "No—the day you get on the plane I will leave college." So again Aunt Amy had to give up her plans.[22]

Amelia never met Amy on that trip to New York but she did meet George Palmer Putnam. George was busy that day and sent his friend Dr. George McCracken by taxi to collect Amelia and bring her to his office.[23] When she arrived, George was in a meeting and Amelia was asked to wait. She had to wait for a long time and his cavalier dismissal of her time annoyed her, so that when she was finally shown into his presence, she was fully prepared to dislike him considerably.[24] "She was as sore as a wet hen!" George was to relate later. "She didn't like me one little bit and she didn't take much pains to conceal her dislike. . . ."[25]

Railey had undoubtedly already mentioned to George Amelia's physical resemblance to Lindbergh. George, busy as usual, was prepared to be patronizing.[26] Instead, he was intrigued, recognizing at once her personality and potential. He disguised his true feelings behind a brusque manner and this is what Amelia later recalled. But although she remembered "no special feelings about Mr. Putnam at first—I was too absorbed in the prospects of the trip and of my being the one to make it, to notice any one person at that time," she also related that "before I had talked to him for very long I was conscious of the brilliant mind and the keen insight of the man. I recognized his tremendous power of accomplishments and immediately respected his judgement. . . ."[27]

George was so impressed that he decided at that meeting that Amelia should be the woman to make the flight.[28] However, all too soon Amelia had to leave to catch a train to Boston. George accompanied her to Pennsylvania Station and later Amelia confided to her sister that "she wished the ride had been longer because he was so interesting," but she also noted that he had hurried her aboard her train and departed without offering to pay her fare home![29]

BOOK THREE:

AMELIA
and
GEORGE

Amelia Earhart knew me better, probably, than
anyone else ever can. With her discernment, why
she married the man she did was often a matter of
wonder to me. And to some others.

> — *George Palmer Putnam,*
> Wide Margins *(New York: Harcourt,*
> *Brace and Company, 1942), p. 282*

How does "being in business" (for flying is a
business) affect marriage? Obviously I can offer only
my own answers—from a woman's viewpoint. It
seems to me that the effect of having other interests
beyond those exclusively domestic works well. The
more one does and sees and feels, the more one is
able to do, and the more genuine may be one's
appreciation of fundamental things like home, and
love, and understanding companionship.

> — *Amelia Earhart, "My Husband,"*
> Redbook *magazine, Sept. 1933*

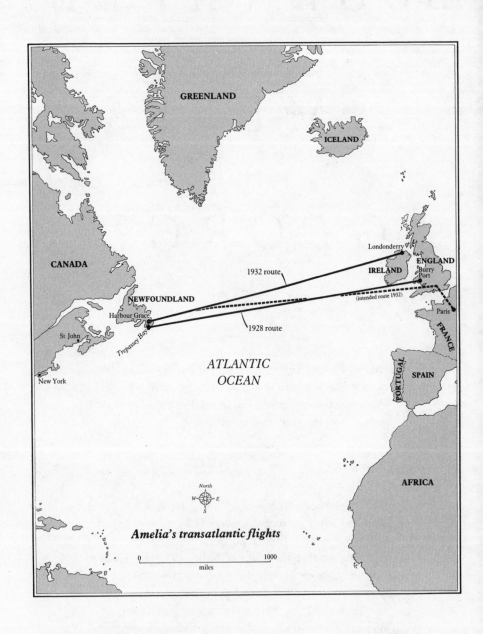

Amelia's transatlantic flights

0   1000
miles

1. Studio portrait of Amelia, 1928.

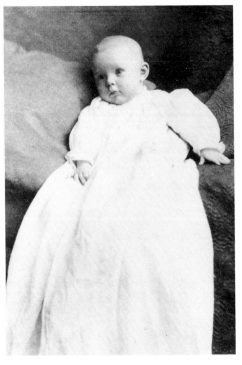

2. Amelia in her christening robe, October 1897.

3. Amelia's parents: Edwin and Amy Earhart.

4. Amelia (Millie), with toy lamb, and Muriel (Pidge) on the front porch of their Kansas City home, c. 1904.

5. Amelia was born at her grandparents' home in Atchison, Kansas. It is now a museum.

6. Amelia (third from right) learned automobile mechanics in this all-female class (taught by the male in center).

7. Amelia in the uniform of a Voluntary Aid Detachment nurse, Toronto, Ontario, c. 1918.

8. Amelia (at right) and Anita (Neta) Snook, California, c. 1921.

9. Amelia's first crash in 1921, south of Los Angeles. Crashes were a frequent hazard in the early days of flying.

10. Amelia picnicking on the beach in 1924.

11. George Putnam, age twenty-three, in Bend, Oregon.

12. "There I was…in the roaring west," George wrote, "I wanted to hear it roar." Bend, Oregon, in 1910.

13. George Putnam, newspaperman (second from left), outside the offices of the Bend *Bulletin*, c. 1911.

George Putnam, adventurer. He liked
ng better than saddlepacking alone
e mountains. Bend, Oregon, c. 1912.

George in uniform during World
I.

16. Poster for one of George's lecture tours.

17. George Putnam, explorer (right), with
Carl Dunrud, taken during the Greenland
Expedition in 1926. Dunrud was a cowboy
and expert lassoer. It was intended that he
would lasso a polar bear!

18. Amelia and George in Boston, May 1928, a few weeks after they first met.

Chapter Eleven

1 9 2 8: *Before the Flight*

T wo days after the meeting in New York, Amelia was told that the flight would be made and that she had been selected as the woman commander, "if she wished."[1] She was, however, to receive no remuneration for her part in the venture.

However, "under the circumstances," Amelia wrote later, "I couldn't say no."[2]

To mark the occasion George presented Amelia with a gift. It was a leather-bound diary, trimmed and inscribed in gold with the words:

> A.E.
> FROM
> G.P.
> 5/15/28

It was an elegant and expensive trifle to which Amelia was to commit her personal thoughts and experiences during the flight.[3]

At the time of her acceptance, Amelia's personal financial situation could only be described as dire. Her regular salary had at last enabled her to repay the debt incurred years ago in Los Angeles, when she had the operation to relieve her sinus pain. Matters were slowly improving but she was still in debt, sometimes borrowing against her next salary check in order to survive.[4]

Amelia would have quickly recognized the opportunities that the flight held for her. Immediate fame, of course, if the attempt was successful, and George, or G.P. as she quickly came to call him, would not have been slow in pointing out the potential for earning substantial amounts of money from personal appearances, lecture tours, and articles. Amelia would also have been tempted by the thought of the flight itself. She was already wholly committed to aviation and its development, and though she was practical enough not to pass up fame and fortune, it is likely that she would have made the flight if there had been no obvious rewards—purely for the experience.

Amelia having formally accepted the offer, another meeting took place in Boston on May 18, 1928, with Layman and G.P. For the time being, she was told, it would be better for everyone if the whole matter was kept secret, mainly to avoid press attention while preparations were under way, but also to avoid alerting any competitive attempt whose preparations might be more advanced. No announcements would be made until they had actually taken off.

For her part, Amelia had made it clear from the start that the role of passenger did not appeal to her much and that she wished to take a turn at the controls.[5] She had no experience with multi-engine flying, however, nor with instrument flying, so it was agreed that if weather permitted, she would be allowed to fly for some of the time. All the same, those present recognized it was important that Amelia was seen to be in charge of the flight, whose entire purpose was to promote the circumstance of a woman flying the ocean. Her role as "commander" was therefore covered by a document drawn up at that meeting. There was no other formal contract.

BOSTON MASSACHUSETTS
MAY 18TH 1928

Wilmer Stultz
Louis E. Gordon
J. H. Lewes Gowner [sic]
and anyone else concerned:

This is to say that on arrival at Treppassy [sic] of the tri-motor Fokker plane "FRIENDSHIP" if any questions of policy, procedure, personnel or any other question arises the decision of Miss Amelia M. Earhart is to be final. That she is to have control of the plane and of the disposal of the services of all employees as fully as if she were the owner. And further, that on arrival of the plane in London full control of the disposition of the plane and of the time and services of employees shall be hers to the same extent until and unless the owner directs otherwise.

David T. Layman
Attorney in fact for the owner

A specimen of Miss Earhart's
signature appears below[6]

Amelia had already been to see the *Friendship* where it was jacked up in the rear of a large hangar at East Boston airport, awaiting the fitting of pontoons that were being worked on by welders nearby. Just under fifty feet in length and with a wing span of seventy-one feet, two inches, it was by far the largest airplane in which Amelia had yet flown. The plane had been registered by Byrd under an experimental license, NX4204 (the experimental status being designated by the *X*), and was painted international orange (a red orange) with gold wings, "the latter described as a warm amber from many coats of spar varnish over birch veneer."7 The color, originally specified by Byrd to facilitate location should he go down in the sea or on ice, would serve the same purpose for the oceanic flight. Amelia saw the *Friendship* only once more prior to the departure from Boston, and she never got the opportunity to fly in it until then. She was too well known at local airfields to risk being involved in the preparations. If she had been seen taking too close an interest, it would have precipitated the type of rumors they were all anxious to avoid.

It had been hoped that the *Friendship* would leave Boston for Trepassey Bay, Newfoundland, during mid-May, exactly a year after Lindbergh's flight. Hilton Railey, at Amelia's request, sailed for Europe to organize things at that end. Similar to Lindbergh's flight, though, the *Friendship* enterprise was frustrated by poor weather. Long gray days through to the end of the month kept them in Boston. G.P. was there all the time. His relationship with Byrd was known and accepted and his presence excited no comment. Mr. and Mrs. Layman visited sometimes, as did Dorothy Putnam. Amy Guest's sons, Winston and Raymond, cautiously made an appearance, not wishing to give anything away.8

To help pass the time, Amelia took G.P., and sometimes Stultz, Gordon, and Gower (Stultz's understudy) sightseeing in her Kissel roadster. "On rainy days the top leaked too much for comfort, so we walked."9 They experimented, going to a different ethnic restaurant each evening and also to all the theaters.

G.P. and Amelia discovered that they shared a well-developed sense of the ridiculous and one particular show that they attended especially amused them. It was a tragedy in which all the characters, save one, drowned, and a recurring line, "the fish are dearly paid for," struck them as hilarious under the circumstances; the crew of *Friendship* instantly adopted it as a motto, "emblazoned under a goldfish rampant."10

Perhaps it was this shared sense of humor that formed the initial attraction between G.P. and Amelia. However, G.P. was naturally drawn toward intelligent people and the cool poise of Amelia in the face of the Atlantic flight together with her obvious ambition and dedication to her work and her enthusiasm for the future of aviation must all have played their part.

Her personal preparations had been minimal and were completed quickly. Her clothes would consist of those she wore as she climbed aboard: high laced boots, brown broadcloth breeches, white silk blouse with red necktie, her by-now genuinely aged leather coat, a brown sweater, flying helmet, goggles, a white and brown silk scarf (for elegance), and she also carried a very necessary heavy fur-lined flying suit borrowed from a friend—Major Charles H. Wooley of Boston, who was unaware of the true reason for Amelia's borrowing it.

Her small knapsack contained a toothbrush and comb, two handkerchiefs, and a tube of cold cream. Layman loaned his camera and G.P. loaned his ex-Arctic binoculars; besides that, a small log book, an autographed copy of *Skyward* that Amelia had promised to deliver by hand to Amy Guest, and some personal messages to be delivered by hand from those associated with the mission comprised her sole luggage.[11]

Amelia's will, listing her possessions and debts, is revealing of her financial precariousness.

MAY 20, 1928

This is hardly a will for I leave no appreciable estate.

I owe several hundred dollars to the Morris Plan. This will be taken care of by insurance if I die.

I owe the Medford Trust Company $700, with the New Jersey Power Bond as collateral.

I owe Jordan Marsh	$25.00
Filenes	140.00 (Fur coat)
Educational	
Services Bureau	50.00 approximate
Garage (City)	53.98
	(plus current rental)

My car is to be sold and the garage bill paid. The remainder is to go toward the payment to Miss Rafferty, who is owed for her instruction in embroidery for the who [sic] season. Miss Perkins can explain the situation here.

I have ten shares of stock in the Dennison Aircraft Corporation which will go to my mother. That in the Kinner Airplane and Motor Corporation also shall go to her. I hope they will pay, and think they will.

My board bill at D.H. [Denison House] is to be paid from my June 1 salary. It will be approximately $50.

My regret is I leave just now. In a few years, I feel I could have laid by something substantial for so many new things were opening for me.

Selah.[12]

To G.P., she entrusted letters addressed to her parents to be given to them in the event that she did not return.

MAY 20, 1928

Dearest Dad

Hooray for the last grand adventure! I wish I had won but it was worth while anyway. You know that.

I have no faith that we'll meet anywhere again, but I wish we might.

Anyway, goodbye, and good luck to you.

Affectionately, your doter,
MILL[13]

To her mother, she wrote:

. . . Even though I have lost, the adventure was worth while. Our family tends to be too secure. My life has really been very happy, and I don't mind contemplating its end in the midst of it. . . .[14]

Apart from her fiancé, Sam, and her employer, Marion Perkins, Amelia confided in almost no one from her immediate circle. Even her mother and sister were excluded from the secret, although there were also two unnamed friends who were invited to attend the *Friendship*'s departure.[15] It was to be Sam's job to tell the family personally the moment the *Friendship* left Boston.

George tried to get preparations for Amelia's story of the trip under way, but in Amelia he had met his match. Fitzhugh Green, then working as G.P.'s staff ghostwriter, recalls a meeting between the two:

I thought I had Lindbergh in my office, but it was Earhart. The likeness was astonishing. Tall slimness, fresh coloring. Blue eyes flashed a Lindbergh grin of white teeth [and the] resemblance did not stop at being physical. "Now," said businessman George P. Putnam, "we'd better line up the film people don't you think?"

"No," said Amelia.

"Then why not let's get the book into focus?"

"Because I haven't made the flight yet."

"But heavens, woman, don't you want to arrange the business end of this now?"

"No."

It wasn't a "NO!", or a "no, no"; nor even a "nope."

"No." Just that smiling sort of "no" that Lindbergh followers know so well.[16]

In fairness to George Putnam and his team, who have been accused of manufacturing this supposed likeness of Amelia to Charles Lindbergh, the comments of Lindbergh's wife, Anne, in a letter to her family after meeting Amelia in 1930 are illuminating.

> The biggest surprise, though, was Amelia Earhart, who was here the first four days. She is the most amazing person—just as tremendous as C., I think. It startles me how much alike they are. . . . C. doesn't realize it, but he hasn't talked to her as much. She has the clarity of mind, impersonal eye, coolness of temperament, balance of a scientist.[17]

It had been agreed that Hilton Railey would leave almost immediately for London to make preparations to welcome Amelia upon her arrival. Amelia spent some time at the Railey home working on a biographical sketch that Railey could give to reporters there. Railey's wife, Julia, found herself in sympathy with Amelia's frustrated cry: "But I don't know *how* to make myself interesting to order! School—college—war nursing—social work—a couple of planes of my own and a little flying—what more can I say? What *is* there to say?"

Julia and Amelia (both were social workers and felt they had something in common) went off to dinner together:

> At the curb we climbed into the worst looking automobile I ever saw, bar none. Its rear end was cigar shaped and its ground color a sick canary. She said she had it in California, it was second hand to begin with and five years old. People got out of the way of it I noticed. [We] scudded through the traffic like a car possessed [and] with something like a flourish drew up at last at "The Old France" restaurant.[18]

Over dinner Julia told Amelia something of George's impressive history, which could only have enhanced the attraction Amelia already felt for him.

The weather continued unsuitable until early June and during this time, Stultz and Gordon had managed to make a few test hops in Boston. When the weather was clear in Boston, fog surrounded their destination in Newfoundland. When it was clear in Newfoundland, they could not take off from Boston. Amelia fretted about the use of floats, receiving conflicting advice as to their usefulness. While they might enable them to make a forced landing at sea, they would make the takeoff considerably more difficult.

Virtually all record-breaking aviators wrote with emotion about the waiting period before takeoff. Many found it the most difficult part of their enterprise. It was certainly so for the crew of the *Friendship*. To kill time, G.P. and Amelia often visited Richard Byrds' Boston home, where Amelia took great interest in the preparations for the Antarctic venture. In contrast to Amelia's own meager supplies, the house was filled with provisions and equipment. She would not, she said, have been surprised to see a team of huskies harnessed to a sled. Sometimes she met with Stultz and Gordon to go over flight plans and charts.[19]

Amelia's friendship with G.P. grew daily. By now, she had started calling him by a nickname, "Simpkin," in their private moments together (it was to be many years before he discovered the reason). It was already obvious to her that G.P.'s attentions were somewhat more than necessary for the sake of the project, and despite her own attraction to him, Amelia clearly fielded any passes by saying that she had Sam to consider. For his part, G.P. was very attracted to Amelia, but perhaps even more than any romantic reason, he saw the challenge of real fame. "It wasn't so much that he was romancing her," said a friend, "as that he was romancing a property."[20]

On Sunday June 3, the weather was ideal—enough wind to lift them off the water and reports of clear skies all the way to Newfoundland. A small party consisting of the crew, G.P., Robert Elmer (technical adviser), some cameramen, and a few sundry others left the Copley Plaza Hotel at 4:30 A.M. and boarded the tug *Sadie Ross* on "T-Wharf" for "a fishing trip."[21] Actually, they headed across the harbor toward the Jeffrey Yacht Club in East Boston, where the *Friendship* was moored.

Sam Chapman, Marion Perkins, and two other close friends of Amelia's joined the party, aboard another tug. It was the third such trip in as many days and the mood was relaxed rather than tense. Who knew if the whole thing would simply be another rehearsal? They loaded sandwiches and thermos flasks of coffee aboard the airplane, and G.P. had carefully provided a small supply of oranges.[22]

The wind created a light ripple on the water as Stultz held the airplane into the wind and opened the throttles, but, as Amelia wrote in her log, "the drag of the pontoons held us down." In fact the plane hardly got up onto the steps of the pontoons. They offloaded six five-gallon cans of gasoline—of the eight they carried for emergency—and tried again, unsuccessfully. The 180 pounds they had gained in dumping fuel was not enough. They tried two further runs of greater distance without unsticking. Without saying a word, Lew Gower, knowing what was necessary, quietly collected his flying suit and the small personal package that was the sum of his luggage. G.P. and Elmer came alongside in a launch and took Gower off. That made the difference. It took sixty-seven seconds to take the *Friendship* off the water and head north.

Although there was no fog, a light haze and blinding sun made visibility poor. By the time they reached Halifax, a flight of 410 miles, they ran into thick fog and were forced to land. They took off an hour later, planning to follow the coastline, but the fog was too thick, so they returned to spend the night.

In her personal diary for that night Amelia wrote, "12pm. Two reporters and camera men are in the next room trying to persuade Stultz and G. to dress and have a flashlight picture taken. I am displeased with their thortlessness [*sic*] in keeping the men awake and am dropping things in my room to make the men realize I am still awake and disapproving. I don't know whether the newspaper men know I'm here so I am not shouting my sentiments. . . ."[23]

News of Amelia's participation had preceded the fliers, however, and when they sat down to breakfast, they read about themselves. Reading the quotes from her mother, Amelia realized how hurt Amy must have been and how worried she must be. She sent Amy a telegram explaining why she couldn't tell her and asking her not to worry. Next day—despite attentions from local pressmen—they were able to get away reasonably early and reached Trepassey by mid-afternoon on June 4.

As soon as they left Boston, the story had broken. Sam had not even reached the Earhart home in West Medford before reporters laid siege to Mrs. Earhart and Muriel. They knew nothing of the flight, of course, but were able to provide pictures of Amelia as a child and tell of her history. They must have felt bewildered, perhaps even cheated, until Sam arrived to give them Amelia's personal message.

It would be unreasonable to suppose that George had not broken the story, given his record in publicity. Now that the crew were—to all intents and purposes—beyond the reach of newspapermen, he wanted as much hype as he could muster as part of his overall strategy. Lindbergh had been beyond his grasp, but with Amelia he could, he must have thought, control one of the most important news stories—and its aftermath—of the century. Some people were unkind enough to suggest that this wasn't so much of a story, after all. George paid scant attention; if necessary, he knew he could *make* it the most important story. Not all newspapers received the story with unalloyed pleasure, nor fell for the "Lady Lindy" tag in his press releases, and one editorialized:

> By manipulation of pictures and publicity, Amelia Earhart, the Boston girl who is crossing the Atlantic with Wilmer Stultz, is to be made a feminine Lindbergh, unless plans go awry. The stunt is financed by George Palmer Putnam, publisher of *We* who now plans a similar book, it is understood, called *She*. . . . Amelia Earhart has been in training, coached by the promoters, to emulate Lindbergh in every respect, in attitude, pictures and behaviour.[24]

Unfortunately, far from crossing the Atlantic, once at Trepassey the fliers were effectively trapped. Successive days of gales or fog meant they could not attempt to take off. At first, they were only mildly disappointed and Gordon used the time to make repairs to the oil tank, which had developed a crack, while Stultz tinkered with the radio. On the fourth day of the delay, they attempted a takeoff, but the wind increased and the water became too rough. In the days that followed, unable even to attempt takeoff, they passed the time by playing cards and looking around Trepassey. It was cold and uninviting and all three became dispirited.

They had only one aviation map with them—Bill Stultz's chart of the North Atlantic—and on this map, each day, they outlined the series of fronts and storms cabled to them via George from the Met office. Amelia called in at the local convent school and persuaded the nuns to loan her some geography books with maps and a large globe and she pored over these in an attempt to help pass the time.[25]

Amelia's mood was lifted briefly by a telegram from G.P., who, knowing she had no change of clothes with her, wired, SUGGEST YOU GO INTO RETIREMENT TEMPORARILY WITH NUNS AND HAVE THEM WASH SHIRT ETC.[26] To which she replied, THANKS FATHERLY TELEGRAM NO WASHING NECESSARY SOCKS UNDERWEAR WORN-OUT SHIRT LOST TO SLIM AT RUMMY CHEERIO A.E.[27] As a matter of fact, personal hygiene was becoming a problem to all three crew members, who had to borrow clothes while their own were washed. Amelia did spend thirty-five cents on a pair of hose, and a khaki shirt was another purchase. It was far too big, but she took a tuck in at the back with a safety pin.[28]

Amelia continued to make faithful entries each night in the diary that

George had given her. Written in pencil in her untidy scrawl she recorded after a week:

> I got a wire from M.P. [Marion Perkins] asking permission to publish one of my poems . . . as the subject was "courage." I refused as I know the luck it would bring forth. Anyway I can't remember whether I liked it. [Note: despite Amelia's refusal the poem was published in an article by Marion Perkins.][29]

After a week of waiting, there seemed, on the evening of June 11, to be favorable conditions. Stultz wired G.P., advising an attempted takeoff the next morning and asking for full Atlantic weather conditions. Next morning, he confirmed their intentions and received a reasonable weather report from George. The wire, however, also carried bad news: MABEL STARTED SEVEN AM ALLEGEDLY FOR HARBOUR GRACE STOP BYRD BELIEVES 900 GALLONS AMPLE FOR FRIENDSHIP. . . .[30]

Mabel Boll, also known variously as the "Queen of Diamonds" and Señora Hernando Rocha-Schioos, was making a strong challenge to be the first woman across the ocean, in the single-engined *Columbia* (now suitably renamed *Miss Columbia*), which had formerly carried Clarence Chamberlin and his crew safely across the Atlantic (to Germany), setting a distance record.[31] In March, Stultz had piloted her and showman Charles A. Levine on the first nonstop flight from New York to Havana, Cuba. Already planning her transatlantic attempt, she claimed to have hired Stultz for the project for a reputed sum of $25,000, and she thought he had accepted.[32] What became clear, however, was that Dick Byrd had talked Stultz into accepting that the Earhart flight was more likely to succeed. The remuneration offered was the same in both cases. But before making up his mind, and without telling the Guest/Putnam consortium of his plan, Stultz met Mabel Boll in New York. What happened at that meeting is unknown, though Stultz obviously revealed nothing of the alternative project despite the great pressure placed on him to contract to the Mabel Boll camp. Later, he declared he had opted out because the entire enterprise smacked of the circus and unprofessionalism (Chamberlin had much the same to say about Levine's participation in the successful flight to Europe).

The thwarted Miss Boll signed WWI flying aces Oliver C. Le Boutillier and Captain Arthur Argles as her crew, and the publicity-conscious Levine backed the venture. Mabel Boll allegedly wore sweaters woven of pure gold links, and with her dark eyes, vividly blond hair, and tempestuous Latin temperament, she made good newspaper copy.[33] She was undoubtedly a threat to the *Friendship*'s more sober venture, and her flight could only have increased the frustration and sense of entrapment felt by the three crew members. In all their minds must have been the fact that with *Miss Columbia*'s conventional undercarriage, Miss Boll could take off in any fine weather, whereas they had sea conditions also to take into consideration.

Amelia's diary entry reveals her anxiety: "Our competitors are gaining on us by the delay." But she was not so concerned about Mabel Boll as by Thea Rasche, whose plans were well advanced but totally secret. "Rasche is the one to fear . . . ," Amelia wrote. She dreaded hearing that Rasche had somehow been able to overtake by leaving from the mainland as Lindbergh had done.[34]

On the morning of June 12, G.P. sent three detailed weather forecasts spaced an hour apart, and with these in mind, Stultz tried for four hours to take the *Friendship* off. Unfortunately, as Amelia recorded in her daily log:

> This has been the worst day . . . the receding tide made the sea so heavy that the spray was thrown so high that it drowned the outboard motors. As we gathered speed, the motors would cut and we'd lose the precious pull necessary . . . we unloaded every ounce of stuff from the plane—camera, my coat, bags, cushions etc. She would have gone but for the motors. There was salt water above the prop. hubs.
>
> I received some letters today and . . . "day after the takeoff" papers from Boston. I couldn't read them under the circumstances of this day. We are all too disappointed to talk. The boys are in bed and I am going soon. We rise at six.[35]

With the letters and papers came a further cable from G.P., advising that Mabel Boll was due imminently at Harbour Grace, Newfoundland, and that she had announced that she would start for London early next morning. Commenting on Stultz's intention to try again on the following day, G.P. said, HOPE YOU MAKE IT AT DAYLIGHT . . . BYRD AFTER CAREFUL RECKONING BELIEVES EIGHT HUNDRED SEVENTY GALLONS AMPLE IF TAKE-OFF WEIGHT ESSENTIAL.[36]

Stultz wired back, querying Byrd's calculations on fuel, and received in return a startled reply: WIRE RECEIVED STOP IT SAID SIX HUNDRED GALLONS PRESUME SHOULD READ EIGHT HUNDRED WHICH BYRD SAYS PROBABLY SAFE ALTHOUGH 830 PREFERABLE. . . . More advice from nonpilot Byrd followed regarding takeoff time and landing points.[37]

Given that Stultz would have taken off in the middle of the night if he could have lifted *Friendship* off the water, this advice must have made him grind his teeth, but he wired Byrd in a friendly manner and received back this reply: THANKS MESSAGE HARD LUCK IF NOT TOO ROUGH SUGGEST MIGHT GO OUTSIDE FOR TAKEOFF STOP YOUR SUCCESS MEANS MUCH TO ME STAY WITH IT COOPERATING PUTNAM HERE REGARDS ALL HANDS BYRD.[38]

Amelia, meanwhile, had her own problems. On reading the papers that appeared the day after takeoff from Boston, she found her private telegram to her mother openly and widely quoted. Furious at the breach of privacy and no doubt overreaching due to frustration and disappointment, she fired off a blistering letter to her sister before joining the men for another takeoff attempt. Even worse, she was worried because Stultz and Gordon had turned to drinking heavily—to alleviate the frustration and boredom.

> The boys went after bad booze and got it last night. They had to push the [automobile] for eight miles because the belt broke. They arrived home about six o'clock tired but with happy memories. I could choke Frazer. It doesn't matter whether he drinks but it certainly does whether my gang do. . . . I am not easy now as the men are all together in [the landlord's] room and have been for more than an hour. It is so important that Stultz's judgement be good in the crisis. . . .[39]

That evening, Wednesday, June 13, 1928, a thoroughly disheartened crew returned from yet another day of fruitless effort. "The days grow worse," Amelia wrote in her log. "I think each time we have reached the low, but find we haven't. . . . Today Bill and Slim tried to take her off after she had been degassed by 300 lbs. The left motor cut and they couldn't get her off light. . . ."[40] They arrived back to find a cable from G.P., suggesting they consider the Azores as a possible destination. This would enable them to lighten the load further.

The evening cable from G.P. read, . . . IF IN MORNING YOU CAN POSSIBLY TAKE OFF EVEN MINIMUM GAS IRELAND FAR BEST BET STOP SUGGEST TRY TAKEOFF AWAY FROM HILLS . . . IF THIS FAILS REDUCE [GAS] AND GO FOR AZORES STOP IF AZORES SURELY NOTIFY ME SO ARRANGE GAS WEATHER REPORTS . . . STOP PROBLEM THERE NAVIGATION DANGER MISSING ISLANDS HOPE YOU HAVE SEXTANT FOR OBSERVATION SENDING POSITION RADIO IF FORCED DOWN STOP MABEL SENDS WORD HERE NO START TOMORROW STOP WEATHER REPORT BOTH FOR IRELAND AND AZORES TEN PM DARN SORRY BUT YOU WILL EMERGE ON TOP WE ALL KNOW YOU ARE DOING YOUR BEST.[41]

All the cables had so far been between Stultz and various members of the management team. Mrs. Guest was obviously worried about this, for that evening a wire arrived for Amelia from Layman, asking for her personal confidential report on the situation—particularly as to the fuel capacity and a possible change of destination. Amelia's reply is lost, but Putnam subsequently wired Railey in London, BEG CHIEF NOT WORRY SHIP OK DECREASING LOAD HAVE ANNOUNCED OUR PLANS UNINFLUENCED COMPETITION MUST PROCEED PATIENTLY.[42] And, a day or so later, he wired to Stultz, CONFIDENTIAL GUEST SAYS ACCOUNT WEIGHT DIFFICULTY TAKEOFF IF YOU COULD CONSIDER LEAVING SLIM WHO WOULD BE PAID AS AGREED EYE IMAGINE IMPRACTICAL ACCEPT YOUR JUDGEMENT. . . .[43]

Since Amelia had not the necessary ability or experience to act as copilot or navigator across the Atlantic, the suggestion that they leave Gordon behind was specious, to say the least. Perhaps to convince himself that it was possible to fly from Trepassey at all, Stultz pumped out 135 gallons of fuel (810 pounds) and made a thirty-four-minute test flight.[44] Then, bad weather kept the plane moored at the buoy for another three days and in that time the only good news was word that the *Southern Cross* had successfully crossed the Pacific from San Francisco to Australia, via Hawaii. This was an identical airplane to the *Friendship*, except that she had a conventional undercarriage instead of pontoons.

In a confidential cable to Amelia (the date of which is not decipherable), George suggested, . . . FOR OCCUPATION MIGHT WRITE SKELETON THOUSAND WORD STORY FLIGHT THUS FAR HALIFAX TREPASSEY WITH NAMES DETAILS TO ENLARGE HERE AFTER YOU UNDER WAY JUST SAVE PRESSURE CABLE TOLLS OTHER END ADDRESS QUOTE NIGHT PRESS COLLECT TIMES FOR PUTNAM . . . MRS. GUEST SENDS LOVE EYE DITTO SAM PERMITTING OR OTHERWISE THINK OF FRESH WARDROBE IN LONDON AND GRIN. SIMKIN [SIC].[45]

In truth, there was precious little to grin about. Apart from the frustrations and tedium, Amelia was concerned by Stultz's increasing drinking. At one point, she considered wiring George to send Gower as a replacement pilot, but as George was later to write, "AE was a scrupulously fair person and she knew that she could not do that without great damage to Stultz; knew also that any such last-minute switch might well bring the whole project tumbling down about her."[46] Stultz was quite simply the best there was and although barely twenty-eight, his experience was vast. In Amelia's mind, too, may have been the suspicion that if she appealed to Putnam and Layman to replace Stultz, they might think she was merely looking for a way out, having lost her nerve.

Nothing could have been further from reality. For days she had been trying to persuade Stultz to take a chance and set off for Ireland or the

Azores. She pleaded with both men but Stultz would not make an attempt to take off with unfavorable conditions forecast. She pointed out the competition and the fact that "thousands [of dollars] were tied up in the project." But Stultz would not be moved and Amelia turned to lecturing them about drinking less and sleeping more.

On June 16 her nightly diary entry is despairing: "Just now the boys are at Paddy Mortons and I know liquor flows . . . they went on a walk this afternoon and had some then. I shall get them home at nine or know the reason. I loathe watching men. Why can't they be more responsible? . . . There is a madness about Bill which is not in keeping with a pilot who has to fly."[47]

On the following morning, June 17, after more than twelve days of waiting, the weather and tide were suddenly all set fair—or reasonably so. Unfortunately, as Amelia feared, Stultz had drunk heavily the night before and was hung over. Gordon and Amelia spent some hours pouring black coffee into their pilot and finally "she knew the start had to be made then or probably never. So she simply got hold of her pilot and all but dragged him to the plane."[48]

At 11:15 A.M., after two abortive attempts to get off in the heavy sea, the crew agreed upon a desperate solution. Realizing that even with the forecasted favorable tail winds, they were leaving no margin for error, they pumped out further fuel, and with 700 gallons remaining taxied out to try again, hoping to reach Ireland. The decision to lighten their load had been Amelia's in the end, but the situation was one of crisis.[49] It is easy to recognize the desperation that Amelia and Lou Gordon were experiencing and that made them continue in the face of this situation. Amelia later confided to G.P. that that hour seemed to her to be the most dangerous of her life, and certainly the most dangerous of the flight. She had simply trusted that Stultz's considerable flying instinct would take over.[50]

The first run was aborted because the spray-soaked engines were spluttering too badly to give sufficient power. On the second run, they were able to reach the required speed of just over fifty miles an hour, and staggered into the air after "a desperate takeoff run of almost three miles,"[51] despite the fact that the two wing-mounted engines were spluttering from a thorough soaking in saltwater spray, one so wet it was an hour into the flight before it achieved full power.[52]

With little optimism, Amelia had left a cable to be sent to G.P. thirty minutes after their departure. It said simply VIOLET STOP CHEERIO.[53] This was the coded signal to G.P. that they had, in truth, left. Only a few villagers saw them off, for there had been so many unsuccessful attempts that the majority had lost faith in the aviators, as had many American newspapers, who criticized the crew, particularly Amelia, for a seeming reluctance to get going.

1 9 2 8: The Transatlantic Flight

*E*ARHART PLANE SOARING OVER ATLANTIC; REPORTED NEARLY HALF WAY TO IRELAND EIGHT HOURS AFTER LEAVING TREPASSEY. This is was how the readers of *The New York Times* learned on the morning of June 18, 1928, that Amelia and her two companions had departed at last. Takeoff was at 2:51 P.M. British Summer Time (Amelia's log recorded 10:51 A.M. Boston time).

As the *Friendship* passed Cape Race at 5:20 P.M. (BST), Lou Gordon transmitted two radio messages, one for George Putnam: OUT OF FOG NOW CLEAR WEATHER, and the other to Bill Stultz's wife: EVERYTHING GOING FINE.[1] Reports of satisfactory progress filtered in from ships' radios en route; the *Friendship*'s call sign, WOX, and transmission frequency of six hundred meters had been well publicized for two weeks. Some ships had made radio contact without seeing the airplane; some had heard the engines but had been unable to raise any contact on the radio.[2]

Back at Harbour Grace, Mabel Boll protested that she had not been given the same weather reports as Amelia and thus had been unable to make the decision to get away. In fact, she was correct. Although her reports were issued from the same source, she was receiving merely the standard transatlantic weather reports put out by "Doc" Kimball at the Met office and aimed at shipping. But George, alert to the fact that the weather was such a key factor in the success or failure of the venture, had arranged to pay for special reports tailored to the fliers' needs. Miss Boll wisely decided to sit and wait. If the *Friendship* was unsuccessful, the *Miss Columbia* would have a clear field free of other contestants.

The clear spell of weather did not last and Amelia and her companions were soon in thick cloud again. While the two men occupied the cockpit seats, Amelia sat in the empty main cabin, squeezed between the two large fuel tanks, to take advantage of any warm air blown back from the cockpit. She perched on the three flying suits, since all extraneous items such as cushions had been left behind. Immediately, she started making entries in an informal logbook, her often untidy, quick scrawl made worse on this occasion by vibration. There was, in truth, little to write about beyond her observations of clouds and fog, but she recorded items she thought might be of interest later. "... we have only the small thermos filled with coffee for the boys. I shan't drink anything probably," she wrote with irony, "unless we come down. ..." Later, she wrote: "4000 feet. More than three tons of us are hurtling through the air. We are in the storm now. Three tons is shaken considerably."[3]

Toward evening, they made contact with a British ship, the *Rexmore*, which gave them a bearing and promised to inform New York of their position; and Bill managed to get several fixes through the patchy fog before the sun went down. After that, all Amelia could see through the one cabin window was "glowing meteors" from the exhausts. "I think I am happy," she wrote at this point, "[a] sad admission of scant intellectual equipment."[4]

Amelia continued to make logbook entries after dark, using her left thumb to mark the starting point of each line. They were never entirely clear of fog, but now and again they were able to catch glimpses of the sea and, at last, as the fuel was used up and the load lightened, they were able to gain sufficient height to climb to five thousand feet, six thousand feet, and finally at ten thousand feet, they were over the massed, lumpy cumulus that made flying so uncomfortable. It was extremely cold at that height; all three donned fur-lined flying suits and, striving to keep alert, watched for the first welcome sight of dawn. Amelia spent a short time in the cockpit when Slim went aft to the chart table; but conditions were always too rough for her to take the controls and she spent most of the time in the cabin, sometimes with her nose pressed against the small single window, earplugs in place to prevent being deafened. As the night wore on, she developed a bad headache and slept for half an hour to relieve it.

When light came, Stultz decided to lose some height. He hoped that the favorable tail winds might mean a fast passage and in this case they ought to be able to see Ireland before too long. Amelia's log book entry read:

We are going down, probably ... going through. Fog is lower here too, haven't hit it yet but will so far as I can see from the back window. ... Everything shut out. Instrument Flying. Slow descent, first. It takes a lot to make my ears hurt. 5000 feet now. Awfully wet. Water dripping in window. Port motor coughing. Sounds as if all motors are cutting. Bill opens her wide to try to clear. Sounds rotten on the right. . . .[5]

In her book, *20 Hrs. 40 Min.*, Amelia frankly admitted that she was afraid at this point. At three thousand feet, they broke into patchy clouds and could see the sea again, but the radio appeared to be dead and they could not raise an answer. The port engine continued to give trouble and they were all quietly aware that only two hours of fuel remained. At any time, they expected to see land, and lines of dark cloud lying on the horizon several times tempted their straining eyesight into thinking they *could* see it. By all calculations, the coast of Ireland ought to have been in sight anytime within the preceding hour.

By accident, Amelia discovered a bottle of alcohol, smuggled aboard by Stultz and hidden in the tool bag. She agonized at first about what to do, finally moving it to a new hiding place. Perhaps the memory of her father's violent reaction when she had emptied *his* bottle down the drain, all those years ago, came back to her. However, Stultz never went looking for the bottle; he was fully occupied and had no need of artificial stimuli.

Just before 9 A.M., Greenwich Mean Time (GMT), and in a state of grave anxiety about their position, the three fliers saw several ships cutting across their course, which, though a welcome sight, perplexed them. Surely, the ships should be sailing a course parallel to their own? The radio was still useless. After discussion, they decided to stay on course, though by now they were down to an hour's fuel supply.

Another ship, the oceangoing liner S.S. *America* (though they were unable to identify it at the time) passed some miles away and they detoured, using up precious fuel to reach and circle around it while Amelia scribbled a note, tied it around one of the Boston-bought oranges, and bombed the ship. It missed, as did a subsequent effort. The ship made no obvious attempt to signal the airplane. Amelia and her companions discussed whether they should land alongside then, while they could be certain of rescue and/or refueling, but they abandoned the idea because the sea was so rough they knew they would never get off again. At last, they decided to fly on.

Unknown to the fliers, the captain had just given an instruction to paint the ship's position on the deck in large white letters, but the *Friendship* flew off before this could be done. Amelia took a photograph of the liner and they retraced the twelve miles to their original course. The ceiling dropped to below five hundred feet and all they could see was gray mist as the *Friendship* droned on with its crew in a state of silent, mounting anxiety.

After half an hour—an interminable period of time, it must have been—they saw a fishing boat; and then several more—a fleet of them! And all going in the same direction as the *Friendship*.

Another hour passed before, out of the mists, a shadow, hardly darker at first than the mist but gradually becoming bluer, claimed their riveted attention. It was land. Slim, who had nervously started to nibble a sandwich, yelled with relief and tossed his snack out of the window. Even Bill permitted himself a smile.

They flew over several small islands and followed the coastline in an easterly direction, trying to match the coastline to their charts. They were over a huge bay that narrowed into an estuary offering sheltered landing conditions from the big seas running in the bay. The tide was out and large sandbanks were exposed, but there was a smooth patch of water beside a small town and, knowing that their fuel was almost exhausted, Stultz decided to land.

They had no idea where they were. They assumed it was Ireland, but in the relief and delight at having made a landfall, their chief concern was to taxi to a buoy and tie up.[6] They opened the door in the side of the airplane and peered out through thin veils of rain. Slim dropped down onto a pontoon and made the plane fast to a mooring buoy. They could see houses and factories behind the muddy beach. There were three men working on a railroad track and the crew waved and yelled to them.

> Finally they noticed us, straightened up and even went so far as to walk down to the shore and look us over. Then their animation died out and they went back to their work. The *Friendship* simply wasn't interesting. An itinerant trans-Atlantic plane meant nothing.[7]

After a while, a few people gathered on the beach but the aviators' shouts raised no answer. Amelia tried waving a towel, and one friendly soul took off his coat and waved back. It was almost an hour before the first boats came out. At low tide, it was a long row from the dock where the nearest available rowing boat was kept. At this stage, the crew of the *Friendship* were still anticipating refueling in order to fly on to their intended destination, Southampton.[8] A check of their fuel tanks while they waited revealed that there were nearly fifty gallons remaining, which, for practical purposes, meant the supply was exhausted due to the gravity feed-fuel supply; indeed, Stultz later told reporters that fuel had already ceased to flow to the carburetors on the landing run. Amelia recorded:

> I wish now I had cheered the first boat that came alongside. It was
> a most ordinary greeting that they gave us. One man in the boat
> [called out] "Ship Ahoy!" He asked what we needed. Stultz leaned
> out of the window and said we had flown across the Atlantic.[9]

The fliers learned to their surprise that they had landed in Burry Port, a
small town in South Wales, and not Ireland as they had assumed.

This accounted for the ships crossing their track—at that point they
had been flying over the Irish Sea, having flown south of the Irish coast.
Bill Stultz went ashore in a dory to contact Railey, send radio messages
to George Putnam, and organize refueling, so that they could carry on to
Southampton. Amelia, meanwhile, exchanged greetings with the occupants of the small fleet of boats that had begun to swarm around the
airplane. However, to all requests for information about the flight, she said
nothing.

After a few hours, Railey arrived by seaplane from Southampton, accompanied by *New York Times* journalist Allen Raymond, and they were
taken out to the *Friendship*. Stultz decided that it was too dangerous to
attempt a takeoff against the flooding riptide, so the *Friendship* was
moved to a sheltered mooring in the town's harbor while Amelia and Lou
Gordon were taken ashore.

The inhabitants of Burry Port now made up for the slow reaction to
the arrival of the aviators. All through the afternoon, word had passed
from mouth to mouth and, determined to make up for their lack of
welcome, a huge crowd gathered, its numbers swollen to two thousand or
more by visitors from nearby Llanelli.

Amelia had tied her silk scarf bandana-style over her head and as she
climbed the steps of the harbor, a hand reached out and pulled it off. She
looked around in surprise but could not see who had taken it. It was to
be the first of many such incidents. Enthusiasm was such that the police
escort had a hard time keeping their charges on their feet and the high
sheriff of Carmarthen joined with the town's three policemen and a few
friends to form a ring of locked arms to escort Amelia from the harbor
to the Ashburnham Hotel.

After welcome hot baths came the first interviews by squads of reporters
who gleefully informed Amelia that she was being called "Lady Lindy."
Amelia had her revenge, to some extent. Railey told them all that her story
had been sold in advance to *The New York Times* and that she was
prepared to answer only the most general questions. Consequently, many
stories were filed stating her likes and dislikes in clothes and makeup. "She
would rather read than eat, rather sit on the floor than on a chair, rather

fence than play bridge,[10] rather drive her car than any of these. . . . When asked if she ever thought of giving up the flight she replied: Never! I thought all this out in the first five minutes and I [knew I wanted] to go . . . I'm going because I love life and all it has to offer. I want every opportunity and adventure it can give, and I could never welch on one of them."[11]

Later, she spent some hours with Allen Raymond, recounting her story and showing him her log of the flight. Then while Amelia went off to her hotel, Raymond occupied himself at a typewriter at the office of a local factory for most of the night. "As he finished each sheet the local policeman was waiting to take it by car to be wired by the General Post Office at nearby Llanelli."[12]

The three fliers managed to get five or six hours sleep before awakening to a sackful of congratulatory telegrams, one from President Coolidge: TO YOU THE FIRST WOMAN SUCCESSFULLY TO SPAN THE NORTH ATLANTIC BY AIR THE GREAT ADMIRATION OF MYSELF AND THE UNITED STATES. . . .

At eleven o'clock, they took off in light rain and patches of mist for Southampton. Stultz had hoped for the escort of an Imperial Airways flying boat to Southampton, but engine trouble had prevented it from taking off, so he decided to fly to Southampton accompanied by the seaplane chartered by Railey and Allen Raymond. It was unfortunate that they could not have waited fifteen minutes longer. Unknown to them, Sir Arthur Whitten-Brown, famous for his part in the first successful nonstop crossing of the Atlantic with Sir John Alcock, was being rowed out to the *Friendship*. The plane took off almost as he reached it and a dramatic moment was lost.

Burry Port, its brief period of fame over, subsided once again into comfortable obscurity. Two years later, its citizens subscribed to a commemorative monument celebrating the day when *Friendship* put the name of their town on the front pages of cities around the world. The plaque, unveiled by Sir Arthur Whitten-Brown, reveals a small mystery, for it cites the duration of the flight as being "20 HRS. 49 MINS." Yet the official time was later given as twenty hours and forty minutes; it is recorded as such in the record books and Amelia subsequently named her book *20 Hrs. 40 Min.* Amelia's logbook, however, recorded that the *Friendship* took off from Trepassey at 10:51 A.M. Eastern Standard Time (2:51 P.M. Sunday, BST) and landed at 7:40 A.M. (12:40 P.M. Monday BST); therefore twenty hours forty-nine minutes would seem to be the correct figure. The plaque is still in place today in Burry Port's leafy Felindan Square, bearing the legend 20 HRS. 49 MINS.[13]

As the *Friendship* approached Southampton, an Imperial Airways Sea

Eagle flew out to meet the fliers and guide them in through the low clouds over Southampton Water. A green light from a Very pistol signaled the *Friendship*'s landing run and this time she had hardly finished taxiing when the launches were snapping at her heels. First to greet the aviators were Amy Guest and her son Raymond.

Meanwhile, the story of the successful crossing had been flashed around the world. George had syndicated the stories cabled in Amelia's own words through Raymond, and they made front pages throughout the United States, generating an enormous interest in the fact that a woman had flown the Atlantic. Amelia told how delighted she was to have made the crossing and explained that most of the journey had been flown blind.

> I was a passenger on the journey—just a passenger. Everything that was done to bring us across was done by Wilmer Stultz and Slim Gordon. Any praise I can give them . . . they ought to have. You can't pile it on too thick . . . I did not handle the controls once, although I have had more than 500 hours solo flying and once held the women's altitude record. I do not believe that women lack the stamina to do a solo trip across the Atlantic, but it would be a matter of learning the art of flying by instruments only, an art which few men pilots know perfectly now. . . .[14]

Edwin Earhart had been tracked down in Los Angeles and interviewed at great length. He unwittingly revealed his hurt at being left out of his daughter's plans: "When I first discovered she was [learning to fly] I told her I was strongly against it, but that was all I could do in the circumstances. That was about 1921. . . ." "Amelia," he continued, "had had every advantage that money could provide for a person . . . she had a remarkable mind but her remarkable scholastic ability was not due so much to an unusually brilliant mentality as to the fact that she had never had any financial worries or other such distractions. Why she is making the trip I am at a loss to explain. . . . I can't see that it will aid the science of flying. . . ." He went on to talk more generously about Amelia's love of adventure, however. "She has ridden horses all her life and once in Toronto she won a prize to any man or woman who could ride a certain outlaw horse at a fair. She rode it even though she was almost killed in the process. . . ."[15]

George Putnam had spent the previous twenty-odd hours in a state of anxiety. He tried unsuccessfully to work and, instead, paced the floor at his home in Rye, jumping each time the telephone rang. Often it was a reporter seeking the latest news. There were six ship's radio reports in the first five hours, followed by silence for more than four hours before the British steamer *Elmworth* heard "barely audible wireless signals" on six hundred meters. This was followed by another five hours of radio silence until just after midnight, when Mr. Battison of Cambridge, Massachusetts, heard a fragmentary message that they were about halfway across. A further seven hours were to drift by with no further word.

When at last George could stand the waiting no longer, he went to *The New York Times*'s offices to await any news of the *Friendship*'s arrival. The S.S. *America*'s sighting of the airplane some seventy-five miles southeast of Queenstown, Ireland, was the first news to come through on the tickertape. The relief at knowing that the fliers had made it safely across the ocean and were within striking distance of land must have been enormous, but George was suddenly too busy to record his own reactions. He started by drafting a cable to Railey, instructing him what to do upon Amelia's arrival, and went to work with a reporter to draft the headline story for the next edition of the *Times*. It was nearly two hours later that news of the safe landing was transmitted, and one of his first actions was to send word to Amelia's family.

It genuinely distressed Amelia to see Stultz and Gordon ignored by the reporters and she continually attempted to bring them forward into the limelight—to no avail. It was the woman they had come to see; or rather "the girl," as they insisted on calling her. She insisted that Raymond send back a story in Stultz's own words. This was published in *The New York Times*, underneath Amelia's story, but it changed nothing. It was Amelia to whom the press wanted to talk, about whom they wanted to write, and whom the crowds came to see. Even President Coolidge had cabled his personal congratulations addressed to Amelia, to which she replied, THE CREW OF THE FRIENDSHIP DESIRE TO EXPRESS THEIR DEEP APPRECIATION OF YOUR EXCELLENCY'S GRACIOUS MESSAGE STOP SUCCESS ENTIRELY DUE GREAT SKILL OF MR. STULTZ STOP HE WAS ONLY ONE MILE OFF VALENCIA AFTER FLYING BLIND FOR TWO THOUSAND FORTY SIX MILES AT AVERAGE SPEED ONE HUNDRED THIRTEEN MPH AMELIA EARHART.[16]

George was later to write that in his opinion Amelia had persistently returned the credit to Stultz because she was moved that he had accomplished "a perfect job in the face of personal, as well as aeronautical odds."[17] She had personal knowledge of the devastating effect of alcoholism.

After being greeted by Amy Guest and her son, the crew made a triumphal procession to Southampton's South Western Hotel—known to countless seagoing transatlantic passengers—where, dressed in the only clothes she had with her—a beige sweater, white shirt and red tie, with dark breeches and black boots—Amelia took tea and tried, a little shyly, to cope with the multitude of questions from the press.[18] Over the next few days, hundreds of thousands of column inches would be written about her, a lot of it pure invention: that she had undertaken the flight to redeem a mortgage on her family home; that she had been racing Mabel Boll; and so on. Hilton Railey was always at her side and she looked to him constantly for help when things got out of hand.

From Southampton, Amelia and her party traveled to London (stopping briefly at Winchester to enable Amelia to see the cathedral), where the fliers had been checked in at the Hyde Park Hotel. Amelia was immediately engulfed in a whirl of engagements organized by the Guests. Stultz and Gordon were "completely ignored. . . . Both were well content to be left alone." "All we want to do is sleep," said Stultz.[19] After a few days, it was decided to move Amelia out of the hotel. It was too public and she was too easily subjected to the crowds and publicity. She looked tired and pale, despite the constant smile, and Amy Guest insisted that Amelia move into the Guests' Park Lane home to recover from the strain of the trip. For the remainder of their stay, Stultz and Gordon became the forgotten men and drifted about London, sightseeing, virtually without being recognized, and visiting airports such as Croydon, headquarters of the London–Paris Air Service, to look at the latest in European airliners. Undoubtedly, Amy Guest considered that the two men had been hired as "crew" and had been well recompensed for their work. They had done their job, and done it well; and that was that.

For Amelia, however, it was lunches and dinner parties; tea dances; visits to Ascot on Gold Cup day and to Lady Astor's home, Cliveden; to the Olympic Horse Show with Lord Lonsdale; an evening visit to Aldershot to watch an Air Tattoo. Cables and letters (Railey hired a team of four secretaries to answer them all) flooded in and there was always the constant barrage of reporters and other callers. Amelia managed a few shopping trips and bought some clothes, for initially she had to borrow from her hostess and had to appear in dresses that the newspapers were quick to note were "several sizes too large." For Amelia, the crowded days passed quickly. A letter from George came by the first ship and received the simple reply, THANKS CHEERING LETTER WILL TRY BE GOOD SIMPKIN SWELL GUY. EARHART.[20]

Not all press reports were kind to Amelia. Some pointed out that she was merely luggage and had contributed nothing toward the success of the flight. An especially sniffish one came, somewhat predictably, from the irascible founder and editor of *Flight,* the prestigious British aviation magazine.

Well, the first lady passenger has crossed the Atlantic by air, although what special merit there is in that is not altogether easy to see. In these days of sex-equality, such a feat should not arouse any particular comment. Compared with the solo flights of lady *pilots* as Lady Bailey and Lady Heath, the crossing of the Atlantic as *a passenger* does not seem to us to prove anything in particular. If it were intended to demonstrate that a machine can now cross the Atlantic carrying a full crew and even a passenger, then that was proved by Commander Byrd's flight last year and very much more convincingly. . . .

The machine itself was in some ways . . . a curiosity: a high winged monoplane, with three engines and twin floats. But it got across, even though the margin was uncomfortably narrow. On alighting at Barrow [*sic*], the pilot is reported to have said he had not enough petrol to take off again.[21]

Such reports hurt Amelia, but she was only too aware of the truth in them. The fact was that in those early days of flight *any* transatlantic venture was a heroic feat. No one could simply take off and be sure that they would make it. It was an adventurous—if somewhat foolhardy—thing to have done, but the fact remained, luggage or not, she was the first woman to have crossed the ocean by air. Air-minded women were more generous, and Lady Heath, in particular, was kind and supportive.

318 ST JAMES COURT

Dear Miss Earhart,

I did not go on to dance after I found you weren't going to stay but I've come home to tell you my address and phone number and to tell you that if you phone me I'll throw down whatever I'm doing to come and fly with you or talk—unless I'm on business connected with your luncheon. . . . Ring me!

Yours,
S. Mary Heath[22]

Lady Heath was to become a friend, and a week later she arranged a secret rendezvous at Croydon to enable Amelia to fly the Avro Avian in which Lady Heath had flown solo from South Africa to England, in what was arguably the most impressive flight made by any woman to date. Amelia told no one about this plan, slipping out of the Guests' home just after dawn into a car sent by her conspirator. Mrs. Guest was awakened and told and, after collecting Hilton Railey, pursued Amelia, arriving at Croydon in time to see Amelia landing a Gipsy Moth in which she had flown with Captain A. H. White to Northolt. Later, she flew a few circuits in Mary Heath's famous Avian.

Amelia had not been able to fly solo, not having been checked out in either the Moth or the Avian, but once in the air she took the controls and flew both airplanes part of the time. Well aware that her flight in the Avian would be reported, now that the reporters had arrived, and still smarting from the innuendo that she was a passenger rather than a pilot, she indulged in a mild display of aerobatics and landed grinning enthusiastically, declaring that she was so impressed with the Avian that she would like to buy one and take it home.[23]

Perhaps carried away by the moment, Mary Heath offered to sell that very plane to Amelia, who bought it without hesitation. Subsequently, she arranged for it to be crated up and shipped back to the United States with the *Friendship*.[24] Quite where Amelia got the money for this transaction is not known. Probably George had told her before departure what she was likely to receive by way of payment for syndication rights to her story should the trip be successful. Amelia must have anticipated that this income would cover the cost of purchase and transport.

French aviation leaders had wanted Amelia and her two male companions to fly to Paris for a reception and air carnival, but after some discussion and cables with G.P., it was decided that they would sail home within a week. Putnam had been able to arrange a civic parade in New York and wanted them back home to capitalize on the immense public interest. Amelia drove to Sheffield to visit a former Denison House colleague who was living there, motored back, and spent a day in London's East End, visiting Toynbee Hall, the settlement house that was the model for Denison House.

At the luncheon given by the Women's Committee of the British Empire, Amelia sat between Lady Astor, who appears to have been totally captivated by the young aviatrix, and Winston Churchill. Amelia delivered a short serious speech on the future of aviation in the United States. Wherever she went, she put over her theories on aviation in general, and women in aviation in particular, convincingly.

> Just now with aviation in its most fluid state, there is every chance for women; perhaps almost as many chances as there are for men. The woman who can create her own job is the woman who will win fame and fortune . . . there are many possible openings in aviation for women; some of these are as saleswomen, as founders of flying schools for women, as developers of flying fields, as pilots, as organiz-

ers of "air taxi" companies, as designers, perfecting or inventing in the field of many needs of a profession still in its infancy. . . . The field is clear for the pioneer and if the pioneer has good ideas nobody will ask whether the pioneer is man or woman. . . .

. . . Here is where Atlantic flights by women, or any other good flight helps—it starts other women to think. In our country a man may learn to fly at government expense, if he passes the requirements of the United States Army schools. I do not know of any such instruction for women. So, until some pioneer woman has arranged better chances for young women fliers [they] must learn to fly in some private flying school.[25]

On the eve of her return, Amelia dined at Lord Lonsdale's home and the next day she attended Wimbledon and watched Helen Wills win a tennis match, then she drove to Southampton. Stultz and Gordon had gone on quietly ahead of Amelia and were already on board the liner S.S. *President Roosevelt* when she arrived at Ocean Terminal. When Amelia boarded, she met the captain, Harry Manning, and little did either know what an important role he was to play in her life some years later. Manning, understanding Amelia's need for privacy after the hectic days in London, allowed her free access to the bridge deck. Of that return voyage, Amelia wrote:

. . . it was then we came to realize how much water we had passed over in the *Friendship*. Eastbound the mileage had been measured in clouds, not water. There never had been adequate comprehension of the Atlantic below us.[26]

A cable from George Putnam advised that thirty-two cities had invited the fliers to civic welcomes. How did Amelia feel about accepting? he asked.[27] Amelia felt it was too much but agreed to accept invitations from New York, Boston, and Chicago.

New York welcomed the fliers as only New York can. They were taken off the *President Roosevelt* in Mayor Jimmy Walker's private barge, then rode in a convertible roadster, smiling and waving through a storm of tickertape and torn paper, to a civic reception at city hall, where Amelia received the key to the city from Mayor Walker. Attentively in the background throughout was George Putnam—watching, working, smiling, missing nothing, and instantly materializing at Amelia's side at a single glance from her. When the city's key was presented, for example, she looked over her shoulder at George, who came forward and took it from her.[28]

On the following day, Amelia returned home to Boston, where she received a similar reception from cheering crowds. Never again for the remainder of her life would Amelia enjoy the ability to go about freely, unrecognized. She had become a public figure and she frankly enjoyed the attention, the fame, and the publicity. For her, the obvious inconveniences were outweighed by the success, which meant freedom from worry about finance, for, despite her father's remarks to the Los Angeles *Times,* [29] it is obvious that Amelia had never been free of such concern from the moment Edwin had lost his job.

Waiting quietly in West Medford was Sam Chapman, Amelia's fiancé. After yet another welcoming reception there, attended by Amelia's mother and sister, Sam took Amelia off to Marblehead for the day. Very little has been written of Sam, of what his reactions to Amelia's adventure might have been, or what he thought of the amount of time she was spending with George Putnam. The truth is that the only two people who knew—Amelia and Sam—never spoke of it. One can only guess at the uncertainty and anxiety—in addition to pride—he must have felt in her accomplishment.

Next day Amelia went to Chicago, and then returned to New York. According to Muriel, Amelia never saw either Stultz or Gordon after this period; both men resumed their careers and their paths did not cross. George saw no reason to involve them in the ongoing publicity campaign he had planned for Amelia. In fact, Stultz had "disappeared just before starting the drive to city hall" in Chicago, and George, worried that Amelia's reputation would suffer if the parade was canceled, donned Stultz's flying helmet and impersonated him in the parade, afterward sending his apologies to the mayor that a stomach upset prevented him (Stultz) from attending the luncheon. No one ever guessed. [30]

Initially, Amelia assumed that she would write the book George had been pressing her to write, collect what rewards she might be able to reap from public appearances and lecture tours, and then go back to work at Denison House. However, there must have been, at the back of her mind, the hope that her new fame would enable her to play a more constructive part in the future of aviation.

George and Dorothy Putnam gave a grand private party at the Westchester Biltmore in Rye; among the guests were leading women pilots Thea Rasche and Ruth Nichols. Amelia was determined to further the cause of women in the field of aviation and even before she left on the Atlantic venture, she had been at work with Ruth Nichols in an attempt to organize an association for women pilots. The problem was, she thought, that at that time there were only about twenty-five licensed women pilots in the United States.

Indeed, Amelia's own "license" was actually an FAI certificate issued in 1923—Amelia claimed incorrectly that it was the first issued to any American woman—but under legislations in force in July 1928, this did not entitle her to a federal license without examination.[31] Further, her attempts to arrange U.S. registration for the Avian (G-EBUG under its British identification) were complicated by legislative difficulties. "She has two courses of procedure," a representative of the Department of Commerce wrote to Porter Adams, who was agitating on Amelia's behalf at George's behest.

> One is to merely identify [the airplane] and fly it noncommercial as an unlicensed ship. The other is to submit complete engineering data in accordance with the Air Commerce Regulations and in that manner get it approved for license. The latter is somewhat complicated and inconvenient so perhaps she would prefer the former and operate it as an unlicensed aircraft.
>
> Her decision in the foregoing would determine the necessity of a license for herself. In the event she merely identifies the ship then she herself would be obliged to operate as an unlicensed pilot. If she adopts the alternative, then we would indeed be pleased to facilitate the issuance of a license for her without publicity. This is somewhat hard to control, however, because the newspaper people, as you know, keep rather close track of such things. You may assure her of our good intentions. . . .[32]

Amelia decided to take the more difficult alternative, applying for a full license for the Avian and for herself. She took the federal examination in total secrecy, flying from the Bowman Clarke polo ground at Rye, and the press were not informed.[33] The wily dyed-in-the-wool journalist George Putnam knew a thing or two about when to call in the media and when not to.

For example, when the manufacturers of Lucky Strike cigarettes offered fifteen hundred dollars each to Stultz, Gordon, and Amelia to endorse their product, Amelia, who did not smoke, turned down the offer. It was George who persuaded her not to, on the grounds that this would disqualify the two men, who needed the money and who did smoke. If she felt so strongly, he argued, why could she not present the money to a good cause—Dick Byrd's Antarctic venture? Amelia agreed, signing an endorsement that read factually, "Lucky Strike were the cigarettes carried on the *Friendship* when I crossed the Atlantic."

It did make good reading when the exchanged letters were published in full in *The New York Times*.

> *Dear Commander Byrd,*
>
> I have wondered if you know how much your help meant in connection with the *Friendship*'s flight to England. You not only aided with your sympathetic interest, but your technical pioneering and vision largely made success possible. Perhaps you noticed my "endorsement" of the cigarettes which were carried by the men in the plane. I made this deliberately. It made possible my offering a modest contribution to your Antarctic expedition which otherwise I could not have done. I enclose the $1,500 received to help you reach the South Pole. . . .[34]

The reply was an equally carefully worded epistle, thanking Amelia for "an act of astonishing generosity." Indeed, fifteen hundred dollars *was* a great deal of money in 1928; after all, it was only weeks earlier that Amelia had been a thirty-five-dollar-a-week social worker. The letters were calculated—and almost certainly drafted by George—to secure public respect and impressive publicity for both clients.[35]

Unfortunately, although it achieved the primary objective, the plan backfired, for George had been in the final processes of arranging a contract for Amelia with *McCall's* magazine, where she had been offered the position as aviation editor. This association of the nation's heroine with smoking—still considered "fast" in a woman—caused *McCall's* to withdraw the offer. Months later, following representations by George, *McCall's* renewed their offer, but by then Amelia had been offered the job of associate editor with *Cosmopolitan* magazine.

Chapter Thirteen

1928-1929

In the aftermath of Amelia's return, George maximized every opportunity and exploited every possibility of obtaining publicity for her, and, although she never earned the enormous amounts of money credited to her by the newspapers, Amelia was in great demand on the lecture circuit and there were several career offers under consideration. Her immediate future was financially comfortable due to lecture fees and syndicated articles she wrote about the flight. This and her full schedule led inevitably to the conclusion that a return to work at Denison House was unlikely. Her career and her enthusiasms now lay elsewhere.

Amelia was pictured frequently in the newspaper, often among an elite circle of famous men and women pilots: Wilkins, Byrd, Chamberlin, Lindbergh, Rasche, Balchen, Nichols, and Landis. Through George's vast connections, she met hostesses of international repute, politicians, and celebrities. She opened buildings, gave public speeches, and was interviewed and feted everywhere she went, possibly never realizing quite how much of the public's sustained interest was due to George's behind-the-scenes stratagems. Although initial attention was paid to those transatlantic flyers who crossed the ocean by air subsequent to Lindbergh—Chamberlin and Byrd, for example—public and media interest soon waned unless there was some new achievement in the offing. It took publicity management on a brilliant scale to keep a flier's name in the forefront of everyone's mind and on the pages of national newspapers.

It is a popular misconception that George used Amelia and drove her too hard, with the implication that he did this for his own ends, and of course he was earning a management fee from Amelia's earnings (probably the same percentage as he earned from all his clients). But, in fact, George was simply ensuring that the maximum amount of benefit was gained from a unique opportunity. He realized that once Amelia's name dropped out of the newspapers, she would be just another woman aviator. No one would pay to hear her speak once the next record breaker seized the daily headlines. Amelia would undoubtedly have recognized the sense in this, too.

Amelia also saw the career George sketched out for her, and she wanted it. She was just as much committed to the property "Amelia Earhart" as George and, if anything, was probably self-driven. Constant publicity would ensure that backers could be found to finance future projects; it was a necessary part of the job and though George's carefully built image of Amelia portrayed her as shy, self-effacing, and hating publicity, she was— at least in those early days—as keen as he to achieve media attention.

George insisted that Amelia stay at his Rye estate while she worked on her book about the Atlantic flight. There she could be assured of privacy and peace, and he could help her with advice. More practically, there were secretaries to transcribe her logbook and working notes. Amelia had taken a course in shorthand and typing in California and was a reasonably proficient typist, but the sackful of mail that arrived daily needed answering. There were proposals of marriage, invitations of all sorts, pleas for money, offers of jobs, poetry written in her honor, cranks by the score—it amounted to hundreds of letters a day.

As usual, George was in a hurry. There was no question of Amelia being allowed to take months to write her book. He needed it in weeks, agreeing with Amelia how many words she would have to produce each day. Despite the tight schedule, she managed to fit in some riding, swimming, dancing, friends, and parties "in tantalizing driblets," as well as several trips to New York.[1] There was a dinner there with Mr. and Mrs. Richard Byrd and Mayor Jimmy Walker,[2] and, on another night, a trip to the theater, accompanied by George. On the strength of her new income, Amelia wrote to her mother, "If you know something [Muriel] wants, get it for her and I'll pay. Also you. My treat, at last." In the same letter, she exhorted Amy not to worry about her safety: "I am well protected here . . . if the Hearst reporter annoys you, wire me and I'll have it stopped." There was already a new tone of confidence about her letters to her family.

RYE, AUGUST 26, 1928

Dear Mammy,

I got back to Rye with hardly a recognition . . . perhaps you'd better not talk [about] my intimate details of salary and business with Pidge.

I don't want her to spread the news and always fear she will. I think I have an apartment, but will let you know later. . . .

Please throw away rags and get things you need on my account at Filenes [a large department store in Boston]. I'll instruct them. I can do it now and the pleasure is mine.

When and if the reporters come to you, please refer them to Mr. Putnam. Don't even say yes or no if you don't want to. Just say you can add nothing to their tales and ask me or GPP. . . .

> Your doter,
> A.E. [3]

From this point onward, Amelia invariably referred to herself as A.E (something that her contemporaries regarded as a piece of Putnam affectation).[4] She had fallen into the habit of calling George "G.P." almost from the first, as everyone else did. A few days after she wrote this letter, just as she was putting the finishing touches to her book, she received word that the Avian, which had been uncrated and assembled at Curtiss Field, had been flown to Rye. "Finally the little book is done," she wrote. "Tomorrow I am free to fly."[5] Amelia dedicated her book "To Dorothy Binney Putnam, under whose rooftree this book was written."

This done, Amelia bought an assortment of air-navigation maps and after a test hop from the nearby polo field, she took off on what was to be a transcontinental "vacation" flight to California, where the National Air Races were being held. It was the reverse of the trip she had planned some four years earlier.

George, never far from Amelia's side, was to accompany her on part of the trip. Although adventurous by nature, he was not fond of flying; it was not his element and he was not happy in a situation where he was not in control. He also suffered from airsickness.[6] They landed and had lunch at Bellefonte Field, and then headed for Pittsburgh, where Amelia ground looped on landing, claiming to have hit a hidden ditch while taxiing. She stated mendaciously that it was "her first crash." The undercarriage and left wing were smashed and the propeller damaged. George took over and faced reporters.

> Miss Earhart had made a perfect landing and was taxiing to a stop when the plane struck an unmarked ditch and went into it. The plane made what is called a ground loop and nearly turned over. Miss Earhart feels it is unfortunate that the accident should have happened, particularly as it occurred through no fault of hers.

Miss Earhart had been visiting at my home and while there we
decided to take a little jaunt. As she was just "playing around" with
no particular object in view, she headed her ship for Pittsburgh
. . . there was no incident of any kind until we ran into that ditch
at Pittsburgh.[7]

George telephoned New York for replacement parts, but as the airplane
was not a common type, it would be a week or more before some items
could be located. "The men in the hangar worked all night putting the
new wings on my old ship . . ."[8] Amelia wrote in her diary, but their work
was in vain. In view of the delay, she and George returned to New York
where the proofs of Amelia's book *20 Hrs. 40 Min.* were ready. It was
rushed into the bookshops with George's customary aggressiveness.

After repair, the Avian was flown to Dayton, Ohio, where Amelia was
to pick it up. She traveled there by train, accompanied by George. "Dayton is a pleasant little city. We were driven to the Miami Hotel by two
reserve officers in a rattletrap Ford. GPP and I had a leisurely dinner
served by colored waiters and weren't recognized. He left on the eleven
o'clock train for N.Y. and I was called at 6:30 next morning . . ."[9]

Within a few days, Amelia's intention to fly to California became
known, and publicity followed her progress across the continent, but the
hours of solo flight were balm to her spirit after the tumult of the Atlantic
venture and its attendant publicity, the constant pressures of her position
as a "personality," and, not least, by her attraction to G.P. and his
constant attentions to her. All she had to think about as she flew across
the continent was each leg of the journey, becoming the first woman to
make the air flight solo from the Atlantic to Pacific coasts.

That this had not been done before was small wonder. There were few
organized airfields. Those few dirt or grass strips that existed were invariably unmarked and difficult to identify. One town looked much like
another from the air. "Oh, for a country-wide campaign of sign painting!"
Amelia wrote.

Coming down through a hole in the clouds, any flyer is thankful for
a definite check as to his location, even if it is only to check on his
navigation . . . imagine automobiling without signs! Imagine trying
to recognize a new town the way flyers do—a hundred-mile-an-hour
look at a checkerboard of streets and roofs, trees and fields, with
highways and railroads radiating and criss-crossing and perhaps a river
or two to complicate—or simplify—the geography lesson.[10]

On one occasion, Amelia's map, which she had pinned to her shirt, tore free and blew away; lost and short of fuel, she landed in the wide main street of a small town. She was greatly amused at her appearance in the mirror, for the wind and sun had tanned and burned her face to a ruddy glow except where her goggles covered the area around her eyes, which remained white. In her logbook Amelia noted that she would resemble a horned toad by the time she reached her destination.

By mid-September 1928, Amelia was in California, where she renewed old acquaintances, visited her father, and attended the National Air Races. George kept in constant touch by letter and cable. On one occasion, after having seen an unflattering picture of Amelia in a newspaper report, he fired off with his usual verve:

> Your hats! They are a public menace. You should do something about them when you must wear them at all! Some of them are cataclysms! But I hasten to add the Pittsburgh bonnet is a peach, as are several of the floppy ones with brims. . . .[11]

After this, Amelia was hardly ever seen in a hat in public; she never again wore the tight-fitting cloches that George loathed and indeed whenever asked about hats declared that she hated wearing one. The hatless tousled curls became a part of her image.

Amelia set out on the return journey at the end of September, but engine trouble forced an emergency landing in Utah, where the only available space was scrubland, bumpy and littered with tumbleweed and mesquite. The Avian was damaged and had to be shipped to Salt Lake City for repairs,[12] and it was October 16 before Amelia reached New York, becoming the first woman to make a solo-return transcontinental flight. George was quick to send out a press release stating that the problem had been a mechanical one. Amelia had many forced landings and crashes over the years (as all pilots did in those days), but according to her press statements, none was ever due to pilot error in her case. Meanwhile, her appointment to *Cosmopolitan* had been made public,[13] the contract calling for eight articles a year on the subject of aviation, but this load was considerably weighted by the vast amount of correspondence from readers.

A series of lecture tours organized by George to publicize her book took her to as many as thirty different venues in a month and this punishing routine was to be repeated many times over the years. Whenever possible, Amelia flew to her engagements in order to publicize the practicality of aviation. Amelia enjoyed speaking in public; her naturally friendly, unaffected, and humorous personality was projected into the lectures that she quickly came to know by heart, creating an almost instantaneous bond between her audience and herself. In addition, she was so enthusiastic about her subject that her audience was seldom bored.

Throughout November Amelia traveled as part of the Putnam "team," consisting of Amelia; George, who lectured on his Arctic explorations; and Dick Douglas, a boy scout who had accompanied Martin and Osa Johnson on safari in East Africa and had produced a book for Putnam's based on his adventures.

George was an old hand at the lecture circuit and prior to the tour he had written a memo to advise Amelia that

> . . . you are apt to take less time than you think you will take. Have plenty of spare ammunition on cards to fill the gaps. To this end I suggest your mapping out your talk on the small cards I am having handed to you with your films.
>
> Remember you will be working with a pointer (get a pointer!) with the slides. You will have a tendency to turn your back on the audience. This is a difficult trick. You really have to remember to always talk into your microphone and explain.
>
> Remember too your tendency is to let your voice drop at the end of sentences. And perhaps most vital of all is the necessity of ending matters crisply and definitely. Many a good speech, like a railroad, is ruined by lack of good terminal facilities.[14]

In mid-November, Amelia met Sam in West Medford, Massachusetts. She had probably already reached a decision about him on her "gypsy tour" of the continent. Her life had grown dramatically beyond that of this quiet, intellectual young man, for in a way he represented her past, while George was the exciting present. On November 23, 1928, she announced publicly that she had broken her engagement. "I am no longer engaged to marry," she told reporters. And then, with a twinkle, said, "But you never can tell. If I was sure of the man I might get married tomorrow. . . ."[15] Sam remained a close friend for the rest of her life.

Another incident that intruded into Amelia's busy schedule concerned a teenage girl. Elinor Smith, who at the age of sixteen was the youngest licensed woman pilot (her FAI certificate was signed by Orville Wright!), had set an altitude record and made headlines when she flew, illegally, under four bridges on New York's East River. Now Elinor was practicing for an attempt on the endurance record and was achieving a significant amount of publicity.

George's intention was to project Amelia to the public as the foremost woman pilot. Women such as Ruth Nichols and Louise Thaden were modest by nature, not headline seekers, and while they may have been better pilots, they created no competition for Amelia; indeed, they were to become great friends. But this young attractive girl who had already acquired a full Department of Commerce license (which A.E. did not possess), and a hunger for adventurous flying in the fullest sense, was a positive threat to George's plans.

Elinor Smith was thrilled when she received a telephone call from George asking her to meet him in Chicago, where she was scheduled to appear at an air show. George and Amelia were in Chicago as part of their tour, the venue probably organized so that Amelia could attend the air show. Amelia flew in, with Louise Thaden as her passenger. Two weeks earlier, Louise had given birth to her first child and her doctor was appalled when his patient told him she was going to the air races. He forbade her to take an eleven-hour, jolting train journey, but he consented to a three-hour plane journey.

To Elinor Smith, George's call seemed the answer to her prayers. Her ambition was to make a successful career in aviation and here, it seemed, was the key. She knew that Putnam had put Amelia's name "into orbit and it was common knowledge that Amelia was earning $500 a week for her public appearances and talks. . . . I looked forward to this meeting on two counts." In Elinor's memoir, *Aviatrix* (written in 1981), she recalled the meeting:

> I was about to meet my personal heroine, and maybe, just maybe, Mr. Putnam would have some ideas on how to solve my problem. . . . With my daily appearance at the show and Amelia's own activities our meeting was delayed, but we finally managed to have breakfast one morning in her suite. . . .
>
> My last minute nervousness was dispelled by her friendly warmth. There was nothing cold-fishy about her handshake either. Taller than I, she was slender as a reed. A tracing of tiny freckles across her nose enhanced a perfectly natural complexion. I hadn't realized until that moment that there was a noticeable spacing between her front teeth.
>
> I was able to distinguish . . . the Putnam publicity touch from the very real and warm individual I was facing. The image of a shy and retiring individual thrust against her will into the public eye was a figment of Putnam's lively imagination. Amelia was about as shy as

Muhammad Ali. I do not mean to imply that she wasn't modest
. . . but she was already a woman of thirty who knew what she wanted
and where she wanted to go. She left no doubt in my mind that it
was the same direction as I. . . .[16]

As a matter of fact, Amelia was extremely self-conscious about the gap in
her teeth and after a whole series of unflattering pictures taken in the
aftermath of the transatlantic flight, she was learning to smile with her
lips closed. Her slight, boyish figure made her a good camera subject,
though there were inevitably some photos that caught her with an unflattering expression; her natural humor enabled her to laugh at these and she
even included a crop in early editions of *20 Hrs. 40 Min.* Amelia's other
unhappiness was her ankles. Long and slender her legs may have been, but
they were somewhat shapeless from knee to ankle and her feet were apt
to swell. When she later adopted trousers as her normal mode of dress,
she told friends it was to hide her "thick" legs. Elinor continued:

> George Palmer Putnam was a handsome man. He was over six feet
> tall with snapping dark eyes and close cropped hair, and you could
> feel his electricity across a room. Wiry and dynamic, he exuded the
> authority of a bank president or millionaire, which he was. If that
> weren't overwhelming enough, his manners were impeccable. Before
> I knew it I was agreeing with his implied opinion that our meeting
> was one of the high points of his long and successful career and wasn't
> it a shame that our paths hadn't crossed until now.[17]

Overawed by Putnam, but wooed by Amelia's obvious sympathy, Elinor
listened while George outlined his suggestion that "some sort of company" should be set up to manage the affairs of top pilots and provide
backing for record flights and arrange appearances. Unaccountably, he
seemed angered by her query "Do you mean something like a literary or
theatrical agent?" Brushing it aside brusquely with the comment that
what he had in mind was a strictly professional organization, he stressed
that he could not, at the time, make any offer, but he asked her to outline her future plans. She did, and later was to regret it deeply. What she
said that disturbed George more than anything was in answer to his
query "What is your ambition?" Her aggressively naïve reply—"To take
Amelia's place as number-one woman pilot!"—raised his hackles.[18]
    Both Amelia and George reacted again when Elinor mentioned that so
far no woman had been allowed to fly the large and powerful airplanes
being manufactured by Fokker or Bellanca—at least no more than hold

the controls. "Certainly no female has ever taken one off or landed it," she informed them. George must have instantly recognized the latent publicity opportunity inherent in this statement.

Elinor returned home, but the call George had promised to make as she bade the couple goodbye never came; and for a long time she was to find constant pinpricks and minor barriers placed in her way by officials and the media, many of which, she was to claim in her memoir, she was subsequently able to trace directly to interference by George. This was particularly apparent in the case of publicity. She found it more difficult to get reporters to cover her aviation feats, which—prior to her meeting with George—would have automatically attracted attention. Sometimes, when reporters had attended some exploit, the story was printed as a tiny piece at the bottom of a column, or more often, it never appeared. This was disastrous for Elinor. She had no private income and without publicity she could not attract the necessary sponsorship to further her career.

George, meanwhile, had decided that he wanted "a first" of his own. He conceived a first nonstop flight from New York to Bermuda with Bill Lancaster as pilot and Harry Lyon (previously navigator on the successful Pacific crossing by the *Southern Cross*) as navigator. They took off from Port Washington, Long Island, in a characteristic blaze of publicity, but, George wrote later, "our undertaking lost no time in becoming a comedy of errors."

Midway along the New Jersey coast, the engine failed and they made a dead-stick landing in a "gummy mass of mud." An incoming wave picked up the airplane and "bounced [it] into the air for a hundred feet or so and nearly broke the plane in pieces." After a rescue they took off again for Atlantic City, where they found that there was water in the fuel tank. Between Atlantic City and Norfolk, Virginia, they got hopelessly lost and George, perhaps not surprisingly, wondered whether there was something besides water affecting their navigation. They landed at Norfolk, where the station commander, having received a report on the plane's equipment from his engineers, suggested that if it was suicide George was bent on, there were easier ways. George took the hint and sheepishly entrained for New York, where Amelia met him at Pennsylvania Station. George later related, "She never once said I told you so. She had, and I should have listened."[19]

Meanwhile, despite her continuing punishing schedule, Amelia was delighted to accept official invitations to government installations in Washington, D.C., to see experiments in wind tunnels, and to discuss the role of civil aviation. She reveled in this, for it implied that she was playing a constructive role in aviation's future. It also fit well with George's plans for her, so there were constant introductions to politicians and government figures. What he wanted was the name Amelia Earhart synonymous (in the mind of the general public) with the term *best woman pilot*. At the same time, he had booked Amelia into such a tight, nonaviation, public-appearance schedule that even when she was offered the chance to accompany Bobbi Trout in an attempt on the world's endurance record, she had to turn it down.[20] Bobbi later made the attempt with Elinor Smith and the two set a record (for women) of forty-two hours three and a half minutes using in-flight refueling to stay aloft. Perhaps, though, George simply did not want Amelia to share her glory with anyone.

When Mary Heath paid a short visit to New York with the purpose of organizing her speaking tour in the spring of 1929, Amelia gathered together as many women pilots as she could to honor her friend. George threw a dinner party for them both and talked to Mary Heath about her plans. Like Elinor Smith, Lady Heath would soon regret sharing her confidences.

George took his family to Havana and Panama in late December 1928,[21] and Amelia spent Christmas in New York in her apartment at the American Women's Association Club at 353 West Fifty-seventh Street. Amy came to stay with her and during the holiday Amelia and her mother flew over New York City and the Statue of Liberty as paying passengers on a fifteen-dollar pleasure flight.[22]

As winter gave way to spring, the constant workload began to take a toll. Amelia carelessly turned her plane on its nose at Curtiss Field and when, only days later, she was on her way to Los Angeles by train, she wrote to her mother saying how tired she was. Even on the train she could not relax, for it was in snatched hours such as this that she wrote her magazine articles.

Often it was necessary for Amelia to fly to an engagement with an entourage of secretary and pressmen. George, too, was a constant companion on these trips. When this happened, a larger airplane than the two-seater Avian was needed. The British pilot Captain Bill Lancaster, who had flown to Australia a year earlier with a woman passenger (achieving the first two-person flight between England and Australia), was hired as Amelia's mechanic, but in fact he was the pilot rather than mechanic on these flights. Amelia did not take easily to flying large aircraft and found them difficult to handle, but Lancaster later told Mary Heath that he had been sworn to secrecy over his actual role because "Putnam wanted Amelia always to be given the credit and publicity for flying the airplanes."[23]

There was a certain amount of talk about Amelia and George in aviation circles at this time. It is hardly surprising, for the two spent a great deal of time together and even when they were accompanied by others on trips, they were more often than not apart from their traveling companions—very much a couple. Whether this gossip ever reached the ears of George and Amelia is not known, but there is reason to believe that Dorothy Putnam was increasingly aware of the situation and was less than happy about it.

In March 1929, Lancaster and Amelia flew into New Castle airport (in Delaware), where young Elinor Smith, still suffering (though fighting) the effects of George Putnam's powerful opposition, was working as a demonstration pilot for Bellanca. That Elinor was on the roster of select pilots that included Clarence Chamberlin, Martin Jensen, and Bert Acosta speaks volumes for the young woman's ability as a tough precision flier. It was only two years earlier that Bellanca had refused to allow Lindbergh to fly one of his airplanes across the Atlantic (a Bellanca had been Lindbergh's first choice of airplane before he went to a Ryan). Although Elinor did not know it at the time, Amelia had in her pocket a bank draft for twenty-five thousand dollars, with which she hoped to purchase the Bellanca.[24]

Amelia's test flight in the machine appalled Elinor, for, as she recalled in her memoir, as Amelia took over the controls "our big calm bird suddenly lurched out of control and wobbled all over the sky." After they landed, Amelia quietly asked Elinor whether they could go up again, alone. The Bellanca flew with the nose well below the horizon, rather than on it, the usual position for small aircraft, and Elinor thought this might have confused Amelia. After guiding Amelia through some gentle banks and turns, Elinor handed over the controls: "Again we slipped and skidded all over the sky. I was baffled, for the ship's flying position had been established, the rest of it should have been like flying a small biplane."[25] Although she said nothing to Amelia, Elinor privately concluded that Amelia's flying ability was considerably less than she had been led to believe. She had been told as much by Lady Heath but hadn't believed it.[26]

Bellanca, who chose his customers carefully in order to protect the reputation of his product, refused to sell to Amelia, despite a great deal of hassle from George. Elinor thought it just as well. Amelia, she felt, simply hadn't the ability to fly the big ship and for her to enter it in competitive events (which was what George apparently had in mind) would have been highly dangerous.[27]

A few weeks later, Amelia hit the newspapers again with a forced landing when the Avian's engine stopped near Utica, New York, where

Amelia had been visiting her sister. When Muriel married Albert Morrissey in late June 1929, Amelia was almost late for the wedding, for she was delayed first by fog and then by a damaged propeller. She traveled to the wedding by train and had to suffer the attentions of reporters still trying to make a romantic link between her and Sam Chapman, who was an usher at the ceremony. Sam "begged" the reporters "to leave me alone," while Amelia, when asked whether she had any plans for a wedding of her own, stated, "I would make a poor wife, running around the country as I am."

On March 29, 1929, Amelia had been granted her aviation transport license.[28] One requirement for this was that the pilot, who had to be the holder of a Department of Commerce license, must have logged a minimum 250 hours of flying time. According to Amelia's second logbook, she had "brought forward a total" of 559 hours and 46 minutes flying time. This was the first entry, dated July 20, 1929, in the new logbook; but it is frankly difficult to see how, with the financial restrictions she had suffered during her time in Los Angeles and the small amount of flying she had done between 1924 and 1928, she managed to build up this very considerable number of hours.[29] It is also known that Amelia was given private instruction, flying from the Bowman Clarke polo field near Rye, before taking the flying test; and this in itself is strange, for any pilot with five hundred hours should need little in the way of instruction to take a basic flying examination.[30]

During that summer of 1929, the airline industry was striving to improve its image. Commercial flying remained very much a novelty, not helped by the media, who fastened on every crash with almost ghoulish detail. Aviation was growing up, however. In his book *Wings over America,* Harry Bruno stated, "In the ten years which followed the first flight of the Wright brothers at Kitty Hawk [1903], airplanes changed only a little, but the decade after the Lindbergh flight to Paris [1927] saw practically every new plane rendered virtually obsolete within six months of its creation."[31]

Bigger, faster airplanes were readily available with more features than Amelia and her friends at Kinner Field had even been able to predict five or six years earlier. All eyes were fastened hopefully on the experimental work in blind flying being carried out by the Guggenheim Fund for the Promotion of Aviation, under James Doolittle's direction. Once flight schedules could be made truly independent of normal weather conditions, the airlines could truly be said to be providing a regular commercial service. Meanwhile, there were numerous local airline services and a few brave attempts at national ones.

In July, Amelia was appointed assistant to the general traffic manager of one of these national airlines—Transcontinental Air Transport (more popularly known as TAT and the foundation company of today's TWA)—with special responsibility for attracting women passengers onto the airlines.

Amelia's satisfaction and pleasure at her new appointment was marred by the news that Bill Stultz had been killed in an accident at Roosevelt Field. He had taken up two passengers who wanted to experience some aerobatics. After several perfectly executed maneuvers, the Waco performed a loop, but at the bottom of the loop, the plane went into a tailspin from which it never recovered. Witness testimony makes it obvious that seconds before the plane hit the ground, killing all three occupants, Stultz applied full power in an attempt to recover. But it was some time before the cause of the accident was understood. One of the passengers had jammed his feet under the rudder bars to brace himself. With no rudder control, Stultz would have found it virtually impossible to recover, and at four hundred feet, he had no chance. The shoes were wedged there so tightly from the pressure that Stultz had applied in an attempt to use the rudder that when the passenger was pulled out of the wreckage, the shoes remained jammed in place.[32]

A few days later, Amelia was on the inaugural flight of TAT's "East to West" passenger service aboard the Ford trimotor *City of Washington* for the outward flight to Los Angeles. Simultaneously, Charles Lindbergh was flying a similar airplane from Los Angeles on the eastbound inaugural flight. The two planes landed in Arizona, where Lindbergh changed airplanes and flew the *City of Washington* on to California. Amelia was quick to point out to her colleagues that "luxuries" such as refreshments might attract more women to the airlines, and once women were happy to fly, they would persuade their men to fly also. She felt very strongly that if the newspapers would only take a different attitude toward reporting "incidents," her campaign would stand a better chance of success. While Amelia had a point (the media did fasten on to even the most trivial bump of an airplane), it is fair to point out that serious crashes were still far from few; Wilmer Stultz's crash, for example, was the third fatal accident *that week* at Roosevelt Field alone.

Dorothy Binney Putnam attempted to aid Amelia's campaign to get women into the air by traveling to Los Angeles and back in seven days, becoming "the first woman passenger to use Transcontinental Air Transport for a round trip." George's publicity machine never slept![33]

Amelia felt a responsibility to educate women to the practicality of flying, and to disassociate the dangers and informality of so-called sport flying from that of the strictly regulated civil commercial aviation. Her articles from this point became harder edged and concentrated not only on attracting women into aviation but also on making them aware of their equality with men.[34] She advocated setting up a formal separate classification for women's aeronautical records—just as there was for athletic and sports records—and qualified her stance: "Of course such regulation does not mean that when a woman is capable she cannot compete with men on equal terms. I'd like to see men's and women's records, and [also] a sexless thing called a World Record. . . ."[35]

In other articles, Amelia pointed out the track record of passenger-carrying airlines in the United States:

> Though everyone knows that regularly scheduled planes fly from London to Paris across the Channel, not many are aware that about fifty-three thousand passengers were carried in 1928 on similar lines in the United States. As I write there are forty-four operators who carry passengers or mail or express, or both, flying more than sixty-two thousand miles every twenty-four hours *on schedule.*[36]

On her return to New York, Amelia found George had fixed up an unusual item, guaranteed to attract newspaper coverage. With George and Dorothy, in a Loening amphibian piloted by its designer/builder Grover Loening, she flew to Block Island. There, with the submarine *Defender* (described as the smallest submarine in the world and the only privately owned one) on the surface, she was lowered over the side wearing deep-sea diving equipment. She never reached the bottom because she noticed a leak in her suit and signaled by pulling on the line to be hauled in. On the following day, after repairs to the suit, she dived successfully with instructor Frank Crilley (one of the world's most famous divers—he received the Congressional Medal of Honor in 1915 for his daring rescue of a diver trapped in wires), and walked along the seabed at a depth of thirty-five feet, as far their lead ropes would allow. There was little to see. They found only a clamshell and an empty milk bottle, so after fifteen minutes or so, Amelia started to feel cold and they came up. Later, dressed only in a swimsuit, she escaped from the diving compartment. She wrote about it, saying:

> On the bottom of the submarine is an unusual contrivance. It is an airtight chamber. By making the air pressure equal to that of the water one may step gayly [sic] forth into the Atlantic Ocean with

never a drop coming into the chamber. The phenomenon is that of the inverted tumbler in a bowl of water where the water creeps up the tumbler only so far as the pressure of the imprisoned air will allow. Yes, I walked out the strange door into the green sea and swam through it into the sunlight. A swimsuit was the only equipment needed as the exit was only fifteen feet under. . . .[37]

Amelia's own version was a chatty, unexciting—though informative— magazine article in which she was at least as interested in the process of getting into the diving gear as the dive itself. The newspapers, however, could be relied upon to hype the incident into adventure and some had her "fired from the torpedo tube of a submarine at 100 ft.," presenting a very different picture from the actual event.[38]

George was now so protective of Amelia's interests that others in the flying world were beginning to be directly affected by his aggressive strategy to make her the leading woman pilot. Lady Heath and Bill Lancaster, for example, had come to America that summer of 1929 for a lecture tour that had been booked months earlier (as Mary Heath had confided to George on a previous visit). On arrival, they found that most of their engagements had been canceled due to lack of interest, and Amelia had been booked into every canceled slot by the head of the lecture-tour company. Lady Heath claimed later, in a conversation with Elinor Smith, that she had since discovered this had been engineered by George, but she felt she could not sue due to her husband's disapproval of litigation. Her friendship for Amelia quickly waned at this point.

Throughout late spring and into summer, Amelia had been working in conjunction with other women on two projects: the first, to form an association for women pilots; the second, to organize a cross-country air race for women pilots. The race, called the Los Angeles to Cleveland Women's Air Derby, was to be the opening event of the National Air Races. It was a major achievement and well organized, so Amelia was less than enchanted when humorist Will Rogers termed it "The Powder Puff Derby." The name stuck, however, and even Amelia eventually found herself referring to the entrants as "powder puffers."[39]

There was no handicapping system (though there were two classes, one for the heavier planes and one for the smaller "sport" types), so the bigger, more powerful airplanes would obviously stand the best chance of winning. The first woman home in the class for larger airplanes would be the one who got the acclaim and publicity. Knowing what the other competitors were using as their mounts for the race, Amelia had recognized that not only would she be outclassed in the Avian but also would have to fly in the small "CW Class" if she raced it. She therefore set about looking for another airplane.

It was July before Amelia settled on the right plane, a Lockheed Vega, registration number NC6911, previously flown by Charles Lindbergh as a demonstrator model and sometimes used as New York mayor Jimmy Walker's hack. Lockheed had loaned the Vega to TAT for trials during the summer of 1929 and Amelia had the use of it during this time. In July, she sold the Avian and bought the big cabin monoplane, but within a few weeks she had swapped it for a later model (registration NC31E) Vega that Lockheed Aircraft was using as a demonstrator. It was NC31E that Amelia flew to California in early August to compete in the race.

When Elinor Smith heard about this, she was uneasy. The Vega was undoubtedly the fastest airplane available, but Elinor "didn't like it."

> The cockpit was high off the ground and your legs rested practically under the engine mount, making the heat build-up pretty uncomfortable at times. I'd flown it just once, and everything the Bellanca was, the Vega wasn't. Fast, unstable, tricky near the ground with a monocoque, "no-longeron" fuselage that would collapse like a packet of cornflakes in a crash. . . .[40]

Bearing in mind Amelia's performance at New Castle in March, Elinor was concerned that Amelia would not be able to handle the Vega, but shortly afterward she received a phone call from George Putnam. He hadn't forgotten her, he told her, and had her career very much in his mind. At the meeting that followed, he explained that Amelia would be flying in the Women's Air Derby and following it with a nationwide lecture tour. He then offered Elinor seventy-five dollars a week (an enormous sum in 1929) to pilot Amelia in the derby and around the country. Elinor was to do the difficult cross-country flying, because as George said, ". . . Amelia is not physically strong, you know. But of course she must appear to be doing it. When pictures are being taken at the various stops you must stand to her left, so her name will always come up first in the captions. . . ." When Elinor refused the offer, George resorted to bullying threats: "You may *think* you have other plans, but believe me, if you don't sign this you will never fly professionally again and certainly never in the New York area. You have my word on that!"[41]

The youngster was upset, only too well aware that George had the powerful contacts and the necessary influence to carry out his threat, but she stuck to her decision. Rumors were circulating that Amelia was taking secret refresher flying lessons at a private field near Rye, but Elinor still wondered how Miss Earhart would cope with the big airplane that Elinor regarded as "unwieldy."[42]

The entrants in the derby included two leading women pilots from overseas: the Australian Jessie "Chubby" Miller, who had flown from London to Darwin as copilot to Bill Lancaster; and Thea Rasche from Germany. Lady Heath filed an entry but was unable to find a suitable airplane in time.[43]

Virtually every American woman pilot of note was lined up as the starting flag went down at Clover Field, Santa Monica, that Sunday afternoon of August 18, 1929. Elinor Smith had hoped to enter but was offered a job putting on flying displays for the crowds who awaited the women racers in Cleveland. Amelia said there were only thirty women eligible under the entrance requirements, which insisted on a current license and one hundred hours of flying time, and of these thirty, twenty turned up on the starting line.[44] Nineteen started and one, Mary von Mach, turned back before reaching the first control point. Although this put her out of the race, she followed the others and completed all the stages.

The race consisted of nine stages. That first day, they were required to fly less than a hundred miles to San Bernardino, but from then on the competitors rose before dawn each day and were in the air by sunup to complete what can only be described as an endurance test of women and airplanes.

On the second leg, the newspapers had a field day. Marvel Crosson's airplane was seen to dive into the ground (her body was later found entangled in her parachute, which had not had time to open as she bailed out at too low an altitude). Thick mesquite undergrowth delayed the searchers and meanwhile reports of sabotage began to circulate, for Claire Fahy's OX5-powered Travel Air was forced down when the wing braces snapped. Investigation led to the suspicion that drops of corrosive acid had been strategically placed at the site of the damage. Thea Rasche was forced down with sand in her fuel tank, and when reporters got to her, she produced a cable, received on the eve of the race, warning her to be on the lookout for sabotage. Bobbi Trout was also forced down with suspected sand or dirt in her fuel and there were immediate and predictable demands (notably *not* from the fliers) for the race to be called off to protect the lives of the fliers. These demands were sensibly ignored by the organizers.

Amelia led on the second leg, but on a refueling stop at Yuma, she overshot the field and upended the Vega in scrub when she hit a ridge.

She blamed the crash on the fact that "something had gone wrong with the stabilizers," but it was more likely that in the extreme heat and resultant thin air resistance, the landing speed of the Vega was higher than she had previously experienced; sand had drifted over the runway, making it difficult to identify, and she overran it. The propeller was bent but a new one was flown in from Burbank within hours and she lost very little time.[45]

There were many forced landings during the race—not unusual in those days, when all pilots were used to landing, making mechanical adjustments, and taking off again with a minimum of fuss. One forced landing, recorded by Amelia, was made by Ruth Elder, who landed in a field of cattle. Having rolled to a stop, the pilot sent up a silent prayer: "Dear God, let them all be cows!"[46]

Some contestants got lost or were blown off course and had to land to discover their whereabouts and/or to refuel.

Margaret Perry felt unwell at the start of the race but took off anyway, despite her flulike symptoms. Two days later, she was hospitalized in Texas with typhoid fever. Blanche Noyes was flying at more than three thousand feet over the western desert in Texas when she looked over her shoulder to see her plane on fire. She landed, put out the fire by throwing sand on it, and took off again despite having damaged her undercarriage.[47]

These incidents, widely reported due to the amount of public interest generated in the "race of flying beauties," caused more than one editor to react: "Women have proven conclusively that they cannot fly." There was renewed backing of the earlier call for the race to be abandoned. In fact, the race was a great success, for sixteen finishers made it to Cleveland; one—Mae Haizlip—had joined them late as she had been unable to make the official start. Sportingly, the other contestants agreed to allow her to compete.[48]

Amelia was to write later that, despite the adverse criticism, this was the highest percent of finishers in any cross-country race to date, for men or women. In reality, it was a highly commendable performance given the unreliability of aircraft at that time, the fact that there were no navigational aids other than magnetic compasses, and that aviation charts were still so basic that the competitors used those that were available in conjunction with Rand McNally road maps.[49] Feeling they had proven a point, the competitors asked for, and got, representation on the race committee in subsequent years.[50]

Waiting for Amelia in Cleveland became unbearable for George, so, with Bill Lancaster to pilot him, he flew west to Cincinnati in a Great Lakes Trainer to meet her. "Bill's entry in that race was Chubby Miller, mine A.E.," he recalled. After lunch with the women, the two men took off ahead of the contestants, but the engine stalled and they were lucky to climb out of the airplane in one piece, having "ripped through the top branches of several trees" before doing a pancake landing in a cornfield. As they rubbed their bruises, they heard aircraft engines, and the entire field of powder puffers passed overhead. Although the men waved, they were not spotted. Later, when George asked whether Amelia would have come back for him if she *had* seen him, she grinned wickedly and said, ". . . you wouldn't have wanted me to drop out of the race. . . ."[51]

The race was won by Louise Thaden in a Travel Air with Gladys O'Donnell's clipped-wing Waco a close second. Both women had airplanes powered by the Wright Whirlwind J5 200 hp engine—as did Amelia and six other competitors. The Vega was generally considered to be "the fastest ship" because of its streamlined design, but Amelia was a poor third and when elapsed times were calculated, she was a disappointing two hours behind Louise Thaden. Elinor Smith recorded Amelia's poor landing at Cleveland as the Vega bounced across the length of the vast airport with Amelia frantically braking and attempting to avoid a ground loop.[52]

"I was filled with admiration for her," Elinor said. "It was barely five months since the New Castle incident . . . and there was absolutely no way she could have built up enough air time to be at ease behind the controls of the fastest heavy monoplane in the air." The landing speed of the Vega was at least a third faster than any other plane in the race and Amelia must have been only too aware that if she allowed the speed to drop, she could stall. "One look at her drawn countenance when she flipped up the cockpit hood" told Elinor and several other pilots who had watched the performance that "this was gut courage that transcended the sanity of reasoning."[53] If Elinor's assessment of Amelia's piloting ability was accurate, then Amelia put up a first-class performance in achieving third place in what was a very select gathering, especially flying an aircraft that was so difficult to handle.

A few days after the race, Amelia called a meeting of women pilots in her hotel suite. She outlined a plan formulated by herself, Gladys O'Donnell, Ruth Nichols, Louise Thaden, and Phoebe Omlie to commemorate the derby by forming an organization that would consolidate the gains made by the women in the race. Elinor Smith was delighted to be invited and went along with the intention until Amelia insisted that they should press for equality in racing with male pilots so that they could compete for big purses in free-for-all competition.

At this stage, Elinor and several others (Phoebe Omlie and Mary Heath among them) objected. To date, few women had any experience in flying the big, fast, pure-racing machines in which the men competed—and these could only be described as huge engines with fuel tanks to which were attached, almost as an afterthought, small wings. They were called "widow-makers," and they were certainly lethal to many fine pilots. Those opposed to the idea argued that to expose themselves to this type of competition could only betray the women's lack of experience. Because of this disagreement over policy, Elinor Smith declined to become a charter member of the group that would ultimately become the Ninety-Nines, arguably the most prestigious organization for women pilots.

The name supposedly arose because of a widely believed legend that there were one hundred licensed women pilots in the United States at that time and all except one joined the organization (Neta Snook, Amelia's first instructor, incorrectly claimed in a magazine article that she was the one who declined), leaving ninety-nine assenting women pilots. This legend, however, is not borne out by either the Department of Commerce or Ninety-Nines's records. There were more than 120 women with licenses of one type or another when the invitations were sent out, and in the following year when the charter deadline expired, ninety-nine applications had been received; hence the name. In 1930, Amelia would be elected first president of the organization whose laudable aim was "to provide closer relationship among pilots and to unite them in any movement that may be for their benefit or for that of aviation in general. . . ."[54]

Putnam was rumored to be annoyed with the derby placings and later blamed Amelia's third place on the fact that the airplane had not been properly tuned before it left the Lockheed factory. The public statements by George became almost a joke in the flying industry, for any adverse incident involving Amelia instantaneously called up an announcement from George blaming the airplane or some mechanical defect. While this naturally irritated other pilots, not to mention manufacturers of equipment, this unscrupulous behavior was George's way of protecting his "property." His recipe for success had always been aggressive action. Amelia's willingness to allow these announcements to be made is less understandable.

Those affected adversely by George's methods smarted and disliked him intensely. He had the ability to create fear because of the power he wielded and it took a tough personality such as that of Charles Lindbergh or Elinor Smith to stand up to him. It is equally fair to say that there was a softer side to George Putnam, for he was capable of great kindness and gentleness when he liked someone and would go to considerable lengths to help anyone with genuine talent and ability. The mistake some people have made about George is in assuming that the way he behaved to them was also the way he treated Amelia. They could hardly have been more wrong!

His relationship with Amelia had long since passed the point where she was a mere client, and their obvious close rapport had not gone unnoticed. In the previous November in Chicago, for example, at her first meeting with George and Amelia, Elinor Smith had been in no doubt that their "love affair was in full swing . . . for one thing there is an electricity between lovers that you can't miss, and the subtle pats and touchings between the two were unmistakable. . . ." Nor did the sharp-eyed youngster miss the fact that the two were clearly sharing the double bed in the adjoining room of the suite.[55] Rumors of a romance were quashed, but Amelia's claims that he meant nothing to her beyond a friend and business partner were negated when Dorothy left George shortly after Amelia returned from the air races and went to stay at Rye. For Dorothy, Amelia's arrival at the Locust Avenue mansion was the final straw, and the writer Corey Ford actually witnessed her departure at George's "handsome home at Rye, its duplex rooms decorated, appropriately enough, with the pelts of dead lions." It was during

> . . . a publication party he gave to launch one of his books, a celebrity-studded outdoors barbeque on the lawn behind his house with GP in chef's hat and apron presiding over the grill.
>
> At the height of the wing-ding, I left in search of the men's room, and wandered around to the front of the house. An express truck was parked outside, and as I opened the door I saw two movers carrying a trunk from the second floor. Dorothy Binney Putnam, GP's charming and vivacious wife, followed them downstairs, dressed in traveling clothes.
>
> "Didn't you know? I'm divorcing George," she said quite casually. "He doesn't need me anymore."
>
> I strolled back to the party, where GP was gaily spearing frankfurters for Amelia Earhart. . . .[56]

Dorothy went to Reno in September to establish residency in order to file for a divorce, which became final in December.[57] Some years later, Amelia was to tell of her early feelings for George in what was possibly the only interview where she discussed her personal life with any frankness:

> I had no special feelings about Mr. Putnam at first. I was too absorbed in the prospects of the trip and of my being the one to make it

... of course after I had talked to him for very long I was conscious
of the brilliant mind and keen insight of the man. . . .

She then related how she had made the flight and gone to the Putnams'
home to write the book:

Mr. Putnam and I found that we had many things in common; I was
interested in aviation, so was he. We both loved the outdoors, books
and sport. And so we lunched together, and dined together, took long
horseback rides together. Usually we were surrounded by many people, both he and I had many friends and were invited to the same
parties. We came to depend on each other, yet it was only friendship
between us, or so—at least—I thought at first. At least I didn't admit
even to myself that I was in love . . . but at last the time came, I don't
quite know when it happened, when I could deceive myself no longer.
I couldn't continue telling myself that what I felt for GP was only
friendship. I knew I had found the one person who could put up with
me.[58]

Given George's record for always getting what he wanted, little imagination is needed to envision his pursuit of Amelia. That he loved her is
beyond doubt, for he would never have parted from Dorothy over some
light attachment; and contrary to popular belief that his interest in Amelia, and hers in him, was strictly business, their relationship became one
of great depth according to George's elder son, David.[59] Many people
interviewed testified that when George wanted to charm someone, he
became devastating, so, for Amelia, the situation must have been a difficult one. Reared in a morally strict convention, she must have been torn
between her feeling for him and her avowed friendship for Dorothy, and
not least by the knowledge that the Putnams' separation was due, at least
in part, to the amount of time she and George were spending together
and George's discussions with Dorothy about the exact nature of his
relationship with Amelia.

For George, too, the matter must have been painful. He had been
married to Dorothy for nearly twenty years. She had been a loving partner,
a good friend, and an eminently suitable wife throughout those years and
they had two sons whom they loved. His subsequent record as a husband
(see Chapter Twenty-two) reveals a man who needed a warm and loving
relationship with his partner. Now he found himself in love with Amelia,
possibly without any encouragement from her, although clearly she had
been strongly drawn to him from the first. However, George knew only

one way: If you wanted something, you went all out and you got it, letting nothing stand in your way.

At about this time, Amelia had a meal with Elinor Smith and said to her:

> "GP has asked me to marry him. What do you think?" I said I didn't think a lot of it and the press wouldn't either. [At the time of this conversation, Elinor had not heard of the Putnams' separation.]
>
> She laughed and said, "That's pretty much what I thought you'd say." However, she said she was already too involved and couldn't give him up. I don't know that she meant this emotionally, necessarily; I thought she saw what GP could do for her and she needed his power and push.[60]

Chapter Fourteen

1929-1931

The ground upon which Dorothy Binney successfully sued for divorce in December 1929 was George's failure to provide for her and her two sons. Since leaving George, she had met and fallen in love with Captain Frank Upton, formerly an officer on the liner *President Roosevelt*. A holder of the Congressional Medal of Honor, Captain Upton was also known for a heroic sea rescue of a stricken shipful of passengers. Neither George nor Dorothy wanted unpleasant attention from the newspapers, particularly any speculation about possible future partners, so they made a private agreement out of court providing George with equal custody of the two sons and he was to contribute toward their support.[1] Dorothy did not need his money and this was simply a method of obtaining a divorce with a minimum of fuss.

George's success in promoting Amelia was not mirrored in his own career, however. The financial crash of 1929 spelled disaster for the publishing industry, too, and G. P. Putnam's Sons was as affected as everyone else by falling sales. Putnam's was also suffering from an internal situation. The president of the company was George's eighty-five-year-old uncle, Major George Haven Putnam (his title dated from service in the Civil War, part of which he spent in a Confederate army prison). The Major, as he was exclusively called in the publishing industry, had spent his entire life in publishing and though he had given George a free hand to build up the house using his modern publishing methods, the old man was clearly nostalgic about those lost days of the nineteenth century when publishing was a slow and gentle process, without the need for hype and angles and contrived best-sellers. This wily old man saw the crash coming and pulled all of his money (presumably including that earned from the profitable previous ten years) out of Putnam's months before the crash and applied it to his estate, leaving only his original one-third shareholding.[2] This was a wise move on his part, but it adversely affected the company's cash flow at a vulnerable time.

Amelia spent the last months of 1929 in Los Angeles, working for TAT and staying with the Madduxes, accompanied by her secretary, Nora Alstulund.[3] On November 22, she wrote to her mother that she had been having a lovely time and flying a great deal. "Today I think I broke the women's speed record in average time of 184.17 m.p.h. I did one lap in 197 . . . in the new arrangement I am half time with both eastern and western divisions of T.A.T."[4]

Visiting her father, now married to his second wife, Helen, and living at what was then known as Eaglerock, near Los Angeles, Amelia found him thin and ill and worried about meeting his mortgage payments because he was unable to work. Amelia subsequently repaid the outstanding mortgage of two thousand dollars and made over a freehold tenancy to her father and, after his death (which she feared was not far off), to his widow. She spent Christmas in California and was disappointed when the FAI contest committee replied to her claim on the speed record:

> Please be advised that there is no category recognized by the F.A.I. for speed trials over a one mile straightaway course; therefore this record can only be recognized as a "Miscellaneous aircraft performance." Maximum speed trials are only recognized by the F.A.I. when flown over a three kilometer course and timed by an electrical timing device which has been approved by the F.A.I. . . . At the last meeting of the F.A.I. it was decided that when aviatrices surpass an F.A.I. world record in their class, their performance shall be entered on the list of women's records and on the list of World's Records. . . .[5]

George traveled to Paris and London, where he adopted a desperate measure to obtain maximum publicity for a book that he hoped would be a best-seller and thus would help to retrieve the failing fortunes of Putnam's.

The book had been written by Francesco Nitti, nephew of the former Italian premier, and the first man to escape from the fascist penal colony on Lipari Island in the Mediteranean. The manuscript apparently exposed appalling prison conditions and spoke out against Mussolini. On December 17, in Paris, George claimed that he had received an anonymous letter threatening retribution if he went ahead with the book's publication.

Adopting a manner of amused unconcern, George stated to the press on that occasion that such threats would not stop publication of the book.

But on December 30, in London and reportedly acting on the advice of Frederick Guest, he went to the police at Scotland Yard with two further letters, both decorated with fascist symbols and supposedly from the same group of fascists in Paris who threatened to kill George ("Pig . . . you will never reach New York alive") and blow up the Putnam offices in London and New York.

This time the police offered George round-the-clock protection until his planned departure on the S.S. *France* on January 4. The matter was reported widely in both the British and American newspapers, thus providing the publicity he sought.[6] The publicity helped the book's sales a great deal and many years later George was to recall this successful publicity stunt (for that is what it was; he later confessed to his family and friends that he had written the letters himself) and attempt to use it again.[7]

When George arrived back in New York, it was to the news that Dorothy was about to marry Frank Upton in the West Indies that week.[8] This must have assuaged any feelings of guilt he had over Amelia, who was in town to meet him and to whom he immediately proposed.

Several writers have claimed that George proposed six times to Amelia, but George states in his biography of Amelia, *Soaring Wings*, that he "proposed twice, at least."[9] On this first occasion, Amelia must have refused him, or asked for time to think about the matter. In any event, a marriage so soon after George's divorce would surely have confirmed the previous speculation about their relationship, which would not have helped Amelia's image.

George's attempts to make the Nitti book a best-seller became somewhat superfluous in February, when the Major died suddenly, leaving his Putnam's shareholding and his personal wealth to his son, Palmer Cosslet Putnam. Palmer returned at once from Africa, where he had been a mining engineer, fired with enthusiasm to become a publisher and take his place at the head of the family business. He was in a powerful position, thanks to his father's foresight, for he had that valuable commodity "ready cash" when there was little after the financial crash of the previous year. On examining the books, he expressed concern about the state of the firm, which at that stage was in need of a substantial capital injection, and he suggested bringing "new blood" into the house at senior-executive level.[10]

In the ensuing family row ("to be avoided at almost any price," George was to write later), George offered to buy his cousin's stock and named a price that Palmer thought was considerably below its value. George, then vice-president of the company and only too well aware of the state of the publishing industry, considered the valuation he had put on the stock so fair that he quickly offered to sell his own holding to Palmer at the same valuation. This put George's holding at $100,000.

> My cousin bought, for which, at the time, I was glad . . . [but] a few years later he went into bankruptcy while he still owed me $75,000, which was very sad indeed. It was sad too for the House of Putnam. For after the engineer took over the controls, what with the depression and internal inflations of one sort and another, soon there were no more Putnams in the House our grandfather had founded.[11]

After George left Putnam's, Palmer arranged a merger with Melvin Minton and Earle Balch (both of whom George had met in his army days and introduced into publishing). They had become Minton, Balch and Company and within a few years, just before its hundredth birthday, they would own Putnam's. George was sorry to leave the family firm, but he recognized that nothing could be the same with his cousin in such a controlling position.

Reporting these events, *Time* magazine said:

> The departure from G. P. Putnam & Sons [*sic*] of G. P. Putnam was almost as newsworthy as the deal itself. In the past decade he has made himself conspicuous on the publishing scene. He is a man with a dangerous combination of literary ability, business acumen, and energy. . . . What Publicist Putnam intends to do in the future is not known. He may expand his cinematic activities, may publish on his own, may retire, may go off exploring. Perhaps he will do all these things. His cryptic statement of plans last week was "If you played golf twelve years, you wouldn't stop all at once would you?"[12]

Throughout the spring of 1930, Edwin Earhart's health deteriorated. Amelia, who was commuting between Los Angeles and New York, saw him whenever she could, but in a letter to Amy, Edwin stated sadly that "even when she is in Los Angeles we do not see much of her so my information about her I get from the newspapers."[13] During those months, two of Amelia's former colleagues, Gene Vidal and Paul Collins, had left TAT and she was working with them to form a new airline that offered hourly round-trip service between New York, Philadelphia, and Washington—the first shuttle! Gene Vidal recalled that "she was a very interesting person, a tomboy who liked all men's games, enjoyed being with the mechanics working on airplanes, and yet was a little girl in some respects. Although often in trousers, she was very feminine and quite romantic in some ways."[14]

In addition, Amelia was writing articles for *Cosmopolitan* and various other journals such as *Aero-News and Mechanics* (and dealing with the massive correspondence that resulted from these); continuing her work with TAT; and engaging the NAA in correspondence regarding establishing a committee to eliminate the headlining of aircraft accidents. "You have no doubt noticed the exceptionally misleading and prominent reports which have appeared lately," she wrote.[15]

Amelia fitted in numerous speaking engagements while she traveled and was still plugging away at her old hobbyhorse—the organization for women pilots that had been mooted in Cleveland the previous summer. In March 1930, the Ninety-Nines held its first meeting, at which Amelia was elected president and Louise Thaden, secretary. Amelia made it her special responsibility to try to attract big prize money for women air-race competitors.

Amelia was also already toying with the idea of a solo transatlantic flight—a "first" of her own—but then, every woman pilot of note had the same ambition. Although she denied such plans to reporters, to a friend she confided that she would like to do it, admitting frankly that she hadn't yet the necessary flying and navigation experience. "Give me, say, eighteen months or two years," she wrote.[16]

George, too, was busy. He was still managing Amelia and other clients while attempting to pick up his own publishing career. They spent time together whenever possible but there were "long intervals of communication only by letter or telegram." Later, George remembered that he had bombarded her with instructions, and Amelia was so busy that often "the answers to my letters were usually my letters returned, with notations in pencil in the margin."[17]

When they were together Amelia entertained George with amusing stories about her trips. After one lecture, a woman had buttonholed her, saying, "Do you know what my little boy said about your lecture today?" "No," Amelia had replied, asking dutifully, 'What did he say?' "Well, he saw your picture beside the box office and came running home crying, 'Mommy, mommy, Colonel Lindbergh's mother is going to speak at the theatre.' "[18] Amelia's ready sense of humor never deserted her no matter how pressured she was, or how cornered by fame.

When in New York, Amelia continued to stay in the AWA Club and, perhaps to assuage her mother's concern, her secretary, Nora Alstulund, moved in there, too. She never mentioned George to her mother during this period, though she wrote regularly, always sending a little something to help financially. Amy was living with Muriel, who had given birth to a son, David, in April, but whose marriage was undergoing difficulties.

Finances were tight and Amy had frequently to ask Amelia for help. There were calls on her assistance, too, from Edwin and Helen Earhart, though these were less frequent.

On one occasion Amelia wrote, obviously in reply to a query from Amy:

> *Dear mother,*
>
> Enclosed is some cash. I just found your letter today and didn't realize you'd be short of funds so soon. I shall not be in New York very long I think, as I am going west again to pick up my ship. There are several dates in the mid-west I must keep too. Please let me know how Pidge fares.
>
> I am not marrying *anybody.*
>
> *A.E.*[19]

Amy's concern was no doubt prompted by misreported quotes. To a close friend, Amelia wrote at greater length: "I am still unsold on marriage. I don't want *anything* all of the time. . . . I think I may never be able to see marriage except as a cage until I am unfit to work or fly or be active—and, of course, I wouldn't be desirable then. . . ."[20]

Early in the year she had written explaining that she was making formal arrangements to provide for Amy, and her letter gives an indication of her financial success:

> I am enclosing a check for $100. Hereafter you will receive it monthly from the Fifth Avenue Bank. I have put all my earnings into stocks and bonds and the yearly income in your name. The list includes the $1000 dollar bond of yours which you may have, of course, at any time. . . . Nora Alstulund and I are living together in a large double room at about half the rent of the suite. I am thus able to live easily on what I make and you can have the other. I sent clothing on because I thought it would please Pidge and was probably needed and you wouldn't have purchased it. . . . I have just returned from Washington and Pittsburgh and am off again to the west soon. I now have a job [it was a public-relations position organized by George] with the Pennsylvania R.R. besides T.A.T. Maddux. I plan to work very hard this year and [do] little else but fly. . . .[21]

When Amy voiced concern about the amount, Amelia responded that her mother should "not think you are taking my hard earned money"—it was merely the interest earned on her investment—"that is extra to what I earn. I am living with Nora and very economical so there will be more

and more accruing."[22] These obviously satisfactory arrangements, no
doubt engineered by George, must have put Amy's mind at rest, for from
this point on she did not hesitate to ask for help when it was needed.

June found Amelia at Grosse Isle Airport in Detroit. She had not taken
lightly the refusal to acknowledge her speed record of the previous autumn. After much correspondence from her, and lobbying of the FAI by
George, she was allowed to make an official attempt on the woman's speed
record over one hundred kilometers, which she set at 174.897 mph. The
same day (June 25), she claimed the record over the same distance,
carrying a five-hundred-kilogram payload, at 171.438 mph, in a Vega
owned by the Detroit Aircraft Corporation.[23] Ten days later, she set a
world speed record for women over the internationally recognized three-
kilometer course, clocking 181.18 mph. On her return home, she found
a letter from her father. He was very ill and, with no time to write, she
forwarded the letter to her mother by way of explanation, with a note
scribbled on the back: "Am heading West and will see him there." She
had only recently told Amy that Edwin was suffering from cancer and was
probably too weak for surgery.

In August 1930, George joined the publishers Brewer and Warren as
vice-president.[24] After visiting her father, Amelia returned to New York
and was hard at work with preparations for the new airline, which had its
inaugural flight on September 1. Called the Ludington Line, it started
with high hopes and with George's help, they organized "free flights for
reporters," which gave valuable free publicity, such as this interview
Amelia gave to reporter Janet Mabie:

> When we started the first of this month we hoped for a lot but we
> didn't expect anything. We expected the service would take hold
> gradually . . . that is the thing with transport in this country. We can't
> learn by European transport. We've our own conditions and we have
> nothing to go by.
>
> We didn't expect to make money for a long time, we knew we'd
> make mistakes and have to find correctives. But what we build we
> intend to build solid and I think we have. . . . The ten-passenger
> Stinson has justified itself as far as this service is concerned. Only
> once in 3900 hours of flying have we had a scrap of motor difficulties,
> a nut broke loose and fell into the crank case. The motor was replaced
> overnight without disrupting services. . . .
>
> We've got twenty landing fields on a 200 mile route. We sit down
> without any fuss if the weather turns. . . .[25]

In September, Helen Earhart cabled Amelia in New York, advising her that her father was dying and wanted to see her. Amelia flew out immediately and spent a week there. He died peacefully a few hours after she left him on September 23. She hurried back east, where she had the usual round of engagements to fulfill, and on September 25 she was in Norfolk, Virginia, where, according to newspaper reports, she "made a spectacular visit to the city. Her plane nosed over in landing at the Naval air station and she suffered scalp injuries which necessitated that she wear a turban" to cover the bandages around her head.[26] Her passenger suffered a broken finger.[27] She had apparently been reaching for the brakes and leaning against the door when it opened and catapulted her backward into the cabin. The plane ground looped and ended up on its back. A few days later (October 2), "full of tetanus," she wrote to her mother about Edwin's death and explained the crash:

> I just returned from Dad to have a little crackup due to mechanical failure. The lock on the pilot's cockpit opened and let me out as I was leaning on it. I wasn't hurt much and neither was [the] Lockheed.
> About Dad. The diagnosis was correct . . . he waged a hopeless fight against a thing which took all his nourishment. . . . His big case was lost and we told him he had won. He couldn't have stood the disapointment so it was for the best. . . . He asked about you and Pidge a lot, and I faked telegrams from you all.
> He was an aristocrat as he went—all the weakness gone with a little boy's brown puzzled eyes. . . .
>
> *AE*[28]

Amelia's explanation of the crash to her mother was a considerable glossing-over of the facts, for the Lockheed was so badly damaged that it required a new fuselage and repairs to all flying surfaces.[29]

Later that month, Amelia accepted a proposal of marriage from George, though two weeks later, to reporters, she again denied any intention of marrying him.[30] On the following day, however, she was with George when he admitted, smilingly, that he had obtained a marriage license, though they had no idea just then when they might use it.[31] The sudden media interest may have been stimulated by George's cryptic dedication to Amelia in his new book, *André: The Record of a Tragic Adventure*, which read: "To a favorite aeronaut about to embark on a new adventure."[32]

The license had been obtained by George on November 8, 1930, and the couple planned to get married quietly almost immediately. After the secret became public, however, there could be no hope of the "no fuss" occasion that Amelia particularly wished, so the wedding was postponed, necessitating the judge to apply for a waiver because the law in Connecticut set a defined period between the filing of intention and issue of a marriage license.

A few weeks later, beleaguered every time they appeared in public, the couple were still saying no to reporters. George had a stock reply: "In answer to the two questions I am constantly asked: 'Am I getting married?' the answer is 'No.' 'When?' the answer is, 'I don't know.' " Meanwhile, Amelia assured her mother in a letter that she was still living with Nora Alstulund: "N.A. and I are still going strong at the AWA." According to Muriel, Amy opposed the marriage because George was older and a divorced man, though since Amy herself was a divorcée the latter seems an unreasonable prejudice. Amelia would never have let such considerations color her judgment, however, nor would her mother's disapproval have weighted her decision. Any reservations she had concerned her personal freedom and George had clearly convinced her that he was prepared to accede to her wishes in this respect.

Amelia's letters to her mother continued over Christmas and into the New Year. They were chatty letters full of family matters, such as instructions about the suit she had sent for Christmas: "Please go to a decent tailor and have the suit fitted. . . . I want you to go into town with Nancy and buy a little brown hat to go with [the] suit (a shade or two darker maybe) and a couple of pairs of gloves . . . then while you're at it get a dark blue hat . . . charge these and send me the bill. . . . What is happening in the family? . . ." There was also business news, such as "I have taken another business with another woman; we've gone into partnership, I'll tell you the circumstances next time we meet."[33] They were letters full of everything but the most important news; but she had never included her family in her important plans.

This dated back to the oceanic flight when Amelia had been distressed at Amy and Muriel's willingness to discuss with the press what Amelia considered to be very personal matters. She had now assumed a matriarchal position of provider and was in the throes of arranging a mortgage to enable Muriel to purchase the house in West Medford, which both Amy and Muriel felt sure would improve her domestic situation.

On Wednesday February 4, in response to an invitation to visit her mother, who had the Challiss cousins staying with her, Amelia wrote a short note to say she wouldn't be home for the weekend but invited Amy and her guests to visit her the following weekend. "I am due in Washington tonight and have a luncheon in Newark today. Cheerio. AE"[34] She planned to spend the weekend with George. That Friday evening they decided, apparently on the spur of the moment, to use the marriage license taken out on November 8, three months earlier.

On Saturday, February 7, 1931, Amelia and George were married in George's mother's home in Noank, Connecticut. "For [Amelia]," George wrote, "it was a heroic decision, touching something in her very much deeper than any mere problem of marriage which must be worked out with the . . . demands of a publicly important person. Her attitude towards responsibility was strict and methodical . . . she could toss off a scrambled word or phrase for fun's sake, but anything she thought enough of to undertake she could not play at." George, too, had been warned by his attorney of the dangers inherent in the proposed marriage; "it may not be easy being married to a public character."[35]

Nevertheless, George telephoned his mother on Friday evening to tell her they were driving up on the following day with the intention of getting married there; he also telephoned a friend of the family, Judge Anderson, to make the arrangements for the ceremony.

It was a clear cold day in the small New England fishing village on that Saturday. There were no guests at the wedding, just the witnesses (one of George's uncles and the judge's son) and George's mother, who had not time even to arrange flowers to decorate the house. A large fire crackled brightly in the low-ceilinged sitting room that looked out over Long Island Sound and it had all Amelia asked—secrecy. She wore a simply cut brown suit and crepe blouse, with brown lizard-skin shoes— "no hat, of course."[36]

Just before the judge was due to arrive, Amelia handed George a letter and from the look on her face he realized that it was of vital importance to her. He wrote of the letter, "It was penciled longhand, with a terrible kind of care for each word, that it be fair and honest. A slip or two in spelling meticulously corrected; a few words crossed out, replaced by others monastically simple."[37] It was undated, written on two pages (four sides) of gray writing paper headed The Square House, Noank, Connecticut (George's mother's home):

> *Dear Gyp,*
>
> There are some things which should be writ before we are married—things we have talked over before—most of them.
> You must know again my reluctance to marry, my feeling that I shatter thereby chances in work which mean most to me. I feel the

move just now as foolish as anything I could do. I know there may be compensations, but have no heart to look ahead.

On our life together I want you to understand I shall not hold you to any medieval code of faithfulness to me, nor shall I consider myself bound to you similarly. If we can be honest I think the difficulties which arise may best be avoided should you or I become interested deeply (or in passing) with anyone else.

Please let us not interfere with the other's work or play, nor let the world see our private joys or disagreements. In this connection I may have to keep some place where I can go to be myself now and then, for I cannot guarantee to endure at all times the confinement of even an attractive cage.

I must exact a cruel promise, and that is you will let me go in a year if we find no happiness together.

I will try to do my best in every way and give you that part of me you know and seem to want.

AE[38]

An edited version of the letter was first published by George in his biography of Amelia, *Soaring Wings,* but it is believed that this is the first time it has appeared in a book in its *unedited* form. It is a most extraordinary testament. Few brides today, even given the relaxed conventions of the last decade, would suggest to a bridegroom that sexual freedom for both parties was implicit in the marriage agreement.

That the points contained in the letter—or most of them, anyway—had been discussed by the couple indicates the level of their previous relationship, and that Amelia was content to continue the liaison in its existing form. It was George who wanted marriage, not—as his detractors have claimed—because he wanted to manipulate Amelia, but because that was how George was. He did not possess Amelia's free-thinking approach and, being a romantic at heart, he wanted marriage with the woman he loved and to be a full partner in every sense of the word.[39]

Clearly when she wrote this letter, Amelia was not madly in love with George and her feelings for him were still those of a close friend. But his reaction to her written appeal reveals perhaps the reason why she was prepared to marry him despite this. "In her heart," he said, "she knew . . . that for good or ill, she must keep freedom in a measure which is not always possible in marriage. She had no selfish dream of the anatomy of freedom, but she did know it for an element without which she personally could not do, as some plants can do without water but cannot survive without air."[40]

Amelia's fear of marriage may have been the result of her parents' experience, of having watched two intelligent, loving people turn sour and embittered in the confines of their union. Perhaps also she still remembered the restrictions against which she had silently chafed when, even in her early twenties, she had been considered a daughter and not an independent adult. Her success had provided her with an intoxicating independence both spiritual and financial, and much as she wanted the close companionship that she felt should be possible in marriage to George, she was not prepared to *trade* the former for the latter. She wanted both. George felt he could accommodate her wishes.

Amelia has been described as emotionally undemonstrative, but Gore Vidal (Gene Vidal's son) explains: "I can tell you that she was a very passionate person who felt things deeply. Of course it didn't always show with her—perhaps suppressed passion would be an accurate description."[41]

After the wedding ceremony, for which they had to borrow his mother's platinum ring, not having had time to obtain one, Amelia sat with the judge's son and talked about the development of a new autogiro aircraft in which she was interested. Then, after a glass of wine, she slipped a fur coat over her suit and the couple drove off to a secret destination—but not before George had telephoned his secretary, Jo Berger, to ask her to release the news. Within an hour, the village was inundated with reporters, but the scent was cold. The village postmistress was bewildered: "Wedding? I don't think there's been a wedding here today. . . ." Mrs. Putnam senior gave only the briefest interview. "They didn't tell me where they were going so that I shouldn't be able to tell." The statement released by Jo Berger gave merely the barest details of the marriage but did reveal that Amelia would retain her own name for business and writing purposes and that both would be back at work, as usual, on the following Monday morning.[42]

Amelia sent a cable to her sister asking her to break the news gently to Amy. Later, Amy gave a short dignified statement to the press. "If Amelia is happy, and I am sure she is, then I am. I knew it was to take place, of course, and I know Mr. Putnam very well, but I didn't know the exact date. . . ."[43] Remembering her mother's disapproval, Amelia wrote to her:

Dear Mother

I want you to know I appreciate more than I can say the interview you gave . . . about my marriage. I was so proud of you. I am much happier than I expected I could ever be in that state. I believe the whole thing was for the best. Of course I go on in the same way as before as far as business is concerned. I haven't changed at all and will only be busier I suppose.

I have given up my A.W.A. [apartment] and moved to 42 W 58th Street, just a few blocks away. I want you to come over as soon as you wish and see the apartment. I have two canaries and you know I've wanted one for ever so long. You can stay here at the hotel in another room or if you prefer at the A.W.A. Nora has moved uptown to the Columbia district. . . .

I sent Muriel the $2,500 promised, I hope it will mean a lot to her, moving into a decent house. . . . I am asking Pidge down here, maybe we could have a blowout together before she becomes too tied down [Muriel was pregnant again]—or is it obviously too late for her? Write me your plans.

AE[44]

Much has been made of the fact that Amelia retained her own name after her marriage, and it was very unusual at that time, but, in fact, George as well as Amelia saw much to commend this decision. After all, Amelia Earhart was an established property; the public would take time to react to the name Amelia Putnam. Undoubtedly, Amelia did relish the individuality this gave her, but she was never bothered when she was addressed as Mrs. Putnam, and in private she often referred to herself in this manner, while George frequently joked that he was often referred to as Mr. Earhart.[45]

Chapter Fifteen

1931-1932

George wrote: "When we were married our desk calendars were so full of pressing appointments that there was no time for a trip. I think that for AE there was a certain savor in the fact that the question of allowing even the gravest single step of her life up to that point to stand in the way of carrying on with her commitments, simply didn't arise."[1]

The commitments of which George spoke are borne out by newspaper archives. Both were deeply committed to their solo careers at that point and one or the other was constantly in the newspapers for attending functions, often as a guest speaker. George never failed to push out regular press releases. There were some newsworthy events in that year, however. After her marriage, Amelia broke away from the Ludington Line following an undisclosed policy disagreement. Shortly afterward, George approached the Pitcairn company, manufacturers of an autogiro—an aircraft that was half airplane and half what we know today as a helicopter—about purchasing one.[2]

In the previous December, Amelia had—"just for fun"—made a test flight in an autogiro, which was still new enough to make headlines. With virtually every prestigious flying record already captured or broken by one of the dozen or so top women pilots, Amelia and George were looking for something that would keep Amelia's name a headliner, and the autogiro, they hoped, was just the vehicle.

On April 8, 1931, Amelia set an altitude record in the autogiro at Pitcairn Field, Pennsylvania, reaching an unofficial height of 19,000 feet on her first attempt and a recorded 18,451 feet on her second. Amelia claimed this as an officially recognized height record. It is not recorded as such, but the resultant crop of headlines confirmed that here was something worth cultivating. Amelia was the only woman flying an autogiro at the time. On May 22, she bought the Pitcairn PCA-2, registration NC10780, stating that she wished to be the first person to fly an autogiro from coast to coast.[3] A few weeks later, George arranged to sell the aircraft to Beech-Nut Packing Company, the chewing gum manufacturers, who promptly loaned the airplane back to Amelia, paying her a retainer to perform the role of flying ambassador. Amelia actually enjoyed flying the weird-looking machine, as well as finding it a challenge.[4]

After a few weeks recuperation from a tonsillectomy, Amelia set off from New York on May 29, accompanied by her mechanic, Eddie de Vaught, on a tour that would take her to Los Angeles via dozens of cities. George's son David still remembers being roped in to help with the publicity dreamed up by his father and Beech-Nut before Amelia took off. "We had giant packets of Beech-Nut—about three feet long—which we were giving away."[5] The autogiro had *Beech-Nut* emblazoned on its side.

At the end of her much-publicized transcontinental flight in what the newspapers insisted on calling "the flying windmill," Amelia reached Los Angeles on June 7 to find that a previously unheard-of pilot, twenty-five-year-old Johnny Miller from Poughkeepsie, New York, had made the trip a week before in an identical machine. Amelia was disappointed and George was furious. His explosive overreactions were well known but could be alarming to anyone witnessing them for the first time. In fact, his tantrums lasted only minutes and subsided instantly; they were more a release of tension, or an expression of frustration, than a reflection of a violent nature.

After some discussion, it was decided that Amelia should return at once to New York, thus becoming the first person to make the return transcontinental flight in the autogiro. She certainly made headlines on this return flight, though they were not those for which she or George had hoped. She stopped over in Abilene, Texas, on the return journey in order to attend an air fair. Naturally, the crowds were fascinated to see the autogiro and its woman pilot, and Amelia made several demonstration flights during the day and gave some rides before deciding to leave. "The crowd was desirous of seeing the gyroplane closely," she explained later, "and I was taking off close to the crowd on that account. . . ." As she took off, a rotor clipped a landing light and fluttered thirty feet, to land among parked cars, of which several were damaged. It showered the crowd with shards of damaged rotors and other debris. Both Amelia and the mechanic were uninjured, but it was felt that the spectators had been put at grave risk and Amelia received an official reprimand from Clarence Young, then Assistant Secretary of Commerce for Aviation.[6]

Amelia answered the charges of carelessness by saying she had underestimated the distance required to get off safely and had been hit by a gust of wind, but that she retained control of the craft at all times and no one had been in danger. A replacement autogiro was hurriedly shipped out and Amelia continued her trip to Newark without further incident. A few hours after she handed the replacement aircraft back to its regular pilot, he crashed it on landing.

Amelia continued to send hastily scribbled notes to Amy and in an invitation to her mother to visit Rye, she also explained the reprimand: "The reprimand wasn't one really, mostly a chance for butting the Ludington Line and I [am] the goat. I am not a careless pilot and the letter doesn't say so."[7] The reprimand *was* galling, however, particularly as she had been voted vice-president of the NAA shortly before setting out on her transcontinental trip.[8]

Amelia found time after her return to write lengthy letters of thanks to citizens of Abilene who had been kind to her after the crash, especially one family who had insisted on her staying with them and using their telephone. She arranged for George to call on them on his way to California a few weeks later. She spent the summer working from Rye—"The city is so warm and it is hard to leave the sea even to fly. . . ."[9]—and writing articles in which she stressed the safety aspect of flying and exhorted more women to take up flying.

In early September, Amelia was demonstrating the autogiro at an air show at the state fairgrounds in Detroit when it crashed on landing. George, who had driven there, was in deep conversation with someone in the crowd and did not see the crash but heard the sound and saw the look of horror on his companion's face:

> As I swung round I saw the giro, its rotors splintered, disappear in a cloud of smoke. I vaulted the rail and raced for the wreck. Never have I run so fast, until one of those guy wires caught my pumping legs exactly at the ankles. I did a complete outside loop, up into the air and over, landing full on my back. . . . Coming to my senses— some of them at least—I saw AE emerge from the welter of dust (it wasn't smoke) and wave her hands in the air to show she was un-hurt.[10]

George cracked three ribs but immediately put out a statement that the crash was due to a structural fault, claiming that a landing strut gave way as the wheels touched. The resultant heavy landing crashed the fuselage to the ground, breaking the wires that supported the rotors, which then dropped and sheared off the tail and propeller. The aircraft was wrecked.

"My giro spill was a freak accident," Amelia reported to her mother after the predictable headlines had appeared.

> The landing gear gave way from a defect and I ground looped only. The rotors were smashed, as usual with giros, but there wasn't even a jar. GP fell over a rope running to pick me up and as he limped up I said "It was all my fault," meaning that he was hurt. The papers got it I said the crack was mine, which isn't accurate. . . ."[11]

However, despite Amelia's steady stream of letters, her relationship with Amy and Muriel had begun to take a downturn. Under increasing pressure, Amelia found the demands of her family irritating. Their concerns seemed to her to be petty and a critical note appears in her letters to Amy, particularly about Muriel and Albert, who had not yet formalized the loan agreement for the twenty-five hundred dollars Amelia had provided for their house, and who were still finding it difficult to cope financially. Forgetting the days when money was not so readily available to her, Amelia wrote curtly: "Let me know how Pidge and Albert progress, I don't know any way I can help them or you except by trying to be banker for part of your funds for a while. If you want to reach me you can do so through Nora at Rye."[12]

Later, she allowed open exasperation to fill her letter:

DECEMBER 1ST 1931

Dear Mother

I am enclosing a check for $33. This plus the $17 I sent last month makes $50. I am depositing the rest of the amount [of $100, the amount Amelia paid monthly to Amy] to your credit here. I am very displeased at the use [to which] you have put what I hoped you would save. I am not working to help Albert, nor Pidge much as I care for her. If they had not had that money perhaps they would have found means to economize before.

I do not mean to be harsh, but I know the family failing about money. As for your paying board, such a thing is unthinkable as you have done all the house-keeping which more than compensates. I would not, if I could, buy the bond. If there were any assurance that things were run on a businesslike basis, there might be some reason for helping.

It is true that I have a home and food but what I send you is what I myself earn and it does not come from GP. I feel the church gets some of what should go to living expenses and I have no wish to continue that to Pidge's loss. . . .[13]

Amelia's position as a public figure had revealed a natural assertiveness, which was encouraged by George, and so it seemed natural for Amy and Muriel to turn to Amelia for help and guidance. Amelia's background, however, had instilled a degree of financial prudence and while, initially, she had enjoyed the novelty of being able to provide treats for her family, she now resented the fact that her generosity was, to a certain extent, being taken for granted.

Muriel, in the throes of marital difficulties, was stung by her sister's stance and it may be that both she and Amy blamed George for Amelia's new attitude, for neither woman really liked him.[14]

Under constant pressure, Amelia more and more treasured her time with George at the spacious house in Rye, about thirty miles northeast of New York. Flanked by sandy beaches, the town had a number of grand estates among old oaks and elm trees and the Putnam home was a pleasant place, vibrant with mementos of George's many trips and adventures and with some startling interior decoration. One guest recalled sleeping in a room whose walls were decorated with jungle flora; another room was painted with water plants and tropical fish, so that one seemed to be sleeping in a fish tank.[15] From an informal English-style garden, guests entered the house through a reception hall, tiled, somewhat startlingly, in sea-green ceramic tiles inset with Chinese medallions.

This led into a huge sitting room with windows along the length of one wall overlooking the terrace and gardens. A huge stone fireplace, kept well supplied with logs by George, who "loved to swing an axe,"[16] was flanked by deep comfortable armchairs. Imported Chinese and Guatemalan rugs, Eastern embroideries, Chinese vases, and Rockwell Kent paintings offered muted accents to the antique dark oak furniture. George's collections of exotica from his various travels around the world—from bearskins and walrus tusks to shrunken human heads and an old Spanish chest—filled rooms lined with books. In the studio, where guests liked to gather after dinner, Amelia's trophies were displayed on the grand piano and in two alcoves. Portraits of George and Amelia hung over the carved staircase. With Amelia's peripatetic youth in mind, the old house must indeed have seemed truly a home at last.

It is doubtful that the time spent at Rye was always peaceful, for George was a lavish entertainer and the house was never empty of the writers and famous personalities that he constantly attracted, but Amelia felt no requirement to shine for visitors. Guests found her quiet, and a serene foil for George's brilliant magnetism.[17] When not working, she loved to ride, play golf, or swim in the Sound, and she found great relaxation in working in the gardens, where pink and white dogwood bloomed each spring; she enjoyed the company of George's two sons, who came to stay. She was especially close to David, who was now twenty-one years old, but the younger son, George, had contracted polio shortly after his parents' separation and constant physiotherapy meant he was unable to visit his father as often as did his elder brother.

As the year moved to a close, the Putnams sent out a cheerful cartoon Christmas card depicting them both in an airplane flying between New York and Los Angeles.

At some point after their marriage Amelia had realized, as she told a reporter, that what she had taken for so long as "only friendship" had deepened into love.[18] There was clearly no need for Amelia to exact payment of her "cruel promise" of a year earlier. That she had found happiness with George was obvious from a poem she wrote for him:

> *To touch your hand or see your face today*
> *Is joy. Your casual presence in a room*
> *Recalls the stars that watched us as we lay.*
>
> *I mark you in the moving crowd*
> *And see again those stars*
> *A warm night lent us long ago,*
> *We loved so then—we love so now.*[19]

Probably there could have been no better match for Amelia Earhart than George Putnam. She was, he fully recognized, "a loner" by nature[20] but her desire to live her own life fitted in well with his own lifestyle. Both were busy with their own careers, and so there was no question of dependence, but, rather, a pooling of resources. If George understood Amelia's needs, then she understood his, too, was tolerant of his aggressive, sometimes overbearing methods, and found no difficulty in handling his brilliance, or his often-bewildering mood changes.

Once, he presented to her a marketing venture to sell children's hats bearing her name. George could see only the fact that at a cost of fifty cents and a selling price of three dollars, it was a profitable project. Amelia examined the hats and pronounced them cheap, firmly telling him she would not allow them to go on sale because she would have nothing to do with cheating children. One can only imagine George's frustrated reaction to Amelia's veto, but the contract was canceled, nonetheless. There was a pronounced stubborn streak in Amelia and George must have realized immediately that on this occasion she was not going to change her mind.

During the winter months, Amelia worked on a new book, which she later called *The Fun of It*, [21] but in the back of her mind a plan was crystallizing. George stated that, one morning, she asked him over breakfast, "Would you *mind* if I flew the Atlantic?"[22]

He knew that what she had in mind was a solo flight. "I must have known for four years really that she wanted to. We talked of it from time to time, but always casually." And he wrote of experiencing "the fusion of a clutch at the heart, and something akin to elation, in the presence of so adventurous a spirit; but one could not *mind* her flying the Atlantic in the sense of putting out a proprietary hand to hold her back. . . ."[23]

There were several good reasons for Amelia's wish to make that flight, but first and foremost was a personal need to prove something to herself and to those critics who had jeered that she had been merely a passenger on the 1928 flight. Probably her own severest critic, she was well aware that her career had been built on a flight in which she played no active role and it hurt to have this pointed out. In the intervening time, she had learned her craft, become an experienced and competent pilot, and in a sense had "earned" her place in the newspapers, yet she wanted and needed to prove that she *was* the best woman pilot. Thanks to George's skill in the field of publicity, she was already firmly established as the *best-known* woman pilot.

There were other considerations. Several other woman had preparations under way to make the flight, and from the publicity angle, George must have seen clearly that if another woman were to be first across the Atlantic, it would not help Amelia's career. The most serious contestant was Elinor Smith, who still made headlines despite George's efforts to subdue the girl whom newspapers had now nicknamed the "Flying Flapper." To George's chagrin, Elinor had walked off with the annual award for "Best Woman Pilot"[24] in 1930, despite his best efforts to undermine her to gain advantage for Amelia.

Elinor had acquired a Lockheed Vega similar to Amelia's with which to make the flight when the spring weather declared the transoceanic-flight season open. Indeed, she had intended to make the attempt during the previous summer but an accident in August at Garden City had wrecked the "high speed [presumably retractable] landing gear" and by the time repairs had been made, including a conventional undercarriage, the weather slot had gone and the Atlantic "season" was over for another year.

Amelia felt she had the necessary experience to make the solo attempt on the Atlantic and she badly wanted to take that record. She also had the ideal plane, the Vega, which—since its rebuild the previous fall—had been chartered to the Ludington Line, flying on a scheduled service between Philadelphia and Washington. There was one more factor: like George, Amelia relished the idea of adventure. There could be no question this time of her not realizing how much water she had to cross, or of the fears of a transoceanic flier. She knew to a degree how accurate her navigation would have to be and how much reliance she would be placing on her plane and instruments, not to mention her own ability and endurance.

Bernt Balchen was invited to Sunday lunch at Rye and over a game of croquet in the weak early April sunshine Amelia told him of her plan. "Am I ready to do it?" she asked him when she had finished. "Is the ship ready? Will you help me?" After a brief moment of thought, Balchen replied, "Yes, you can do it. The ship, when we are through with it, will be OK. And . . . I'll help."[25] As before, only a very few were let in on the plan: her cousin Lucy ("Toots") Challiss, who was visiting at Rye; and Eddie Gorski, her mechanic. Amelia wanted to reserve the option to pull out at any time and therefore did not want the pressures of reporters, family, friends, or even commercial interests. Nor did she wish to take the risk of precipitating a competitor into sudden flight.

As a cover story, the press were informed that the Vega had been leased to Balchen. He was in the early stages of preparing for an already-publicized polar flight and the plane was shipped to the old Fokker plant at Teterboro, New Jersey. There, under Balchen's instruction, Gorski went to work. It was first necessary to strengthen the fuselage to take the additional fuel tanks in the wings and cabin, which would enable the Lockheed to carry 420 gallons of fuel and thus give her a range of over 3,200 miles. A new engine was also fitted; the old Wasp, which had done sterling work over the past three years, was removed and a new super-charged Wasp engine that developed 500 hp was installed. The airplane in its smart red and gold livery was not given a name. Although it had become customary to name airplanes on record-breaking attempts, George was opposed to anything that might have detracted from the publicity and credit that would accrue to the name of Amelia Earhart. The airplane would not, therefore, be allowed to become a "personality"; it was merely a vehicle for Amelia.[26]

The proposed flight date was set by George, with his keen sense for a story, and it was hoped that Amelia would leave exactly five years to the day that Lindbergh had made his flight—on May 20–21, 1927. Amelia went along with this, recognizing the news value of the coincidence but ready at any time to abandon the project if Balchen concluded that she should not make the flight for any reason, or if she herself wished to cancel.[27]

In early 1932, no other person had successfully flown the Atlantic *alone* since Lindbergh, and though there had been some twenty flights by crewed airplanes (including the *Friendship* flight), what Amelia was planning was in itself a major venture.[28] Knowing that she would be castigated by certain elements of the media, she made it clear in her earliest statements that she was not trying to prove anything and was well aware that the flight would not contribute anything to the science of aviation. "It was clear in my mind that I was undertaking the flight merely for the fun of it. It was in a measure, a self-justification—a proving to me, and to anyone else interested, that a woman with adequate experience could do it."[29]

That it was *necessary* to prove that a women could succeed becomes evident from the attitude of Mary Heath, once a friend and now, because of George's behavior, openly hostile toward Amelia. In an article in *Liberty* magazine entitled "Why I Believe Women Pilots Can't Fly the Atlantic—an outspoken warning by Lady Heath," this world-famous, experienced pilot confidently stated that it could not be done. "It is plain suicide for any woman today," she claimed, and she had previously delivered her opinion in several lectures. Though almost certainly unaware of Amelia's imminent intention, Lady Heath was a close friend and confidante of Elinor Smith, who had made no secret of her proposed transatlantic attempt. Coincidentally, the article hit the newsstands on the day Amelia took off, enabling a classic, though completely unintentional, piece of nose-thumbing from Amelia. In sending the article to *Liberty*, Lady Heath's accompanying note had read, ". . . do make an appeal if you can for women not to fly the Atlantic, even if you can't use my scribble. It is madness for them to attempt it and at least the first dozen will be drowned. . . ."[30]

It was decided early on that Amelia would not set out to duplicate Lindbergh's route, for Balchen doubted her ability to endure such a long flight. It was agreed that she would aim for Paris as a provisional destination, with the British Isles as the prime objective, but her departure point would be Harbour Grace, Newfoundland (Lindbergh had flown from New York), and to enable her to start in as fresh a physical condition as possible, Balchen would pilot the plane to Newfoundland. If, after her first landfall, she felt able to continue to Paris, well and good; otherwise, she was to set down anywhere.

That spring Amelia carried on with her usual round of speaking engagements. Most were fee-earners, but some were performed in a spirit of social concern, such as an address to the inmates of the Welfare Island workhouse, after which she was stopped for speeding and received a suspended sentence. From April, she worked almost exclusively on the preparations for the flight, equipping the plane with additional instruments, though in retrospect they seem basic enough: a drift indicator, and both aperiodic and gyroscopic compasses to supplement the magnetic one already fitted. With expert help, she worked out the fuel system and how to best use it so that weight would be evenly distributed as each tank emptied. In this, she was assisted by Major Edwin Aldrin.[31]

Instruction in blind flying techniques was vital and once the Lockheed was ready, Amelia practiced instrument flying whenever possible, "until I felt really confident of my ability to handle the ship, without looking outside of the cockpit—that is, flying it solely with instruments."[32] Through the middle weeks of May, George and Amelia studied the Atlantic weather-pattern charts with increasing interest. Once again, George had recruited the personal assistance of Doc Kimball at the New York U.S. Weather Bureau to provide detailed information of a "weather slot" or window in which Amelia could safely get across. Doc Kimball, having seen seven women perish in attempts to fly the Atlantic, cooperated reluctantly, declaring, "When weather is at all possible we *may* tell a good man that he might make it.[33] To all women we say NO. Unless conditions are extraordinarily good. And that is very seldom."[34]

Amelia's letters to her mother were full of domestic trivia; her secretary was on vacation and it was difficult coping with her heavy correspondence; the garden was just coming into spring flower; she advised her mother to make use of the "scrub woming" hired to help out at Muriel's home; she sent a book for Sam Chapman—"Will you forward it to him?"[35] There is no hint of the important event that was now occupying virtually her every waking thought.

On May 18, the outlook weather pattern made the projected departure date (May 20) look doubtful. A persistent trough of low pressure stationed over the eastern Atlantic threatened to dispense its rain and low cloud for a week or more. There was no improvement on May 19 nor on the morning of May 20. George went to Doc Kimball's Weather Bureau office at the top of the Whitehall building in lower New York City, while Amelia, who had virtually abandoned the idea of a departure for some days, decided to drive over to the airfield. When she arrived at Teterboro Airport, Eddie Gorski told her that George was on the telephone. He and Kimball had just gone over the morning weather reports coming in from Atlantic shipping and key weather stations; not only was there clear weather over the Atlantic but also there was good visibility all the way to Newfoundland—"St. John's, anyway," he told her, adding, "And by to-

morrow the Atlantic looks as good as you're likely to get it for some time."
This slot would not last, however.[36]

Amelia had a hurried conference with Balchen and decided immediately that she could be ready to leave at three o'clock. She drove home to change into flying clothes (riding jodhpurs, silk shirt and scarf, sweater, and loose jacket), pack her leather flying suit, maps, and a few odds and ends such as the elephant-toe bracelet that George had brought back from Liberia in 1929, and which it is said she regarded as a good-luck charm (though she is on record as saying she didn't believe in luck: "The best mascot is a good mechanic!").[37]

> Five minutes was enough to pick up my things. Plus a lingering few more to drink in the beauty of a treasured sight. Beside and below our bedroom windows were dogwood trees, their blossoms in luxuriant full flower, unbelievable bouquets of white and pink flecked with the sunshine of spring.[38]

This was possibly the worst moment. Seeing the safe, calm old house with its peaceful garden full of sunshine and spring flowers, Amelia must have wondered why she was risking her life when she could, without loss of face, remain safely at home. "The actual doing of a dangerous thing, it seems to me, may require little courage. The preparation for it—the acceptance of the inevitable risks involved—may be a far greater test of morale," she once had said.[39]

Amelia allowed only moments for these fleeting thoughts before racing back to the airfield, reaching there at 2:55; by 3:15, the Lockheed was in the air with Balchen at the controls and Amelia and Eddie Gorski resting in the cabin behind the auxiliary fuel tank.

They flew via St. John's and when they arrived at Harbour Grace, they found that weather reports were promising, though far from perfect. Knowing that George would have, by prearranged plan, now told Amy and Muriel about her flight, and remembering the contretemps of the previous flight, Amelia wired an instruction to George: TELEPHONE MY SISTER DIRECTIONS FOR PRESS INTERVIEWS. She also requested advice regarding her own media contact: IS RADIO BROADCASTING LOCAL STATIONS OK?[40] George replied that she should avoid all broadcasting; he needed maximum impact to command the greatest fee from syndicating the scoop of the flight through *The New York Times*. Almost hourly reports on Atlantic weather conditions were cabled to Harbour Grace, as well as encouraging forecasts from London.

Even the most detailed of these, however, seems little enough information with which to set off on such a hazardous journey in view of the number of times the words *perhaps* and *probable* occur in the text: To Amelia Earhart, Harbour Grace, NF May 20:

NOON EST LOOKS SATISFACTORY. ONLY PROBABLE DIFFICULTY THOUGHT POSSIBLE EXTENDING FROM EASTERN ATLANTIC LOW SOUTH WESTWARD TO LATITUDE FORTY LONGITUDE FORTY-SEVEN PROBABLY CONSIDERABLE CLOUDINESS. FORECAST HARBOUR GRACE LONGITUDE THIRTY-FIVE WILL BE FORWARD SOON. EASTERN SITUATION APPARENTLY CLEARING UP SATISFACTORILY. FOLLOWING JUST RECEIVED FROM LONDON OUTLOOK TOMORROW EASTERN ATLANTIC FRESH NORTHWESTERN OR WESTERLY WINDS. SKY HALF TO HEAVY COVERED. CLOUDS FIFTEEN HUNDRED FEET SHOWERS VISIBILITY GOOD. BRITISH ISLES WIND SOUTH OR SOUTHWEST TWENTY TO THIRTY MILES AT TWO THOUSAND FEET BUT VARIABLE IN EASTERN DISTRICT. VARIABLE CLOUDS PERHAPS THUNDER AND RAIN. LOCAL FOG IRISH SEA ENGLISH CHANNEL. WESTERN EUROPE WIND SOUTHWEST OR WEST MODERATE TO FRESH VARIABLE CLOUDS PERHAPS THUNDER SHOWERS. GP 2:50 PM[41]

In the early afternoon, while Balchen and Gorski completed the final mechanical check, Amelia went off to have a nap, and it says a lot for her self-confidence that she was able to sleep. Just after 6:30 P.M. (local time), she was awakened and returned to the field. Balchen recalled her quiet and unobtrusive demeanor in his diary:

She listens calmly, only biting her lip a little, as I go over with her the course to hold, and tell her what weather she can expect on the way across the ocean. She looks at me with a small lonely smile and says, "Do you think I can make it?" and I grin back: "You bet." She crawls calmly into the cockpit of the big empty airplane, starts the engine, runs it up, checks the mags, and nods her head. We pull the chocks, and she is off. . . ."[42]

Amelia remembered only Balchen's parting words: "Okay. So long. Good luck."[43]

Despite the load, the Lockheed rose easily and Amelia headed out over the open water in fair weather into a "lingering sunset."[44] As planned, it was exactly five years to the day that Lindbergh had set off on his historic flight across the Atlantic. A cable was sent to George: AE TOOK OFF 712 NFLD PERFECT PERFORMANCE. . . ."[45] For George, it was to be a long and anxious wait.

For a few hours, the flight was uneventful but then, as she cruised along in the moonlight at twelve thousand feet, Amelia's altimeter failed. In all her experience of flying, she had never had this happen before and George later wrote that her reaction was one of awe rather than horror. From this point on, she had no indication of her true height, a vital factor in instrument flying; however, she carried a barograph, which would at least give her an indication of her climb and descent.[46]

Shortly afterward, a severe storm with lightning buffeted the Lockheed for about an hour and Amelia later thought that she had probably wandered off course during this interlude. About four hours into the flight, the exhaust manifold seam parted due to a bad weld. Noting the vibration, Amelia must have stood up and peered over the instrument panel through the gap under the rim of the cowling; there she could see the glow of flames and she immediately guessed what had happened.

Amelia would have remembered a similar fiery glow from the *Friendship*'s exhaust on her previous ocean flight, and would not have been concerned per se by the flames, which she knew were caused by the burning of fuel and air under pressure and present in all vehicles (even in modern cars, but not seen because of the long exhaust pipe), but particularly visible on aircraft with short or stubby exhausts and at night. She was then "sorry she had looked at the break at all because the flames appeared so much worse than they did in the daytime."[47] She must have been concerned about the damage causing further problems, however, and indeed as the night wore on, the manifold began to vibrate with increasing intensity. Later, she admitted to being tempted, at this point, to return. After some thought, however, she decided that she was four hours out, requiring a four-hour return trip and necessitating a night landing in Newfoundland with a big fuel load. On reflection, she decided that eight hours of flying time would put her more than halfway across the ocean and she elected to fly on.[48]

After a while, Amelia flew into clouds and decided to get over the top of them. She climbed for half an hour and then noticed that the plane was feeling sluggish; a film of slush on the windscreen had just alerted her to the fact that she had picked up ice when suddenly, without further warning, the Lockheed went into a spin.

> How long we spun I do not know. I do know that I did my best to do exactly what one should do with a spinning plane and regained flying control as the warmth of the lower altitude melted the ice. As we righted and held level again, through the blackness below I could see the whitecaps, too close for comfort.[49]

She wrote that a glance at her barograph showed that she had lost three thousand feet in the spin, and now, still with no idea of her exact height, she flew under the clouds until she ran into fog and decided that it was too dangerous to fly so low without visual checks. She climbed again, trying to find the medium between the fog and the ice and flew for some hours purely on instruments until dawn came. Flying eastward against the sun's passage, she found the night was fortunately short, but even so, that first glow of daylight must have been a welcome sight. The various incidents and problems had helped her to stay awake but she carried with her a small bottle of smelling salts to help maintain concentration. Later, she confessed to almost "losing her nerve over the ice," but remembering that Lindbergh had experienced a similar problem had given her courage.

As the sun rose, Amelia found it more comfortable to fly just inside the top of the clouds at about ten thousand feet, for the sun's brilliant reflection dazzled her if she flew on top; but as the morning wore on, she decided to fly under the layers, even though "they were very near the water."[50] About two hours from her estimated first landfall (Valencia Island in County Kerry, southwestern Ireland), she turned on her reserve tank only to find that the cabin fuel gauge was leaking and that there was a steady drip of fuel into the cockpit and onto her left shoulder.

Prior to this, the metal of the exhaust manifold, burned for many hours by flames fueled by hot gases, had split even further and the vibration had increased, causing Amelia extreme concern for the past hour or more. She now became worried that the fumes of leaking fuel would reach the exhaust system and be exploded by the flames that she knew were there, although they were not visible in the daylight. At this point, she decided to put down at the first sight of land, wherever that might be.

Considering Bernt Balchen's expertise, that he was a very thorough and cautious man and that he had given the plane a painstaking preflight check, it is surprising that so many things had gone wrong in such a short time.

Doc Kimball had warned that there was a belt of rain south of Amelia's course, so when she ran into storm clouds in late morning, she thought she was too far south and turned northeast, hoping to reach the southern tip of Ireland. Later, she claimed that she probably had been more or less on course, for when land came into sight, she found she had "hit Ireland about the middle," but, in fact, her first landfall was Teelin Head, County Donegal, in the northwest corner of Ireland. She was some two hundred miles north of her stated track, which should have taken her across Dingle Bay in the southwest corner; indeed, had she been another fifty miles north, she would have missed Ireland altogether and flown on to Scotland.

Probably more exciting than actually sighting land was seeing a small
fishing vessel about 100 miles off the coast. I was going by, as I
wanted to reach land, but then decided to circle, that all might know
I had got so far, anyway. I circled and received an answering signal.
A whistle and some kind of bomb was sent off. Of course I could not
hear them, but I could see the smoke and the steam from the whistle.
It was the first human contact since Newfoundland.[51]

Even when she sighted land, Amelia had no way of pinpointing her
position, and with no altimeter, she was reluctant to fly on indefinitely
with no information about the height of any mountains she might encoun-
ter in the glowering thundery clouds that were all around her. When
flying around the United States, she had often used railroads to aid
navigation, and now, fortunately, she spotted a railway track. A railroad
must, she reasoned, lead to a major town where there would be an airfield.
She had yet to learn that Britain and Ireland were (and still are!) poorly
served in the matter of landing fields and was surprised when the town
she flew over had no airfield. Deciding that she would land anyway, she
selected a large pasture and, after several low reconnaissance passes,
landed in the long sloping meadow, hoping to avoid the grazing cows. A
lone, astonished farm laborer saw her land.

Amelia cut the switches, climbed out of the plane, and, as the man
approached the plane, called out, "Where am I?"

Danny McCallion replied obligingly and with excruciating accuracy.
"In Gallegher's pasture."

Chapter Sixteen

1932 - 1933

Although she had allowed for a flight of 3,200 miles, Amelia actually flew 2,026 miles in fourteen hours and fifty-four minutes, landing at Culmore near Londonderry in Northern Ireland at 1:45 P.M. (British Summer Time) on Saturday, May 21, 1932.[1] Having used only 350 of the 420 gallons of fuel carried by the Vega, she had enough left to fly for a further three hours or so. She considered the possibility of flying on to Croydon, near London, having established her position, but the condition of her airplane and her own physical fatigue convinced her to end the flight in Londonderry.

McCallion was not sure whether Amelia was man or woman when she emerged from the Vega, her boyish figure dressed in jodhpurs and shirt, her short hair untidy and uncombed.

"Have you come far?" he asked her. "From America," she replied. "I was all stunned and didn't know what to say," he recalled later.

Having only sipped at a small can of tomato juice during the entire flight, Amelia asked where she could get a drink of water, and McCallion led her to a nearby peat-roofed cottage, where she drank several cups of tea while he ran for William Gallegher, who owned the farm.[2] After investigating the truth of the unlikely tale carried by his normally sane cowman, Gallegher located a car, which took Amelia to Londonderry, some five miles away. Meanwhile, the local police were alerted and it seems that it was they who notified the *Londonderry Sentinel*, the first newspaper to receive the news. As teleprinters across the world chattered out details of her arrival, a reporter on the *New York Sunday Mail* reached immediately for the telephone and called George. He was lucky enough to break the news before anyone else. The scribbled notes made by

George's secretary survive in the National Air and Space Museum library at the Smithsonian Institution in Washington, D.C.

> Landed in pasture
> Londondery Island [*sic*]
> 5 miles from London [*sic*]
> Plane OK
> 8:35 <u>Ireland</u>
> London

These notes indicate that the reporter's geographical knowledge was poor; however, the telephone call ended a period of great anxiety for George, who, interviewed during the flight, had remarked tensely, "I guess I'm doing as well as can be expected!" "He was wild like a bear," his son David recalled, remembering his father's endless pacing.[3] Now George was elated: ". . . tell her to telephone me wherever she is, all I want is to hear her voice and tell her she is the greatest woman in the world. . . . I knew that if any woman could do this great feat she was the one; but I have been in deadly fear of the terrors of the Atlantic all night. For Heaven's sake tell her to telephone me at once. I shall not leave the phone. . . ."[4]

George's nervousness had reached a crescendo when a telephone call from the Press Association advised that Amelia had crashed near Le Bourget. It was a mistake; a plane *had* crashed but it was "twelve interminable minutes," George recalled, before he was told it was a false alarm and that, in fact, there was still no news of Amelia.[5]

For Amelia, though her physical weariness was obvious from telltale dark smudges under her eyes, it must have been a moment of great personal satisfaction. For now *she* had flown the Atlantic—on her own—and in doing so had broken several records:

- She had become the first woman (and only the second person) to fly the Atlantic solo.
- She had become the only person to fly it twice.
- She established a record for crossing it in the shortest time in any direction (previously held by Alcock and Brown in a time of sixteen hours and twelve minutes).
- She established a record (2,026 miles) for the longest nonstop distance flown by a woman (previously held by Ruth Nichols with a distance of 1,977.6 miles).

On arrival in Londonderry, Amelia went straight to a post office, where she sent cables before telephoning a London number where authorized newsmen were standing by for her firsthand report of the flight. Only when she had performed this prearranged duty did she book a transatlantic call to George. Even as she waited, congratulatory cables and calls started to flood in, but she would have been prepared for this, of course.

When her call to George came through, Amelia was able to tell him a little about her flight: She had chosen for the last hours to fly low over the ocean, she said, because "I'd rather drown than burn. . . . "[6] After giving George an outline of the flight for *The New York Times*, she was able to wash and eat before returning to Culmore with two mechanics. She had earlier accepted an invitation to stay the night at the home of a Mrs. McClure, chatelaine of a large house (Brook Hall) near Gallegher's farm, no doubt reflecting that she stood a better chance of a peaceful night's rest there than in a Londonderry hotel.

Next morning, having received the mechanic's report, Amelia decided not to fly the plane to Croydon but to have it dismantled and shipped over. She had received several offers to fly her to England—from such diverse quarters as the formidable Lady Bailey, and James and Amy (Johnson) Mollison. On George's advice, however, she was not prepared to share her limelight. Lady Bailey, in fact, flew to Londonderry to greet Amelia but arrived shortly after Amelia had left in a plane chartered from National Flying Services by Paramount newsmen (Movietone in England) who had bought exclusive rights to filmed interviews.[7]

First, though, there was breakfast, followed by photo calls and interviews. Amelia was patient and chatty. She had taken off with literally what she was wearing; she would have to borrow some money and clothes, for all she had with her was twenty dollars; she had no intentions of flying back to New York. Certainly more adept with reporters than after her previous flight, Amelia talked about the flight in general terms, throwing in a few colorful terms such as "Atlantic rollers." She showed them some of the more impressive telegrams from the President of the United States, the Prime Minister, Lord Londonderry, Andrew Mellon, Charles and Anne Lindbergh, and Governor and Mrs. Roosevelt.[8] She kept to herself one that read, WE KNEW YOU COULD DO IT AND NOW YOU HAVE STOP CHEERS CONGRATULATIONS MUCH LOVE MOTHER AND MURIEL.[9] Although she had accepted the invitation of the American ambassador to stay at the embassy in London, she was delighted to receive a cable from Lady Astor duplicating the invitation and offering to lend her a nightgown.

Amelia was persuaded to don her leather flying suit, start up the airplane, and taxi it around the meadow for newsreel cameras; then, as she stopped the engine and emerged from the Lockheed, the small crowd that had gathered there cheered and threw hats in the air. These pictures were circulated to cinemas within days, purporting to be live film of her landing after the flight—a harmless subterfuge aimed at an unsophisticated cinema-going audience.

In the early afternoon of May 22, Amelia left Gallegher's and departed for London in a Desoutter airplane that weighed less than the Vega's fuel load. Her arrival in London was to enthusiastic crowds and her short speech was heralded by a deafening clap of thunder and heavy rain, which made her laugh. This unaffected behavior endeared her to the crowd, especially as she showed no hurry to leave but stayed talking for a while, her short hairstyle undamaged by the weather. What Amelia did not see was physical fighting between Pathé and Paramount newsreelmen who were vying for the best filming position. Two of Pathé's men ended up with broken ribs in the scuffle! Amelia had already been distressed to learn that a plane carrying two reporters returning to London from Culmore had crashed, killing both occupants.

Amelia's days in London were filled with dinners and public appearances, initially attended wearing borrowed clothes until she was able to buy some of her own; "I lived mostly on credit," she said afterward. George roared with laughter when told his wife was short of money. "It won't be the first time she's landed in London broke!" he quipped. Amelia had spoken to him several times and in a conversation on May 24, she asked him to join her for the remainder of her visit. In a letter to her mother, Amelia said she hadn't been able to face the thought of going home alone.[10] George made plans to sail on the twenty-sixth, on the S.S. *Olympic* and meanwhile, though he was busy with plans for her New York reception, he took time to write to Amy:

> *Dear Mrs. Earhart:*
>
> Thanks for the note. Of course I will take over the letters to Amelia. I am sure your cable addressed to her, London, has reached her.
>
> . . . I am glad I am going over. We are coming back on a slow boat deliberately planned so A.E. can get a good rest, and naturally I will be able to shield her from much buffeting.
>
> Will you let me know, please, if you and Mrs. Morrissey, or either of you, care to come to New York to be here when Amelia arrives? Our friend Capt. Railey is caring for all these things while I am away. Just write me here and my secretary will see that Capt. Railey gets your word. Accommodations will be arranged for you at the Hotel

Biltmore, where we will stay, if you care to come. It will, I imagine, be a pretty hectic time. Likely we will be going to Washington that midnight.

Of course we would love to have you. On the other hand, possibly you would prefer to keep out of the circus and come to us a little later at Rye for a quiet visit.

Sincerely,
GPP[11]

In all her interviews, Amelia made it clear that she had made the flight for purely personal reasons. She doubted that she would ever do it again. "For one thing," she said in a speech to the Institute of Journalists, "it would take more than four years to convince my husband. . . . " She claimed no advances for aviation as a result of her flight, though she did state firmly that she believed it would be only a short time before a commercial air service, probably in flying boats, would be crossing the Atlantic regularly.

Watching film of her arrivals in 1928 and 1932, one is immediately struck by the change in Amelia's attitude toward reporters. In 1928, though she answered questions readily, she was diffident and shy. In 1932, she "hosted" the interviews, tossing in amusing remarks and playing with the reporters in a friendly manner. It is she who wound up the sessions with a confident "Are there any other questions?" In a radio interview at the BBC, she was not afraid to throw in words of her own invention. When the Lockheed picked up ice, she said, "it felt bloggy." And she broadcast a message to the American people after being told that she was to be awarded the Distinguished Flying Cross by Congress.

In what little time she could spare from the arduous round of public appearances, Amelia wrote a final chapter for her book *The Fun of It*, describing her flight in a brief, practical way. This was cabled to her publishers, Harcourt, Brace, in New York—"a postscript," she said, "from overseas." Predictably, she was pictured daily with famous statesmen and socialites, celebrities from stage and aviation. Jim Mollison and Amy Johnson made regular contact—it would not be long before Mollison would make his own spectacular east-to-west flight across the ocean, the *hard* way, which experts said was virtually impossible due to constant adverse winds. She not only met the Prince of Wales (later Edward VIII and subsequently Duke of Windsor) when he formally received her at Buckingham Palace on May 25, but also danced with him three times a few days later at a charity ball. Amelia was a good dancer and made no secret of her enjoyment of the pastime. The two were reported as chatting happily together, and later Amelia told reporters, "Like all flyers he dances well," and "I hope the prince was amused." She was distressed at newspaper reports of the incident when she was reported as drawling "Waal . . . " at him.[12]

The Lockheed Vega, which had meanwhile arrived in London, was reassembled and put on display at Selfridges. The busy round of personal appearances continued until, on June 3, Amelia left England for Cherbourg, France, on C. R. Fairey's yacht *Evadne*. There she met George for a private reunion before they entrained for Paris. It had been fifteen days, he recalled, since he'd taken leave of her:

> Fairey met me at the landing ladder of his yacht. "Hello," he said. "She's in there."
>
> AE was standing in the doorway. "Hi!" she said casually.
>
> It had a fine sound, that characteristic greeting. It took account of nothing—the strain and exactions of the flight, the chances that it would fail in mid-ocean—and it took account of everything. She was there, and there was nothing to be excited about. . . .[13]

Later, over breakfast with the others on the *Evadne*, Amelia teased George with gentle humor. "Generous allowance for a trip to Europe," she said with a grin, referring to the twenty dollars he had handed her at Teterboro, and later she reflected how shocking it was that she'd "had to fly the Atlantic in order to get a new wardrobe."[14]

In Paris, entranced by the city she had wanted to visit since earliest childhood, Amelia carried on the arduous tasks of a celebrity, but in the photographs of her, there is a new luminosity in her face. There can be no question that George's presence meant a great deal to her and he was a constant shadow. He was no stranger to Paris and his support gave Amelia a confident warmth in her handling of duties that might otherwise have received merely her practical, good-natured touch. Sometimes they appeared hand in hand—unusual, for both of them were intensely jealous of their personal lives and such public demonstrations of their relationship were very few.

Informally, the couple were lavishly entertained by the international set based in Paris for the early summer—the outrageous Lady Mendl (Elsie de Wolfe) and Elsa Maxwell, for example, and a couple whose contact were later to prove so valuable: Jacques and Violette de Sibour.[15]

Formally, Amelia was presented with the Cross of Knight of the Legion of Honor, laid a wreath at the tomb of the Unknown Soldier, attended the Air Races, and always, always, the couple were surrounded by happy crowds wanting to see and touch Amelia. Everywhere they went, she was showered with bouquets of flowers and their rooms were banked with them. This caused a problem for George, who suffered from hay fever and "when introduced to an interested public was seen to be red-eyed and weeping."[16] Amelia was modest and took a practical line about her achievements; when her courage was praised, she replied, "If it took courage I wouldn't have done it. . . . I undertook the flight for my own pleasure and in a sense to justify myself."[17]

This line was clearly meant to deflect criticisms of the flight, which in some cases came from influential quarters: "Amelia has given us a magnificent display of useless courage," began M. E. Tracey in the New York *World Telegram*. Equally typical is this acerbic contribution from C. G. Grey, editor of *The Aeroplane:*

> On Saturday, May 21st, Mrs. G. P. Putnam, known professionally, or for purposes of publicity, as Miss Amelia Earhart, landed at Londonderry, in or near the Irish Free State, from Harbour Grace, Newfoundland. This proves that in 1932 with a modern aeroplane, a modern engine, and the latest navigational instruments, a woman is capable of doing what a mere man did in 1919, but in three hours less than the man's time.
>
> We cannot think why she did it, except of course for her own gratification. It does nothing for the good of aviation. And . . . we all know that a good woman pilot is as good as an equally good man. And we all know that quite a number of men who are not by any means good pilots have got across the Atlantic whereas others who were remarkably good pilots have fallen in.
>
> . . . Any further information on the subject of this flight may be gained from the daily press, and the cheaper the paper the more information the reader will get for his or her money.[18]

In a letter to the president of the NAA (Amelia was vice-president), one apparent misogynist wrote: "Only an average flyer, she has pushed herself to the front by following the tactics of the feminists. . . . Using a man-made perfect machine, tuned by men mechanics, trained by men flyers, [and a] course laid out by a man, by a lucky break she just managed to make the hop. . . ."[19] It is difficult to know why Amelia attracted this sort of criticism (and there was more in the same vein even from other leading American newspapers), for though the flight in itself offered no particular breakthrough, the mere fact that there were pilots prepared to risk all to gain records encouraged manufacturers to further technological effort. In a sense, this was Amelia's—and all the other record-breaking fliers'—contribution to aviation.

In the public eye, too, the flight was a triumphant success at a time when newspapers carried daily reports of fatal air crashes. So her success encouraged confidence in aviation as a principle. Strange this need to criticize the ability that is given to so few to reach out further than one's fellows; however, Grey's comments regarding "cheap" newspaper reporting were accurate. Colorful accounts of Amelia landing with hardly a drop of fuel, within six feet of a hedge that would have wrecked her plane, killing cows as she landed, and various imaginary incidents that were supposed to have occurred during the flight are a trap for unwary researchers. Fortunately, in the many speeches she was to make over the next months, Amelia took the opportunity to mock these spurious accounts: ". . . and no cow died, unless it was from fright!"

After Paris, Amelia and George traveled to Rome, where they were granted an audience with the Pope and later met Mussolini, who had sent a massive bouquet of red roses to her on her arrival in the Eternal City. But the main purpose of the trip was to attend the Congress of Trans-Oceanic Airmen organized by General Balboa, the Italian Minister for Air. George was particularly amused that apart from Amelia, the only person to have flown the ocean twice, the convention members were exclusively male and "well weighed down by medals." There was no medal for Amelia—although she was to receive one later. "It really was a troublesome situation. As far as Italy was concerned AE's sex was simply wrong. . . ."[20]

Within days, the Putnams were in Brussels for a private meal with the king and queen of Belgium, where Amelia was presented with the decoration of Chevalier of the Order of Leopold.[21] George, in morning suit, had had to borrow a top hat. Unfortunately, it was several sizes too small and he carried it around uncomfortably, hoping no occasion would arise when he might have to put it on his head. At a dinner party in Amelia's honor, the couple met André Picard, the internationally renowned balloonist; George spent the evening unsuccessfully trying to persuade him to write a book.

It must have been a great relief to Amelia when on June 15, nearly a month after she had taken off from Teterboro, New Jersey, she boarded the liner *Ile de France* to sail for New York. She looked surprisingly relaxed as she acknowledged the cheers of those on the quayside, and was delighted when three light airplanes appeared over the ship to bomb her with flowers.

A few days of rest on the ship were followed by the cacophony of New York at its most exuberant. Amelia was given a tickertape parade and mayoral address; welcoming crowds of thousands cheered the motorcade of dozens of cars containing civic dignitaries and aviation notables. Some of them were rivals in the field of aviation. When Elinor Smith, for example, warmly congratulated her, Amelia was quiet for a moment, recognizing the magnitude of the young flier's disappointment that she had not been the first woman to make the flight. Then she said, "Thanks, Elinor. It means a great deal to have you say that."[22]

Amy and Muriel did not come to New York, perhaps because of George's eve-of-sailing letter, and on the following day, George flew with Amelia to Washington, where she was to receive from the President of the United States the Special Gold Medal struck by the National Geographic Society.

The Society had, from time to time, honored a select band of geographical pioneers, but Amelia was the first woman to be so chosen. There were the usual rounds of lunches and dinners, including dinner at the White House, "a solemn occasion," George recorded. On the day of her arrival, the Senate approved the proposal to award Amelia the Distinguished Flying Cross.[23] Newsreel film shows that throughout it all, Amelia's slim and feminine presence seems calm, slightly amused. Almost always dressed in brown, according to newspaper reports, she is often the only woman without a hat, her fair, curly hair lifted by summer breezes.

After Washington, there were other cities, other parades, other welcomes. There were thousands of letters and cables each day. George was Amelia's constant support, not always able to be at her side but shadowing, occasionally taking her arm to steer her through a crowd, watchful, listening. This was his *business*, after all. Sometimes a reporter looking for a different "angle" interviewed George. His forthright views on feminine equality must have made good copy. Stating that it did his ego good to have his wife do something better than he, he finished:

> There is no question of my ever approaching Amelia's skill as a pilot
> . . . but I have licked her at plenty of things. If she were a gloating
> feminist, always harping on about her career and her success and
> never letting me get an oar into the conversation, I should probably
> have to sock her.[24]

George then disposed of the idea that "a woman's place is in the home" with the scornful rejoinder that it was a "lot of bunk. AE does seem to me a particularly good sport who gets all the fun there is out of what goes on, whether it be flying or gardening or fan mail."[25] This statement of George's seems to embody Amelia's entire approach to life: to put her entire concentration into whatever she was doing at the moment—work or play—and to *enjoy* it.

Amelia's book *The Fun of It,* [26] with Amelia's postscript that told the story of the Atlantic flight, was published to coincide with her return. Each copy of the first edition contained a small phonograph record of the speech she had made over the transatlantic radio link. This was George at his brilliant best, as a publicist par excellence.

When first contemplated, the book was to be written primarily to promote flying and in particular to encourage women to take up flying. As such, it might have sold in reasonable quantities to anyone interested in aviation, or to women college students and graduates, but that final chapter ensured its place on the best-seller lists.

Honors of all kinds continued to be heaped upon Amelia and the keys to various cities were bestowed at civic receptions; but perhaps the most valued award was honorary membership in the National Aeronautic Association. Fourteen men had previously received this distinction. "I appreciate the honor very much," Amelia wrote to Hiram Bingham, president of the NAA. "Indeed I do not think my exploit deserves it."[27] Her diary for the remainder of 1932 was so full that when, in late June, Bingham asked for a convenient date on which he might arrange a dinner honoring Orville Wright, Amelia was hard pushed to come up with a free evening until December: "I will endeavor to let you know six weeks in advance exactly what dates are open."[28]

George's career also took a new turn at this point. In the months he had been with Brewer and Warren, he had failed to make any significant impact, though his wealth of contacts had been invaluable. As he arrived back in the United States from Europe, it was announced that he had been appointed chairman of the editorial board of Paramount Studios, where he was required to do for movies what he had done for publishing, that is, identify viable projects from the hundreds of scripts submitted monthly, and to come up with original ideas. He would have to spend more than half his time in Los Angeles, but as Amelia loved the California climate, this presented no great hardship.

On June 29, there was a civic welcome in Boston, where Amelia briefly saw her family, but she stayed only one day. The Vega had been assembled and was available to fly and on July 1, she flew George and his son David to California, primarily to attend the Olympic games later in the month, but where Amelia and George both had business matters to pursue as well.

Barely ten days later, Amelia announced that she would make her trip back east a nonstop one to Newark, New Jersey.[29] No woman had so far flown nonstop from coast to coast. Ruth Nichols held the woman's record for the fastest coast-to-coast crossing—though not nonstop—in a time of twenty-nine hours, one minute, forty-nine seconds.[30]

But Amelia told reporters she hoped to beat the time set by Frank Hawks,[31] and the Met office predicted favorable tail winds. Amelia had merely to achieve the average speed she made on her transatlantic flight to beat Hawks's record of eighteen hours, twenty-one minutes, fifty-nine seconds, set five years earlier.

A forced landing (immediately, and somewhat predictably, blamed on component failure—a faulty fuel line—according to George's press release) in Columbus, Ohio, put the all-comers record out of reach. When Amelia landed, she was more than an hour behind Ruth Nichols's flying time and she stated that she felt more tired than after her oceanic flight. She had been seated very uncomfortably on her parachute; " . . . I didn't carry one on the Atlantic flight because it wouldn't have done any good over the ocean. . . . "[32] She said she had no plans to attempt the record in the near future but hoped to "one day, but would install special equipment for the purpose so she could fly at high altitude." On this trip, Amelia said she did not exceed thirteen thousand feet as she crossed the Rockies.

Although Amelia had not beaten Hawks's time, her elapsed time of nineteen hours, fourteen minutes, forty seconds (flying time seventeen hours, fifty-nine minutes, forty seconds) set a new woman's record for the crossing, knocking nearly ten hours off Ruth Nichols's time. "I wasn't trying for a record," she told an Associated Press reporter. "This flight was merely for practice in navigation."[33] This statement should be viewed in the light that her course had been plotted, and full navigation notes were prepared for her, by former naval navigator Clarence S. Williams; but it was eminently sensible of her to have taken advantage of the best professional advice available. It must be remembered, however, that such assistance may not have been available to other women fliers. Amelia returned to California—and George—without further incident, though a few days later, she was forced down again in northern California (it was a mechanical fault, again), when returning from a speaking engagement.

After a few days spent at the 1932 Olympic games, accompanied by George and David, Amelia returned to her packed schedule, commuting several times each month between the east and west coasts. On August 25, she made another attempt on the coast-to-coast record and this time achieved her goal of a nonstop flight (the first woman to do so). While her time had still not, as she had hoped, bettered Frank Hawks's, she broke the cross-country distance record (2,478 miles) and her time of nineteen hours and five minutes broke her own record for the fastest flight by a woman.

For some months, Amelia had been trying to persuade her mother to visit her in Rye that fall, but Amy had declined to accept. It seems that Amy disliked George from the start and though, for a while at least, she later came to accept him, her dislike never entirely disappeared. This may have been rooted in jealousy. Amelia had so little time to spare for Amy and their contact was reduced to the regular letters that told her mother little about her real life, concentrating in the main on mundane domestic matters. Each month, Amelia sent Amy's allowance, and the accompanying letters often had a disappointed tone when Amelia believed her money was being spent frivolously by Muriel.

In October, Amelia was voted Outstanding American Woman of the year; she accepted on behalf of "all women."

> When heavier-than-air craft were invented women followed just a few years behind men in their operation, and today women hold various records, 34,000 feet altitude, 254 miles an hour speed, 3,600 mile non-stop, non-refueling flight and recently two women remained in the air for eight days. I don't see how they did it!
>
> But just as important as these spectacular achievements is the everyday flying that 500 women are doing in this country. These women fly on all sorts of missions of business and pleasure, and I accept the medal for them too.

Recounting a laudatory article in the French press that compared her in glowing terms to Lindbergh, Amelia continued with a grin:

> All of it was too good to be true, and I knew there must be some catch in it. There was. The article ended with this query: " . . . but can she bake cakes?"
>
> So I accept these awards [the title, a plaque and a chamois purse containing $1,000 in gold] in behalf of the cake bakers and all of those other women who can do some things quite as important, if not more important, than flying, as well as in the name of women flying today.[34]

Amelia's speeches always contained a firm but gentle reminder that women were the true equals of men. She was not blind to the fact that the attitude of some women was responsible for sexism: "Sex," she once said, "has been used too long as a subterfuge by the inefficient woman who likes to make herself and others believe that it is not her incapability but her womanhood which is holding her back. . . . "

Amelia *was* a feminist but never resorted to the extremes of blatant feminism, nor did she need to do so. Indeed, apart from her membership in the Ninety-Nines and the National Women's Party, she maintained an opposition to any women-only organization. Her thinking, her entire philosophy, was based on her certain knowledge that she was the equal of anyone, and in her marriage to George, she was able to live in harmony with her concept of life. She actually denied being a feminist, disliking the connotation, saying that her opinions were merely "modern thinking." Her constant speeches on the subject, however, were made because she could see discrimination, even if she did not experience it herself. In this, too, George, was her aide. He had smoothed her path in countless ways, and this should not be forgotten nor discounted in assessing Amelia's career and achievements.

What did Amelia give George in return? The reflected kudos of her international celebrity, of course, partly created by him, but she was no Trilby to his Svengali. George had provided the means for Amelia's own ability and courage to bubble to the surface. Had George wanted such celebrity for himself, it is obvious that he could have achieved it in some way or another. It was not fame per se that he hankered after, but the success of anything to which he put his brilliantly active mind. What is surprising is how well Amelia grew into the mold that George created for her as a publicity image. Or perhaps it was that George identified the greater qualities in Amelia long before they were apparent to anyone else.

Amelia, too, was practical in ways that George was impractical. She smoothed his exuberant excesses. She also shared with him a love of books, gardening, adventure, meeting and entertaining interesting people, music, the outdoor life, and a constant reaching upward and outward. She obtained from everything she did, no matter how trivial, the utmost enjoyment, and this characteristic of hers was very dear to George. On the evidence of Elinor Smith, the two were already lovers shortly after Amelia returned from the *Friendship* trip; and Amelia's sister, Muriel Morrissey, was quite sure "that it was a normal marriage in every sense of the word."[35] To George's other wives (see Chapters Twenty-one and Twenty-two) and family members, he was a warm, loving, sometimes extravagantly emotional man. He would not have settled for, and never could have been content with, a cold impersonal management/client arrangement.

In an interview in that fall of 1932, when asked about her husband, Amelia smiled and replied that she was

. . . awfully proud of him. He is such a good sport about my flying. If he hadn't been I never could have made that ocean flight. Of course I wouldn't have expected him, and knew he wouldn't think of forbidding me to make the solo flight. But he could have tried to dissuade me, or he could have whined and made it unpleasant. If he had it would have taken too much out of me. Too much nervous energy to have opposed him . . . but he trusted my judgment. He doesn't know anything about flying, but he knows that I wouldn't have attempted anything that I didn't think I could do, that I wouldn't just dash into a thing without thought or preparation. He trusts my judgment about my ship, just as I trust his about books.[36]

There was no publicity, and no mention by Amelia in correspondence, about a frightening incident on October 22, 1930. Amelia was landing in a crosswind when a Braniff Airlines aircraft somehow got over the top of her. Fortunately, the incident was merely a near miss, and was formally logged as such in the FAA files.

In December 1932, Amelia was awarded an honorary degree (Doctor of Science) by Thiel College, the college that her father had attended. In her speech, Amelia declared that her life was divided " . . . fifty fifty— aviation and marriage—and I guess one job is just about as big as the other." Later, in a letter written to her mother on Christmas Eve, she unwittingly revealed the full tragedy of her father's life, and his early promise:

I had an interesting time at Thiel. I met several people who were in Dad's class and others who knew him. I found his record for scholarship, ie., age of graduation, has never been equaled. He was fourteen when he entered college and only eighteen when he got his degree. . . . Every one remembered Dad as so handsome and bright. His nickname was "Kid." I didn't know that slang was popular then. "Kid Earhart" now sounds like a prize fighter. . . .[37]

Throughout the winter and into spring 1933, Amelia's schedule of engagements was breathtaking. Her monthly letters to Amy are scattered with references to various cities, such as, "I am just rushing to catch the [train] to Chicago." Two days after this, she had an engagement in Portland, Oregon, to which she flew in the Vega; then on to California.[38] This schedule, which worried Amy, seemed to have a bracing effect on Amelia: "I am quite able to stand and weigh now as much as I ever have in my life. I have been drinking cream and gained ten pounds—so that's that."[39]

Her letter in the month of April was extremely brief but it had a certain novelty value, if only for the headed writing paper:

> THE WHITE HOUSE,
> APRIL 20TH 1933
>
> *Dear Mother,*
>
> GP and I are staying here tonight. You may hear of our visit officially but this is a personal note. . . .

Two paragraphs of unimportant trivia follow, the mouthwash she recommends Amy to use and a mention of some family photographs.

> . . . that display of garter on sister's fat knee [Muriel's daughter, Amy Morrissey]. Do please have Pidge let the children wear sox so they don't look like bumpkins. And why the silly hair ribbon? I'll buy 'em 6 pairs of sox each if she will use them.[40]

An element of disapproval had crept into many of Amelia's letters and she often lectured her mother and sister on their clothes, sometimes sending money to buy a specific garment such as a dress or suit, upon which she then gave minute instructions about accessories. Unintentional or not, there is often an unpleasant air of patronage toward her family, which she alternatively loved and nagged. She showed more genuine affection toward her Challiss cousins, who often stayed at Rye, but then she never felt any responsibility toward her cousins, whereas she was Amy's support and resented the fact that she was also, sometimes, indirectly keeping the Morrissey family. Atavistically, she echoed her grandfather's deep-rooted conviction that a man should be able to provide for his family.

On a previous visit to the White House, when Hoover was President, George recorded the solemnity of the occasion and noted the gloom that seemed to pervade the entire building. He had felt chilled. Now his boyhood acquaintance, Franklin D. Roosevelt, had become President and the atmosphere had apparently lifted dramatically. "The President's dwelling house," George observed, "miraculously became an American home—rather fabulous, to be sure, but homely in its simplicity, enormously informal, a sort of combination clubhouse, workshop and drawing room, with rollicking overtones leaning at times to the slightly lunatic. . . ."[41] The relationship between the two men may have been of long standing, but George was "GOP to the core" and never deserted his

19. One of a series of publicity shots taken on the roof of the Copley Plaza in Boston prior to the 1928 transatlantic flight.

21. The plaque at Burry Port in South Wales bearing the legend, 20 hours and 49 minutes—the correct time according to logbooks but probably not snappy enough for Putnam's book title.

20. The *Friendship* arrives in Southampton, June 1928.

22. Amelia in the doorway of the *Friendship* in Southampton, 1928.

23. Amelia surrounded by crowds in Southampton, June 1928. Stultz and Gordon have been left on the periphery of the crowd. The woman wearing the feathered hat is Amy Phipps Guest.

24. Amelia with Captain A. H. White
after a flight to Northolt from Croydon.
London, June 1928.

25. Amelia at Ascot with Lord Astor,
1928.

. Bill Stultz (left), Amelia (center), and Lou Gordon (right), are welcomed back to the U.S.A.

Miss Amelia Earhart
"Lady Lindy"—the First Woman to Fly the Atlantic

AND

George Palmer Putnam

Arctic Explorer, Boy Scout Enthusiast and Publisher

Tomorrow at 2:30
Horne Auditorium, Seventh Floor

Miss Earhart, the first woman to cross the Atlantic by aeroplane, will tell of her thrilling flight about which she has written the book, "20 Hours and 40 Minutes."

Mr. Putnam will give a talk on his Arctic explorations which he will illustrate by moving pictures. He will also present and tell the story of Robert Dick Douglass, Jr., Boy Scout who was his guest on a safari with Martin Johnson into British East Africa.

At the conclusion of the talks, Miss Earhart, Mr. Putnam and Scout Douglass will autograph books purchased.

Extraordinary arrangements have been made to accommodate the great crowd that will be here to meet and hear these celebrities.

Boy Scout, Girl Scout and Campfire Girls Meeting at 8 P. M.

All Scoutmasters and their troops are invited to a special meeting in the Joseph Horne Co. auditorium, at which Miss Earhart, Mr. Putnam and Robert Dick Douglass, Jr., will speak.

. Amelia shortly after her return from the nscontinental flight in 1928.

28. Poster for Amelia's first lecture tour, October 1928.

29. Amelia's Avro Avian after its ground loop in Pittsburgh, Pennsylvania, in 1928. The plane was quickly repaired to enable Amelia to make her return transcontinental flight.

30. Amelia after taking the altitude record for autogiros in 1931.

Amelia and fellow contestants in the 1929 Women's Air Derby: (left to right) Louise M. Thaden, Bobbi Trout, tty Willis, Marvel Crosson, Blanche W. Noyes, Vera Dawn Walker, Amelia Earhart, Marjorie Crawford, Ruth der, and Florence "Pancho" Barnes.

32. Amelia, Ruth Nichols, and Louise Thaden, c. 1931.

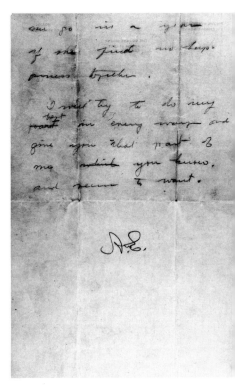

33. Letter that Amelia presented to George Putnam on the day of their wedding, February 7, 1931.

Republican beliefs.[42] It sometimes made for lively discussion in a Democratic administration. Amelia, though, supported FDR to the hilt, even trying to persuade her sister to vote for him.[43]

The Putnams were guests of the Roosevelts on a number of occasions (indeed, this was not their first visit; they had dined there some months earlier, had been personal guests of the President at his inauguration, and had attended a private reception party afterward), and though it would be incorrect to say that they were close friends with the Roosevelts, they undoubtedly enjoyed a relationship that was mutually rewarding.

Over dinner on this April 1933 visit, Eleanor Roosevelt confided that she had never flown at night and would like to see the lights of the capital city. Amelia immediately telephoned Eastern Airlines and organized a flight. Dressed in their evening clothes, the two women drove to the airport and were taken on a flight over Washington and Baltimore. Sometime later, the First Lady, who talked of getting a pilot's license, actually went so far as to acquire a student permit, but nothing ever came of this somewhat wistful ambition despite Amelia's promise to give the First Lady personal tuition.

Meanwhile, Amelia's visit to Washington had a serious note. On the day after her dinner at the White House, she was the guest speaker at a conference of three thousand members of the influential Daughters of the American Revolution. Amelia's hard-hitting speech criticized them sharply for agitating for strong rearmament without doing anything to obtain equality for women in the military organizations. Unless they were willing to bear arms for their country, she told them, they had no business adopting resolutions favoring a buildup of weapons. Her speech drew gasps of surprise, but many saw the sense of her arguments.

In fact, Amelia was a self-confessed pacifist. As a young woman, she had seen at first hand too much of the waste of war to see any glory in it. Within days, there was another hint of the steely side of Amelia Earhart. The NAA, of which she was not only an honorary member but also vice-president, announced that its house magazine was being farmed out to private enterprise for the agency's profit. For some months, Amelia had become increasingly dissatisfied with the way the NAA was conducting its affairs and the bureaucratic approach that its president, Hiram Bingham, had adopted.

Amelia's public opposition to this move caused open conflict between herself and Hiram Bingham and resulted in a great deal of publicity, which most people thought was adverse to the interests of aviation. Eventually, she announced her resignation because of their policy differences—"Your viewpoint and mine are too dissimilar concerning fundamental policies to make any association desirable"[44]—amid further publicity and in a series of extremely polite but bitter letters between her and Bingham.

Later, Bingham wrote to Richard Byrd to ask him to stand as vice-president in Amelia's place, and he commented briefly that the whole affair had started because George "became excited about the magazine," alleging that this was because George had planned to start a new magazine himself. In fact, he had probably misinterpreted George's jokey announcement that he was thinking of starting a club, with a house magazine, for "The Unknown Husbands of Famous Women."

Chapter Seventeen

1933 - 1935

With Amelia's career firmly established, George now concentrated on his own work. His ability to evolve new ideas and contrive special projects was given free rein in Hollywood and he was responsible for a number of innovative ideas. For one film, he brought together ten top screenwriters, each to write a single chapter of a mystery story. As each was handed the cumulative results of the work of the previous writers, the new twists and turns of a different mind were added. The finished story was used for the film *Woman Accused,* and was modestly successful, but it is now remembered chiefly for George's novel conception.

Amelia occasionally visited George at the studios and there was a crop of publicity shots of her pictured with stars such as Cary Grant, Mae West, and Marlene Dietrich. In an interview about one of George's films, *Christopher Strong,* in which Katharine Hepburn played the part of a woman pilot, Amelia was asked for her thoughts on aviation movies and she quickly warmed to a theme.

> . . . I think it's too bad when aviation movies depend for their excitement on plane wrecks and lost flyers and all that sort of thing. Perhaps that's good drama but it certainly isn't modern aviation. . . . There was a picture based on Air Mail, not long ago, in which planes crashed right and left. But that's no more representative of the air mail service than a train wreck every half hour or so would be truly representative of rail transportation.[1]

Asked in George's smiling presence whether war aviation movies (an obvious reference to *Wings,* the first film in which George had been involved before he met Amelia) did not throw the same melodramatic spotlight on flying in general, Amelia spoke her mind:

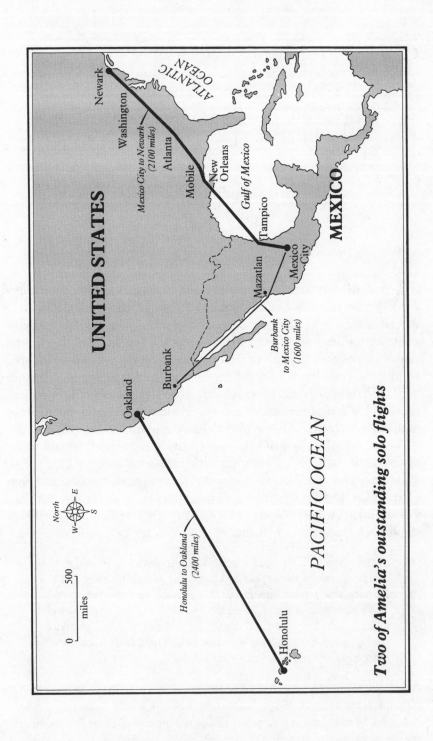

UNITED STATES

MEXICO

ATLANTIC OCEAN

Newark

Washington

Mexico City to Newark
(2100 miles)

Atlanta

Mobile

New Orleans

Gulf of Mexico

Tampico

Mexico City

Mazatlan

Burbank
to Mexico City
(1600 miles)

Burbank

Oakland

PACIFIC OCEAN

Honolulu to Oakland
(2400 miles)

Honolulu

North
E
W
S

0 500
miles

Two of Amelia's outstanding solo flights

As an individual I'm opposed to war, anyway, and naturally I think it is extremely unfortunate that war should be emphasized, and to some extent glorified, in any kind of film . . . the destructive possibilities of aviation are its least important attribute and . . . to put chief emphasis on the airplane as a weapon of war would be to distort its true place in the scheme of things. Aviation has grown up, you know, it isn't a plaything anymore. It has become a useful and serious industry. . . .[2]

In radio broadcasts, personal appearances, and lectures Amelia constantly pushed her theme of women in aviation, and the safety of aviation as a method of transport, and by June 1933 she was busy organizing her own participation in the first of the National Air Races to be opened to men and women pilots. To her disappointment she and Ruth Nichols were the only women contestants, but this at least ensured that the spotlight was firmly on Amelia. Ruth Nichols had to withdraw temporarily because her plane was not ready, but she and Amelia came to a private arrangement to fly against each other's elapsed times for the twenty-five-hundred-dollar woman's prize. In addition, together with the five men in the race, the two women were competing for the Bendix Trophy and a ten-thousand-dollar prize; but given the powerful machines the men were flying, it was extremely unlikely that either woman seriously thought she had a chance of winning. Amelia's engine was 450 horsepower, whereas the men's machines were powered by engines of 700 to 800 horsepower and more.

Prior to the race, there was a minor family squabble by correspondence; partly because Amy had been helping Muriel financially again, and partly because Amy suggested taking her two young grandchildren on vacation. Amelia lectured:

> . . . you are not to have both children. . . . I will not permit it under any circumstances. You are not the kind of woman who has no other interests but brats and I do not see the necessity of your being a drudge and nurse maid.[3]

Subsequent letters continued the theme:

> *Dear Mother,*
>
> I am sorry I cannot change about your taking two children at one time. I do not like to be arbitrary but I do not see any other way of doing things.[4]

Her next letter went further:

> I want your solemn word that you will not try to [take] the two
> infants with you. I shall be compelled to withhold the monthly check
> if you do . . . it is bad for you and for them too, and as I have pointed
> out, for the Morrissey's. *It is absolutely out.*[5]

These letters, with their somewhat overbearing tones, created a painful
period of relations between the two households, but Amelia (who continued to send the monthly allowances) held the upper hand. Eventually,
Amy spent her vacation at Rye later that summer.

Amelia turned her attention to the Air Races.

The time to beat was Roscoe Turner's transcontinental record of twelve
hours and thirty-three minutes. Amelia did not finish with the other
contestants. Although used to flying back and forth across the States, she
was delayed when her hatch cover broke loose in a rainstorm and she
reported almost losing control of the plane. She landed for repairs, losing
nearly an hour, but her arrival in Los Angeles was more than six hours
behind that of her male competitors. Typically, within a day or so she
publicly announced that her return journey to New York would be an
attempt on the west-east record—her own, incidentally.

George was waiting in Newark, New Jersey, to greet Amelia after she
clipped almost two hours off her previous record in an elapsed time of
seventeen hours, seven minutes and thirty seconds. This was still disap-
pointingly short of the men's time, but she reported being bothered by
fumes from a broken fuel line, and the hatch cover had again blown open.
She had been forced to fly for seventy-five miles holding the hatch down
and had sprained her hand in doing so.[6]

Amelia spent most of the summer of 1933 at Rye. Originally, she had
planned to accompany George on a trip to Europe but when Jim and Amy
Mollison successfully piloted their de Havilland Dragon *The Seafarer*
across the Atlantic "the hard way" (east to west against the prevailing
winds), Amelia invited them to recuperate in Rye as her guests. After
circling Stratford Airport near Bridgeport, Connecticut, Mollison had
been so exhausted that he underestimated his approach and the plane
crash-landed in a swamp. They were both injured but not seriously.

During their visit, a "North Atlantic Flight Club" was founded, its
membership restricted to those who had flown alone across the ocean. On
that basis, only five pilots were eligible for membership: Charles Lindbergh, Wiley Post, Jim Mollison, James Mattern, and Amelia.

George's son David had also returned home after adventuring in South

American jungles. Amelia was extremely fond of David, and the feeling was mutual, so this was another reason for Amelia to stay home.[7] Finally, Amelia's mother consented to visit Rye, though whether Amy's change of heart was connected with the fact that George was away for eight weeks is not known.

It was a quiet summer, but when George returned from Europe, the tempo increased, as it always did, and the usual crop of celebrities was to be found at Rye—Sir Hubert Wilkins, Bernt Balchen, William Beebe, Roy Chapman Andrews—to name a few. Dinner parties inevitably finished up in the studio, where guests sprawled comfortably to talk into the early morning of past adventures and future plans. George, restless even as a host, often left the table to telephone San Francisco or Los Angeles as a new idea occurred to him.

Nothing escaped George, and his concerns ran over into so many areas, it is difficult to know how he found the time to hold down a full-time job with Paramount. Despite his many activities, however, and contrary to popular belief, he was not a wealthy man; most of his private income had been lost when his cousin had taken G. P. Putnam's Sons to the verge of bankruptcy and George never recovered the amount he had left invested in the publishing house. Nor was Amelia a wealthy woman. Between them, thanks to George's management and the fact that both were workaholics, they earned a considerable sum, it is true, but their constant entertaining, Amelia's airplanes, the upkeep of Rye, the salaries of their retinue, and a high-profile lifestyle used up their income almost as fast as they earned it. While they were certainly not financially strapped, there was, equally certainly, no huge fortune behind them. The millionaire tag was all simply part of the Putnam image.

Amelia kept busy traveling and lecturing all over the United States. Her usual fee for a lecture was $250, but often she had to settle for less than this at "fill-in" lectures or for small organizations and colleges. The problem was that it was some time since Amelia had done anything *really* newsworthy and her lecture subjects—flying and opportunities for women—were a little worn, no matter how well she put them across.

George continued to commute between New York and Hollywood. Their Christmas card that year depicted a model of an old sailing ship and the printed message read, "This is the Merchant Sailing Ship, George and Amelia . . . although no models ourselves at least we're still afloat, hopeful that in 1934 *your* ship may come in. . . ."[8]

In the early part of 1934, Amelia launched a fashion house to manufacture and market clothes of her own design. They were sensible, classic-line clothes and would not be too out of place today: shirtwaisted dresses, classic silk shirts, blouses with tails long enough not to ride up and reveal a midriff, slacks with permanent pleats, blazers, and hip-length jackets. She specified washable fabrics and cool pastels, as well as classic navy and white combinations, and the whole effect was quiet and tasteful. Amelia was confident that practical, no-nonsense, well-made clothes selling for reasonable prices would be a surefire success. There were a few touches of genuine originality in the aviation theme that ran through the collection: Tiny silver propellers served as buttons; silver screws fastened up a jersey dress; parachute silk was used as detail on blouses.

Amelia's first shop opened in Macy's in New York. It was a novel concept then—a shop within a store—and reported a brisk trade. Others outlets followed, but it was a brief success. By the end of the year, the venture was shut down. There was the inevitable lecture tour in late spring 1934, but when in the fall George attempted to set up a new series of winter lectures for Amelia, it rapidly became apparent that there were few takers at the $250 premium to which Amelia had become accustomed. Some new exploit and further newspaper coverage would be needed to bring her name into the forefront of the public mind.

Amelia had a new venture in mind already, though it would not reach fruition until the following year. Some months earlier, Amelia had told a friend, Dot Leh, that her airplane needed an expensive overhaul and that she would have to spend ten thousand dollars to fix it up. She was therefore thinking of selling it.[9] As the result of Dot Leh's connections and inquiries, the Vega was sold in June for seventy-five hundred dollars to the Franklin Institute in Philadelphia as a permanent exhibition display.[10]

Before parting with the "little red bus" (as she affectionately called it), Amelia removed the upgraded Wasp engine and substituted an obsolete model; she wanted her well-tried engine for the new airplane, also a Lockheed Vega. It was a later model, in which Elinor Smith had been preparing to be the first woman to fly the Atlantic, a plan abandoned after Amelia successfully took that record. It was originally built to exacting specifications for Henry Mears of New York, who had a round-the-world flight in mind. Called the Vega, Hi-speed Special, it carried the registration 965Y and was equipped with special fuel tanks, radio, and streamlined landing gear and cowling. These latter appointments, together with a Hamilton Standard Controllable-Pitch Propeller, gave the plane a speed of 200 mph and Amelia had her eye on further records as well as her constant journeys across the continent.

For the first time since their marriage, George and Amelia found time in the summer of 1934 for a long vacation when they saddle-packed into the wild mountainous country of the Absaroka Mountains in Wyoming where an old friend of George's (Carl Dunrud, a member of George's Greenland expedition) had a ranch. With Dunrud as guide, Amelia quickly came to understand her husband's lifelong love of mountains. They both rode well—it was one of the ways they relaxed together during Rye weekends—and now George tried to teach her to fish. Later, she was to observe engagingly:

> Whether I'm a good flyer is debatable. Whether or not I'm a finished fisherman isn't.
>
> I'm not!
>
> "Now" I hear my husband admonish, "drop your fly *there*—the dark eddy by that rock."
>
> In that particular pool are several dark eddies and any number of rocks. Not that the exact locality makes any difference anyway because I'm not yet able to persuade my line to go where I wish it to.
>
> "Not there. *There!*"
>
> "Holy Cats!" the Lord and Master-Fisherman is becoming apoplectic. "Let the line run out! Keep the tip up . . . gently . . . give the trout a chance. Now try another cast."
>
> I do.
>
> "Hell's Bells!" That's not a flail—that's a rod—only four ounces of delicate bamboo . . . just your wrist and forearm. . . ."
>
> So it goes.
>
> "After all," . . . it's only human to talk back when he complains too bitterly because I've snapped the line and lost a promising trout . . . "after all what do *you* know about taking a plane off a small field?"
>
> "Or a large one!" His grin is disarming.

Amelia's record of the vacation conveys the warmth and depth of their relationship and reveals a typical George, always expecting perfection—he was at his best out of doors, even more so than in business—his characteristic and unrealized excitement in the moment, the rising frustration that died in a laugh as suddenly as it had erupted. About the same vacation, Amelia wrote:

> In contrast . . . to the worries of a bewildered world was the crisp peacefulness of the Wyoming mountains with all the needs of living right at hand on the pack horses, a concentrated world of ones own, refreshing, restful, and remote.[11]

It was an intensely happy period for them both and Amelia told George she'd like to spend more time there. Before the end of their vacation, they filed a mining claim and commissioned the building of a small log cabin near the Dunrud ranch in Meeteetse.[12]

Shortly after their return to Rye, Amelia sprang another of her apparently artless remarks upon George. Just as she had mulled privately over her solo transatlantic trip, so she had quietly decided on her next venture—a transpacific flight from the Hawaiian Islands to California, a flight of some twenty-five hundred miles. George heard the news as he arrived home from the office.

> One night in the autumn of 1934 she sat in golden crepe pyjamas on the "liver-toaster" [club fender] round the fireplace at Rye reading the evening paper. As I came in from the train she looked up in the way of a person thinking out loud and said, "I want to fly the Pacific soon."
>
> I had a brief-case and an armful of evening papers, but instead of going into the Hencoop (AE's disrespectful name for the office) to dump them I leaned against the arched doorway and said, "You mean from San Francisco to Honolulu?"
>
> She straightened a topaz link in one of her cuffs thoughtfully. "No; the other way; it's easier to hit a continent than an island."
>
> "When do you want to do it?" I asked
>
> "Oh, fairly soon. . . . "[13]

When Amelia made such plans, George knew he would have to arrange the funding to prepare and equip the plane, and organize the logistics. For example, the plane would need a thorough overhaul and would have to be shipped to Hawaii; special equipment for a transoceanic flight would need to be purchased and fitted. A record flight of this nature required not only planning and courage and practical organization but also cash. George knew just what to do for a contact in the advertising world. Sydney Bowman had for some weeks been running a $125,000 publicity campaign for the Hawaiian Sugar Planters Association in order to fight the Jones-Costigan Act (sugar control) adopted by Congress. Bowman was quickly convinced of the value of climaxing this campaign with a successful record flight by Amelia and happily agreed to George's suggestion that the association sponsor Amelia for a ten-thousand-dollar purse, with five thousand dollars payable on signing of contracts and the balance payable on the success of the attempted flight.[14]

In October, the Putnams left Rye for California, where the Vega was to be overhauled by Lockheed. As in the past, George had organized an expert to oversee the technical aspects of the entire operation. On this occasion, the expert was Paul Mantz.

George had met Mantz in 1928 during his involvement with the film *Wings*. Then the young pilot's dream had been to break into the movie business and he had provided a small team of stunt pilots to act out dogfights for the cameras. Mantz was a pilot of great brilliance with an instinctive feel for flight, and his experience of performing difficult stunts in the intervening years had taught him the value of precise planning to obtain successful results. He was an ideal man for the task of masterminding Amelia's flight, for he knew everyone worth knowing in the industry and was conversant with the latest developments in aviation technology.

Amelia and Paul Mantz worked well together and when a house near the Mantzes' home in North Hollywood became available to rent and George returned to New York, Amelia moved out of the Ambassador Hotel suite where she and George habitually stayed and into the house at 10515 Valley Spring Lane, inviting Amy to join her there.[15]

In late November 1934, George telephoned Amelia with news of a fire that had destroyed a large part of their home in Rye. George had been staying with his mother in Noank, Connecticut, prior to joining Amelia in December for the transpacific flight attempt. Since the house was to be empty all winter, the caretaker had drained the water tanks but locked the house without turning off the boiler. The resulting fire already had taken a good hold when a neighbor spotted flames and called for help.

One entire wing of the house was gutted and George's irreplaceable collection of Rockwell Kent paintings, as well as books and papers, were lost. Everything in the dining room was destroyed; the silver (much of it inherited from Earhart and Putnam ancestors) was a shapeless mass in a pile of ashes that was once an antique rosewood cabinet. A trunk containing all of Amelia's papers accumulated from childhood, including her poetry, letters, and some stories on which she had been working, had vanished.

Amelia's first thought, though, was for George's most treasured possessions. "What about your father's books?" Fortunately, they had been protected in a heavy glass-fronted bookcase that had been smoke damaged and charred but had not burned, and the books were largely undamaged. She was upset to learn that her papers (her "peppers" as she called them) were gone. Among her papers were her writings, especially her poetry. Gene Vidal recalled that she wrote a number of poems: "She wrote poetry for magazines under another name and often showed me the poems before mailing them."[16] The fire was sad for both Amelia and George, for they deeply loved their home. Practical as ever, George immediately commissioned the rebuilding program.

During December, preparations for the flight were finished and on December 22, the Putnams and the Mantzes sailed for Hawaii aboard the S.S. *Lurline,* with Amelia staunchly denying any suggestion of a transpacific flight. Her declared intention was a short series of lectures and flying around the islands.

Amelia wrote to her mother from the ship explaining how they were running the Vega's engine:

> . . . and it has barked a cheerful "howdy" each time. . . . the radio on the plane has been working wonderfully. At midnight I could pick up and talk to regular airway stations. Kingman Arizona heard perfectly. . . . I'll have GP cable you when I start. My hope is to go on east so I shall not see you until later if that plan materializes. . . .
>
> Please try to have a good time. You have had so many squashed years. . . . G.P. said you were an awfully good sport to stay alone in the little house. I said I had known that a long time. I have taken possession of the stuff in the zipper compartment of my brief case. Put it away until I turn up and if I don't—burn it. It consists of fragments that mean nothing to anyone but me. . . . [17]

Amelia's plan was to land and refuel in California and fly on to Washington, D.C., and although the transoceanic route had been flown before (by Sir Charles Kingsford-Smith), no person, male or female, had flown it solo. In January 1935, news of the sponsorship of Amelia's flight broke in the newspapers and was vociferously denounced by editors as a mere stunt. Nothing could be gained, they averred; Kingsford-Smith had already charted the route; such flights should be attempted only in large planes equipped to stay afloat for several days. The papers calculated that under ideal conditions she might have only fifty gallons of fuel left [that is, more than two hours flying and over three hundred miles] if she was to make California. If she was to ditch, a costly search, risking the lives of naval pilots, would have to be undertaken. There were some grounds for this attitude, for only a month earlier a fully crewed plane had disappeared on the same route, entailing a fruitless forty-seven-day full-scale search by army and navy planes and ships.[18] Ten pilots had already lost their lives attempting to make the crossing, and if Amelia failed, it could damage aviation in the eyes of the public.

As the papers thundered a concerted condemnation, the navy refused to clear Amelia's departure, saying that her radio equipment had insufficient range for safety requirements. While they appreciated that she could receive transmissions over the distance, they questioned the ability of her radio to transmit over the twenty-five-hundred-mile distance to Los Angeles station KFI. Paul Mantz, whose expertise ensured that Amelia carried the latest radio equipment, immediately flew the Vega to twelve thousand feet and was able to reach Kingman, Arizona, and exchange conversation, effectively quashing the objection. In fact, Amelia's flight across the Pacific was the first in which a civilian airplane carried a two-way radio telephone. Because of the cost and weight, such equipment had previously been limited to larger transport aircraft.

The next snag was the sponsor, who, fearing that bad publicity would damage the campaign, opted to back out of the venture. Amelia faced the association's committee and scathingly told them that she could sense an aroma of cowardice in the room. However, she said, she fully intended to make the flight with or without their support. She got their support.

All that remained was the weather. While Amelia waited for ideal conditions, she and George stayed at the plush home of a wealthy friend of George's, attended by a large staff of Japanese servants. Amelia wrote to Amy: "We have lived like kings . . . GP and I wonder if we'll ever be satisfied with only one or two servants again. . . .[19]

It was January 11 before conditions were right and Paul Mantz would agree to Amelia's departure. He was confident that the plane was as ready as he and mechanic Ernie Tissot could make it, and the weather forecast was favorable. The Vega was loaded with five hundred gallons of fuel and together with various extra equipment weighed more than six thousand pounds.[20] Mantz, however, reckoned that even with the excessive load, the plane should lift off in three thousand feet, and Wheeler Field had a six-thousand-foot grass strip. The army, whose airfield it was, had mowed a takeoff strip and planted distance flags to aid Amelia in the takeoff run. Heavy rain made the strip sticky but even so she lifted off as Mantz had predicted, in just under three thousand feet—but not before she noticed the ambulances and fire trucks standing by, servicemen with hand-held fire extinguishers, and several women "with handerchiefs obviously ready for any emergency." She also saw the anxiety in the dead-white face of Ernie Tissot as she pushed the throttle open and released the brakes.[21] Two hundred people and various newsreel cameras witnessed her departure.

For George, who had not slept the previous night and would not sleep while Amelia was airborne, the takeoff was a period of supreme anxiety. He was no airman and no mechanic, but he knew very well that this was the most dangerous moment of the flight. Beside him, Paul Mantz was willing the Vega into the sky. "Get that tail up! *Get that tail up!*" he yelled at the top of his voice, adding various profane trimmings.[22]

As Amelia eased her aircraft into the air, George sighed with relief and a reporter asked him how he felt. "I'd rather have a baby," he said, smiling, meaning rather than fly himself (though perhaps it was also an ironical comment on the reversal of normal husband/wife roles). This was published nationwide as a frustrated wish to become a father and stories that Miss Earhart's husband wished she'd give up flying and have a baby proliferated.

This time there were no frightening incidents and from her detailed description of the flight, Amelia really enjoyed the experience. The Vega behaved perfectly and the only incidents that broke the apparent monotony were Amelia's regular radio contacts at quarter to and quarter past each hour, when she reported in a somewhat unprofessional manner that "Everything is okay."[23] Once she saw a ship and was delighted to receive a Morse-code transmission from the radio operator, indicating that at nine hundred miles out, she was dead on the course professionally laid out—as usual—for her by Clarence Williams.

A few hours out, Amelia heard the radio announcer of the KGU commercial radio station in Honolulu suddenly announce, "We are interrupting our musical program so that Mr. Putnam may try to communicate with his wife." Typically, George could not pass up such a wonderful opportunity for publicity:

> And then some hundreds of miles out over the Pacific, I heard my husband's voice as though he were in the next room.
> "A.E." he said, "the noise of your motor interferes with your messages. Please speak a little louder."
> A few minutes later I talked to him, through the little cup microphone—louder, as requested.[24]

The radio was a revelation. "Miraculous!" Amelia said later. Using the call sign KHABQ, Amelia could receive and transmit on frequencies 6,210 and 3,105 kilocycles. The confidence that this equipment gave Amelia was incalculable and though she disliked the effort involved in reeling in and out the long antenna through a hole in the cabin floor, she was delighted with the regular contact with radio stations. Once, after flying over a solid fog bank for hours, she spoke out loud to herself: "I'm getting tired of this fog." This was picked up by radio stations as "I'm getting tired" and was carried on the news broadcasts of West Coast news stations, causing anxiety to her friends. For George, however, the regular sound of her voice was a tremendous comfort, a tenuous link with Amelia. "At least . . . this feature was a pleasant contrast to previous Atlantic flights with their long blank silences."[25]

Amelia was some twenty miles south of her targeted landfall—the Golden Gate Bridge and Oakland—when she reached the California coast; but climbing up over the hills, she could see San Francisco Bay under her port wing tip. By radio, she announced, "Am on course, will be in any moment now." She landed at Oakland some eighteen hours after leaving Honolulu.

Throughout the night, her radio-telephone broadcasts had been heard on commercial radio stations, and the public at large felt personally involved. At no point did she reveal her position, so that even Clarence Williams, who had prepared her charts, was unsure whether she would opt for a Los Angeles or San Francisco landfall, but after she announced at 7:55 A.M. that she was heading for Oakland, people began to surge to the airport.

The crowd of thousands—various estimates range from five to ten thousand—were at first not even sure that Amelia had arrived, for she landed at the far side of the field, almost out of sight, though her landing run and taxi toward the daunting reception was captured by newsreel cameras. After a short rest, Amelia announced her intention to take off again for Washington, D.C. She was tired after the flight, however, and despite the buoyancy created by success, she recognized it would be foolish to fly on without rest. She spent the night in an Oakland hotel after cabling George, SORRY I DID NOT DO BETTER.[26]

George, relieved, cabled her a jokey telegram—SWELL JOB BUT HOPE IT DOESN'T BECOME A HABIT[27]—before he boarded a ship to return home the slow way. President Roosevelt also sent congratulations and a long letter: "You have scored again . . . [and] shown even the 'doubting Thomases' that aviation is a science which cannot be limited to men only."[28]

A few days later, Amelia met George's ship and after a civic reception, the two flew back to New York by scheduled airline.

Now there was no problem in finding organizations to book lectures at $250 each. For the following months, Amelia was on the road almost nonstop, too busy even to write to Amy. Every night, she telephoned George, sometimes asking him to contact Amy and send her a check. Consequently, he wrote:

FEB 11TH 1935

Dear Mrs. Earhart

In the first place, here is a check for the rent. Secondly here is a check for $50 to help out immediate cash requirements. Third I am sorry to report that it looks as though we are going to be delayed in getting back to the coast. At least there is not much chance of A.E. getting there until about 20th of March. Most anything can happen to me. Affairs are even more than usually hectic and uncertain! Anyway I will keep you informed.

Now here's one thing that seems to me important. I have just learned that apparently we are paying $15 a month for the board and lodging of a dog in an animal hospital. That is quite absurd. That amount would support two starving people and there are plenty of *them!*

Amelia is away in the middle west lecturing and so I am a bit hazy in my knowledge. But as I understand it, we have some obligation to take care of this dog. In paying the rent will you please tell agent that I will not accept further responsibility for this dog. The owner or someone else, will have to take him off our hands. And so please get him out of the hospital, terminate the arrangement there, and give him to the agent. I absolutely refuse to waste money in this minor and unjustified way. I suspect you will sympathize with me. I would much rather you bought a string of pearls or even a diamond bracelet!

AE is rolling around in the middle west in her Franklin lecturing every night, heaven help her, and is expected back on the 26th. Incidentally you might mark on your calendar that she is on the Beech-Nut broadcast (Red Davis) on March 11, 13 and 15th.

Sincerely
GPP[29]

Two days later, a cable from Amelia in Wisconsin, dispatched after she had spoken to George by telephone, advised Amy to DISREGARD WHAT GP WRITING ABOUT DOG WILL WRITE YOU MYSELF FIRST MINUTE HERE IS VALENTINE CHEERIO. A[30]

The dog was part of the rental agreement and George's choler would have, she knew, probably vanished even before the letter was posted; he once admitted that his best letters were filed in the wastebasket. Even so, it is not difficult to see how Amy's dislike of George could have become so deep-rooted.

When the prestigious Harmon Awards were announced that spring, for

1935, Amelia was awarded the title of America's Outstanding Airwoman. Both she and George had hoped for the title World's Outstanding Woman Aviator, which she had held after her solo transatlantic flight, but the committee was divided because of Jean Batten's east-to-west solo flight across the South Atlantic. Eventually, the honors were shared between the two women. George counteracted Amelia's disappointment by referring to Amelia in subsequent interviews as "The First Lady of the air," an obvious play on the title accorded to President Roosevelt's wife.

At the same time, in a poll conducted by New York University's journalism students, it was found that of world figures the best-known men were President Roosevelt and Hitler, while the best-known women were Eleanor Roosevelt and Amelia Earhart. This was hardly surprising since not a week passed without Amelia's name appearing in the papers for some reason or other. Much of this had been due to George—now without a full-time business interest of his own—but the natural cumulative effect of fame was also starting to take effect. Some newspapers wondered whether Amelia was planning a world flight since she had, after her Pacific crossing, said on radio that it would be good practice and experience for future flights. Now, asked to explain, she said enigmatically, "Everyone has his dreams. I like to be ready. . . ." However, she denied plans for a world flight. When the reporter expressed a hope that she wouldn't attempt any more ocean flights, Amelia reacted quickly and seriously. "Why?" she asked. "Do you think my luck might run out? Do you think luck only lasts so long and then lets a person down?"[31]

Having finished her tour of the midwest, Amelia traveled to New York, where at a reception she met the consul general of Mexico, who suggested she should make a goodwill visit to Mexico City. "It's the first time I've ever been asked anywhere," she said later to George. "I just *went* to Ireland."[32]

Although Lindbergh had flown to Mexico City in 1927 from Washington, D.C.,[33] the possibilities for Amelia inherent in this trip were not lost on George. A flight from Los Angeles to Mexico City with a return to the New York area would generate yet another crop of valuable publicity. With characteristic enthusiasm, George catapulted into action, flying to Mexico City to organize the project.

The Mexican government agreed to issue a special postage stamp commemorating the flight and George recognized that he could finance most of the costs of the flight by organizing a limited edition of what are now known as first-day covers. Seven hundred and eighty stamps[34] were produced. Four hundred and eighty had to be placed on public sale in order to satisfy international postal regulations, but three hundred were purchased by George to be carried by Amelia on her return to Newark, New Jersey, placed on autographed covers, and sold to collectors.[35] To protect the rarity value of the issue and ensure that no further stamps could be produced, nor forgeries made, George provided the tube of special colored ink and personally destroyed the line cut.

George always maintained that "Amelia never made profits from any flight . . . no single flight showed direct returns in black on the balance sheet."[36] This statement is probably accurate (though very disingenuous), for the flights themselves created no direct revenue and were costly to finance. Any profits came from peripheral activities such as lecturing, books, and so on. George's idea to sell stamps was not only novel but also typical of his brilliance at innovative publicity and money-making schemes.

The flight to Mexico was planned for mid-April and meanwhile Amelia flew to Washington, where she stayed at the White House for a few days while undertaking several engagements—among them a speech at the National Geographic Society—before going home to Rye. She wrote Amy to say, a little wearily, "I returned to New York and found myself signed for the most strenuous lecture engagement ever undertaken. . . . I hope to start west the middle of this month. GP has left Paramount and is in a state trying to decide what alley he will run down. There are so many things to do."[37]

In an interview in Washington, Amelia was asked what she thought about the White House cuisine. Amelia replied that she had been so busy fulfilling engagements outside the White House that she'd hardly had any meals there. This became construed as a comment that she loved staying at the White House but never got enough to eat. She had already written a charming thank-you note, offering George's services for a matter under Mrs. Roosevelt's consideration, but now, exasperated and embarrassed, she quickly cabled a denial of the article and followed with a letter explaining the misunderstanding:

> Wall, I sure am glad to be here, and gosh, I sure do hope I'll meet the Prince of Wales," was the quotation attributed to me in 1928 after the *Friendship* flight. It happened that I *said not one single word on the subject.* The whole was fabricated out of one reporter's imagination. I can laugh at it now. I only hope that one day I can laugh also at the preposterous "starvation interview" the Press has had me give concerning my stay at the White House.
>
> I believe you know me well enough to be sure I *would* never put out the kind of smart ungracious stuff it contained. Something I said

(I can't think what yet) must have been misinterpreted and got passed round by word of mouth, since more than a week elapsed before it got into print.

I am humiliated that any incident should have occurred to mar what was to me so delightful an interlude. . . . Perhaps you will let me raid the ice-box sometime, not because it's necessary but because it's fun.[38]

To which her hostess replied:

You were such a perfect guest that I welcome you back at any time and you need not feel that you have to be out for every meal! We all feel we have not seen enough of you.

Affectionately
Eleanor Roosevelt

A handwritten P.S. reveals the First Lady's sense of humor and perhaps the relationship between the two women: "I shall give you a key to the ice box next time!"[39]

On April 19, Amelia left to fly to Mexico, where George awaited her. Before takeoff, an act of sabotage was discovered. A drop of acid had been placed on the rudder cables and they were almost eaten through.[40] Eventually, after an otherwise uneventful flight, Amelia lost her way and landed some fifty miles short of her destination in a dry lake bed. Redirected by peasants, she flew on to Valbuena Airport, where George and Presidente Lázaro Cardenas were waiting to welcome her. At an altitude of eight thousand feet, Valbuena was too high to enable Amelia to take off with a full fuel load, so the Mexican army prepared a three-mile-long runway in a dried-out lake bed at Texcoco. Amelia's return was delayed by poor weather, and George had to leave by commercial airline ahead of her.

It was May 8 before Amelia was able to leave, and although this leg of the venture, too, was uneventful, Amelia had fretted about the long water crossing and promised herself that after this she would do no further long flights over water with only a single engine.[41]

As usual, George hyped the flight for all it was worth. The result on this occasion was "a frenzied mob of between 10,000 and 15,000 people" waiting in Newark, New Jersey, and determined to touch Amelia or pat her as she alighted exhausted from her airplane. The police were unable to get close enough to protect her, and George, frustrated and angry, could only shout, "This is the most disgraceful scene I have ever witnessed. . . ."[42] Previously, only Lindbergh had provoked such scenes. The crowd, however, was determinedly good-natured and carried Amelia, shoulder-high, to the hangar where the official reception committee, and the frustrated George, waited with ill-concealed impatience.

Without a break, Amelia returned to her packed lecture schedule, though she managed to spend a few days toward the end of May in Los Angeles, where she and Paul Mantz signed a partnership agreement. Amy had gone east to stay with the Morrisseys and George's mother had traveled out to visit the Putnams in Hollywood. The Putnams had planned to fly to Wyoming to repeat their vacation of the previous year, but neither could find time.

One of the alleys that George decided to run down, having left Paramount, was to join a consortium of businessmen to manufacture a training unit for parachute jumpers. Having been sold on the idea that pilots should be able to practice using parachutes in a safe environment, and realizing the potential for sales of such a system to military sources, George went into partnership to market two-hundred-foot towers to which a safety line attached a standard parachute harness. Nowadays, everyone is familiar with these devices, but then it was a novel concept.

George launched his publicity campaign by having Amelia make the first jump in public (others had tested it privately), and she was followed by a team of experienced parachute jumpers, Fay Gillis (a fellow member of the Ninety-Nines), an actress from a Broadway play, and a reporter. George wondered whether, in addition to the aviation industry and the army and navy (for whom it had primarily been designed), he might sell the idea to amusement parks and country fairs. The reporter doubted that the idea would catch on.

But there was a serious side to the circus atmosphere; army and navy chiefs were there to watch and place orders and Gene Vidal, director of Air Commerce, had flown up for the demonstration and was persuaded by George to jump. George wrote to him next day:

> *Dear Gene,*
>
> In case you missed it here's what the New York *Herald Tribune* did this morning—front page and first page of second section. All the papers are correspondingly good. All four newsreels, I think, will carry a yarn—they have some good stuff. Publicitywise it was just about 100% success—far better than I had dared expect.
>
> *Sincerely,*
> *GPP*[43]

The Putnams' peripatetic existence meant they had little time to spend at the newly reconstructed house in Rye, so they rented it to a doctor for a year and based themselves in a New York hotel when in the east and the Valley Spring Lane cottage when in California. The heavy demands made on Amelia that spring took an inevitable toll, for in June she became ill with the old recurrent sinus problems. An operation was followed by an attack of pleurisy and she was bedridden for ten days. George, who had been in New York, flew to her side. "[He] arrived yesterday, which helps," she wrote Amy. Her constant headache did not prevent Amelia's usual instructive lecture when writing about the vacation Amy was to take with Muriel:

> About clothes. Please remember you and Pidge attract attention as my relatives so spare me blowsies. I'd prefer you to get a few simple decent clothes, both of you. Not awful cheepies, so people who don't look below the surface won't have anything to converse about. Things you get now are cheaper and can be used next year. . . .[44]

For some time, Amelia had hankered after a small house of their own in North Hollywood. She loved the climate and the way of life there, and her business partnership with Paul Mantz would require her presence on a regular basis. George was opposed to the idea of buying in California, but, not unusually, Amelia got her way without any fuss; George was disposed to be amenable, having worried about Amelia's longer-than-usual convalescence. In late July 1935, Amelia wrote to her mother from California:

> Today we bought a small house here. GP has been letting off steam since he arrived how he could not leave the east etc. But Paul and I have kept him so busy with the funny businesses we have stirred up that his bleat has grown less and less.
> Imagine my surprise when day before yesterday he asked me to drive him around Tolucca Lake district—where he had been busy pointing out the impossibilities of renting even for a short time. Well at the very end of Valley Spring Lane (I don't know whether you ever walked there or not) was a little house with a "For Sale" sign on it. It was on a square lot with two sides on the golf course and a hundred foot lot on the other, now vacant.
> We got home and he said "I think I'll just call that real estate man and see what he has to say." The result was in four minutes we were seeing the place and next day made an offer for it. GP left at one

today via United and actually two minutes before the plane took off the real estate man rushed up and reported our offer accepted. Whew.

. . . My ship is still undergoing repairs, that is repainting and re-upholstering and when it is finished I shall put it with Paul's fleet for charter. We are going to start a flying school and plan all kinds of things. GP is as keen as are we. . . .[45]

Earlier in the year, Amelia had announced that she had accepted an appointment at Purdue University in Lafayette, Indiana, as a consultant in the department for the study of careers for women. Although both she and the college's president (Dr. Edward C. Elliott) were aware that her involvement would be limited to a few weeks each semester, Amelia was very keen on this appointment.

Amelia had met Elliott the previous year at a luncheon and so impressed him with her talk and positive attitude toward careers for women that he asked if she would visit the college and lecture the women students.[46] As a result, a contract was negotiated with Amelia as a visiting faculty member at a salary of two thousand dollars a year. In addition to the Women's Careers Department, there was an aeronautics department operating from the college's own airfield. Here was an opportunity to encourage able young women not only to forge worthwhile careers but also to take up flying—two subjects close to her heart. She continued to work determinedly at her honorary position in the Ninety-Nines and wrote surprisingly long personal letters to female inquirers who were seriously interested in taking up aviation.

Throughout the summer of 1935, Amelia spent her spare time with Paul Mantz, planning the flying school and charter business. Sooner or later, she knew, she would have to give up record flying and when that day came, this business would provide an income.

Amelia enjoyed Paul's company. He was fun and knew how to enjoy life. He played in a way George never could play, but he was also a fine pilot, respected by Amelia and others for his knowledge and expertise. He also had something that George had not: a *real* love of, and feel for, flying similar to her own. Furthermore, he had the entrepreneurial spirit to use his ability to make money. In a sense, he was a Putnam who could fly, and who could share all aspects of the flying experience with Amelia.

In late August, acting on a whim, Amelia and Paul decided to fly to the National Air Races in Cleveland, Ohio. Once there, they made another spur-of-the-moment decision to enter the Bendix Trophy Race, after Paul worked out that, with their combined experience and the

Vega's performance, they could probably take fifth place. They duly cranked up and, taking fifth place, won five hundred dollars. For Amelia, it was sheer fun, offering freedom from absolute responsibility. With Paul's overtly flirtatious manner, the feeling was that in some way they were behaving deliciously childishly.

Amelia was kept so busy that fall that her notes to her mother were often no more than a line or two. It fell to George to write to Mrs. Earhart, keeping her in touch with her daughter's progress and sending her photos of the new house and pictures taken when they had flown with Paul over the Grand Canyon.

Chapter Eighteen

1935 - 1937

Amelia's involvement with Purdue University was almost more a period of rest than another part of her schedule. She fitted in well with campus life, invariably staying at South Hall (now Duhme Hall) on her visits there. Of the six thousand students on campus, almost one thousand were women, and female faculty members were as scarce as female students.[1] Her lectures were oversubscribed but it was in off-duty hours that the students felt they got to know the woman they had previously read about in newspapers:

> South Hall residents vied with each other to sit at Miss Earhart's table in the dining room . . . buttermilk became an overnight favorite beverage because it was her choice. . . . These were the days when table manners were considered somewhat important . . . one thing you were supposed to do was keep your elbows off the table. Amelia's posture at table, when she was deep in conversation was apt to be sitting forward on the edge of her chair—both elbows on the table— and chin cupped in hands. Naturally the question was "If Miss Earhart can do it why can't we?" The stock reply was "As soon as you fly the Atlantic, you may!"
> . . . after dinner . . . as many students who could would follow Miss Earhart into my room and sit around on the floor and talk and listen . . . she sat on the floor too—she was adaptable, easy and informal. It was during these times especially that we got to know some of the underlying beliefs and hopes and dreams that motivated our distinguished guest.
> The conversations invariably centred around Miss Earhart's belief that women should have and really did have choices about what they could do with their lives. She believed and said that, of course women

should be engineers or scientists; they could be physicians as well as nurses; they could manage businesses as well as be secretaries to managers. She believed in women's intelligence, their ability to learn, and their ability to do whatever they wanted to do . . . she saw no limitations on the aspirations [of women students].

There was no question that she, through her own achievements and persuasiveness, was an effective catalyst to heretofore unthinkable thoughts for all of us.[2]

Amelia took her role as visiting faculty member seriously and luckily some of her class lecture notes survive at Purdue, indicating her practical approach to encouraging the young women.[3]

A questionnaire she drafted for her students, inviting the answers to questions probably to be used in debate, also survives.

Why are you at College?

Do you really want a career?

Or are you doing it because your aunt says you ought to do it?

Or because you think it is the thing to do?

If you are married how does your husband fit into the picture?

What do you expect of him?

What part does he play in your life?

Ninety-two percent of the women students who answered wanted a career.[4]

The demands on Amelia's time gave her few opportunities to write to her mother, and the few letters she did write at this time reveal an abruptness with Amy's affairs that was also visible in earlier letters when the pressures upon Amelia had been very great. Now, George was often Amy's correspondent, and, as it is well documented that Amelia telephoned him every evening, it is probable that he performed this small chore at her request, as on one occasion when Muriel arranged a dinner party with Amelia as guest of honor. Amelia wrote the briefest of notes, canceling it without explanation. Amy wrote and told her plainly what she thought of this arrogant behavior, and George read this to Amelia over the telephone. Although they agreed that George should write and explain, Amelia must have subsequently recognized that her curtness had caused hurt, for she scribbled the following note:

Please tell Pidge when I wrote her about canceling a dinner she was planning at Cambridge, I did not mean that GP and I would not be glad to eat at home with *just the family* if she wishes. That is if she will have a maid come in for whom I will gladly pay. . . .

George wrote simultaneously:

I guess we will have to leave the decision in all this to Amelia. For self protection she simply has to be hard-boiled about getting away from people. Realize, please, this is a problem repeated two or three times a day every day for the last few months. I am meeting Amelia in Buffalo on Thursday and will take your letter with me.[5]

George fully recognized that the stresses of the past months were having an effect on his wife. However, despite the strains of her busy life, Amelia showed no desire to take even a temporary retirement. In a speech in December 1935, she hinted at what the future might hold for her. "I'm looking for a tree on which new and better airplanes grow, and I'm looking for a shiny new one to shake down," she said.[6] In fact, she already had fixed in her mind the airplane she wanted.

In late November, Paul Mantz had obtained a quotation on behalf of George and Amelia for a Lockheed Model 10E Electra. Prior to this, other manufacturers had been canvassed and George wrote to Paul telling him that he had received a quotation from Sikorsky for one of their S-43 flying boats. At a price of $110,000,[7] it was not under serious consideration, but George suggested to Mantz that he let Lockheed know that Amelia would not automatically choose Lockheed, despite her past successes with their products. Amelia had recently scoffed at suggestions that she might be planning a round-the-world flight, but it is obvious from the correspondence to airplane manufacturers that she had had such a venture very much in mind for some time. The price quoted by Lockheed was more than thirty-six thousand dollars for a basic airplane; sophisticated equipment would cost as much again and would need to be fitted for the venture she had in mind.

News clippings of the period reveal that if Amelia was tired, she never allowed it to show in her public life. To reporters, she was always gracious, charming, and available for interviews, and while she relied on George to contact Amy, she had not forgotten Edwin's widow and clearly visited her stepmother from time to time on her frequent visits to Los Angeles. The little house in the California hills in which Edwin had died was no longer part of an isolated community. When Helen Earhart found that development taxes threatened to bankrupt her so that she might lose her home, Amelia stepped in and bought the house for three thousand dollars, clearing all outstanding assessments at the same time. It is also obvious from her letters that in addition to supporting Amy and, often to her chagrin, indirectly helping Muriel's husband, Amelia also contributed every month to the upkeep of two Challiss cousins who were in financial difficulty.[8]

Amelia relied on George's support more and more. When she checked in each night by telephone, he masterminded the logistics of her tour, advising whether she had spoken at the same venue in the past so that her lectures, from specific descriptions of her record-breaking flights to "Flying for Fun," could be altered to avoid giving the same speech. He provided information on whether the audience was likely to be a public one or consist of members of a private club.[9]

George and Amelia's nightly chat was important to both of them, but occasionally she finished too late to phone and sometimes when this happened she would send a cable next morning. A typical one reads, SORRY MISSED CALL LAST NIGHT APPRECIATE ROSES SEE YOU SOON. A.[10]

If there was a hint of difficulty in their marriage at this point (as future events were to suggest), and if the constant separations caused some coolness between the two, there was no evidence of it at Christmas when George took Amelia for a walk one Sunday morning in bright, cold sunshine along New York's Park Avenue. He told her he wanted to look at some bronzes of bears in a gallery there. Instead, showing her a magnificently carved chest he had commissioned many months earlier, he mumbled, "There, how do you like that?" It was a few moments before Amelia realized that her initials were carved into a crest on the front and that the sides were encrusted with allegorical references to her various record flights—fishes for the oceans she had crossed, a shamrock for the landing at Culmore, etc. It was typical of George that having given so much thought to what was a precious item made by a brilliant master craftsman, he should present it in such an offhand manner. In fact, it was his replacement for the rosewood cabinet that Amelia had treasured but that had been lost in the fire at Rye.[11]

The couple was to need confidence in their relationship. Shortly afterward, they received a verbal warning from Paul Mantz that his wife, Myrtle, was suing him for divorce, alleging extreme mental and physical cruelty but, more important, alleging his adultery with Amelia. Without question, Paul was a ladies' man (a fact never denied by him), and Amelia had been drawn to him, but it is unlikely that their relationship ever went further than a mild attraction. She had spent a great deal of time with him. Often the two were alone on flying trips and certainly they spent long hours together planning their business ventures. She had been a guest at the Mantzes' home for a month on one occasion and for odd weekends over a period of about a year. Myrtle was unable to offer any evidence to back up her charge against Amelia, and Paul took the witness stand himself precisely to clear Amelia from any damaging charges.

Unfortunately, this well-intentioned act merely gave the newspapers an opportunity to run riot with sensational copy. Paul denied that he and Amelia had ever acted improperly. He also cross-charged mental cruelty, relating that Myrtle had once appeared in his bedroom and shot at him with a revolver and was insanely jealous without any foundation.

One witness for the plaintiff claimed that she had attended a conference between Paul and Myrtle, held to attempt a reconciliation. Myrtle was said to have stated on that occasion, "I know I am upset and jealous but I believe that if Miss Earhart would take her clothes and leave our house we would have a better chance of getting along."[12]

The Mantzes' maid swore that Amelia and Paul had never been alone together in the house overnight. Indeed, this had been the source of a violent quarrel, for when the maid told Myrtle this some months before the divorce case, Myrtle summarily dismissed her for lying. When Paul took hold of Myrtle to stop her rounding on the unfortunate servant, a fierce physical fight had started in front of embarrassed dinner guests.[13]

Amelia's name was cleared, but she would have been naïve not to have recognized that to some extent she had laid herself open to the accusations. George had been unhappy for some time about the amount of time Amelia spent with Paul, but it was not in his nature (nor in the spirit of their marriage contract) to question her behavior.

In one of George's letters to Amelia's mother, he mentioned the affair briefly after giving her details of Amelia's itinerary.

> If you have seen any of the clippings relative to Paul Mantz's divorce mess in Los Angeles, there is nothing to worry about. It was simply an effort by a cheap lawyer to get publicity for himself by perpetrating some innuendoes involving A.E.'s name. There was nothing we could do about it. Now it is all over.[14]

This time Amelia wrote at greater length:

> Poor old Myrtle Mantz. She had to get nasty in the trial. The only two women she had not driven away from Paul paid for their loyalty by being dragged into a divorce suit. The silly accusation fell of their

own weight and I cannot but feel she will eventually do something so disgraceful that the world will know what she is. Because, of course, after her self-inflicted publicity she will be watched. I really have been fortunate, for anyone who has a name in the paper is a target for all sorts of things. . . .[15]

The question of whether Amelia *did* have an affair with Mantz has been asked many times. It is highly unlikely; Amelia was simply not Paul Mantz's type of woman. He was flamboyant by nature and his romances were with passionate, more obviously beautiful and extroverted women than Amelia. Even after his second marriage, which was a happy one, Mantz indulged in casual love affairs, but he was also capable of treating a woman on equal terms, and in Amelia he probably recognized an equal spirit. Any excitement the two shared emanated from a kindred love of flight and plans for their proposed business ventures. Amelia enjoyed Mantz's company (few women would not), but if George was jealous of the time Amelia was able to spend with Paul (which is probable given his comments at a later date), it was most likely to have been because the respect and reliance she had previously placed only on George was now placed also on Paul.

In particular, Amelia relied on Paul's advice in her plans for a round-the-world flight. Why did Amelia wish to fly around the world? She had surely already proven herself as a pilot of note and her newsworthiness was established beyond question. It was necessary for a variety of reasons. Initially, she made record flights for publicity in order to secure her reputation and to launch her career. Then, after she had received public acclaim, she felt unease that her career, which meant so much to her, was based on what she considered a fabrication; she had not *earned* any credit by merely being Stultz's passenger. Her Atlantic solo flight had put to rest any doubts about her ability, for she had worked hard to acquire the necessary knowledge and experience that, together with her inherent courage, had enabled her to make that flight.

Since then, Amelia's various exploits had established her as a competent pilot—the best-known woman flier in the United States, thanks to George's superb management—and now she wanted and needed to make a final gesture. Both she and George could not have been unaware that the public were tiring of record-breaking flights. Virtually every major record worth taking had been taken, and short of faster and faster flights from point A to point B, there were few that would capture public attention. One was flight in the stratosphere—an area of aviation that had been under exploration by Amelia's friend the late Wiley Post before he was killed in an air accident in August 1935. (Wiley Post and Will Rogers were killed in a Lockheed Sirius equipped with floats. Undoubtedly the reduced performance of the airplane, due to the floats, had some bearing on the accident.) The other was a flight around the world by a woman.

The world had already been successfully flown—as early as 1924 by a U.S. Army Air Service team—but probably more notably by Wiley Post. For good measure, Post had flown it twice in his Lockheed Vega, the *Winnie Mae*. On the first occasion, in June 1931, the one-eyed, partially deaf aviator had taken a navigator (Harold Gatty) and completed his transglobal circumnavigation in eight days, fifteen hours, and fifty-one minutes.[16] This flight, Post readily admitted, did nothing for aviation, although it established his own reputation; at one point after a rough landing, he had to beat the propeller back into shape with a hammer and a rock—colorful stuff, but it did not reflect the professional image of aviation that he wished to project.

Post subsequently set to work to learn about instruments such as the new automatic pilots and radio direction finders—primitive as they were in those early days of aviation—to prove that flying could be made safer and more precise by modern technology. Two years later, in July 1933, using these instruments, he successfully accomplished a solo round-the-world flight in the *Winnie Mae* in seven days, eighteen hours, and forty-nine and one-half minutes. His biggest problem, obviously, was lack of sleep, but he ate only enough to keep himself alive; hunger, he said, helped to keep him awake! He had proven the value of instruments in aviation, however, and on his return he said that if man wanted to fly long distances safely and faster, he would have to go higher—into the stratosphere. There, big winds—jet streams—were known to exist that could add up to 200 mph to the speed of an airplane. He was working on this theory when he died and had achieved spectacular success when, wearing a pressure suit of his own design, he "rode" the jet stream from Burbank, California, to Cleveland, Ohio, at an average speed of 227 mph in an airplane with a designed maximum speed of 168 mph.[17]

So Amelia's ambition to fly around the world would provide her with a major "first"—she would be the first woman, if successful—but also, as she was later to confide to the President, her course was unique. Previous attempts always had been made to create time records and therefore the shortest possible route had been taken. Amelia decided to travel the longest possible distance by traversing the world at its waist, obviating the necessity to compete against existing records.

Amelia would never claim that this flight was being made purely for the fun of it, but she was quoted as saying that she was doing it to achieve a personal desire and "I want it to be a thorough check of modern equipment. I expect to keep a log of what happened to personnel and machine under various conditions. Records such as these, be they of success or failure can do much to safeguard subsequent flights."[18]

Funding for such a project was a critical factor. George and Amelia had no access to the necessary sum to buy and equip the Lockheed Electra that Paul Mantz and Amelia had already decided was the most suitable for the proposed flight. (Even had they been able to contemplate the $110,000 plus needed to buy the Sikorsky, it was not an airplane that Amelia could have flown with confidence, though Paul Mantz later claimed he would have been happier if Amelia had selected a seaplane.) In 1936, the amount required, even for the Electra, was a great deal of money and the Putnams certainly were not in a position to raise it on their own recognizance.

According to independent accounts by George, Amelia, and President Elliott of Purdue University, it was George who first planted the idea of a "Purdue flying laboratory" in Elliott's mind. There it bubbled around for a while, until in the autumn of 1935, at a dinner party at the Elliotts' home, Amelia outlined her dreams for women and aviation, which coincidentally seemed remarkably similar to the aims and ideals of Elliott. Before the evening was over, fellow guest David Ross offered to donate fifty thousand dollars as a gift toward the cost of providing a machine suitable for the flying laboratory. Further donations totaling thirty thousand dollars in cash and equipment were received from J. K. Lilly (of the Eli Lilly drug company), Vincent Bendix, and manufacturers Western Electric, Goodrich, and Goodyear.[19]

The $80,000 formed the basis of "The Amelia Earhart Fund for Aeronautical Research"; its primary aim was to "develop scientific and engineering data of vital importance to the aviation industry."[20] Many years later, when it was suggested that Amelia's flight was a spy mission, various writers would suggest that this sum had been provided by the government and paid through Purdue merely to provide a cover. However, R. B. Stewart (then secretary-treasurer of Purdue University), who masterminded the fund, is adamant that there was no government involvement whatsoever.

> The PRF gave this money [from Ross and Lilly] to Miss Earhart
> so that she might buy her airplane. . . . Contrary to popular belief,
> the money was not supplied by the United States government and

Purdue University was not used as a smoke-screen to disguise any association with this mission. I sincerely hope you can set the record straight.[21]

A man of significant financial brilliance, Stewart had developed the Purdue Research Foundation five years earlier to fund a building program and to provide fellowships. His skill at raising money in large amounts is demonstrated in the way he masterminded the college building fund.

> We were issuing Purdue University bonds to build dormitories and the Union building—all of them tax exempt. So I could receive a gift of a million dollars worth of stock on which the donor was getting interest and paying taxes on that interest. And I could say to that person, "I'll get you out. I'll sell that stock to the research foundation. The foundation will pay cash of sufficient amount to buy you Purdue bonds and that income will be tax-exempt so your net income will be the same. Now, when you die, then we cancel the Purdue bonds. The effect is—this is a deferred gift. There is no gift until you die. Actually, you're making money on it . . . "[22]

It was this same brain who masterminded the fund to buy Amelia a "flying laboratory." Almost everyone at Purdue was impressed by Amelia and her record; there was general and genuine pleasure that she was part of their team and great enthusiasm at any chance to play some part in her career.

There were only a few critics; some of the older women—wives of professors, in the main—were shocked that Amelia wore slacks not only around the dormitories but also in Lafayette's drugstore/soda fountain. Once, she even went down to dinner wearing slacks, which was not accepted dress in the conservative midwest.

Dean Potter huffily announced that Amelia was not scholastically qualified to be a member of the university faculty. A woman faculty member retorted that the dean was a scholar and didn't recognize the importance of motivating young people as well as educating them. Amelia merely mentioned that she had taught Harvard University extension courses as long ago as the mid-twenties and felt she was qualified. Indeed, in terms of practical experience there was probably no one better qualified.

George had been placed in charge of administrative arrangements for the airplane by Elliott and Stewart[23] and in March 1936 he advised Lockheed that the financial arrangements had been completed and he was in a position to make the initial payment, but in view of the circumstances he looked for some price reduction. The equipment manufacturers, he felt, should be willing to supply their products at cost because of potential publicity and especially since Amelia would make nothing out of the plane, "all proceeds going directly to the Purdue Fund for aviation research."

"Delivery is required June," George wrote, "so please step on it." A month later, he was writing again at great length advising Lockheed on technical matters such as engine size, fuel system, a special hatch cover, and to say that, in Amelia's absence, Paul Mantz's approval was the final authority on all technical matters. Stressing the need for confidentiality, he instructed that the plane should be registered in his name and specified the Electra Model 10E, which came with two Pratt & Whitney Wasp S3H-1 engines, each capable of developing 550 horsepower. With the fuel loads she would be carrying in the extra tanks, Amelia would need the power of the largest engines issued by Lockheed for the Electra.[24]

Much thought was given to the radio equipment. Amelia (and George) had been extremely impressed with the radio telephone she had used in the Vega on her transpacific flight and she was reluctant to revert to telegraphy, which she said she had not practiced for a number of years (probably not since the 1932 Atlantic solo, if then). Western Electric supplied a standard transport 50-watt radio transmitter (13A) and a new, continuously adjustable, four-band receiver (20A) with suitable power and remote-control apparatus.[25] The equipment transmitted on 6210 kcs. (kilocycles, but now referred to as kilohertz) during the daytime and 3105 kcs. at night—standard aircraft frequencies—but was modified to incorporate an emergency frequency on 500 kcs, which she could, if necessary, use in conjunction with a code-transmitting key. To work effectively on 500 kcs., a 250-foot trailing aeriel was required. These aerials were technically effective but cumbersome to use, as they were heavy and had to be let out and reeled in by means of a handle, a tiring job just before landing, when there were many other jobs taking up a pilot's attention. They were also mechanically unreliable, for in order to prevent the wire from lashing about, the aerial terminated in a heavy lead ball, which was apt to break off under the strain imposed by the aircraft's speed through the air; the antennae then became useless.

Both the radio and the code transmitter were able to be used by either the pilot or navigator from their respective positions in the cockpit and rear cabin.[26]

While George and Paul Mantz worked out the administrative details, Amelia continued her lecture tour, writing to her mother, "The rumor about the world flight in June is applesauce. Confidentially I shall have a new airyplane to play with then, I hope, but as I'm busy lecturing until

May or thereabouts I shall not hop off in June. It would take months to prepare for such a trip—maybe a year." Amy's hopes may have risen about her daughter settling down by the line in this letter: "I have a grand surprise for you. I can't tell you now but it's a swell one."[27] This was followed in several subsequent letters with a tantalizing promise that she would "probably come north to see you and unfold the great secret."[28]

Taken out of context, these sentences have been used to suggest that Amelia may have been pregnant, but several letters in the archives at Radcliffe College's Schlesinger Library reveal merely that she and George had planned a surprise trip for Amy to visit Europe with a young cousin, Nancy Balis, as companion.

Everything had been planned by Amelia for Amy, including lengthy lectures on *exactly* what to pack and how to pack it, even how to launder it. "I have given you very decent stockings. Also everyday ones. Keep separate . . ."; detailed instructions followed on how to don silk (pre-nylon days) stockings, and how to remove them to prevent them from sagging. More followed: "If raining do not wear kid gloves. They'll spot. . . . Keep manicured and have hair done every ten days. . . ." Lists of minutiae contained what Amy might do, where she might go, and what she might say: "Please don't down the Roosevelt administration. It's all right to be reactionary inside but it is out of step with the times to sound off about the chosen people who have inherited or grabbed the earth. You must think of me when you converse and I believe the experiments carried on today point the way to a new social order when governments will be the voice of the proletariat far more than democracy ever can be. In all cases be careful of reporters. . . ."[29]

On July 21, 1936, Amelia was in Los Angeles to test-fly the Lockheed Electra 10E, registration R16020, with Lockheed's test pilot, Elmer C. McLeod.[30] The inevitable news stories that accompanied the event described the airplane as being capable of flying up to forty-five hundred miles nonstop and detailed the special state-of-the-art equipment on board. Amelia took formal delivery of the plane on July 24, her thirty-ninth birthday.

Amelia was no doubt delighted with her new "ship," but there were some drawbacks. It was no easy switch from the Vega to the Electra with its sophisticated controls and twin engines. It was a physically taxing airplane to fly and Amelia's reserves of physical energy did not run deep. With Paul as her tutor, however, she began learning how to master it. There were times when Paul grew angry at her seeming inability to grasp what to him were fundamentals of flying and he drove her hard. It was at Paul's insistence that she spent time in a Link trainer that he installed in his hangar at Burbank; and there she learned about instrument flying in simulated conditions. However, Paul, in fact, was never entirely satisfied with her ability to fly the Electra, no matter how much she practiced, and despite his personal respect for her.[31]

A month earlier, George had written to Eleanor Roosevelt on Amelia's behalf :

> . . . to avail ourselves of the help which you kindly offered when we last saw you. Our wish is to be put in touch with the proper person in the State Department whose aid can be enlisted in connection with A.E.'s proposed world flight. We want appropriate guidance in securing the required permissions. . . . Do please emphasize that the project is for the present confidential. As you know A.E. likes to avoid advance discussion of flights—their realization depends upon so many factors.[32]

In referring this letter to Richard Southgate, Chief of Division of Protocol, the First Lady's secretary wrote:

> Mrs. Roosevelt, upon her return to Washington, the other day, found Mr. George Palmer Putnam's letter to her and learned that you had kindly consented to take care of the things he wished done in the State Department.
>
> Mrs. Roosevelt asked me to send you this special note to say that she had promised Mr. Putnam to keep this matter confidential. She is sure you understand and that you will be *very* nice to him.[33]

The constant obsession in government papers for confidentiality regarding Amelia's flight appears to stem from this letter and, having received patronage on such a level, George was never slow to hint at the relationship that Amelia and the First Lady enjoyed.[34]

Meanwhile, George was liaising with Gene Vidal, once Amelia's colleague at TAT and now director of Air Commerce.

> I am told that hard surface runways are being installed in the Navy Field [Luke Field]. This is down at Pearl Harbor at sea level. On A.E.'s former flight she used Wheeler Field, which is Army and has some altitude and no hard surface runways. What I want to get is an exact description of the new runways, the total length of the pavement, the extra run and nature of the approaches. If they are not finished, I would like an estimate of what the condition will be as of, say, February. I do so hope you can get the information from the Navy Department.[35]

A week later, George's follow-up letter had an intriguing paragraph implying that he was aware of something that Vidal wished to keep secret:

> By the way I golfed Saturday with George Leisure, the lawyer.
> *Remember?* . . . Well, George is kinda peeved at you. He says each
> time he meets you you have apparently forgotten him entirely—go
> through the motions of being introduced again. He felt you were just
> trying to high-hat him and pretending you never had that night
> meeting with him. I told him I knew that wasn't true but that you
> are sometimes dumb about names and faces! He asked me how many
> times you would finally have to meet him before you'd remember
> him. I am sure you do recall that he did render you a very great service
> one night. And naturally it is not unreasonable for him to be peeved.
> When are you coming up for more tennis?[36]

But only a month later, Amelia cabled quixotically on Vidal's behalf,
direct to Eleanor Roosevelt.

> . . . CONCERNING A MEAN AND UNFORTUNATE INSTANCE OF POLITICAL SCHEM-
> ING. . . . AVIATION IS MY VOCATION AND AVOCATION. I SHOULD RATHER HELP
> THE INDUSTRY THAN PROGRESS MYSELF. THUS I FEEL THE PRE-EMPTORY DIS-
> MISSAL OF THE DIRECTOR OF AIR COMMERCE AND TWO ASSISTANTS SUBSTITUT-
> ING [A] LEGALLY TRAINED INDIVIDUAL FOR ONE OF PRACTICAL EXPERIENCE
> ALMOST A CALAMITY. THERE IS LITTLE USE OF MY TRYING TO INTEREST OTHERS
> IN THE PRESIDENT'S CAUSE WHEN MY HEART IS SICK WITH THE KNOWLEDGE
> THAT AN INDUSTRY CAN BE JEOPARDIZED AND AN INDIVIDUAL'S CAREER
> BLASTED BY WHAT SEEMS A PERSONAL FEUD. . . .[37]

Her plea seems to have stimulated instantaneous action, for although
Vidal had already been dismissed and given one day's notice to clear his
office, on September 17, Amelia cabled Mrs. Roosevelt her thanks.

> . . . FOR YOUR HELPFULNESS IN THE MATTER ABOUT WHICH I WIRED YOU. AN
> INFORMED OUTCOME NOW PROMISES TO BE SATISFACTORY TO VIDAL WHOSE
> LOYALTY MERITS THE FAIR TREATMENT WHICH YOUR INTERESTS SECURING. I
> AM SURE YOU UNDERSTAND THAT I WAS ACTUATED BY DESIRE TO SERVE THE
> INDUSTRY, THE INDIVIDUAL AND THE ADMINISTRATION.[38]

Eugene Vidal had been a close friend of the Putnams since the early days
of Amelia's involvement with the TAT airline. Indeed it was through
Amelia's influence with the Roosevelts that Vidal had been appointed to

the post of Director of Air Commerce in 1935.[39] His son, Gore Vidal, was very much aware of the debt his father owed to Amelia. "Eleanor was in love with Amelia and Amelia used this to get her way over lots of things, such as getting my father into the cabinet."[40] From surviving correspondence, there is no doubt that George and Amelia had used this friendship, trading on Vidal's position and contacts, to short-cut formalities when planning record flights. Permissions that usually took months to obtain were miraculously available to Amelia in days, for example. In particular, Vidal's loss of office at the Bureau of Air Commerce at this moment would have been a severe blow, for he had access to official information that the Putnams could not get from any other source. Fortunately, her direct appeal to Eleanor Roosevelt paid off; Vidal was reinstated.

The summer passed quickly for Amelia. Apart from the usual round of lectures, her lecture file shows that in 1936 she gave 136 speeches and lectures. She usually drove to these because there was seldom a landing strip conveniently placed; driving through the night and sleeping during the day before delivering her speech and leaving immediately for the next venue. Apart from this round of lectures, there was a residential visit to Purdue, and work for the Department of Commerce, in which for one dollar a year she was commissioned to test a new direction finder.

Amelia's correspondence took up a great deal of time; she wrote often to Gene Vidal on matters of aviation generally, and wrote a great number of responses to young women who had requested advice on aviation as a career.[41] In addition, Amelia organized the women's handicap race at the 1936 National Air Races. Consequently, it was George who met Amy in New York when she returned from her European trip; Amelia was simply too busy. In two months, Amelia found time for only two hastily scribbled notes to Amy—the first to enclose pictures of the newly completed house in Hollywood, and the second to say that she and George would visit Boston to discuss her sister's rapidly escalating marital problem.[42]

Despite all the problems created by his divorce case, the friendship between Amelia and Paul Mantz seems to have remained as strong as ever. Her reliance upon his technical advice was total. His knowledge of the latest developments was formidable, and both Amelia and George must have recognized that the level of assistance that Paul could, perhaps uniquely, provide was essential for the round-the-world project.

Throughout these months, George, too, was busy coordinating the logistics of Amelia's proposed flight. His own concerns seemed to have dwindled to ad hoc jobs such as steering a Paramount movie (*Go West Young Man,* starring Mae West) through its New York premiere with all the resultant ballyhoo. George had formed a company, Major Pictures, to promote these activities, but it is clear that he spent most of his time during this period "managing" Amelia Earhart. He wrote streams of letters to government and military departments requesting information on weather and charts of the Pacific. Some of the requested information was classified, he was advised, but the navy would assist where they could and two reports in particular—"Climatic Features of the Pacific Island Region" and "Detailed Information on Seaplane Anchorages and Landing Fields"—that might be of help would be made available for George's examination if he could come to Washington, he was told.[43]

A proposal that Amelia should use in-flight refueling on the longest section of her planned route occupied George for some weeks, as did securing the services of professionals. Former naval navigator Commander Clarence S. Williams would prepare detailed charts of the entire route; and Amelia would take Harry Manning, a distinguished master mariner with the United States Lines, as navigator for the more difficult legs of the trip. Manning had commanded the S.S. *President Roosevelt*—on which Amelia had returned from England in 1928. They had been friends since, and Manning, who was a radio ham and a pilot in his spare time, obtained a three-month leave of absence from his employers in order to make the trip. A full-time mechanic, Bo McKneely, was employed, and Paul Mantz was contracted as technical advisor at one hundred dollars a day.

The area of the Pacific Ocean with its myriad groups of islands over which Amelia would have to fly was not well charted (except by the British Admiralty, who were not consulted). During the previous two years, various surveys had been carried out by the U.S. Navy to correct charts that in some instances contained information provided by the navigators of clipper ships a century or more earlier. Clarence Williams would have known that the only way to get access to the latest information was through official channels—civilian records were pitifully inadequate for the trip Amelia planned. Recognizing that in order to get the full cooperation that she would need from various government departments for the complicated Pacific section of her flight, Amelia wrote at length to the White House—this time to the final authority.

NOVEMBER 10TH 1936

Dear Mr. President,

Some time ago I told you and Mrs Roosevelt a little about my confidential plans for a world flight. As perhaps you know, through the co-operation of Purdue University I now have a magnificent twin-motor, all metal plane especially equipped for long distance flying.

For some months Mr. Putnam and I have been preparing for a flight which I hope to attempt probably in March. The route, compared with previous flights, will be unique. It is east to west, and approximates the equator. Roughly it is from San Francisco to Honolulu; from Honolulu to Tokio[44]—or Honolulu to Brisbane; the regular Australia–England route as far west as Karachi; from Karachi to Aden; Aden via Khartoum across Central Africa to Dakar; Dakar to Natal, and thence to New York on the regular Pan American route.

Special survey work and map preparation is already under way on the less familiar portion of the route as, for instance, that in Africa.

The chief problem is the jump westward from Honolulu. The distance thence to Tokio is 3900 miles. I want to reduce as much as possible the hazard of the take-off at Honolulu with the excessive overload. With that in view, I am discussing with the Navy a possible *refueling in the air over Midway Island.* If this can be arranged, I need to take much less gas from Honolulu, and with the Midway refueling will have ample gasoline to reach Tokio. As mine is a land plane, the seaplane facilities at Wake, Guam, etc. are useless.

This matter has been discussed in detail by Mr. Putnam with Admiral Cook, who was most interested and friendly. Subsequently a detailed description of the project, and request for this assistance, was prepared. It is now on the desk of Admiral Standley, by whom it is being considered.

Some new seaplanes are being completed at San Diego for the Navy. They will be ferried in January or February to Honolulu. It is my desire to practice actual refueling operations in the air over San Diego with one of these planes. That plane subsequently from Honolulu would be available for the Midway operation. I gather from Admiral Cook that technically there are no extraordinary difficulties. It is primarily a matter of policy and precedent.

In the past the Navy has been progressive in its pioneering, and so broad-minded in what we might call its "public relations," that I think a project such as this (even involving a mere woman!) may appeal to Navy personnel. Its successful attainment might, I think, win for the Service, further popular friendship.

I should add the matter of international permissions etc., is being handled very helpfully by the State Department. The flight, by the way, has no commercial implications. The operation of my "flying laboratory" is under the auspices of Purdue University. Like previous flights I am undertaking this one solely because I want to, and because I feel that women now and then have to do things to show what women can do.

Forgive the great length of this letter. I am just leaving for the west on a lecture tour and wanted to place my problems before you.

Knowing your own enthusiasm for voyaging, and your affectionate interest in Navy matters, I am asking you to help me secure Navy cooperation—that is if you think well of the project. If any information is wanted as to purpose, plans, equipment etc., Mr. Putnam can meet anyone you designate, any time, any where.

Very sincerely yours,
Amelia Earhart

P.S. My plans are for the moment entirely confidential—no announcement has been made.[45]

The original of this letter in the Roosevelt files bears a handwritten scrawl across the top of the front page: "Do what we can and contact Mr. Putnam." A formal memorandum was written to the Chief of Naval Operations, in which "the President hoped the Navy would do what they could to cooperate with Miss Amelia Earhart in her proposed flight and that in this connection, contact should be made with Mr. Putnam."[46]

Appropriate naval cooperation was thus secured (though George was advised that Amelia would have to take appropriate instruction on in-flight refueling procedures and bear the costs of the exercise, about two thousand dollars) and because of Amelia's request, all correspondence was stamped CONFIDENTIAL. It was probably through Gene Vidal that George learned of a possible alternative to the questionable flight refueling proposals.

The Department of Commerce was about to establish an emergency field on tiny Howland Island, a convenient stage roughly halfway between the Hawaiian Islands and New Guinea. Indeed, a construction party was due to leave Honolulu in early January to begin working on the project.[47]

The United States had begun a colonization project on the uninhabited island of Howland on April 2, 1935; prior to this, there was some doubt as to whether it was a British or American possession.[48] The declared intention of the U.S. government at that stage was to assert United States sovereignty in order to use the island "for weather observations and reporting and for the clearing of emergency landing strips."[49] As director of Air Commerce, Vidal became involved with the landing-strip project, with the principal aim of providing emergency landing facilities for Pan American airlines, who were then just beginning surveys for proposed air services in that part of the Pacific. In May 1936, administration of the island became the responsibility of the Department of the Interior and there was a certain amount of internal political maneuvering as each department fought for its rights. In June 1936, the Department of the Interior organized an expedition to Howland and the nearby islands of Baker and Jarvis, using the coast guard cutters S.S. *Itasca* and S.S. *Tiger*. The *Itasca*'s navigator took the opportunity to correct the coordinates of the island, which appeared incorrectly on charts, but it was some years before the corrections appeared on new hydrographic charts.

At some point in their many discussions regarding Amelia's flight, Vidal undoubtedly mentioned Howland Island and its proposed landing strip. Such a landing seemed infinitely preferable to refueling in flight, for, apart from the degree of difficulty in the actual task of refueling, there was Amelia's physical condition to take into account. How could she stay awake and alert over the period of twenty-four hours, flying the airplane with no one to spell her occasionally? And how was she to fly the plane and manage the complicated maneuver of "docking" the fuel lines? Paul Mantz had told them plainly that he thought it an inadvisable solution unless completely unavoidable.[50]

Amelia opted to land on Howland Island provided the landing strip was finished in time and if she could obtain the necessary permissions. After much correspondence, these were secured from departments as diverse as the Department of Air Commerce and the coast guard, but the construction of the landing strip had run afoul of bureaucracy at the Treasury Department. Amelia once again wrote to President Roosevelt for help.

> . . . am now informed apparently some question regarding WPA [Works Progress Administration] appropriation in amount three thousand dollars which covers all costs other than those borne by me for this mid Pacific pioneer landing field which permanently useful and valuable aeronautically and nationally. Requisition now on desk of A. V. Keene, Bureau of Budget, Treasury Department. Understand its moving requires executive approval under circumstances could you expedite as immediate action vital . . . please forgive troublesome female flyer for whom the Howland Island project is key to world flight attempt.[51]

In reply, Amelia was advised that federal funds had been allocated to enable the Bureau of Air Commerce to build the emergency landing field and that the working party was scheduled to leave Honolulu on January 12.[52]

George and Amelia spent Christmas 1936 in Indio, California, with financier Floyd Odlum and his wife, the noted aviatrix Jacqueline Cochran. Amelia and Jackie had been friends for some time and Odlum, a multimillionaire, had made some contribution to the round-the-world flight fund. The relationship had gotten off to a rough beginning when George took the same approach to Jackie that he had taken with Lady Heath and Elinor Smith. Just as with those two ladies, in Jackie he met a powerful character; but Jackie had the power of her husband's millions behind her. Of their first meeting, Jackie said:

> He was very patronizing, and said, "Well, little girl, what's your ambition in flying?"
> "To put your wife in the shade," I replied.[53]

Such an unpromising start had not hindered the growth of a genuine friendship. Over Christmas, Amelia and Jackie spent a great deal of time discussing aviation, but, in particular, they shared an interest in mental telepathy and psychic phenomena. They evidently put their interest to some practical use, for an airplane belonging to Western Air Express was reported missing on December 15, 1936. On December 22, Amelia telephoned the airline, claiming to have had some sort of vision in which a trapper had found the wreckage and looted it. A trapper subsequently turned up near Salt Lake City and reported finding the wreckage but disappeared without trace before giving the location. Amelia next predicted that she would make a startling discovery on May 10 concerning this wreckage, but there is no evidence that she ever did so.[54]

Quite what to make of these claims, so unlike the practical, even prosaic Amelia, is difficult, and becomes more so in the light of subsequent events. On December 27, while Amelia was still a guest at Indio, a United Airlines scheduled flight was reported missing. Amelia reportedly telephoned the United Airlines office in Burbank and told them to search for the wreck at Saugas, a small town to the north of Burbank. The wreckage was duly found in the location she had given them.[55]

One further incident in this weird chain occurred two weeks later when a Western Express charter plane crashed. Amelia advised officials to search near Newhall, fifteen miles north of Burbank, where (again) the wreckage was found as she predicted.[56] Later, Jackie Cochran substantiated the newspaper reports of these events and claimed that they had a pact to contact each other in case of emergency.[57]

Throughout January 1937, George continued to work on flight preparations while Amelia completed the last in her current series of lectures. A domestic crisis also intruded at this time when Muriel and Albert Morrissey decided to divorce. In a long letter dated January 31, Amelia berated her sister for "giving in too much" to Albert. "Given a little power over another, little natures swell to hideous proportions," she scolded.

> . . . What's done is done. The problem is what to do now. In order to protect you—from yourself as much as anything—I want several things done. One, the stock which you bought with the thousand dollars Mother gave you is to be made over to GPP. . . . Then Albert is to return the five hundred dollars to you which you gave him in a separate transaction. . . . you will probably have to obtain a legal separation in order to get a monthly income. Please do not go to any old lawyer on this. I am coming east this week and unless events move too fast, hold the legal part until I get to NY. If you have to see someone, go to the man whose name I gave you before. And don't SIGN ANYTHING IN THE MEANTIME. Do not even write letters to Albert on the subject of the divorce or separation. Don't move out of the house away from Albert no matter how tough things may get. . . . Perhaps Albert can be brought to his senses if GPP presses for the notes. I shall write to him to find out. Of course our money is gone [the money the Putnams had loaned before Christmas]. That I can swallow, but it does make me sad to think that hard earned cash did no good. . . .[58]

There was little time to spare for family affairs, however, as the date for the flight moved ever closer. A further factor was advised by Vidal: Pan American Airways intended to carry out a flight survey in March to pioneer a new air route to Auckland via Pago Pago. The U.S. Navy and coast guard had been detailed to provide ships to assist on this survey; if Amelia could plan her trip to coincide with the flight, such assistance as they could render to Pan Am would be available to her also.[59]

In full possession of the arrangements made for the Pan Am escort, George traveled to Washington in early February to talk to chiefs at the U.S. Navy. In their discussions they decided:

> 1. That two aviation mechanics from Pearl Harbor travel to Howland on the coast guard cutter *Duane* for the purpose of servicing the Lockheed; and further, that the U.S.S. *Ontario*, a station ship at Samoa, would

stand by "to act as plane guard" for the flight at some point about one thousand miles southwest of Howland Island and relay weather information to the *Duane* at Howland;

2. That the Governor of American Samoa, Pago Pago, obtain weather conditions from Suva, Fiji, and from Australia and other locations and transmit data to *Duane;*

3. That the U.S.S. *Swan* cruise to a position halfway between Honolulu and Howland Island to act as standby ship in case of an emergency and transmit weather information to Pearl Harbor and the *Duane.* (The *Swan* to return to Pearl Harbor after Amelia's safe landing on Howland).

George then confirmed these requests in writing to Admiral Leahy, Chief of Naval Operations, as part of a high-handed, name-dropping exercise that would be hard to beat for barefaced cheek. He got away with it, as he did with all his other requests—that Amelia might use Wheeler Field at Hawaii, for example.[60]

What does emerge clearly after examination of thousands of documents in American and British archives is that any government involvement in the planning of Amelia's flight was solely at the behest of George and Amelia. Navy chiefs bridled, displaying reluctance and annoyance on occasion, but George bullied, cajoled, and threatened until he got what he wanted. Every new privilege that was extended to this ace bargainer was quickly accepted and further privileges were requested.

On February 12, Amelia, with Harry Manning in attendance, held a press conference at the Barclay Hotel in New York City to announce the round-the-world flight. It was all that George could have hoped for, with batteries of newsreel cameras and gangs of eager reporters. Amelia arrived late, indeed had even forgotten her own wedding anniversary celebration planned some weeks earlier, for which she was teased by George, but she quickly settled into her usual role of hosting the interview.

One of George's main tasks was to ensure that Amelia reaped some financial reward from the flight. Remembering the success of the Mexican stamp issue—when the stamps had quickly become great collectors' items, reaching a value of one hundred dollars within months—he had ten thousand special envelopes printed, which Amelia would carry on the airplane. Once the flight had been formally announced in the press, Gimbel's, the New York department store, started advertising the Amelia Earhart Special Cover in its philatelic advertisements. "Most of the covers carried by Miss Earhart in previous flights are now worth between $25 and $200," the blurb ran. "The covers will be postmarked at Oakland at the beginning and termination of the flight and also at a city in Australia or India. A Howland Island cachet, the first one in its history, will also be affixed to these covers. . . . Price of this usual cover $2.50; same cover with Miss Earhart's autograph $5.00."[61]

In addition to the special covers, George was already booking a post-flight lecture tour for Amelia at five hundred dollars per appearance. Despite the fact that the airplane and basic equipment had been provided for her by Purdue University, the Putnams had sunk a great deal of their personal money into the preparations and supplies for this flight. Indeed it would become obvious before too long that far from being wealthy, the Putnams had few financial reserves and they were relying on the success of the project to rectify this position.

From New York Amelia flew to California, taking Harry Manning, Bo McKneely (the Lockheed's mechanic), and George, to make final preparations for her flight. Alighting in Blackwell, Oklahoma, when a minor fault occurred with the propeller synchronization, the party were forced by bad weather to spend the night. George chose this moment to play one of his famous practical jokes.

While the party were dining, he slipped to the telephone and called the chief of police. Later, when Amelia was driving out to the airport in a borrowed car, she was stopped, booked for speeding, and taken to the police station, with Harry Manning belligerently complaining that they had seen no speed-limit sign. In a hurry to get away, Amelia elected to go to court immediately and pleaded guilty. The police judge, having given Amelia a lecture about speeding, turned to George, apparently not understanding the relationship, and asked, "Are you responsible for this woman?" Relishing every moment of this, George retorted, "No your honor. I'm just a relative and I disown her." The courtroom tittered, and from George's expression, Amelia began to suspect that she had been set up. The judge (who George thought was in on the joke, but was not) fined Amelia the minimum amount of $1, since she was a visitor, and $3.50 in costs. Later, he asked George whether the lady was really Amelia Earhart; "I thought they were trying to kid me all the time," he said.

Afterward, when the "fine" had been returned to her and they were all laughing about it—George more than anyone—Amelia wryly accepted George's little-boy victory. "You've behaved pretty well up to now but I've half a mind to take off without you," she said to him for the benefit of reporters, asking of one, "How much is the bus fare to Burbank . . . for one?" Here she is reported to have called him by a nickname not previously heard before—"Muggy."[62]

Amelia got her revenge in a neat fashion. Although George had long been a regular air traveler, he continued to suffer from airsickness. Shortly after the couple's return to California, he boarded a plane to return to New York and after about an hour he was handed a small package by the stewardess. It was from Amelia. He opened it to find a raw pork chop.[63]

The laughter always present between the two may have helped break the tension that had already started to build up in the team, and for the next month, there was precious little time for laughter. There were countless details to be worked out and checked, such as ensuring that supplies of aviation fuel and oil would be in place all along Amelia's route. Such caches were also arranged at places where Amelia hoped not to have to put down, but where extra fuel should be available just in case. Jacques de Sibour of Standard Oil, whom Amelia had met after her solo transatlantic flight in 1932, had experience flying in the tropics, and many valuable contacts; he was extraordinarily helpful to George in this respect. Not only fuel and oil but also parcels of spares were shipped out to various destinations, to be available should they be needed.

There was, rightly, a great deal of discussion on the difficulty surrounding a landfall on Howland Island, a tiny barren dot in the Pacific Ocean. A half mile wide and two miles long, Howland Island is about forty miles from the nearest land—Baker Island, some twenty-five miles north of the equator. It would take extraordinarily accurate navigation to locate this coral formation whose highest point was only eighteen feet, but Manning seemed confident that he could do so.

Paul Mantz listened grimly to Manning's confident assertions. His own feeling was that using a sextant on the deck of a ship had nothing in common with celestial navigation from the roof hatch of an airplane, and it may have been Paul who suggested that they engage Frederick Noonan, a former navigator on the Pan American Pacific Clipper routes across the Pacific. Noonan had made a dozen or so trips in the area, knew the problems that would be encountered, and had experience at celestial navigation from a plane.

It was Paul Mantz who had designed the navigator's table and work area in the Electra after examining the setup on the Pan American Clippers. Noonan would have found all the equipment familiar. There was a good-sized table on which to spread charts, and a glass inset in this worktop enabled the navigator to use the master aperiodic compass mounted underneath. A chronometer was fitted beside the table in rubber mounts, and other instruments installed at this position were altimeter, air-speed and drift indicators, a pelorus (sighting device for the compass), and a temperature gauge.

Noonan insisted that a bubble octant be installed in addition to the marine sextant because his experience had taught him that the latter was inadequate for shooting from an airplane.[64] The built-in "bubble" level provided an artificial horizon in case the actual horizon was obscured by clouds or because the plane was too high. Further, he required at least one additional chronometer, he said.[65]

Born in Chicago in 1894, Noonan is reputed to have run away to sea in 1908. He rounded the Horn seven times, and served on the largest square-rigged ship (*The Crompton:* circa 1910), sailing under the Union Jack; during World War I, it is said that he served in the British merchant navy in the North Atlantic, and was torpedoed three times. He had learned his navigation at the Weems School of Navigation in Annapolis and in 1925 he joined Pan American Airways as a navigation teacher.[66]

After two years, Pan Am transferred Noonan to active work as a navigator on their Pacific Clipper flying boats, and interspersed with this experience, he had the task of mapping out the air routes to Hawaii, Midway, Wake Island, Guam, the Philippines, and Hong Kong—on which he is reputed to have made more than a dozen flights as navigator. For a while around 1930, he was also stationed at Port-au-Prince, Haiti, as the station manager, and it was rumored among Pan Am employees that he was dismissed from Pan Am's service as a result of excessive drinking. Research has proved this to be inaccurate. He actually resigned because, as a navigator and not a pilot, he could go no further in the company ranks. He had recently married and felt that his navigator's salary was insufficient for his new needs; he was then forty-four years old and wanted to make a new start.[67]

It was Noonan's intention to start a navigation school and he must have fully recognized that being part of Amelia's round-the-world trip would provide him with an incalculable amount of free publicity. However, the stories of his heavy drinking are too widely based to have no foundation. His contemporaries in the aircraft scene in California all knew about this problem of Noonan's. It does not seem to have affected his work, however, and his professional reputation was that he was a first-class navigator. He was a heavy drinker, and this is borne out by the man who was Noonan's boss during his days with Pan American's transpacific operations. Clarence L. Schildhauer said that

> [Noonan was his] best navigator when he was sober, but he was inclined to go on benders. Mind you, Pan-Am started its transpacific services in November 1935 carrying mail only; passengers weren't carried until October 1936. From San Francisco to Manila took five calendar days [hopping via Honolulu, Midway, Wake, and Guam;

this was followed by a few days' stopover in Manila before the return flight]. Noonan developed a bad habit of going on a bender and getting lost among Manila's whorehouses. Before takeoff he'd have to be hunted down and "poured" aboard the airplane. It was a ten-hour flight to Guam; precise navigation wasn't needed until the halfway point so he could have a few hours to sleep it off.[68]

Noonan was given several warnings about his behavior, because—as Schildhauer reasonably pointed out—"it would not inspire confidence among the customers if they were to see the navigator being carried aboard in Manila."[69] Noonan did not wait to be fired, however; he resigned. But it is ironic that Amelia once again should have placed her trust, and the success of her flight, in the hands of a man with a reputation as a drinker.

Amelia said she fully appreciated the navigational difficulty involved in locating Howland Island, but she had four means of doing so: one, dead reckoning (an estimated position based on speed in a given direction maintained for a definite period); two, radio bearings from ships and shore stations; three, her radio direction finder; four, celestial navigation.

It was decided that Noonan would go along as far as Howland and return from there by ship. Manning would continue as far as Australia and Amelia would make the remaining journey alone. Shortly before the flight, it was decided that Paul Mantz would join the crew as far as Honolulu. Mantz claims Amelia asked him to go along,[70] but in an article written on the morning of the departure, Amelia claimed Mantz had asked her specifically because his fiancée, Terry, was on her way to Hawaii and he thought it a good opportunity to join her there. "We are leaving for Honolulu in a few minutes," Amelia wrote for the New York *Herald Tribune,* "and I have just made the most amusing discovery that I'm unwittingly playing the role of understudy to Cupid."[71] Elsewhere, Amelia said that she thought she "had just one more long flight in my system."[72] And then? "My lovely home in North Hollywood . . . California sunshine . . . books, friends . . . many things."[73]

There were days of tedious delay due to bad weather, which grounded even commercial airlines. Oakland Airport had an unpaved runway that turned to quagmire after heavy rain. At last, however, Amelia took off for Hawaii on March 17, 1937 with Manning, Noonan (appropriately, because it was St. Patrick's Day, wearing a bunch of shamrocks in honor of his Irish ancestry), and Mantz on board, together with 947 gallons of fuel. There was no great departure scene—they had been at the airport and prepared to leave on several occasions over the previous few days and the reporters were beginning to tire of the game. One, however, a photographer on the staff of the San Francisco *Chronicle,* rented an airplane and took a memorable picture of the Electra as it flew over the almost-completed Golden Gate Bridge shortly after takeoff.

Sole rights to Amelia's story had been sold to the *Herald Tribune* newspaper group, and as Amelia worked toward departure, George was bombarded with cables from the editor and proprietor (also his good friend), Helen Ogden Reid, stating that the exclusivity deal for Amelia's story meant that she should talk to *no one except Tribune representatives.* George replied that this would make Amelia look ridiculous; she would give interviews explaining her position regarding personal statements to reporters but must be free to answer general questions about her flight. If the *Tribune* was dissatisfied with this, then he would prefer to "washout the arrangement and refund advances . . . rather than cause overmuch grief. . . ."[74]

The flight to Honolulu took only fifteen hours and forty-seven minutes (as recorded by Amelia in *Last Flight*), trimming over an hour off the record held by the Pan Am Clipper service, and this despite the fact that Amelia and Mantz claimed to have throttled back for most of the journey to save the engines for the main flight yet to come. Amelia flew most of the time, with occasional periods of rest when Paul took over.

There were two very minor technical problems: Icing caused an engine to run rough for a short time and a radio generator burned out when Harry Manning held down the Morse-code key to enable a shore-based direction finder to take a bearing on them. Amelia's own commentary is interesting. Even though she was not carrying the full fuel load she anticipated taking on her longest hop, she did not feel able to manage the takeoff alone.

> Paul Mantz and I had carefully worked out the piloting technique of that start. It was a team-play take-off—each with his own job, I at the controls, Paul handling throttles and retractable landing gear.[75]

An hour out from Oakland, the crew sighted a Pan American Clipper "silhouetted against a towering bank of cumulus, sun flecked clouds . . . this was the first time I had ever seen another plane at sea, and later I was to learn that in all their Pacific crossings up to then Pan American pilots had never sighted each other."[76] Coincidentally, the pilot on that Clipper was Ed Musick, Noonan's former commander.

Both Amelia and Mantz were impressed with Noonan's navigation. Manning's role appears to have been one of checking the navigation and working the radio, but to Paul's annoyance, he constantly came into the already-cramped cockpit to shoot star sights through the cockpit hatch. It would have been better, Paul felt, if the hatch was in the main cabin. The flight gave Amelia her first opportunity to use the new radio direction finder (RDF) and Paul recorded that he was happy with her calm and professional approach.[77]

Noonan's navigation was accurate; when they brought the Electra down through the clouds, their landfall was directly in front of them. Paul Mantz's biography, *Hollywood Pilot*, states that Amelia "seemed to be tiring towards the end of the flight" and that as the Electra crossed over Honolulu's Wheeler Field, for a new east-west record (2,400 miles in fifteen hours, forty-seven minutes), "Amelia had asked Paul to land the ship; she looked groggy from the long flight."[78] She mentioned neither of these facts in her various accounts of the story but it does seem beyond doubt that it was at Amelia's request that Paul took over and landed the airplane, and Paul recalled that as he crossed Wheeler Field:

> I wrapped it around in a steep bank to check the wind sock. AE yelled "Don't! Don't!" She was very fatigued and kind of exuberant. She calmed down when I made a normal approach and we landed. . . .[79]

There was a delay in Hawaii before Amelia attempted to take off on the most dangerous leg of her journey: the flight to Howland Island, which lay more than 1,800 miles away. Noonan had flown similar routes on a dozen occasions previously and remained confident if naturally a little tense because of the media exposure. Mantz was to return to the mainland after Amelia's departure.

The twenty-four-hour departure delay was announced to the press as due to adverse weather conditions. In an internal report to the Chief of Naval Operations, however, U.S. Naval Lieutenant Arnold E. True stated as part of his detailed report:

> The forecast issued by me and confirmed by Aerological personnel at Pearl Harbor was for favorable flying conditions over the entire route, except for cloudiness and showers near Pearl Harbor. This forecast was verified by all subsequent weather reports over the route. It is understood that her delay was occasioned by other reasons.[80]

According to Paul Mantz, Amelia was simply too fatigued to leave immediately and needed to rest before setting out on a very physically taxing leg of the trip. Although the Honolulu–Howland leg was some six hundred miles shorter than the Oakland–Honolulu flight, the navigational problems were clearly a source of anxiety. After a day's rest, however, Amelia was ready to leave at daybreak on March 20. In the meantime, Paul flew the Electra on a test flight after a few adjustments had been made to the propeller lubrication bearings, and delivered it to Luke Field near Pearl Harbor.[81] Luke Field's three-thousand-foot paved runway was more practical for a takeoff with a 900-gallon fuel load (this included 590 gallons of high-test military aviation fuel—100 octane, which Mantz had acquired "by pulling a few strings"), to give extra boost at takeoff.

Amelia and her crew sat for an hour in the predawn light at the end of the runway—floodlighting was switched on for her but she waited for the sunrise—carrying out the routine preflight checks.

At last, the Electra started to roll. There was a slight crosswind and Mantz's chief concern was Amelia's habit of correcting any swing of the aircraft on the takeoff run by increasing power in the opposite engine, to straighten up. Countless times he had told her that on takeoff she *must* use the rudder pedals to keep the plane straight—that the *throttles* must be pushed smoothly forward together. Any "jockeying" would create a dangerous yaw in direction and potentially lead to a ground loop. He said many times that Amelia had never seemed to grasp the importance of this advice.[82]

The aircraft gathered speed and was about a thousand feet down the runway—probably ten seconds from takeoff—when the unthinkable happened. The plane appeared to drop its right wing. Amelia corrected by reducing power on the opposite engine and the plane swung to the left out of control in a classic ground loop. The undercarriage collapsed (the right wheel and undercarriage were torn away) and the machine careened along the runway on its belly, spraying showers of sparks before coming to rest. Despite the fact that fuel was pouring out through the drain well in the damaged belly, there was—miraculously—no fire.[83]

Many years later, it would be suggested that this crash was engineered by Amelia to buy time to plan her covert government mission, but only a fool would hope to get away with such a dangerous ploy; and Amelia was certainly no fool. The official U.S. Navy report on the accident, after consideration of the written and verbal testimony of several eyewitnesses, discovered the following:

> As the airplane gathered speed it swung slightly to the right. Miss Earhart corrected this tendency by throttling the left hand motor,

the aircraft then began to swing to the left with increasing speed, characteristic of a ground loop. It tilted forward, right wing low and for 50 or 60 yards was supported by the right wheel only. The right hand landing gear suddenly collapsed under the excessive load, followed by the left. The airplane spun sharply to the left sliding on its belly and amid a shower of sparks from the mat came to rest headed about 200 degrees from its initial course.[84]

Amelia had the presence of mind to cut the switches as soon as she knew she had lost control and the fire truck that had followed along the side of the runway reached the airplane within seconds. Witnesses said that Amelia stood up in the cockpit for a short time before crawling back through the cabin over the catwalk laid across the tops of the fuel tanks (usually she hoisted herself out through the hatch over the pilot's seat). Rescuers were already at the open cabin door and found Noonan calmly folding his charts, saying that he'd be ready to go again next time Amelia wanted to try. As Amelia climbed out, she appeared dazed and Mantz put an arm around her. "Something must have gone wrong," she told him.[85]

Manning was later to say of what he called "the Honolulu fiasco" that the crash was purely due to Amelia's lack of ability as a pilot.[86] She had overcorrected and the heavily overweight airplane had been too much for the landing gear in the resultant ground loop, he said.[87] Predictably the Putnams blamed the accident on mechanical failure: "Witnesses said a tire blew. However, studying the tracks carefully, I believe [that] possibly the landing gear's right shock absorber, as it lengthened, may have given way," Amelia said.[88]

George, waiting in Oakland, had merely heard on the radio that Amelia was about to take off. Later, he was to write that when the telephone rang he picked it up and heard:

> "Putnam?"
> "Yes."
> "Have you heard?" It was the Press Association. "They crashed . . . the ship's in flames. . . ."
> The gang was looking at me.
> "Here Bill [Bill Miller of the Depart of Commerce] . . . you take it."
> I could not listen further. I moved out into the cold morning, trying to walk steadily. In a few minutes they came racing after me. "No fire . . . no fire at all. False report! No one hurt! . . ."
> In 1932 in New York the telephone had told me falsely of a

crack-up ending to the Atlantic solo—uncorrected for many minutes. And now, in 1937, the black wings brushed close again. . . .[89]

Shortly afterward, George heard Amelia on the radio being asked whether she'd try again. "Of course," she said, and hesitated, "if it's possible . . . repairs . . . costs." Immediately, George "shakily scribbled" a cable to his wife. SO LONG AS YOU AND THE BOYS ARE OK THE REST DOESN'T MATTER AFTER ALL ITS JUST ONE OF THOSE THINGS. WHETHER YOU WANT TO CALL IT A DAY OR KEEP GOING LATER IS EQUALLY JAKE WITH ME.[90] An hour later, Amelia telephoned him, "her voice weary with sadness."[91] She told him she wanted to try again.

Practical as ever, George told her he'd make arrangements for the Electra to be shipped back to California. She and "the boys" could take the S.S. *Malolo* back to California; it was sailing the following day at noon.[92] Meanwhile, the ten thousand special covers had to be placed in the secure hands of the Honolulu postal authorities until they were needed again.[93]

In general, the newspapers were kind to Amelia, but a sour note was sounded by Major Al Williams, a highly respected flier and a leader in aircraft development. He stated:

> Like every other human enterprise, aviation suffers from a great number of ingeniously contrived rackets. Daring courageous individuals with nothing to lose and all to gain have used and are using aviation merely as a means toward quick fortune and fame. The worst racket of all is that of individually sponsored trans-oceanic flying . . . . [where] the personal profit angle in dollars and cents, and the struggle for personal fame, have been carefully camouflaged and presented under the banner of "scientific progress."
>
> . . . Amelia Earhart's "Flying Laboratory" is the latest and most distressing racket that has been given to a trusting and enthusiastic public. There's nothing in that "Flying Laboratory" beyond duplicates of the controls and apparatus to be found on board every major airline transport. And no one ever sat at the controls of her "Flying Laboratory" who knew enough about the technical side of aviation to obtain a job on a first-class airline. . . . Paul Mantz was the only pilot in the ship who knew how to take airplanes off and land them.
>
> Nothing is said about the thousands of dollars which she and her manager-husband expected to get for thousands of stamp cachets carried in the "Flying Laboratory." Nothing at all was hinted of the fat lecture contracts, the magazine and book rights for stories of the

flight. . . . No, the *whole* affair was labeled "purely scientific" for
public consumption.

Williams then went on to denigrate Amelia's reputation as a pilot:

> She lost control of the plane during a takeoff on the concrete
> runway on a standard Army airdrome and wrecked the "Flying Labo-
> ratory." And there again the public got a garbled story and a cleverly
> contrived explanation . . . plus a heroic story about cutting the
> switches and saving the lives of her crew. That ship got away from
> her on the take-off—that's the low down.
> Planes have to be held by clever pilots to straight courses on a
> getaway. And neither landing gear nor tires were designed to with-
> stand being jammed into the ground. Her plane was a stock type
> which is carrying passengers and mail in this country day after day
> . . . . It's time that the Bureau of Air Commerce took a hand in this
> business and it's my guess that the bureau will not grant Mrs. Amelia
> Earhart permission to make another attempt—[and] it's high time
> that [they] put an end to aviation's biggest racket—"Purely Scien-
> tific" ballyhoo. . . .[94]

Al Williams was merely voicing what many in the aviation industry felt
about Amelia's constant appearances in the media, and probably she and
George were very much aware of the groundswell of disapproval. George
managed to have the article commented on and refuted by C. B. Allen,
the redoubtable aviation correspondent of the New York *Herald Tribune,*
but Amelia was white-faced and hurt when shown the Williams article.
Her only comment to reporters, however, when questioned for her reaction was, "I'm glad it wasn't a woman who wrote it."[95]

Chapter Nineteen

1 9 3 7: Miami–Lae

G eorge Putnam has sometimes been blamed for Amelia's final and
fatal flight. It is said, and believed by many, that he insisted she
have the airplane repaired and carry on with the original plan. However,
within minutes of the crash at Luke Field, even before speaking to
George, Amelia had already told reporters that she wanted to try again.
In her book *Last Flight* (published posthumously), and in her numerous
accounts of the crash, she claimed that the thought had occurred to her
even as the plane slued to a halt among sparks at Luke Field. "If we don't
burn up I want to try again."[1]

Undoubtedly, George would not have argued with Amelia's decision
and his cable to her, prior to their telephone conversation, was a genuine
statement of his feelings on the matter. Her decision to carry on must
have given George pause, however, for the plane was uninsured (no one
would take the risk), so the financial loss to the Putnam resources was
serious. Much of the cost of the trip had already been expended and was
not recoverable; for example, an engineer had been flown out to Karachi
in order to overhaul the engines when Amelia reached India. He arrived
there, only to find Amelia's flight abandoned, so he was flown back again,
all at Amelia's expense. There was a substantial bill from the U.S. government for the work they had carried out on Amelia's behalf at Luke Field.[2]
The main expense was the repair and rebuilding of the Electra by Lockheed.[3] The financial implications of a possible second failure were frightening.

"Friends helped generously," Amelia recorded, but even so "I more-or-
less mortgaged my future. Without regret, however, for what are futures
for?"[4] However, it was not only her own future that was mortgaged; it
was also George's.

If Amelia had abandoned the entire idea, what then? Their losses were sustainable—but barely. Amelia (using her own money) had invested with Paul Mantz in several new businesses, which were now coming to fruition.[5] There were plans for Amelia and George to start a new airline in partnership with Gene Vidal and Floyd Odlum.

Amelia knew, however, that if she abandoned her plan, she would henceforward be remembered as the woman who once tried to fly around the world and failed. Her previous achievements would be overshadowed by this failure. Worse, her ability as a pilot would always be called into question. It was unthinkable, given Amelia's character, the determination amounting to stubbornness, her pride in the reputation she had painfully acquired, that she would not have tried again.

George's role, as usual, was to provide the means for Amelia to accomplish her goal and to offer support. In the weeks following the accident, it was George who arranged, through the navy, to make the necessary immediate repairs prior to crating and shipping the Electra back to California.

After consultation with Clarence Williams, Amelia decided that since the second start was so much later in the year it would be safer to reverse the original flight plan and fly eastward because of the weather conditions in the Caribbean and Africa. This required new diplomatic clearances as well as the extension of existing ones. George contacted their friend Jacques de Sibour, who once again obtained permissions to fly over alien territories and who relocated fuel, oil, and supplies of spares and obtained new prevailing weather patterns.

It was George who liaised with the navy and coast guard on the subject of guard ships and the provision of radio and direction-finding facilities for the flight; who organized new overlays for the stamp covers (and the marketing of them); who raised the money to pay for the Lockheed repairs and the additional costs of the rearranged flight; who organized in advance the provision of customs formalities at each of Amelia's stops so that she would run up against as little bureaucracy as possible; and who booked Amelia into a series of seventy postflight lectures at a fee of five hundred dollars per appearance.[6]

Amelia concentrated on the Electra and, perhaps chastened by her experience, flew with Paul Mantz to regain her confidence. Many hours were spent on "homework" simply absorbing the information obtained by George's administrative machine about weather conditions, airport facilities, and customs problems that she might meet at each stop along the way. Once again, she planned the inventory, assessing each item in order to remove every ounce of unnecessary weight, now only too aware of the Electra's sensitivity when overburdened.

Manning had told Amelia shortly after the Honolulu crash that he would not be able to accompany her, as his leave of absence would expire before she could make a second attempt. Immediately after the crash, he had publicly praised her coolness in cutting the switches and thus avoiding certain fire. Many years later, however, he was to say he made his decision because he had no faith in her ability, and it is obvious from the rest of his statement that their relationship had not been without its problems.

> Amelia Earhart was something of a prima donna. She gave the impression of being humble and shy; but she really had an ego, and could be as tough as nails when the occasion required it. I got very fed up with her bull-headedness several times. That's why she brought Noonan into the picture—in the event that I were to give up on the flight. AE herself was not a good navigator; and Noonan was a happy-go-lucky Irishman. He wasn't a "constant" navigator; I always felt that he let things go far too long. . . ."[7]

In addition to arranging the practical details of the flight itself, Amelia spent time writing the first five chapters of her book *World Flight*.[8] Her intention was to make notes throughout the flight and mail them back to George at each stop. They would be transcribed and filed to await her return, when she could use them to complete the book for early publication to take maximum advantage of the predictable publicity. Floyd Odlum made a donation of $10,000 to the finances of the second attempt and because of this, Amelia dedicated the book to him: "To Floyd, with gratitude for all-weather friendship." Vincent Bendix, one of the original backers of the flight, donated a further $20,000.[9]

There was always the never-ending flood of correspondence to be answered. On May 14, Amelia received a request from her former employers, Denison House, to send a personal message to "give a boost" to a fund-raising event. "I am sorry my preoccupation with flight preparations prevents my doing anything active for Denison House," Amelia replied. "Further, aviation accidents are very expensive. However, here is $25 for use for *girls* in some way. I hope they have camp privileges these days. . . ."[10]

Amy was still a guest at the house on Valley Spring Lane and at times the atmosphere there was less than harmonious. Amy was now sixty-eight years old—an intelligent woman who had been denied a career by virtue of the times in which she was born and brought up, and who had been denied, by Edwin's behavior, the comfortable family life she felt should have been hers by birthright. Amy had sacrificed much for her daughters and was very possessive of them both; in a sense, she never accepted that they were not still answerable to her. Amelia occasionally chafed at her mother's assumed dominion over her, but in general she was able to cope because her own natural leadership asserted itself. Besides, she loved her mother, without being blind to her faults. She had taken Amy with her on several lecture tours, flying her across the continent on at least two occasions.

The real problem was Amy's relationship with George, whose frenetic lifestyle and often peremptory manners and flashes of temper ruffled Amy. She had not the sense to remain quiet, however, and her way of dealing with the problem was to snipe at George whenever possible, which created tension between Amelia and Amy. Sometimes the constant criticism and acrimonious asides Amy made about George became embarrassing enough to cause Amelia to ban her mother from the dinner table and make her eat in her room until things improved.[11] George, however, was tolerant of Amy's scoldings (he otherwise found her to be a rather sweet, if improvident, person) for Amelia's sake.

At the Putnam home, in addition to Amy, there were Jo Berger, the secretary whom Amelia and George had shared for some years and who often traveled with them between New York and Los Angeles; a young woman general assistant, Margo de Carrie, who worshiped Amelia, did secretarial work in Jo's absence, and otherwise helped in many ways, such as meeting airplanes, ferrying guests around, and entertaining Amy. The house was run by Fred, the Filipino majordomo. There were also numerous casual callers and, just as at Rye, the house in the Hollywood hills could scarcely be called restful, despite its tranquil setting.

One regular caller during May 1937 was Albert Bresnik, a young photographer whom George had designated "Amelia Earhart's official photographer"; it was George's way of attempting to control the release of photographs of Amelia, especially during the round-the-world trip. Originally, Bresnik had been approached with the idea that he would join Amelia for one or two sections of the flight. "The idea was that she would be meeting heads of state and VIPs along the way and if I went along as official photographer then we'd have total control of all photography concerned with the trip. I was twenty-three at the time and it would have been quite an achievement, so I was very disappointed when told I wouldn't be going along."[12]

One morning, a few days before Amelia left on her flight, Bresnik called on Amelia to show her proofs of some photographs he'd taken at a photo session.

> . . . we were in the kitchen having coffee and I asked her what she was planning to do after the trip. I can't remember her exact words but she told me she thought there was a possibility she was pregnant and that when she came back she was going to be "just a woman."[13]

Lockheed worked hard to make the necessary repairs, against a tight schedule. A considerable amount was done to strengthen the Electra against the potential stresses of overloading, for the question of fuel loads was constantly on Amelia's mind after the Honolulu incident. The engines were thoroughly overhauled and on May 18, only a little over a month after it had returned to California, the newly rebuilt Electra was delivered to Amelia.

While the airplane had been undergoing repairs, Paul Mantz had been busy; although the Eclipse flow meter and a Cambridge fuel analyzer appeared to have worked well on the Oakland–Honolulu flight, he returned both to the manufacturers for overhaul.[14] He also worked out a carefully planned table of throttle settings that he felt would enable Amelia to economize on fuel, but there was little else for him to do except occasionally accompany Amelia to Lockheed to oversee the repair work. He had noticed a new coldness in his relationship with George and a distance between himself and Amelia, but at the time he did not pay too much attention, thinking that it would blow over.

Two days after the delivery of the rebuilt Electra, Amelia and Paul flew to Oakland, where they picked up the six thousand stamp covers that had been postmarked in Honolulu and returned for appropriate overstamping with the words *Second Take Off.* She was using the flight to Oakland as a test hop, Amelia told reporters, and she hoped she might get away around the beginning of May (at this point she had not publicly announced that her route would be a reversal of the original plan). After collecting the stamp covers, the Electra returned to Burbank.

Paul Mantz was always bitter about what happened next. Even in the early sixties, nearly thirty years later, he reacted strongly when he spoke of it. Amelia left him in no doubt that she would be spending some days, perhaps even a week or more, in preflight preparations at Burbank, and, naturally, Paul assumed he would be consulted. After their return to Burbank, they discussed various aspects of the Electra's performance and handling. That evening, Paul flew to St. Louis to take part in an aerobatics competition; he intended to be gone for two days, leaving adequate time to assist Amelia before she left. Paul had been deliberately left out of Amelia's real plans, however.

On the following day, accompanied by George, Bo McKneely, and Fred Noonan, Amelia took off on the first leg of her journey—from Los Angeles to Miami. She said that rather than waste time in California, she might as well make that first leg of the world flight a shakedown; then if problems developed, she could simply announce that it had been a proving flight and return the plane to Lockheed. There would be no adverse publicity because she had technically not yet started her trip.

When he heard on the radio of Amelia's departure from California for Florida on May 21, Paul guessed immediately that Amelia had started her second attempt at the world flight, and he was astounded and angry. He'd "wanted to make a final check of her radio equipment, and of her fuel consumption, to run through the list of optimum power settings for each leg." She'd been pushing too hard, trying to meet the tight schedules set up by George, he declared; too much time had been given to money-making schemes, advertising commitments, and public appearances, and not enough time preparing for the flight.[15]

But above all, he was hurt at the subterfuge involved, for he realized that in order to leave on May 21, Amelia must have made her decision sometime earlier, yet she had not mentioned it during their flight to Oakland on the previous day.

In fact, the policy had been decided at least three weeks earlier, for at that time George wrote to Admiral Leahy outlining the details of the planned "sneak take-off . . . which will occur probably between May 13th and 24th."[16]

George was later to write that Amelia had once trusted Paul Mantz implicitly but had lost faith in him prior to the flight and intended to dissolve her business partnerships with him after her return. Whether this is true or whether George was merely sniping at Mantz after their relationship deteriorated dramatically in 1939 is not known. If there was a reason why Amelia treated her former confidant in such a cavalier manner, the only people who could have known were Paul, Amelia, and George, and they never spoke of it to anyone.

But Paul was wrong in his assertion that it was at George's insistence that Amelia undertook the punishing work schedule. Amelia had become a workaholic and needed no urging. This flight was far more important to her than to George and she was especially aware of the financial cost of this second attempt, so she was prepared to work, and the work ethic was atavistically strong in her.

Paul's concern that Amelia had not paid enough attention to preparation was echoed by Amelia's radioman, Joseph Gurr, who was called in prior to the Oakland–Honolulu flight to repair a minor fault in the original radio installation. Gurr also felt that Amelia was too casual in her approach to safety features and preparation. He was concerned enough, prior to the first takeoff, to check things out himself and had spent an entire day with Manning laying out all the safety equipment in front of the hangar, testing—as far as possible—everything. They inflated the life raft, fired flares from the Very pistols, checked water and medical supplies. "I do not know whether Amelia was checked out in the use of the equipment, but then Harry [Manning] was, so no problem."

On another occasion, however, Gurr was even more concerned by Amelia's attitude. He was particularly anxious that Amelia be instructed in the use of the radio and direction-finding equipment; he wanted to show her how to tune the receivers, how to operate the transmitter, learn correct radio procedures and the limitations of the system. Due to her busy schedule, Amelia was generally not available, but at last she came along as Gurr requested and he began what he assumed would be a lengthy session of instruction. However, after only an hour, Amelia said she had to leave for an appointment. "We never covered actual operation such as taking a bearing with a direction finder, not even contacting another radio station," he recalled.[17] Apart from the time she spent flying with Mantz, it is believed that this was her only formal instruction in the use of the radio and communication system aboard the Electra.

After the Honolulu crash, Gurr removed and checked the entire system. He was unhappy about the trailing antennae, and on a test flight, he tried unsuccessfully to raise someone on the 500-kc. channel, with the antenna unreeled. Afterward, he "took the opportunity to re-design the top antennae installing a short stub mast behind the direction-finding loop on top of the cockpit." A wire antenna was fixed from this mast in a V leading back to the tops of the two rudders. "It made a great deal of difference in radiated energy. Also, because of the added wire, this top antennae [sic] would now be more effective on 500 kcs. The reel antennae was left on board."[18]

From Burbank, Amelia and her three male passengers flew to Tucson, Arizona, where they landed to refuel. As Amelia started up the engines, the left one backfired and burst into flames, but this was soon put under control with the plane's fire extinguisher system, and Bo McKneely was on hand to cope with cleaning up the soot and to replace the burned rubber fittings. Next morning, they flew on to New Orleans, where they stopped overnight.

The Electra arrived in Miami on the following day, May 23, and for the next week Amelia and McKneely worked with the mechanics at Pan American Airways to ready the Electra for the flight. According to the *Herald Tribune*'s aviation correspondent, C. B. Allen,[19] no one could fail to be impressed by the calm, unhurried manner in which Amelia went about the preparations for the flight. Allen was an old friend who had been a frequent guest at Rye, and his articles on Amelia tended to be of the devotee type.

She "knew her stuff," he reported, "knew exactly what she wanted done . . . but also knew enough to let [the mechanics] alone while they did it. . . . There was an almost audible clatter of chips falling off skeptical male shoulders." He noted that she especially endeared them by her willingness to join in and help to push the plane in and out of the hangar, to sit on the floor under the plane and listen attentively when some technical matter was pointed out to her, without worrying if her clothing had splatters of oil. She was happy to eat with the men at the airport diner, and although she once plaintively said she'd hoped to do a little sunbathing and swim, she was too occupied at the airport. There in the cockpit of the all-metal plane, with the searing heat beating down on the concrete apron, she spent an hour running up the engines. When reminded she had said she wanted to sunbathe, she laughed and said, "Not the same thing at all . . . I wanted to soak up a little sunshine, not be fired by it." Her smiling and cheerful presence won everyone's support in Miami. However, Allen reported that she told him:

> I have a feeling that there is just about one more good flight left in my system and I hope this trip is it. Anyway when I have finished this job, I mean to give up long-distance "stunt" flying.[20]

She said that she was prompted by a number of reasons. Among them the repeated urgings of George to give up hazardous flight attempts and her own feeling that she had done her fair share in this field. There was inevitable newsreel coverage, and one clip records Amelia and George in their hotel, hamming for the cameras.

> "Now are you *sure* you don't want me to come along?" George asks with a smile.
>
> "Well, of course you know I think a lot of you but one hundred and eighty pounds of gasoline . . . perhaps might be a little more valuable."
>
> "You mean you prefer one hundred and eighty pounds of gasoline to one hundred and eighty pounds of husband?" Mock incredulity.

Amelia giggles and hesitates before looking at him in smiling exasperation: "I think you've guessed right. . . ."

It is almost impossible not to be instinctively drawn to this Amelia with her natural intelligence, cheerful humor, and quick smile. Watching these newsreel clips fifty years after their production, one might believe Amelia to be a product of the eighties, dressed in trousers and shirt, with her short undated hairstyle. She has the confidence of today's successful woman and great femininity.

Amelia hoped to get away on May 30, but a test flight revealed a fault with the radio transmitter and with the Sperry auto-pilot. The automatic pilot problem was resolved by changing the rudder control fitting, but the radio fault was more persistent. The *Herald Tribune* reported on May 30 that, having tried unsuccessfully to raise a local radio station on both 3105 and 6210 kilocycles, the Pan Am technicians inspected the system and decided that the problem lay "with the new antennae recently installed on the flying laboratory." They believed it to be of an improper length to give the transmitter its maximum efficiency and range and "set to work this afternoon experimenting with various lengths and hope to have the problem solved in time for another test flight tomorrow." Meanwhile, Amelia got her wish to do a little sunbathing and fishing from a friend's yacht.[21]

Later, George was to advise Paul Mantz that the radio had given endless trouble. "As I understand it . . . the technicians decided . . . that the longer aerials were improper. One part of them just canceled out the other, so they shortened the aerials and got the thing pretty well licked. . . ." The 250-foot trailing aerial was discarded, possibly in the interest of saving weight, since Amelia clearly believed that it was not essential to the operation of the radio. One Morse-code key was returned to Western Electric and Joseph Gurr kept the other; the Electra carried no Morse-code keys but a carrier signal could be transmitted by holding down the microphone switch.

On June 1, a small crowd assembled in Miami before dawn to watch Amelia and Fred set off for California by the longest route that could be contrived—by flying east. George's son David (accompanied by his wife, Nilla) was there and remembers George's transparent anxiety. Amelia showed no sign of nerves. Their public goodbye was recorded on newsreel film and shows Amelia sitting on the wing looking down at George and holding his hand. If the obvious affection between the two was enacted purely for the cameras, both George and Amelia missed their true vocation. They should have gone into acting. On the previous evening, she had told him:

> I know that if I fail or if I am lost you will be blamed for allowing me to leave on this trip; the backers of the flight will be blamed and everyone connected with it. But it's my responsibility and mine alone.[22]

For their private farewell, George and Amelia retreated into the hangar building.

> There in the dim chill we perched briefly on cold concrete steps, her hands in mine. There is very little one says at such times.
> When Bo called that all was ready, Amelia's eyes were clear with the good light of the adventure that lay before her. But as she walked out to the [airplane] she seemed to me very small and slim and feminine. . . .[23]

Amelia was a hundred miles over the Atlantic when she tuned into a Miami radio station to get a weather forecast, only to hear the report of her takeoff. "In that manner that radio-folk sometimes have, the account of a very normal departure had become breathlessly exciting . . . it held me in cruel suspense as to whether I was going to get off safely," she wrote.[24]

Amelia's first destination was San Juan, Puerto Rico, a thousand-mile hop, but the territory over which they flew was well known to Noonan from his time with Pan Am, and the journey was uneventful. Amelia recorded that with Noonan's expert navigation (one landfall was one minute from the estimate he gave some hours earlier) and the Sperry auto-pilot, "I was beginning to feel that long-range flying was becoming pretty sissy."[25]

George called Amelia that night "to talk over a few things, but especially, I suspect," she recorded, ". . . just to say Goodnight. That was pleasant."[26] On the next legs, to Caripito, and Paramaribo, Amelia estimated that despite bucking headwinds, they had averaged 148 miles an hour.[27] They rested at the next stop, Fortaleza, to refresh both themselves and the Electra before flying on to Natal, their takeoff point for the South Atlantic leg to Dakar in Senegal.

For the nineteen-hundred-mile transoceanic flight, Amelia loaded 850 gallons of fuel and 80 gallons of oil.[28] The crossing was uneventful, taking thirteen hours and twelve minutes. At about halfway, they passed an Air

34. Amelia and companions during the inaugural flight of T.A.T.'s transcontinental service. Amelia and Dorothy Binney Putnam are on the left; Anne and Charles Lindbergh are on the right.

35. Amelia in her Kissel automobile, "The Yellow Peril," outside Denison House, 1932.

37. George and Amelia in Paris, the intended destination of her flight (she had hoped to emulate Lindbergh's feat), 1932.

36. Amelia reads telegrams to Danny McCallion and the Galleghers on the morning after her solo transatlantic flight in 1932.

38. Amelia posing for photographers in Londonderry on the morning after her solo transatlantic flight, 1932.

39. George and Amelia at their home in Rye, New York, c. 1932.

40. Amelia in the *Beechnut* autogiro. It was not an easy plane to fly but Amelia recognized the advantages of its STOL features.

41. Amelia receiving an award from President Herbert Hoover.

42. The welcome accorded Amelia after she completed the first solo flight from Hawaii to the U.S.A., 1935.

43. A design from the Amelia Earhart fashion collection, a range of classic clothes designed by Amelia that would not be outmoded today.

44. Carl Dunrud cuts Amelia's hair while the Putnams take a rare vacation in Wyoming, 1934.

45. Amelia arranged an impromptu night flight over Baltimore, Maryland, and Washington, D.C., for Eleanor Roosevelt.

46. Above, Amelia takes a catnap. Photographed by George Putnam at their Hollywood home, c. 1935.

47. At right, Amelia in Rye, New York. Photo courtesy Cap Palmer.

49. Below, George and Amelia in the garden of their Hollywood home, c. 1935.

48. Above, Amelia with David Binney Putnam (elder son of George and his first wife, Dorothy Binney) on the beach in Rye, New York, c. 1933.

10. Amelia with her Lockheed Vega, which she called her "little red bus."

51. Purdue University provided the funds for Amelia's "flying laboratory," a Lockheed Electra 10E. In an early visit to the university's airport, George is at far left; Amelia, center; and the university's President Elliott, far right.

52. At Paul Mantz's insistence, Amelia spent time in his Link trainer learning to fly on instruments. "Never enough time," he complained. Amelia's secretarial assistant, Margot de Carrie, is on the left.

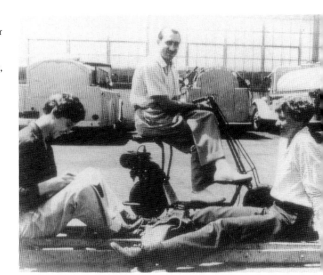

53. Amelia with her "shiny new airplane" and Cord roadster.

France mail plane but could not make contact. Amelia explained, "The mail plane's radio equipment, I believe, is telegraphic code, while mine, at the moment was exclusively voice telephone."[29]

Once, they descended over a ship to enable it to report their position; occasionally Amelia allowed the Sperry autopilot to fly the Electra while she jotted notes in her log. She wrote, "Gas fumes in plane from fueling made me sick again this morning after starting. Stomach getting weak I guess."[30] There are several such notes among her papers and this record of morning sickness adds credence to her confided statement to Al Bresnik that she thought she might be pregnant.

Although there was a catwalk over the fuel tanks that enabled Noonan to join Amelia in the cockpit when he was not working, there was a fishing line and pulley system rigged up between Amelia and the navigator's position, enabling them to pass notes. As they sighted the thin purple smudge of the African coast, Fred passed Amelia the following note:

> 3.36 Change to 36 degrees.
> Estimate 79 miles to
> Dakar from 3.36 pm

Under this, Amelia scrawled, "What put us north?"[31]

Amelia's inclination was to turn north not south. She did not trust Noonan's assessment, perhaps because it was overcast and he had not been able to get a sextant shot to fix their position. For whatever reason, she ignored his instruction and, on reaching the coast, turned left, following the shoreline north for about fifty miles when they found themselves at Saint-Louis, Senegal. Had she done as Fred asked, they would have arrived at Dakar, their intended destination, 163 miles to the south, within half an hour of 3:36 P.M. Amelia was generous enough to admit her error in her cabled report to the *Herald Tribune,* but this insistence of relying on her instinct rather than on Noonan's calculations did not augur well.[32] Next morning, they flew to Dakar, where they stayed for a day to enable a small repair to be made to the fuel meter and to have the engines checked before the flight across Africa.

The stop at Dakar was fairly typical. They did some sightseeing, had laundry done, and parceled up for return to America anything not wanted on the remainder of the journey, such as maps they had used so far, notes Amelia had jotted down for the book, and various receipts and weather reports that would be helpful later in writing her book.

The subsequent flight over Africa via Gao, Fort-Lamy, El Fasher, Khartoum, and Massawa, though hot, tediously long, and only occasionally exciting, was always interesting to Amelia, for she was seeing the places whose romance she had savored as a child. She dwelt on the priceless names in her log: "Qala-en Hahl, Umm Shinayshin, Abu Seid, Idd el Bashir, Fazi, Marabia Abu Fas. . . ."

Noonan thought the navigation across the great continent more difficult than over water, for the few maps that were available were inaccurate and therefore totally misleading. Landmarks were few and information was limited to helpful comments such as, "Swamp in rain; salt pan; rolling desert no trees; many remains of animals; two helig trees about four hundred meters apart ringbarked—they intersect the twenty-fourth meridian." It was probably despite, rather than because of, such assistance that Noonan was able to write to his wife, ". . . we were lucky in always reaching our objectives. In all the distances I don't think we wandered off the course for half an hour, although there were times when I couldn't have bet a nickel on the accuracy of our assumed position."[33]

Leaving Africa, the pair flew down the Red Sea from Massawa to Assab in Eritrea. Originally, Amelia had planned to fly from Assab to Aden en route to Karachi, but at Assab there was some doubt about whether it was desirable to make a stopover at Aden. The Electra therefore took on a full load of fuel and set off on the long flight to India, hugging the Arabian shore.

For this stretch of her flight, Jacques de Sibour had forwarded information and sketch maps of emergency landing grounds, "which I was able to obtain from the Air Ministry here [London] through the good offices of Sir Francis [Shelmerdine]. This data has never been released to an outside source before, so should be quite a help to Amelia when flying along this particular stretch." While expressly forbidden to land on Arab territory, Amelia was carrying credentials in Arabic. These had been prepared in the Cairo office of International Aviation Associates, the firm for whom de Sibour worked, and stated that Amelia was on an important mission on behalf of King George VI and that on no account must she be harmed. "This might be useful should a forced landing have to be made," de Sibour had informed Putnam.[34]

The flight to Karachi was another first; no one had previously flown nonstop from the Red Sea to India before and Amelia was delighted to learn this from de Sibour on her arrival.

"There's a phone call for you," he said, after our greeting.
"Oh, yes." My interest was mild. Probably a local newspaper.
Jacques persisted. "From New York. GP on the wire."

As casual as that! And we were almost exactly on the other side
of the world.[35]

Reports that Amelia had taken off from Massawa (prior to the Assab
stopover) for Karachi had placed the plane long overdue and created great
anxiety for the welcoming committee and for George. In these days of
instant communications, it is easy to overlook the fact that Amelia was
invariably out of contact when in flight. She told George she expected to
be in Lae, Papua New Guinea, about June 23 or 24 and home three or
four days after that.[36] She confirmed this by cable next day after speaking
to the mechanics who were to give her engines a major check and oil
change.[37]

The fuel analyzer was out of order and needed replacing, which was
causing Amelia concern. After discussions with Paul Mantz, George cabled advice and instructions on the installation.[38]

What George did not tell Amelia was that widespread rumors were
circulating in America that at the conclusion of the trip she would divorce
him in order to marry Paul Mantz. He could not discover the source of
these stories and knew there was no truth in them, for Paul had recently
married Terry and was, from his own and other witnesses' statements,
"crazy about her." But George telephoned Paul after Walter Winchell
told his national radio audience that rumors of Amelia divorcing George
after her world trip to marry Mantz were untrue. "Instead," Winchell
reported, "she will marry an aviation inventor."[39]

Paul and George had laughed about it, but Gene Vidal's son, the
American writer Gore Vidal, did not laugh and thinks there might have
been a germ of truth in the rumors. He believes that Amelia was "madly
in love" with his father and states that had Gene given her any encouragement (which he had not), she would have divorced George and married
Gene after the flight.[40] There is certainly no evidence to support any
suggestion of a romance in the surviving letters between Amelia and Gene
Vidal. They are extremely businesslike and convey mere friendship.

Indeed, despite the punishing schedule of the world flight, Amelia
made time to write a personal note to George at each stop—usually a few
scribbled lines on a page torn out of her stenographer's pad.[41] From
Karachi, for example, she wrote:

I wish you were here. So many things you would enjoy. . . . Perhaps
some day we can fly together to some of the remote places of the
world—just for fun.[42]

If there was no time for a letter, she sent George a brief cable, invariably ending ". . . love, A."[43]

From Karachi, the Electra flew to Calcutta on June 17; landing on an already sodden airfield, and with more rain forecast, they elected to refuel and take off immediately for Akyab (now Sittwe), Burma. "That take-off was precarious, perhaps as risky as any we had," Amelia wrote. "The plane clung for what seemed like ages to the heavy sticky soil before the wheels finally lifted, and we cleared with nothing at all to spare the fringe of trees at the airdrome's edge."[44]

By now, Amelia and Noonan had been en route for eighteen days (from Miami); fifteen legs of the journey had been accomplished and they must both have felt reasonably confident with the mission so far. Any remaining doubts about Amelia's ability to fly the Electra competently must have been assuaged by the number of flying hours and, more particularly, landings and takeoffs she made under a wide variety of weather and airport conditions. The airplane had performed well and there had been no major problems.

After a short stop at Akyab, they continued their eastward track, but they had to return to Akyab after running into a monsoon, a navigational feat accomplished by Fred Noonan's "uncanny powers," Amelia observed, for they had zero visibility in the raging tempest.[45]

Flights to Rangoon, Bangkok, Singapore, and Bandoeng followed. In Bandoeng, Amelia was told that G.P. was on the telephone again. In this recorded conversation, Amelia informed George that she would be back in California before July 4, and he immediately set to work to arrange a civic welcome there on Independence Day.

Takeoff was again delayed by monsoon weather for some days, but on June 24, they were able to get away and landed at Soerabaja, Java. En route, Amelia had experienced faults in some of her long-distance instruments, so she returned to Bandoeng for repairs. The instruments concerned—the fuel analyzer, flow meter, and generator meter—were not crucial to flight but would play an extremely important role over the Pacific, where fuel would need to be monitored and conserved.[46] These instruments had all given trouble previously on several occasions and one, the fuel analyzer, had been replaced at Karachi; Amelia wanted to have them working properly for the crucial Pacific Ocean crossing.

The repairs, coupled with monsoon weather, forced Amelia to stay at Bandoeng for some days and she allowed herself to become a tourist.[47] At the nearby town of Batavia (now Jakarta), she toured the markets and purchased a small souvenir for a friend.[48] She also enjoyed the famous local dish, *rijsttafel,* a meal of rice with twenty-one different courses of fish, chicken, meats, eggs, relishes, curries, nuts, fruits, and vegetables.

Perhaps it was as a result of this meal that Amelia was smitten with a nasty and debilitating form of dysentery;[49] she was said to be extremely ill for a day or so, and perhaps this was also the origin of the undated scribbled jotting she made: "Sick again this morning. Must be the petrol fumes."

With health and weather conditions delaying them, it was June 27 before Amelia and Noonan were able to leave Bandoeng for Port Darwin in Australia, via Koepang (now Kupang), Indonesia. At Port Darwin, they had the direction finder repaired. A fuse had blown; this was replaced and the instrument was checked out by Australian Royal Air Force Sgt. Stan Rose, who provided spare fuses and showed Amelia how to replace them. The parachutes were packed and shipped home; they would be of no value over the Pacific, Amelia explained.[50]

The couple reached Lae, Papua New Guinea on June 29, accomplishing the twelve-hundred-mile flight in seven hours and forty-three minutes. At this point, the Electra had flown some twenty-two thousand miles and there were seven thousand more to go, all of them over the Pacific Ocean.

Amelia had hoped to get away from Lae before June 31 in order to ensure arrival in California on July 4, as she had advised George in her phone conversations at Karachi and Bandoeng. Lae Airport was run by Guinea Airways, under their manager Eric Chaters, and it was he who organized mechanics to give the Electra a thorough going-over. Fortunately, they were used to Lockheed aircraft, as there was a sister ship to Amelia's Electra based on the field. Amelia wrote:

> . . . everyone has been as helpful and co-operative as possible—food, hot baths, mechanical service, radio and weather reports, advice from veteran pilots here—all combine to make us wish we could stay.[51]

Oil and oil filters were changed, spark plugs were cleaned, and the engines were checked. The fluctuating fuel pump and the Sperry autopilot had both been giving further trouble and these were repaired again.

Amelia and Fred Noonan spent the day of the thirtieth unpacking and repacking the plane. Every single item not absolutely essential to the flight was parceled up and mailed home. Even Amelia's elephant-toe bracelet was returned and there was not a spare ounce of weight left on the Electra after this exercise.[52] Her obsession with weight may have been taken to extreme lengths, for according to Harry Balfour, radio operator at Lae, survival equipment was also taken off. Balfour claimed that "she unloaded all her surplus equipment on me including her [Very] pistol and ammunition, books, letters and facility books."[53]

Amelia cabled her last commissioned article for the *Herald Tribune:*

"DENMARK'S A PRISON" AND LAE, ATTRACTIVE AND UNUSUAL AS IT IS APPEARS TO TWO FLYERS JUST AS CONFINING. LOCKHEED STANDS READY FOR LONGEST HOP WEIGHTED WITH GASOLINE AND OIL TO CAPACITY. HOWEVER CLOUDS AND WINDS BLOWING WRONG WAY CONSPIRED TO KEEP HER ON THE GROUND TODAY. IN ADDITION FN HAS BEEN UNABLE ACCOUNT RADIO DIFFICULTIES TO SET HIS CHRONOMETERS LACK KNOWLEDGE THEIR FASTNESS OR SLOWNESS. WE SHALL TRY TO GET OFF TOMORROW THOUGH WE CANNOT BE HOME BY FOURTH OF JULY AS HAD HOPED.[54]

In another *Herald Tribune* article, she remarks:

Not much more than a month ago I was on the other shore of the Pacific, looking westward. This evening, I look eastward over the Pacific. In those fast-moving days which have intervened, the whole width of the world had passed behind us—except this broad ocean. I shall be glad when we have the hazards of its navigation behind us.[55]

There were many pictures taken of Amelia and Fred at Lae. Amelia, in particular, looks extremely tired, ill even, with a puffiness about the eyes and sunken cheeks. The boyish smile is still evident, but there is an emaciated look about her face and neck. She had been en route for a month by this time. In addition to spending twenty days actually flying the Electra, she had carried out the duties that might today be expected of visiting heads of state. Met by senior officials of government, she was accorded VIP treatment, which inevitably included a whirlwind sightseeing trip at every stage of her journey, as well as a dinner of banquet proportions.

In her unofficial log, Amelia jokingly referred to "the appalling habit of falling asleep after dinner and rising at 3 am to prepare for the next day's flight" that she and Fred had adopted.[56] By the time the two reached Lae, they must have been close to the end of physical reserves, though Amelia looked to be coping less well with the rigors of the journey than did Noonan.

At every stop, there had been numerous details with which to cope: customs clearance, involving a thorough examination of the Lockheed;

fumigation of the plane and equipment; scrutiny of their health and inoculation certificates; arranging hangarage or tie-down for the Electra; supervising any repairs to equipment that had failed en route; planning for the next stage of the journey; ensuring that all the necessary permissions and flight maps and weather reports were available and that local radio frequencies were known. The long process of refueling had to be watched carefully; all gas had to be siphoned from the storage tanks spotted along the length of her route by Standard Oil (and bearing the name AMELIA EARHART in bright colors), and strained through chamois-cloth filters to ensure no contamination. The details were endless.

Somehow, as well as handling all this, Amelia also coped with reporters *and* wrote a total of some thirty thousand words about the journey as far as Lae, the bulk cabled home and published as a series of articles by the *Herald Tribune*, which were later used to compile a book titled *Last Flight*. One wonders when she found the time to sleep and, indeed, on her own evidence, she slept very little.

Not surprising then that, with her spell of sickness at Bandoeng, Amelia looked tired and ill during her time at Lae. However, the key question is, Did it affect her performance during the subsequent flight? Since the flight was physically taxing, the answer is almost certainly that it did.

A further day's delay was encountered because Fred Noonan had not been able to set his chronometers when the time signals were not picked up on the Electra's radio, and Amelia cabled George:

RADIO MISUNDERSTANDING AND PERSONNEL UNFITNESS PROBABLY WILL HOLD ONE DAY HAVE ASKED BLACK FOR FORECAST FOR TOMORROW YOU CHECK METEOROLOGIST ON JOB AS FN MUST HAVE STAR SIGHTS. ARRANGE CREDIT IF TRIBUNE WISHES MORE STORY.[57]

This cable has been much debated. In general, bearing in mind Fred Noonan's reputation for heavy drinking, often it has been misquoted as "crew unfitness," to back up the theory that it was Noonan who was not fit to fly. However, what if it referred to Amelia's own state of health? Perhaps it was Amelia who was unfit, not Fred Noonan. One has only to look at photographs to see the evident physical toll the flight had taken on her. And what about Amelia's preflight statement to Albert Bresnik that there was a possibility that she was pregnant? There are only her logged notes of being sick in the mornings to offer any substantiation to this; but could her message have been a warning to George? George never confided in anyone on this matter. Alternatively, some years later, there was a claim by her friend Gene Vidal that Amelia was undergoing an early menopause.[58] Clearly both of these possibilities could not be correct; but was either of them? Again, frustratingly, we may never learn the answers.

A great deal of emphasis has been placed on reports of Fred Noonan getting drunk on the night of their arrival at Lae after an argument with Amelia. These reports vary in description, and reliable witnesses who were present that night do agree that he got very drunk but only after Amelia and Noonan had already made the decision not to fly on the following day.[59]

> The argument that caused Noonan to get drunk was over nothing very much. A.E. had been invited to a dinner party. Noonan was not personally invited, though I think this was merely an oversight. Anyway, he came down to the bar of the Cecil Hotel to find Eric Chaters and Jim Collopy all smartened up and ready to go for drinks. When asked if he was going, Fred said, "No, but A.E. is" leaving no doubt that he was disgruntled, and when asked what he'd have to drink, he said, "Whiskey." The other guys were all drinking beer but he stayed on whiskey and got very drunk. Next day A.E. watched him like a hawk to make sure he didn't drink again.[60]

This drinking session of Noonan's was said to have been behind Amelia's cabled message explaining the delay in departure, but clearly it was not the only reason. More than likely, the simple truth was merely that both Amelia and Fred were physically and mentally exhausted, and the extremely difficult leg from Lae to Howland that lay ahead imposed a new stress factor. It is known that she had delayed her flight from Hawaii on the first attempt due to fatigue; perhaps she now felt that a day's respite would enable her to fly more efficiently. Bad weather (it rained most of the next day) and Noonan's problem with setting the chronometers were also more likely factors in the delay than Noonan's rumored hangover. That the two had reached a scratchy relationship is not impossible, of course; Manning has testified that Amelia could be a difficult person with whom to work. Her physical endurance was never great.

In speaking to George from Bandoeng, Amelia obviously gave him no cause for concern, for he continued to book engagements and, prior to her advice (by cable from Lae) that they could not now make it home by Sunday July 4, he had been sending messages to Amelia through the *Itasca:*

FOLLOWING FOR MISS EARHART UPON ARRIVAL HOWLAND ISLAND. FLIGHT CONTINGENCIES PERMITTING IS SATURDAY ARRIVAL LIKELY. SUNDAY LATEST.

EITHER PERFECT. CONFIDENTIAL WANT YOU TO KNOW VERY IMPORTANT RADIO
COMMITMENT MONDAY NIGHT NOTHING ELSE WHATEVER.[61]

Later, when her delayed start had become obvious, he cabled:

PLEASE FORWARD EARHART LAE RUSH. IS THERE ANY LIKELIHOOD OAKLAND
ARRIVAL BY MONDAY MORNING REPLY VIA ITASCA.[62]

The U.S. Coast Guard cutter *Itasca* had been standing off Howland
Island for some days to act as a radio contact for Amelia. The seaplane
tender U.S.S. *Swan* was lying some two hundred miles to the northeast
of Howland to act as plane guard on the Howland–Hawaii leg. However,
for the difficult Lae–Howland flight, the old, coal-burning tug, the U.S.S.
Ontario, equipped with an antiquated radio system, was to be Amelia's
only help. During the original world-flight attempt, the *Itasca* and several
other ships had been in the area for the Pan American survey and Amelia
had planned to take advantage of this arrangement. That the U.S. naval
and coast guard chiefs were prepared to extend help to Amelia's second
attempt was due to George's persuasiveness, which is well documented in
National Archive (Washington) files.

One of *Itasca*'s problems was the amount of commercial radio traffic
that the flight created, from the press and from various officials who had
been involved by George (the cost of which was all borne by George).[63]
Added to this, communications in the area were very poor. Cables for
Amelia had to be routed through Samoa and took more than twenty-four
hours to reach her; *Itasca*'s Commander Thompson spent considerable
time attempting to ascertain Amelia's flight plan, radio schedule, and
communications data, as well as her estimated time of arrival at Howland.

The charts laid out by Clarence Williams had been of immense help
on the journey so far, though Amelia had not adhered strictly to the
original flight plan. For the Lae–Howland flight, reciprocals of the original
Howland–Lae attempt had been prepared, together with the local data
regarding Howland Island that Williams had gleaned from the hydrographer's office in Washington.

It is possible that the following cable, received by Amelia in Lae, may
have decided the fliers to depart from Clarence Williams's recommended
direct course.

THE FOLLOWING FROM NARAU. NEW NARAU FIXED LIGHT LATITUDE 0.32 S;
LONGITUDE 16.55 EAST. FIVE THOUSAND CANDLEPOWER 560FT ABOVE SEA
LEVEL VISIBLE FROM SHIPS TO NAKED EYE AT 34 MILES. ALSO THERE WILL BE
BRIGHT LIGHTING ALL NIGHT ON ISLAND FROM PHOSPHATE WORKINGS.[64]

The island of Narau (now spelled Nauru) lay nearly 1,400 miles into the 2,556-mile flight, and if stars were not visible for celestial navigation, the bright lights would give Noonan an excellent opportunity to check his position. Furthermore, a detour to Narau would involve a deviation of only a few degrees north of the most logical course—a deviation easily corrected on the remaining part of the flight and involving little additional fuel.

Amelia estimated approximately eighteen hours for the 2,556-mile journey, based on the average speed she had achieved over the journey so far—approximately 145 mph. Part of the flight would have to be made at night, however, and since it was essential to reach Howland in daylight, a time slot for the Lae departure had to be worked out.

Calculations were further complicated by the fact that they would be crossing two time zones and the international date line, and that communications from the *Itasca* referred to U.S. Navy time, which divided hourly time zones into two half-hour ones. It was probably Noonan's suggestion that they leave Lae at precisely 0:00 hours Greenwich Mean Time (GMT) in order to simplify matters. This would mean that GMT would also coincide with the elapsed time of the flight (for example, at 14:43 GMT, they would have been in the air for fourteen hours and forty-three minutes, no matter what time zones or meridians they might have crossed) and ensure a daylight arrival over Howland.

During the past fifty years, Noonan's professional skills have sometimes been called into question; but research reveals that he was a careful, even pedantic worker.[65] He had three chronometers in the Electra and at a reasonable guess, one would be set at GMT, one at local time in Lae, and one at local time in Howland. As Amelia stressed, "absolute accuracy in time was vital for the accuracy of celestial navigation. . . . Howland is such a small spot in the Pacific that every aid to locating it must be available."[66]

Both fliers were aware of the magnitude of the task ahead of them—of that there can be no doubt—but Noonan told various people at Lae that he was "confident that he would have no trouble finding the island."[67]

On the morning of July 2, 1937, the weather forecast was reasonably favorable: head winds of twelve to fifteen knots, partly cloudy conditions and rain squalls, but visibility mostly unlimited.[68] All preparations were complete. Amelia made the decision to leave.

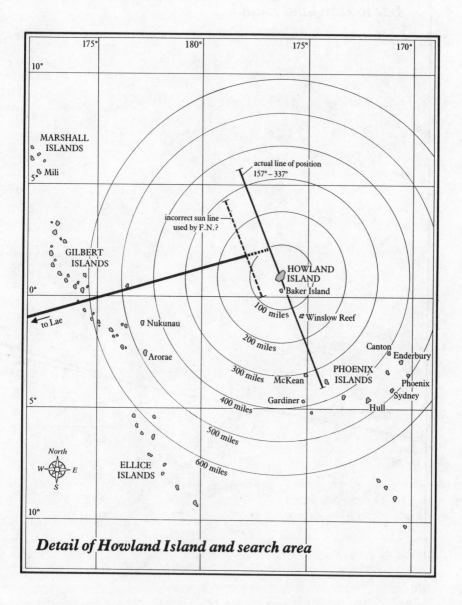

175° · **180°** · **175°** · **170°**

10°

MARSHALL
ISLANDS

5° Mili

actual line of position
157° – 337°

incorrect sun line
used by F.N.?

GILBERT
ISLANDS

0°

HOWLAND
ISLAND

Baker Island

to Lae

Winslow Reef

Nukunau

100 miles

Arorae

200 miles

Canton
Enderbury

300 miles

McKean

PHOENIX
ISLANDS

Phoenix
Sydney

5°

Gardiner

400 miles

Hull

500 miles

North

W   E

S

ELLICE
ISLANDS

600 miles

10°

Detail of Howland Island and search area

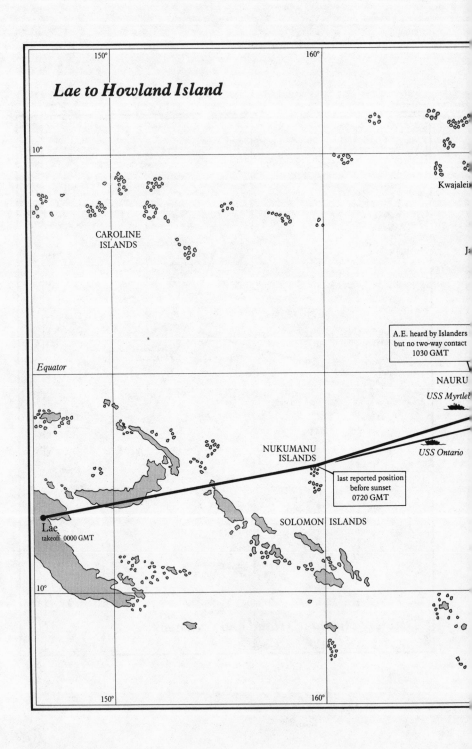

Lae to Howland Island

150°   160°

10°

Kwajalei

CAROLINE
ISLANDS

J

Equator

A.E. heard by Islanders
but no two-way contact
1030 GMT

NAURU

USS Myrtle

USS Ontario

NUKUMANU
ISLANDS

last reported position
before sunset
0720 GMT

SOLOMON ISLANDS

Lae
takeoff 0000 GMT

10°

150°   160°

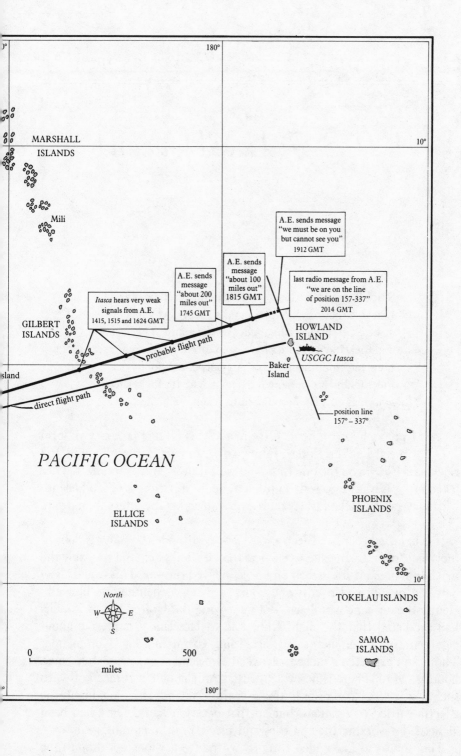

180°

MARSHALL
ISLANDS

10°

Mili

A.E. sends message
"we must be on you
but cannot see you"
1912 GMT

A.E. sends
message
"about 100
miles out"
1815 GMT

A.E. sends
message
"about 200
miles out"
1745 GMT

last radio message from A.E.
"we are on the line
of position 157-337"
2014 GMT

Itasca hears very weak
signals from A.E.
1415, 1515 and 1624 GMT

GILBERT
ISLANDS

probable flight path

HOWLAND
ISLAND

USCGC *Itasca*

island

Baker
Island

direct flight path

position line
157° – 337°

PACIFIC OCEAN

ELLICE
ISLANDS

PHOENIX
ISLANDS

10°

North

W   E

S

TOKELAU ISLANDS

0   500

miles

SAMOA
ISLANDS

180°

1 9 3 7: *Lae–Howland*

Since this book is a biography the author feels no obligation to either reach or propound a theory, which could
at best be speculation, about Amelia's fate. The facts
and the various theories have been carefully researched,
however, from thousands of original contemporary documents, and are presented in appendices for the reader,
who may or may not choose to reach a conclusion.

At precisely 00:00 hours Greenwich Mean Time (10:00 A.M. local
time at Lae) on Friday, July 2, 1937, Amelia Earhart lined up the
Lockheed Electra on the one-thousand-yard runway at Lae and started her
takeoff run. It was 12:30 P.M. on July 1 at her destination, Howland Island,
which lay two and a half time zones away and across the international date
line.[1]

It is believed that the Electra was loaded with one thousand gallons of
fuel (see Appendix B, page 343)—less than its tanks held but probably the
maximum possible for takeoff on Lae's unpaved runway. This would allow
between twenty and twenty-one hours of flying, depending on how efficiently the airplane was flown. Before leaving the United States, Amelia
had predicted that the flight from Lae to Howland would take about
eighteen and a half hours but, according to *Itasca*'s log, Commander
Thompson expected Amelia to arrive at Howland at approximately 19:30
hours (GMT). There is no evidence that Amelia had ever taken off with
such a heavy fuel load prior to this. For the Oakland–Honolulu flight, the
Electra carried 947 gallons, but on that occasion Paul Mantz had been
at her side, working the throttles and retracting the landing gear.

The runway at Lae ended abruptly with a twenty-five-foot drop to the waters of the Huon Gulf and witnesses stated that the takeoff was hair-raising for there was not a breath of wind to help the Electra into the air on that hot, clear morning. Commercial pilot Bert Heath, who was flying into Lae in his trimotored Junkers airplane, watched the Electra's lumbering takeoff run from high above the field. He recalled that close to the seaward end of the runway, a dirt road crossed it. There was a high camber on this road and as the Electra hit the crest, it bounced into the air and "over the drop-off," flying so low over the sea that the propellers were "throwing spray." Mr. Heath noted that the dust kicked up by the Electra over the dirt road hung about in the still air for some time and did not disperse.[2]

A report by James Collopy (district superintendent of Civil Aviation) stated:

> . . . after taking every yard of the 1000 yard runway from the north west end of the aerodrome towards the sea, the aircraft had not left the ground 50 yards from the end of the runway. When it did leave it sank away but was by this time over the sea. It continued to sink about five or six feet above the water and had not climbed to more than 100 feet before it disappeared from sight.
>
> In spite of this, however, it was obvious that the aircraft was well-handled and pilots of Guinea Airways who have flown Lockheed aircraft were loud in their praise of the take-off with such an overload.[3]

In the days that Amelia and Noonan had spent in Papua New Guinea, they made contact with Harry Balfour, radio operator at Lae.[4] Between them, they arranged a radio schedule and after the Electra's takeoff, Balfour listened for Amelia's transmissions on her daytime frequency of 6210 kilocycles; within the hour, he received her first communication. From this point on, the flight can be pieced together only by examination of the various radio transmissions that took place over the following twenty or so hours (see Appendix A, page 336).

The first radio communications between Amelia and Balfour were not logged, but Balfour is on record as stating that he was in contact with her every hour, at which time, position reports and height were received. Amelia's schedule was to transmit at fifteen and forty-five minutes past each hour, and to listen on the hour and half hour to receive messages.

After about five hours, Amelia reported that she was "at 10,000 feet but reducing altitude because of banks of cumulus cloud," and two hours later she told Balfour that she was "at 7,000 feet and making 150 miles per hour." Amelia meant airspeed; the Electra's ground speed would have been significantly less, depending on the strength of the head winds.

At 07:20 hours (GMT), Amelia provided a position: "Latitude: 4 degrees 33.5' South. Longitude: 159 degrees 07' East." This placed the Electra more or less directly on the great circle course for Howland Island, some twenty miles southwest of the Nukumanu Islands—which should have been visible, as it was still daylight—and giving Noonan a perfect opportunity to check his navigation before nightfall. Although this transmission was given only a third of the way into the flight, it was to be Amelia's only position report, and thus it has great significance.

An important factor is that having covered more than 846 miles (735 nautical miles), the Electra had achieved a ground speed of only 118 miles per hour (103 knots).[5] This was considerably less than Amelia would have hoped for with an average airspeed of 150 mph. The shortfall is not unreasonable, however, if one takes into consideration a combination of the excess weight in the early stages of the flight when the Electra was slowly climbing to ten thousand feet, and stronger-than-forecast head winds. The last weather report that Amelia is known to have received before takeoff forecast 12–15 mph east southeast winds, but they were actually 25 mph.[6] Lae had transmitted the increased wind strength of "25 mph to the *Ontario* and 20 mph from there to Howland" but there is uncertainty that Amelia ever received this message due to the twenty-four-hour delay in transmission while cables were routed through American Samoa.

Noonan could have determined the approximate wind strength and its direction, though, by using the drift meter and smoke bombs, and if there had been any doubt at this time about whether they could complete the flight, Amelia would have turned back (as she had at Karachi when conditions were marginal).

From the Electra's reported position near Nukumanu Island to Howland Island is 1,714 miles on the great circle route laid out for Amelia by Clarence Williams. With a decreasing gross weight as the fuel was used up, and head winds forecast to decrease to 20 mph, the Electra was easily capable of averaging 130 mph or better over the remaining distance, but this would give a revised estimated time of arrival (ETA) in the vicinity of Howland of 20:38 GMT, leaving very little margin for error regarding fuel.

At 08:00 hours GMT, Amelia made her final radio contact with Balfour. At this stage, her transmissions were becoming fainter but he was able to make out her message that she was "on course for Howland Island at 12,000 feet." When Amelia informed him that she was changing from her daytime frequency, 6210 kilocycles, to her nighttime one, 3105 kilocycles, Balfour stated, "We asked her to remain on her present frequency but she told me she wished to contact the American Coast Guard cutter *Itasca* so there was nothing to do about it but pass the terminal forecast to her and the upper air report from Ocean Island."[7]

The U.S.S. *Ontario,* designated as Amelia's guard ship on that Lae–Howland flight, was lying 423 miles (368 nautical miles—a nautical mile is equal to 1.151 statute miles), from the Electra's last reported fix near the Nukumanu Islands. The *Ontario*'s position—latitude 3 degrees 9' South; longitude 165 degrees 06' East—put the ship less than ten miles north of Amelia's great circle track. Amelia had previously requested by cable that the *Ontario* BROADCAST LETTER N FOR FIVE MINUTES AFTER HOUR GMT FOUR HUNDRED KILOCYCLES WITH OWN CALL LETTERS REPEATED TWICE END EVERY MINUTE.[8] This was done. *Ontario*'s captain, Lieutenant H. W. Blakeslee, recalls that it was rainy and overcast that night. The ship had no light switched on but had one ready should they hear a plane.[9]

At 10:30 hours (GMT), three hours and ten minutes after Amelia had reported her position near Nukumanu Island to Balfour, residents on Nauru Island reported hearing Amelia say ". . . ship in sight ahead."[10] Assuming that the ship Amelia reported was the *Ontario,* the Electra was then averaging a ground speed of 125 mph, almost exactly what she should have been making with reported 25-mph head winds and a fuel load approaching recommended operating levels. The reports from Nauru of what Amelia said are open to question, however, for some listeners claim Amelia actually said ". . . lights in sight ahead."[11]

It has been suggested that from the Nukumanu Islands, Noonan may have set a course for Nauru, some 607 miles to the northeast, in order to have one last opportunity to check his astronavigation before setting out over open ocean; the sky was overcast and he may not have been able to take sextant bearings on celestial bodies. Such a detour would have added only thirty-one miles to the flight.[12] It is much more likely, however, that he continued on the direct great circle course for Howland, knowing that some four hundred miles on that track the U.S.S. *Ontario* was waiting, its *specific* duty being to act as a guard ship for the flight.

Captain Blakeslee had no notification that Amelia had left Lae nor any acknowledgment from Amelia that she had heard *Ontario*'s Morse signal. A watch was kept, but the crew neither heard nor saw any sign of the Electra. Two hours after the time Amelia was due to pass overhead, the ship, which had been on station for ten days, was ordered to return to port for essential supplies.[13]

Another possibility that has been suggested is that Amelia saw the S.S. *Myrtlebank*. The *Myrtlebank* was headed for Nauru and arrived there at dawn on the following day. At the time of Amelia's report, this ship was lying at latitude 1 degree 40' South; longitude 166 degrees 45' East— some forty-four miles north of Amelia's great circle route.[14]

The suggestion that Amelia flew via Nauru seems unlikely, however, for in order for her to have been within visual distance (thirty-four miles) of the lights on Nauru within three hours and ten minutes after her last reported position, she would have to have been making a ground speed of 170 mph, a significant improvement over the previous calculated performance. On the other hand, from thirty miles off Nauru, she might have been able to see *both* the *Myrtlebank* and the lights on Nauru.

The flight via Nauru would have been possible, of course, if Amelia had transmitted her position to Balfour sometime after it was plotted. Her casual attitude toward radio and reporting procedures makes this not unlikely (in the entire trip from Miami to date, she had provided only seven position reports). The position report could have been provided by Noonan at any time following Amelia's previous radio contact, and it is not beyond credibility that, having received it, Amelia waited until her 5:15 scheduled time to report. From the *Itasca* log alone, it is obvious that she was seldom pedantic about keeping to radio schedules.

The wife of the district administrator on Nauru, Mrs. Garsia, noted in her diary for July 2 that Amelia had taken off from Lae and had been notified of the existence of the new Nauru light and local weather. She recorded picking up Amelia's radio transmissions on a shortwave receiver from 6 P.M. [Nauru time] but though the transmissions became increasingly loud, Mrs. Garsia could never make out what was being said. "Amelia was due near or over Nauru at 9:40 P.M. but though we watched she did not come near."[15] It has been said that Nauru could never have picked up Amelia's radio signals if she had not been within fifty miles of the island, but Amelia had broadcast her position to Lae from almost nine hundred miles away; *Itasca*, subsequently, first heard Amelia's faint transmissions at something close to the same distance; and on the following day, a Nauru resident reported receiving Amelia's transmissions when she was in the vicinity of Howland Island.[16]

There is no real evidence as to the precise track of the airplane after Nukumanu. No one saw or heard the plane fly over, and this fact alone has meant that even the most outrageous theories regarding Amelia's course cannot be refuted. Neither can it be refuted that she flew on a direct course for Howland, in which case she must have flown over the Gilbert Islands at about 3 A.M. [local time], but since no assistance had been requested in advance, no one was standing by to receive a transmission.

From 10:30 hours (GMT), there was no radio contact from Amelia for several hours. At 12:42 hours (GMT), *Itasca* signaled coast guard headquarters in San Francisco, where George was waiting for news, to advise that they had not heard from Amelia but saw "no cause for concern as she is still 1000 miles away." It was 14:15 hours (GMT) before the first transmissions from Amelia were received by *Itasca* on 3105 kilocycles.[17]

In the ship's radio room, Chief Radioman Leo G. Bellarts was accompanied by Radiomen Thomas O'Hare and William Galten. A primary radio log, kept by Bellarts, was backed up by a secondary log maintained by one of his operators.[18] In addition to the two radio receivers, there was a loudspeaker. Others waited in the room to hear Amelia: Commander Warner K. Thompson, *Itasca*'s captain; three of his officers, Lieutenant Commanders Lee Baker and Frank Kenner, and Ensign William L. Sutter; Richard Black (later Admiral Black) from the Department of the Interior but representing George Putnam regarding administrative details on this leg of the flight; and two press agency reporters, H. N. Hanzlick of the Associated Press and James Carey of United Press International.

At first, no one could make out what Amelia was saying above the static, but Bellarts caught her "low monotone voice" saying: ". . . cloudy and overcast." The two pressmen were familiar with Amelia's voice and agreed that it was she but could not decipher what she was saying. Bellarts sent weather forecasts to KHAQQ [Amelia's call sign] at *Itasca*'s scheduled transmission times of 14:30 and 15:00 hours (GMT). Nothing was heard from Amelia during her 14:45 hours slot but this caused no particular concern. She was still a long way from Howland and no one was surprised that reception was poor over such a distance.

At 15:15 hours (GMT), Amelia came in on cue. "*Itasca* from Earhart. Overcast . . . will listen on hour and half hour on 3105." Her voice was clearer this time and understood by others in the radio room. Fifteen minutes later, Bellarts called KHAQQ and gave details of the weather for the Howland Island area before asking, "What is your position? When do you expect to reach Howland? *Itasca* has heard your phone, so go ahead on key. Acknowledge this broadcast next schedule." Each phrase was carefully repeated twice in accordance with the accepted code of practice.

No signal was picked up from Amelia during her next transmission time (15:45 hours GMT), so Bellarts repeated his previous message at 16:00 hours. When Amelia failed to report at 16:15, Bellarts waited eight minutes and transmitted weather by voice and Morse code on frequency 3105 kilocycles.

As Bellarts finished calling, he switched to receive and picked up a faint transmission from KHAQQ that he logged as ". . . partly cloudy . . . ," noting after it the code "S1," indicating a very weak reception (signal strengths being measured on a table of 1–5. S1: Very faint; S2: Faint; S3: Fair; S4: Good; S5: Very loud). A minute later, Amelia transmitted again but so faintly that neither Bellarts nor anyone else in the room could make any sense of it.

The *Itasca's* log reveals that for the next hour and twenty minutes, Bellarts sent weather data and his "What is your position?" message at each scheduled transmission time, but nothing was heard from Amelia. At 17:44 hrs (GMT) she broke in at strength 3: "[want] bearing on 3105, on hour, will whistle in mic—" Her transmission broke off, but moments later she spoke again: ". . . about two hundred miles out. Approximately. Whistling now." She whistled briefly but the transmission was too short for a direction finder to home in on the signal.

Dawn was now breaking, recorded in *Itasca's* log at 17:45 hours GMT (6:15 A.M. ship's time). At 18:00 hours (GMT), Bellarts sent weather and requested Amelia's position. At 18:15 hours (GMT), Amelia's voice boomed in on schedule at strength S4: "Please take bearing on us and report in half an hour. I will make noise in microphone. About one hundred miles out." Bellarts recorded that, once again, she was on the air too briefly to take direction-finder bearings, but all on board the *Itasca* were heartened as the strength of her calls increased, indicating that she was getting closer.

Amelia's report that she was "about one hundred miles out" fitted in well with the time that *Itasca* expected her to arrive (19:30 hours GMT, according to the ship's log), and they all confidently expected the Electra to appear overhead in an hour or so, but they heard nothing until 19:12 hours (GMT) when Amelia's voice filled the loudspeaker. Signal strength S5 this time—maximum reception. Bellarts logged her call: "KHAQQ calling *Itasca*. We must be on you but cannot see you but gas is running low. Been unable to reach you by radio. We are flying at altitude 1,000 feet." But the secondary log reads: "Earhart says running out of gas. Only half hour left/can't hear us at all/we hear her and are sending on 3105 and 500 same time constantly and listening in for her frequently."[19]

These two accounts have been taken by some researchers as sinister evidence. Why, they have asked, is Amelia sometimes quoted as saying "gas is running low" and at other times, "running out of gas, only half an hour left"?

Reading the pages of these logs, and pages of radio transmissions unrelated to the Earhart mission, the reason is obvious. This mission, while interesting, was really not very special. It was just another job for *Itasca;* she had performed a similar task some months earlier for the Pan Am survey. The men keeping those logs had no reason to believe that their scribbled "radio shorthand" notes would be the subject of countless books. Busy with their duties, they recorded the gist of what they heard, rather than the *precise* wording.

The message received at 19:12 hours GMT (7:42 A.M. ship's time) was actually written in the primary log by Bellarts as follows:

0742 KHAQQ CLING [CALLING] ITASCA WE MUST BE ON YOU BUT CANNOT SEE U BUT GAS IS RUNNING LOW BEEN UNABLE REACH YOU BY RADIO WE ARE FLYING AT ALTITUDE 1,000 FEET.

While the second log, in the same radio room, maintained by another radio operator, reads:

0740: EARHART ON NW [NOW] SEZ RUNNING OUT OF GAS ONLY ½ HOUR LEFT CAN'T HR US AT ALL/WE HEAR HER AND ARE SENDING ON 3105 ES 500 SAME TIME CONSTANTLY AND LISTENING IN FOR HER FREQUENTLY

The reported version of what Amelia actually said was made some hours later, after the radio operators and others present in the radio room examined the written log and discussed what *had* been said.[20] The sensational suggestions by several writers that this was done on instructions of the U.S. government to cover up or distort the facts may be discounted if only because of the wealth of information that exists from so many different sources, ranging from the military records to the press (not renowned for keeping secrets) and the inhabitants of various islands. The explanation offered by *Itasca's* commanding officer is more credible:

The transcript of the radio logs from 0200 until 0930 is necessarily not complete due to the rapidity of events and also due to the Earhart exclusive use of voice, only partially received. At these times tuning was so essential that parts of the actual message may not be given. Officers of appropriate rank and experience were present . . . the radio log stands as it was written at the time and has not been changed or corrected. The transcript is an actual transcript [and] the portions [extracted above] form a true representation of the picture.[21]

Amelia's message that she was low on fuel caused some consternation in the radio room, but there was little that Commander Thompson and his crew could do other than set in motion provisional plans to go to the aid of the fliers if they had to ditch. On Howland Island, a high-frequency direction finder had been installed, manned by Radioman Frank Cipriani. However, when contacted by the *Itasca*, he reported that he was unable to get any fixes on Amelia because her transmissions were too brief. The equipment Cipriani was using was in any case very much experimental and in the "breadboard" stage. It had been taken to Howland by Richard Black and was powered by a dry-cell battery arrangement. In use for the whole night while Cipriani tried in vain to "fix" on Amelia's transmissions, by daybreak—when it was most likely to have been of use—the batteries had run down and were insufficient to power the unit.

Itasca was already making heavy black smoke, which, in the light breeze of under 10 mph, drifted very little. Commander Thompson estimated that the smoke should have been visible for twenty miles or so. Over Howland, the sky was clear and the sun already hot, but to the north and northwest, thirty or forty miles away, *Itasca*'s crew could see formations of large cumulus clouds.

Thompson now decided to break with the radio schedule and transmit and receive on a continuous basis. At 19:13 hours (GMT), within a minute of receiving Amelia's message that she was low on fuel, Bellarts transmitted by voice: "*Itasca* to KHAQQ. Received your message signal strength five. Go ahead please." He followed this with a long stream of letter *A*'s transmitted by Morse-code key on the 3105 frequency. This was repeated at 19:17 (GMT) hours with no response. Two minutes later, he tried again. "*Itasca* to KHAQQ: Your message okay please acknowledge with phone on 3105." Again he sent out a long series of letter *A*'s by key.

Tension was now beginning to build in the radio room. Amelia had not once acknowledged receiving any message from *Itasca* and her messages to them were brief and incomplete. However, their apprehension must have been nothing to that experienced by Amelia and Fred Noonan, who had now been in the air for over nineteen hours. They were physically tired; there was no sight of Howland Island, where Noonan clearly expected it to be; fuel supplies were running low; and Amelia had not been able to make any radio contact. This meant that she was not only unsure that her transmissions were being received but also could not take direction-finder bearings on her DF unit. It is not difficult to imagine the concern that Amelia and Noonan must have been feeling.

At 19:28 hours (GMT), Amelia called *Itasca:* "We are circling but cannot hear you, go ahead on 7500 now or on the schedule time on half hour." Again *Itasca* received her message at signal strength 5. Bellarts, confused by the sudden change of frequency, nevertheless immediately sent out a constant stream of *A*'s on 7500 as requested, and called by voice, "Go ahead on 3105."

To the immense relief of everyone in the radio room, Amelia acknowledged receiving their message almost immediately: "KHAQQ calling *Itasca*. We received your signals but unable to get a minimum. Please take a bearing on us and answer 3105 with voice." She then transmitted a series of long dashes for five seconds or so. The time was 19:30 hours (GMT). It was the only time during the flight that Amelia was in two-way contact with *Itasca* and her reception of the transmission was too poor to enable her to tune her direction finder to the signal.

Five minutes later, having tried and failed to take a bearing on Amelia's transmission, *Itasca* radioed Frank Cipriani on Howland, but he had been no more successful. Bellarts called on 3105 again: "*Itasca* to KHAQQ. Your signals received okay. We are unable to hear you to take a bearing. It is impractical to take a bearing on 3105 on your voice. How do you get that? Go ahead." There was no response, so he tried yet again, sending on 7500 kilocycles, since the only satisfactory contact had been received by Amelia on that frequency: "*Itasca* to KHAQQ. Go ahead on 3105 or 500 kilocycles."

For more than half an hour, Bellarts sent voice and code signals on all frequencies that he knew Amelia's radio was capable of receiving. The transmissions in the ship's log are interspersed with the laconic "No answer," but the frustration and concern felt by all present were subsequently to be made obvious through the ship's log.

At 20:14 hours (GMT) the listeners in the radio room heard Amelia's voice for the last time. Volume was still strength 5 although it was not quite so loud as the previous transmission. She was sending on 3105 kilocycles and spoke rapidly; some listeners described her transmission as sounding hurried and almost incoherent: "KHAQQ to *Itasca*. We are on the line of position one five seven dash three three seven. Will repeat this message on 6210 kilocycles. We are running north and south."22

Bellarts immediately replied: "*Itasca* to KHAQQ. We heard you okay on 3105 kilocycles. Please stay on 3105 do not hear you on 6210. Maintain QSO on 3105." He sent this by voice on 3105 and by key on 7500 kilocycles but nothing further was heard from Amelia on any frequency.

Itasca continued to transmit on all frequencies until 21:30 hours (GMT), when Commander Thompson made the assumption that Amelia had ditched. He then set in motion the search procedure.

Commander Thompson had only the small amount of information Amelia had provided on which to base his search. There seemed no other reason for Amelia's report of flying "at 1,000 feet" than that she was flying beneath a cloud base, for it is easier to see over a greater distance at a higher altitude. Since the only cloud in the vicinity was to the north and northwest of Howland, Thompson concluded that the Electra's most likely position was in that sector. Furthermore, if Amelia had been in the clear skies surrounding and to the south and east of Howland, she ought to have been able to see the pall of black smoke hanging over *Itasca*. Notifying San Francisco of his intention, Thompson gave the command to proceed north at full steam.

Apart from the more sensational claims by writers who believe that Amelia and Noonan were not even in the vicinity of Howland when they disappeared, there has been much conjecture about what might have happened in the cockpit of the Electra during that flight. The main theories are that Amelia and Noonan had a disagreement, causing Amelia to disregard his instructions (as she had done at Dakar); or that Noonan was suffering from a hangover and consequently was not up to the mental effort required, so that the Electra was lost due to his incompetence. The permutations and speculation are seemingly endless, but unless the Electra is found, we will never know the answer, and perhaps not even then.

What is certain is that Amelia and Noonan were exhausted. Even had they been fit and rested when they left Lae, which they were not, they had been awake for more than twenty-four hours, and flying for over twenty, when Amelia was last heard on the radio. The dimensions of the Electra's cockpit were, according to an article written by Amelia before her departure from the United States: "four feet six inches by four feet six inches," and for the entire twenty hours Amelia would have been sitting in the same upright seat, unable to leave it at all. She was surrounded by equipment and would have found it difficult to stretch her limbs, though in smooth conditions she could allow the giro to fly the plane from time to time. The ceaseless engine noise in that confined space, and the vibration in the all-metal fuselage with its empty fuel tanks (also experienced by the crew of the 1967 commemorative flight to Howland in a Lockheed Electra), would have added greatly to the physical stress.[23]

Amelia's only contact with Noonan was on the occasions when he crawled over the fuel tanks and sat in the right-hand copilot's seat in the cockpit, when the two would have had to shout over the engine noise in order to communicate. Otherwise, notes were passed between them on the end of a cleft bamboo pole or by using the pulley system.

Although Fred Noonan was able to stand up and stretch his legs in a limited manner, he would have been working all night in the cramped, poorly lit navigation area and would also have been subject to the constant noise. In these circumstances, it is not unlikely that he could have made a mathematical error at some point, which progressed through his final calculations.

The most likely scenario is that the plane was in the vicinity of Howland and may, at one point, have even been within visual distance but missed it either due to clouds in the line of sight (a relatively small cloud would obscure such a small target)[24] or, if the fliers ever emerged into the clear air north of Howland, possibly missed the tiny island in the glare of the rising sun on the water. This, according to eyewitnesses, reduced visibility to a practical fifteen miles or less, although the *Itasca* at that time was making heavy black smoke, which at one point stretched for ten miles.

What seems most likely is that Amelia ran out of fuel and was forced to land at sea shortly after her last verified message to *Itasca* at 20:14 hours (GMT). Using extensive information gathered during eighteen years of research on the subject, Elgen and Marie Long claim to have pinpointed the most likely position,[25] which is "35 miles west, north west of the island . . . in an area perhaps twenty miles wide and forty miles long."[26]

Coincidentally, and perhaps curiously, using an entirely different line of investigation, British researcher Roy Nesbit (a former Royal Air Force navigator) has reached precisely the same conclusion.[27]

The author's conclusion is that Amelia probably went down within a hundred miles of Howland Island. For lack of proof in any direction, it is not beyond the bounds of *possibility* that Amelia and Noonan were picked up by one of the Japanese fishing boats known to be several hundred miles to the north of Howland. Amelia reported running "north and south on a line of position."[28] This would be a line calculated by Noonan using a sun sight taken earlier in the day, but the Electra might have been *anywhere* on that line, because there was no second coordinate given and one assumes from Amelia's message that they were flying up and down the line within the area where they expected to find the island.

There is substantial testimony to support the fact that a Caucasian couple was seen on the Japanese-mandated Marshall Islands (some six hundred miles to the north of Howland) at some time around 1937, but that this couple was Amelia Earhart and Fred Noonan is open to serious doubt. The testimony of many islanders made more than twenty years later may well have been made in the light of rewards offered for information, coupled with a genuine desire to please the interrogator. There is no really convincing evidence that this was Amelia Earhart's ultimate fate, though the Japanese theory is discussed in Appendix B of this book. All the documented facts point to a ditching off Howland Island, which neither flier survived.

It is known that Paul Mantz attempted to verbally prepare Amelia for a ditching in the Pacific in her Vega, prior to her solo transpacific flight; and presumably he may have gone through a similar routine for the Electra. Verbal instructions, however, would have been of minimal help in an actual sea landing.

Amelia would have known that she should keep the undercarriage retracted, but if she was completely out of fuel, as seems likely, she would have had to cope with a dead-stick forced landing on the water. Even over a smooth sea, it is difficult to judge a plane's height above the water surface, and if she stalled too high, the impact alone would have been sufficient to have killed both occupants. In rough seas, it would have been even more difficult to judge and such a stall, or even the effect of the waves in a rough patch of sea, would have caused severe damage to the Electra. When the *Itasca* steamed to the area under heavy cloud to the north of Howland Island, on July 2, she reported a turbulent sea with waves four to six feet high.[29]

Photographs of the Bendix receiver, installed in the Electra immediately before Amelia and Noonan left Miami, were shown to the author by Elgen and Marie Long. They reveal that the unit was sited immediately in front of Amelia's head and was mounted on the top of the instrument panel; its casing was a sharp-cornered metal box. If Amelia had hit her head on this in a ditching process (and it is difficult to see how she might have avoided it, for she had no shoulder harness), it is probable that she would have been knocked unconscious. Noonan may have been in the cockpit, having been warned of a possible emergency landing, or he may have remained aft in the cabin.

Assuming Amelia remained conscious after a forced landing, that everything had gone according to the book, that she had lowered the flaps correctly, glided in perfectly, stalled out at the correct height above the water, and that the plane remained intact, there were other problems to take into account. The floating attitude of the Electra, due to the weight of the engines and empty fuel tanks, was nose down–tail up. With no way of escape through the cockpit hatch (which would have been underwater), Amelia would have had to scramble up the almost vertical slope of the fuel tanks, perhaps with the help of Noonan, or perhaps without his help if he was unconscious.

The life raft and emergency equipment were housed behind the rear cabin bulkhead, at the rear of the plane, and even to have reached this would have required tremendous effort in an upended plane. It would then have been necessary to retrieve this not inconsiderable weight from stowage above head height (due to the plane's nose-down attitude); partially inflate the raft using the CO_2 canister; open the cabin door; throw the life raft into the water and jump after it, continuing the inflation process once safely on it. No trace has ever been found of Amelia's life raft.

There have been at least ten occasions when Lockheed Electras have made forced landings on water. One detailed report reads:

> The pilot experienced engine failure in the right engine and shortly afterwards lost some power in the left engine. He was able to land on a smooth sea, just off the Massachusetts coast, into a 10 mph wind with reduced power in one engine. The plane landed with the tail down to allow the easiest deceleration and therefore lessen impact and as a consequence the pilot and all passengers got out safely and were picked up more or less immediately.

The plane floated for eight minutes before sinking.[30]

1 9 3 7 - 1 9 3 9

A melia Earhart to George Putnam:

> I know that if I fail or if I am lost you will be blamed for allowing me
> to leave on this trip; the backers of the flight will be blamed and every-
> one connected with it. But it's my responsibility and mine alone.[1]

For George, who had been waiting at coast guard headquarters in San
Francisco during the entire flight, the news from *Itasca* was scarcely
believable. There had been many occasions in the past when he had
waited with ill-concealed anxiety for news of Amelia's safe arrival and
when bad news had been passed to him erroneously, but it had all turned
out well. At first, he was convinced that it would be the same this time,
that at any minute news would arrive of Amelia's rescue.

The *Itasca*'s cable to headquarters had reported merely:

EARHART CONTACT 0742 REPORTED ONE HALF HOUR FUEL AND NO LAND
FALL. POSITION DOUBTFUL. CONTACT 0646 REPORTED ONE HUNDRED MILES
FROM ITASCA BUT NO RELATIVE BEARING. 0843 REPORTED LINE OF POSITION
157 DASH 337 BUT NO REFERENCE POINT PRESUME HOWLAND. ESTIMATE 1200
FOR MAXIMUM TIME ALOFT AND IF NON-ARRIVAL BY THAT TIME WILL COM-
MENCE SEARCH IN NORTHWEST QUADRANT FROM HOWLAND AS MOST PROBA-
BLE AREA . . . UNDERSTAND SHE WILL FLOAT FOR LIMITED TIME.[2]

George told New York *Herald Tribune* reporters, "The plane should float,
but I couldn't estimate for how long because a Lockheed plane has never
been forced down at sea before. The plane's large wings and empty tanks
should provide sufficient buoyancy, if it came to rest on the sea without

being damaged. There was a two-man life raft aboard, together with lifebelts, flares, a Very pistol and a large yellow signal kite."[3]

Already steaming north, *Itasca*'s Commander Thompson commenced the search within three hours after Amelia's last contact. His next cable suggested that headquarters contact the navy to request a seaplane to assist him.

In the hours and days immediately following Amelia's last substantiated message, hope was kept alive by constant reports of radio signals purporting to have come from the Electra. The most significant was heard by Walter McMenamy, who worked for Paul Mantz from time to time and who had maintained radio contact with Amelia during her solo transpacific flight. McMenamy claimed that he intercepted weak Morse-code signals on the 6210-kc. frequency about six hours after Amelia's final contact with *Itasca:* ". . . just the letters l-a-t," which he assumed was latitude, followed by indecipherable transmission. Although Amelia's Electra carried no code-transmission key, she could have transmitted a carrier signal by holding down the microphone switch. Later, McMenamy claimed to have heard Amelia's voice, very faintly, calling, "SOS, SOS, SOS, KHAQQ, KHAQQ."

Two hours later, Carl Pierson, also of Los Angeles, claimed to have picked up weak and indecipherable signals on 6210 kcs.

It is interesting that despite the fact that these two amateur radio operators[4] were reporting radio contact throughout the next twelve hours, the San Francisco coast guard said they had heard nothing despite the fact that radio reception was unusually good and that they had three radio stations set constantly to monitor the appropriate wavelengths. Nothing was heard, either, by the coast guard's Pearl Harbor radio station, nor by *Itasca* and *Swan,* who maintained their radio vigil. *Itasca*'s Commander Thompson later concluded that probably what McMenamy and Pierson (and later, many other genuine radio operators) actually heard were the transmissions on 6210 and 3105 by *Itasca* herself, attempting to contact the lost fliers, for there were significant coincidences between the reported times of the messages and transmissions recorded in the ship's radio log.[5]

Due to George's publicity machine, every single known detail was published under banner headlines that Amelia was missing in the Pacific Ocean. It was a boon to hoaxers, for they could invent messages (or send them on home radio sets), knowing which frequencies were applicable, the approximate location of Amelia's disappearance, and enough personal information to enable faked messages to sound convincing.

From the start, Paul Mantz doubted the authenticity of the reported signals, stating that the Electra's radio equipment was not capable of transmitting over any distance (even allowing for "skip," the phenomenon that enables occasional freak radio reception hundreds or thousands of miles away) from sea level. Nor, except for the briefest period, could transmissions be made without the right engine being run to keep the batteries charged—a feat that could be accomplished only if the Electra was on land.

Donald R. Husted, however, who had supervised the fitting of the Western Electric radio equipment, stated that he thought it was *possible*.[6] Joseph Gurr, who spent many hours checking out the system in Burbank, told George that under favorable conditions and if *everything* was still working, it *could* transmit.[7]

It was not on the strength of the radio reports, however, but based on the belief that the empty fuel tanks would enable the plane to stay afloat for an indefinite time, and the knowledge that Amelia carried a life raft and emergency provisions, that a massive search was launched. Personally authorized by President Roosevelt, it involved nine naval ships and sixty-six airplanes, at an estimated cost of more than $4 million.

Only the *Itasca* and *Swan* were on station to start the search immediately;[8] the other ships had to be diverted from other duties elsewhere. The aircraft carrier U.S.S. *Lexington,* for example, which was standing off Santa Barbara when the orders were dispatched, had been scheduled to be the star attraction at the Marine Week celebrations beginning on July 4. Ordered to Howland Island by Rear Admiral Manley on July 3, *Lexington* left immediately but took eleven days to reach the search area.[9]

Within hours of Amelia being reported down, a PBY flying boat with a crew of eight was dispatched from Hawaii to Howland to help in the search, as requested by Commander Thompson. Later, Thompson would pointedly mention in his report that throughout the PBY's flight, *Itasca* had no difficulty in maintaining constant radio contact. The PBY was expected to arrive on the morning of July 3, and *Itasca* therefore left the most likely search area and returned to Howland Island to meet the plane. Some seven hundred miles north of Howland Island, however, the seaplane sent the following radio message in Morse code:

> Last two hours in extremely bad weather between altitude 2000 and 12000 feet. Snow, sleet, rain, electrical storms. In daylight conditions look equally bad cloud tops appear to be 18000 feet or more. Am returning to Pearl Harbor.[10]

Now understandably desperate for information, George pounced on every new rumor that was flashed to newspapers and wire services. His first request was that transmissions be sent every hour on the hour on 3105 kcs. " . . . just her initials, AE, followed by the questions: Land or water? North or south?"[11]

The twenty-four hours following Amelia's disappearance were spent as he had spent the previous twenty-four, at San Francisco's coast guard headquarters, waiting and hoping for a substantiated report. Noonan's wife, Bea, joined George there to await news. Those present remembered how he paced back and forth for hours, in shirt sleeves, and with perspiration streaming from his face. "AE will pull through," he told a New York's *Sunday Mirror* reporter. "She has more courage than anyone I know. I am worried, of course, but I have confidence in her ability to handle any situation." Once, irritated by Mrs. Noonan's stifled sobs, he stopped to say, "It's this way, Bea. One of two things has happened. Either they must have been killed outright—and that must come to all of us sooner or later—or they are alive and will be picked up." This statement was, understandably, no succor to the distraught bride of several months, who promptly collapsed.[12]

George, though, was not able to use the luxury of retreat into helplessness. He was a doer and psychologically unable to allow the organization of the search to be left to others. As the hours and days wore on, he could be seen twisting and struggling with the problem, searching for new avenues of possibilities. After discussions with Clarence Williams and Paul Mantz, for example, he decided that a likely place for Amelia to have come down was several hundred miles to the south of Howland, perhaps in the vicinity of the Phoenix Islands, several of which, he said, were large enough for Amelia to have made "a pancake landing." Using his normal bulldozing tactics to get his own way, George telephoned navy and coast guard chiefs to request that ships be diverted from the organized search pattern to search the reefs in the Phoenix archipelago.

At George's request, Clarence Williams prepared a chart of the great circle "base course" from Lae to Howland and on the assumption that Noonan would have obtained a drift angle soon after takeoff, he estimated drift at 11 degrees (which would have been laid off into the prevailing wind), or to the right of the original course. The prolongation of this track, he said, passed 140 miles to the south of Howland Island. He also warned George that it was just as likely that the opposite might have happened, and drew another track line 11 degrees to the left of the course, which passed 140 miles to the north of Howland. From these two lines, he provided George with what he called a "cone of possibilities," which a staff artist of the Los Angeles *Times* laid out and wired to many of the daily papers around the world.

George immediately begged the navy to instruct the battleship U.S.S. *Colorado* to search to the southeast as far as the Phoenix Islands, taking in the numerous reefs and coral atolls in that area. Acceding to his requests, the *Colorado* made full steam to the area and sent up all three of its 3U-3 spotter biplanes. The three young pilots (Lieutenants John Lambrecht, William Short, and Leonard Fox) could not even locate the reefs that they had been instructed to search. It was concluded that the charts were probably incorrect and, indeed, many years later the reefs were rediscovered by cartographers.

The *Colorado* continued to search for the following five days, covering an area of more than twenty-five thousand square miles. Every island of any size in the search area was visited: Enderbury, Phoenix, Birnie, Sydney, McKean, Gardner, Canton and Hull, though only Hull Island was inhabited and the residents there had never heard of Amelia Earhart. The biggest problem the searchers felt Amelia might have, if she was down in the ocean, was sharks. The waters were so shark-infested that after a survey by the Royal Navy a year earlier, they were considered unsafe for British commercial airliners to fly over and a proposed air route was abandoned.[13]

Gene Vidal claimed Amelia had told him that if she could not locate Howland, she would turn back to the Gilbert Islands and, consequently, the Minesweeper U.S.S. *Swan* called on the Gilbert Islands and found the inhabitants highly excited by the unexpected contact from the outside world, but with no news of Amelia despite their having contacted all the larger islands in the group by radio. Some of the smaller islands in the archipelago lay up to sixty miles out, but they were all eventually contacted without result.[14]

After the aircraft carrier *Lexington* arrived on station, sixty-two of her airplanes covered an area of 151,556 square miles, and the *Lexington* was escorted by three new destroyers—the *Drayton, Lamson,* and *Cushing*—who also participated in the meticulous search, which was eventually estimated to have covered more than a quarter of a million square miles of ocean.

Although the ships detailed from other duties took some days to arrive on the scene, the coast guard cutter *Itasca* spent seventeen days searching, from the first hours that Amelia was reported missing, and two British ships, the S.S. *Moorsby* and H.M.S. *Achilles,* who were in the search area, also immediately joined in the search at the request of *Itasca*'s captain. *The New York Times* reported that the Japanese had detailed two vessels, the aircraft tender *Kamoie* and the survey ship *Koshu,* to search the seas around the Marshall Islands some six hundred miles to the north of

Howland, and in all it was estimated that more than four thousand men were involved.[15] Hopes were raised briefly by the sight of what was taken to be green flares but these turned out to be meteorites or lightning;[16] a radio transmission was picked up by the British ship H.M.S. *Achilles* on 3105, which signed KHAQQ and said faintly, "Give us a few dashes." It was later decided that this probably emanated from *Itasca*. Another radio transmission was picked up by three radio operators on the naval station on Wailupe: "281 North Howland call KHAQQ beyond north don't hold with us much longer above water shut off." Much later this was thought to be a hoax message that had originated in the Hawaiian islands.[17] Even suspected hoax calls had to be investigated, but as Commander Thompson later pointed out, each time a hoax was investigated, it pulled ships and planes away from the "most likely quadrant," the area to the northwest of Howland. This area was searched thoroughly by *Itasca* during the day and night after Amelia's plane disappeared, however, and subsequently a much extended area in that sector was searched during the following seventeen days, but it is doubtful whether the Electra would have still been afloat by that time.

As each new report was cabled to San Francisco by *Itasca* the transmissions were intercepted by wire services and Commander Thompson was inundated with lucrative offers for his unique story on the Earhart rescue . . . and photographs by newspaper editors anxious to scoop their competitors.

But as the vast methodical search failed to turn up a single sighting, hope began to fade. At one point, George was reported to have broken down in nervous collapse, but this brought forth a hasty denial:

> I have not collapsed. I have indulged in no public sobbing. The nearest I have been to a hospital is the home of an old friend, Dr. Harry Clay, who has lent me a helping hand. In the existing circumstances what is said about me is not of the least importance except that false reports heighten the anxiety of relations and friends. If I seem to have thrown in the sponge, it just makes it harder for them. . . . if Amelia is dead it is the way she would have chosen.[18]

But despite his seeming rationality, George was now willing to try anything. His son David had flown to Oakland to join him while they awaited news, and he remembers his father's desperation and the endless pacing of the floor at the coast guard radio station while George considered his next move.

Through Purdue's President Elliott came a cable from a correspondent suggesting that a position 2 degrees latitude and 1–8–1 longitude should be searched. "This position is 100 miles west of Howland," the writer stated reasonably, and considering the much-publicized messages reported three days earlier by Wailupe naval station, it was too coincidental to be ignored. When George requested that this position be searched, however, he received a cable back from Admiral Leahy curtly advising him that it had already been thoroughly searched "with negative results."[19]

One apparently well-founded report emanated as the result of a radio listener who unknowingly had tuned into a popular radio program called *March of Time*, which dramatically simulated the conversation between Amelia and the *Itasca*. The excited listener (an airport manager) immediately reported having heard Amelia, and it was some time before it was realized what had happened.[20]

In her weekly newspaper column in the New York *Telegraph* on July 7, Eleanor Roosevelt noted her great anxiety over Amelia. "I feel sure that if she comes through safely she will feel that what she has learned makes it all worth while. But her friends will wish science could be served without so much risk to a fine person whom many people love as a person and not as a pilot or adventurer."[21]

President Roosevelt asked to be kept informed of the results of the search and on July 20 his secretary, Marvin H. McIntyre, sent the President an internal memo stating that Gene Vidal had been in close touch with the Amelia Earhart story, talking several times a day to George Putnam. "He has some interesting sidelights and some speculations which are probably true as to what actually happened. You might find it interesting to spend 15 minutes with him," he suggested. To which Roosevelt replied that he would be away until July 26 but would like to see Vidal for five or ten minutes.[22] In view of the suggestions that the President had an ulterior interest in the outcome of Amelia's flight, the archives reveal that he was prepared to devote a remarkably small amount of time to the matter.

A little later, George wrote to McIntyre saying how much he appreciated the "friendly personal cooperation which you have extended. Is there any way of ascertaining what the Japanese are actually doing—especially as regards a real search of the eastern fringe of the Marshall Islands? That is one of the most fruitful possible locations for wreckage."[23]

Everyone was still working on the theory that the Electra would float and no attention was paid to Amelia's former radio mechanic, Joe Gurr, who shyly voiced an opinion that the fuel tanks had vent openings in them "through which the water could fill them in a certain length of time."[24]

As the official search wound down, George's own efforts grew more desperate. Though never allowing himself to become the victim of some of the more obvious crank messages that flooded in to him and to Amy, he did focus on some obscure possibilities. Shortly after Amelia's disappearance, for example, he recalled her telepathic experience with Jackie Cochran a few months earlier.

According to Jackie's memoirs, it was she and not Amelia who had located the missing airliners.[25] Further, she claimed, she had correctly "seen Amelia and George having to land at Blackwell, Oklahoma in February" (when George played the silly practical joke), and she had also been aware of the fire in Amelia's engine at Tucson on the first leg of her world flight—from Burbank to Miami. Shortly after Amelia disappeared, Jackie related, George called on her at her Los Angeles apartment "for the kind of help Amelia thought I might be able to give."

> He was extremely excited . . . I told him where Amelia had gone down; that with the ditching of the plane Mr. Noonan, the navigator, had fractured his skull against the bulkhead in the navigators compartment and was unconscious; but that Amelia was alive and the plane was floating in a certain area. I named a boat called the *Itasca* which I had never heard of at the time, as a boat that was nearby, and I also named another Japanese fishing vessel in that area, the name of which I now forget. I begged Putnam to keep my name out of it but to get planes and ships out to the designated area. Navy planes and ships in abundance combed that area but found no trace. I followed the course of her drifting for two days. It was always in the area being well combed.[26]

Three days later, Jackie claimed, she knew Amelia had died.[27] This incident almost certainly lies behind George's intriguing cable to to Daniel Roper, Secretary of Commerce:

> . . . REQUEST YOUR GOOD OFFICES IN OBTAINING COOPERATION OF BRITISH AND JAPANESE IN CONTINUING SEARCH ESPECIALLY REGARDING ELLICE, GILBERT AND MARSHALL ISLANDS, OCEAN ISLAND AND AREA NORTH EAST OF SAME. ALSO IF POSSIBLE REQUEST SOME EXAMINATION OF ISLAND NORTHERLY AND NORTH WESTERLY PAGO PAGO. LEAVE NOTHING UNDONE LOOKING TOWARD SECURING INFORMATION. WHATEVER IT MAY BE POSSIBLE TO DO WILL BE SINCERELY APPRECIATED. FOR YOUR CONFIDENTIAL INFORMATION EXTRAORDINARY EVIDENCE SEEMS TO EXIST INDICATING CASTAWAY STILL LIVING THOUGH OF SUCH STRANGE NATURE CANNOT BE OFFICIAL OR PUBLICLY CONFIRMED.[28]

Virtually the same message was dispatched to the Secretary of the Navy, and within days George offered a reward of two thousand dollars for information, and a guarantee to defray any costs involved in thorough searches of island groups such as the Gilberts.[29]

Estimates of the costs of the huge search were filtering into the newspapers, which had been carrying the story on front pages, worldwide, for nearly a month. Along with the Lindbergh baby kidnapping and the abdication of King Edward VIII to marry Wallis Simpson, the Earhart disappearance has long been regarded as one of the greatest newspaper stories of this century.

There was political criticism of the expenditure (estimated by newspapers at $4.5 million) involved in the search, but most people were able to accept that the ships and the men would have been working at some maneuver in any case. Besides, the search for Amelia was not unique. A similar one had been made in the Pacific for Captain Charles Ulm prior to Amelia's transpacific solo in 1934, and that occupied naval and coast guard ships and personnel for twenty-seven days. A spokesman for the navy told *The New York Times* that the opportunity to operate under service conditions over an important and little-known strategic area of the Pacific was an important by-product of the extensive search for Amelia.[30] Subsequently, Senator Davis, who formally raised the question of costs, was informed by letter that though the actual cost of fuel and oil involved in the search was $81,223.38,[31] the expenditure was not merely philanthropic:

> ... the search made possible flights over Islands and areas over which naval planes had never flown before, permitted a cursory survey of the area, which may help to correct charts and allowed a study of the weather and other operating conditions in a part of the Pacific which is becoming of increasing strategic importance.[32]

By now, the administration felt they had done all they could regarding a purely civilian matter and George's continuous shifts of the scene of action were becoming an irritant. When, through the President's secretary, George asked whether he was sure everything possible was still being done, the Secretary of State (Sumner Welles) wrote to McIntyre sending him the file of cables that they had sent to various missions.

> You will see from this file that we are doing everything we possibly can to be of help and I don't see that there is anything that you or I can say to him in reply to his letter, other than that you have seen

the file of telegrams we have sent and are sure that we are doing everything we possibly can. . . . The Japanese authorities have assured us that all fishing vessels have been told to keep on the lookout on the reefs and waters adjacent to the Marshall Islands. There isn't any way we can check up on what they are doing and we will have to take their word for it.[33]

On July 18, the search was officially abandoned by the ships in the Howland area and George, still desperately seeking any help he could muster, issued a press release from the National Geographic Society, claiming that the search was imcomplete. The Gilbert Islands, he said, had not been properly searched.

The Gilbert Islands are so far west that they mark where the east begins, they lie in the open Pacific just across the International Date Line, about 600 miles west of Howland Island and 1,600 miles southwest of Hawaii. Reason for searching so far from Miss Earhart's goal was the strong ocean current which swirls a titanic stream of the Pacific westward along the Equator in that area. The drift, aided by fairly constant trade winds, would carry a floating object westward from ten to forty miles a day. Natives have taken advantage of this current to make long oceanbound voyages in frail open canoes. There is a record of an "involuntary" voyage of two natives whose boat was caught in the current and finally landed, three months later, 1,300 miles away.

The Gilbert Group consists of 16 coral islands festooned in a thin crescent across the equator . . . governed by Great Britain as part of the Crown Colony of Gilbert and Ellice Islands, of which the 200 square miles of dry land are scattered over a million square miles of high seas. . . .[34]

"This release," George was informed by the National Geographic Society, was "circulated to 600 dailies and all press associations."[35]

At the end of July, despite official opinion that Amelia had perished, George was still following up his own lines of inquiry. He flew to Washington, where he proceeded to badger anyone whom he could get to listen. To Amy, who was still staying in the Putnams' Hollywood home, he wrote, "I am having conversations this afternoon with the White House and with many others. I find an extraordinarily unanimous opinion that somehow, somewhere, Amelia is still alive. We are doing everything possible—at least we are trying to."[36]

George's touching obsession with continuing the search is a powerful argument about his emotional nature and his love for Amelia. No possibility was too obscure to warrant his interest. One of his requests was to ask the American Embassy in London to make a thorough search, at his expense:

> . . . BEGINNING AT THE FOLLOWING POSITION: 174 DEGREES TEN MINUTES EAST LONGITUDE TWO DEGREES 36 MINUTES NORTH LATITUDE. THIS IS ONLY 85 MILES FROM TARAWA, ON MAKING ISLAND BEARING THENCE 106 DEGREES TRUE. MR. PUTNAM BELIEVES HE HAD AUTHENTIC INFORMATION . . . THAT UNCHARTERED [SIC] REEF EXISTS AT THAT POINT AND IS REGULARLY VISITED FOR TURTLES EGGS ETC BY GILBERTESE NATIVES [FISHERMEN].[37]

One by one, George's leads came to nothing, however. "I have the honor to inform you that the High Commissioner for the Western Pacific has reported that Captain Handley has returned after searching for Miss Amelia Earhart in the locality mentioned (174 deg.10 mins E Long; 2 deg 36 mins north Lat) . . . but that he found no trace of the reef referred to, or of Miss Earhart's plane."[38] "Foreign office advises that U.S. vessels visited all Gilbert Islands."[39] Finally, all that was left for them to do was to forward to George the bills for expenses.[40]

The bills created their own problems for George because, to put it plainly, he had no money to meet them. "For many years," he was to explain later to Amy, he had been "pouring my fullest energy and thoughtfulness and, largely, my income, into AE's activities and ambitions. And you know that the final tragedy and its aftermath involved me financially as much as, and even more than the Estate. For which . . . I have no regrets. If we had to do it again, I'd spend everything I had again. . . ."[41] He explained the position carefully on many occasions in an attempt to make Amy understand that the Estate was not wealthy and that there was very little money after all debts had been settled.

> You must realize that she expected, properly, to make a great deal of money out of the results of the flight after her return. For instance she owned the ship entirely [Purdue had agreed to present her with the Electra] which was worth $70,000 or more. Some of its purchase came from her and some from me, as well as the other larger contributors.[42]

George also told Amy that during this period, when he was coming to terms with Amelia's probable death, he was " . . . knocked out and was no good to myself or anyone else,"[43] and this is borne out by friends who knew him. "He was never the same man after Amelia disappeared, he changed a lot . . . became older, somehow . . ."[44] was a typical comment. His pragmatism did not entirely desert him, however, and he was able to recognize the opportunity to obtain revenue for himself and Amelia's depleted Estate immediately by completing the book about the flight, which had been commissioned prior to Amelia's departure by Harcourt, Brace and Company, the New York publishers.

One of the saddest experiences of these weeks had been the regular receipt of mail from Amelia, it having been mailed from various stops along her route. Now he suggested to the publishers that he produce the book based on this informal log of the flight that she had sent back to him. It was mainly a compilation of her personal papers, articles she had written about her early years and her solo transpacific and Mexican flights, added to the already published reports of the early stages of her flight that she had filed by cable with the *Herald Tribune* at her various stops. Her unpublished en-route world-flight jottings on less than fifty pages torn from a stenographer's note pad were more aptly described as aide-mémoires than pages of manuscript. However, George was fully aware that a book written (posthumously, as it were) by Amelia Earhart held more commercial interest than one written about her by someone else.

The book was retitled *Last Flight*, and although George was insistent that it was entirely Amelia's own work, an examination of her notes and the finished product reveals that it owed a great deal to the hand of an editor. Amelia's log, in hard-to-read cramped scribble, made worse by the obvious vibration of the Electra, read, for example:

> Caripito. Rain clouds hung around us this morning as we left. We flew low over the jungle most of the way to the coast then played hide and seek with rain storms until I decided I better give up watching scenery and climb up on top of 8000 feet topped all but highest. First big town Georgetown. Out at sea but could see neat fields along the coast . . . little clouds. . . . white scrambled eggs.[45]

In *Last Flight*, this became:

> Rain clouds hung thick about Caripito as we left on the morning of June third. We flew over jungles to the coast, and then played hide and seek with showers until I decided I had better forgo the scenery, such as it was, and climb through the clouds into fair weather. An altitude of 8,000 feet topped all but the highest woolly pinnacles. In

such a maneuver lies a recurrent delight of flying . . . now and then
[the] sun illuminates mystic caves and roaring fortresses or shows
giant cloud creatures mocking with lumpy paws the tiny man made
birds among them.[46]

To transcribe Amelia's notes and help with the physical production of the
book, George recruited free-lance journalist Janet Mabie. During the
previous eight years, Ms. Mabie had written a number of articles about
Amelia, and could be relied upon to give a favorable slant to any news
story that George had wanted to break. Later, Ms. Mabie complained
bitterly that she was never paid for the work she did on *Last Flight,* nor
the syndicated articles that emanated from it,[47] but that George had
merely advanced her the sum of three hundred dollars, which she claimed
was for expenses. By October 1937, the manuscript was completed and
though Ms. Mabie claimed that she did most of the work, it is equally
clear from his correspondence that George, too, spent a great deal of time
working on the project. Nor, at the time, did Janet Mabie dispute the title
page:

LAST FLIGHT

by

Amelia Earhart

Arranged by George Palmer Putnam.

The matter was not to end there, however.

During the preparation of the book, George was still seeking information, writing letters, and lobbying the administration for any proof of
Amelia's fate. A life raft said to be similar to Amelia's was found off the
Hawaiian coast and raised hopes again, briefly, until investigation proved
it had originated elsewhere.[48] There was uncertainty about the type of life
raft that the Electra actually carried, but Margot de Carrie, George and
Amelia's secretarial assistant, recalled that she had actually inflated it and
tested it on Tolucca Lake near the Putnams' Hollywood home. "It wasn't
very seaworthy," she told reporters.

The U.S. Coast Guard tracked down many of the calls—purporting to
come from Amelia—to hoaxers.[49] A man who attempted to sell George
information regarding Amelia's present whereabouts by using an old scarf
of Amelia's as proof of his reliability was traced and tried for attempted

extortion. He was declared insane and committed to a mental hospital.[50]

By October, George had concluded that Amelia was dead. He tactfully tried to convey this to Amy, who never really accepted that her daughter had perished, but he succeeded only in upsetting her. Muriel was more levelheaded, recognizing that if her sister had survived, they would have heard something in the intervening months. Under mounting pressure from creditors, George filed a petition to be named trustee of Amelia's Estate. This caused a flurry of letters between Amy and her mass of correspondents, many of whom were friends or casual contacts of Amelia's and with whom Amy kept in constant touch. To one, Benigua Green, who wrote protesting that George was "giving up," he replied, explaining patiently:

> It became necessary for something definite to be done to simplify pending business matters. I did not choose to file her will or to take other similar steps that must come if and when we feel the chapter is definitely closed. Rather, on advice of counsel, I have sought to be appointed "trustee for a missing person." To date the law assumes AE is not dead but simply missing. In [her] absence a properly accredited representative is permitted by the court to conduct her business affairs. After an appropriate period if the missing person is not found then the will is probated, etc. So that is the situation. I am sure you would like to know about it.[51]

In November 1937, *Last Flight* was published and though it never achieved the revenue George hoped for, it provided a regular income after the advance of three thousand dollars had been accounted for.[52] George included, as an endpiece, a note from Amelia to himself, probably written prior to the first transpacific flight:

> Please know I am quite aware of the hazards. . . .[53]
>
> . . .
>
> I want to do it because I want to do it. Women must try to do things as men have tried. When they fail, their failure must be but a challenge to others.[54]

In December 1937, George joined an expedition to the Galápagos. He had a commission to produce an illustrated book and had wanted to visit the islands ever since his first wife, Dorothy Binney, had gone there in 1922. He wrote affectionately to Amy, whom he had started to call "Mother Earhart":

I could enjoy it all were the circumstances different. But naturally the thought keeps recurring how AE would have enjoyed it. And there are times when the nightmare on the horizon blots out all else. At that I am glad I have broken away. It will do me much good. Already I am rested and sleeping well. . . . But sometimes I feel that I am running away from something I should face at home. So . . . I am puzzled and far from happy, but there is nothing I can do about it. Mostly the days are filled with an effort to keep from thinking. The total emptiness is appalling.[55]

The expedition covered many weeks and it was spring before he returned. "George," a friend was to tell me, "was capable of the full gamut of emotions."[56] His grief for Amelia was deep and real and it is not lessened by the fact that during those final weeks at sea he found solace in a relationship with Ione Reed, one of the women in the expedition. Given George's passionate nature it was hardly surprising that he would succumb in the confined nature of the expedition to a pretty and intelligent young woman who also found him extremely attractive. The two were discreet and the relationship continued for some months after their return, but eventually it seems George found her company irritating and drove her off in a somewhat cruel manner by deliberately provoking arguments and constantly finding fault.[57]

In George's absence many things had happened. A group of people headed by Elmer Dimity (a parachute manufacturer who had known Amelia during the two years prior to her disappearance), with the approval of Amy, set up the Amelia Earhart Foundation. It was a well-intentioned, though hopelessly inefficient organization whose mission was to raise money to send a search/rescue expedition to the Pacific to discover whether Amelia was still alive or, if she was not, an "explanation of the mystery."[58]

Dozens of organizations with whom Amelia had had connections (some extremely tenuous) erected memorials; others provided tributes in the form of scholarships and other honors in her name. The ball that George had set rolling in 1928 had gathered speed by virtue of his publicity machine in the interim years and now—by an unfortunate accident—it had gathered its own momentum, which nothing and no one could stop. It might be called the Amelia Earhart Legend.

George could not know the long-term effects on the public imagination of Amelia's disappearance, of course. All his energy was presently directed at trying to make a living. As he had told Amy, he had spent the previous two years working primarily on Amelia's behalf. Now, returned and rested after the South Atlantic trip, he took stock of his position. He was fifty-one years old, without a job and unable to use any of the assets in Amelia's Estate, which, though the net value did not amount to much, he had helped to create.

The fact that he was continuously referred to in the press as " 'the millionaire publisher' did not help much," he told Amy, "except to keep creditors happy."[59]

Amy was one of George's major problems. She was convinced, probably by the many sycophantic letters she received, that Amelia had left a substantial Estate. Although the will at this stage had not been published, the nature of its contents was no secret; the bulk of Amelia's Estate had been left to George (it had been assumed that Amy would predecease George), but the net income was to be used to support Amy during her lifetime. If George died before Amy, then everything would go to her and after her death to Muriel. At this time, George was supporting Amy, although he was recording the amounts he sent her and most of these were eventually properly offset against the Estate.

During the summer of 1938, George began to make plans for his future. He set up a small publishing company of his own (George Palmer Putnam, Inc.) in leased offices at 6253 Hollywood Boulevard. Having secured an advance of three thousand dollars from Harcourt, Brace, he contacted Janet Mabie, announced that he was writing a biography of Amelia, and invited her to come to the house at Valley Spring Road and help him write it. He would pay all expenses, he said, and though he could not give her a by-line he would formally acknowledge her help and would reach agreement on her remuneration. Ms. Mabie was delighted and traveled from New York to California to begin work immediately, though in view of her subsequent claims that she had never been paid for the work she had done six months earlier on *Last Flight*, her alacrity in accepting this second commission seems peculiar.

There was a great deal of material: eighteen large scrapbooks crammed with news cuttings dating from Amelia's earliest days in aviation; hundreds of photographs; Amelia's own writings; and George's recollections of events they had shared. Again, Ms. Mabie would say that the entire work was all hers, and indeed perhaps much of the compilation and typing was hers. However, the many surviving letters written by George to friends and relatives of Amelia's requesting information prove that he was not as detached from the project as Janet Mabie was to attest.

A typical letter from George said:

Dear Muriel,

. . . forget the note I sent you the other day about the bronco. I found the verse.[60] Do you know the verse or rhyme or whatever it was that Amelia used to know which concerned Simkin? [*sic*] I think Simkin was a cat. I have a hazy recollection that she was a pussy who wanted to drink her cream and have it too. Anyway at the beginning of our acquaintance AE called me Simkin and I find that in the code we set up for use in my messages to her at Trepassey I signed myself Simkin. If you can help me unravel that I will be grateful.[61]

From Muriel's reply came the following passage in the biography, later published as *Soaring Wings:*

When I'd known AE only a short time she began calling me "Simp-kin."
"Why?" I asked her one day.
It had, it seems, something to do with a book out of her childhood reading. A tale of the Tailor of Gloucester who "lived alone with his cat, which was called Simpkin." Simpkin was a cat who believed that if holding one mouse in reserve against the danger of having time on one's hands—or paws—was wisdom, then holding a good number of mice in reserve . . . was even better. So Simpkin kept a flock—or whatever the grouping of mice is—always available by the simple expedient of housing them, one by one, under inverted teacups.[63]

George went on to explain how Amelia had seen the resemblance in that although she was the center of an important project just then, in reality it was merely one of a group of enterprises in which he was engaged. "And so she privately called me Simpkin," George confided.

It was George who delved into Amelia's childhood and first discovered the often-told incidents such as her riding her sled facedown as the boys did, and on one occasion, unable to stop, steered it straight between the fore and hind legs of a horse crossing her path as she careened downhill.

The end result was an interesting mosaic that has formed basic research for all subsequent biographies. "Essentially informal and often unorderly," it further enhanced the heroic publicity-shy image of Amelia that George had striven to promote, with—it must be stressed—Amelia's full cooperation during her lifetime.

In September 1938, George told Amy in one of his regular letters that the book was almost completed and that he had "been devoting almost all my time for the last couple of months to [it]. . . . As I think you know Janet Mabie has been here for some time helping me. . . ."[63] Following Amelia's disappearance, the relationship between George and Amy had been much closer than previously, but over the the next months, it slowly disintegrated once George made it clear that he intended to try to establish proof of Amelia's death in order to have the will probated and to administrate the Estate in the manner in which Amelia had wished.

To establish the necessary proof for the court, he wrote to Admiral Leahy,[64] who had commanded the search for Amelia, and through him obtained a sworn affidavit from Leigh Noyes, captain of the U.S.S. *Lexington*, on the scope and results of the search. It ended, "No trace of either the Amelia Earhart plane or of its occupants was found."[65]

One of the main contentions between George and Amy, however, was Amy's inability to accept that she must live on an income within the limits of Amelia's provision for her, and that Amelia would not be there to bail her out whenever she got into financial difficulties as she had in the past. In addition, she began to write tediously lengthy letters to George requesting that this or that item belonging to Amelia be sent to her: furs, coats, jewelry, small items of furniture or silver, and so on.

Often these notes have an offensive implication and it is to George's credit that he remained courteous and helpful, never losing his patience at unwritten but obvious innuendos that he was using the proceeds of the Estate, and Amelia's property, for his own enrichment. When Amelia's will was probated, it was proven that George had acted properly and was simply stating the facts when he tried constantly to explain to Amy that there was no great fortune in Amelia's Estate.

> It is also true, as I mentioned before, that the Estate owes some considerable bills. Unless some good luck comes over the hill for me during the next year, which would make it possible for me to absorb some of these charges, there will be precious little left of the Estate. Which is a situation we might as well all face. . . . It has been my own suggestion from the first that, irrespective of the condition of the Estate, I elect to do what I can to care for your future and to help Muriel. . . . Despite your unhappiness because things have not always been done just as you would like them, the facts I think demonstrate that I have done as much as I possibly can to be more than fair and considerate.[66]

Armed with the necessary statements from Richard B. Black and Captain Leigh Noyes (of the U.S.S. *Lexington*), and in the company of his employee Charles "Cap" Palmer, George went to Los Angeles city hall to file evidence—all, it seemed likely, that there ever would be—of Amelia's death. It was accepted by the court and the will was duly probated.

In essence, Amelia left all her household furniture, clothing, and personal effects and jewelry to George. In addition, "all the rest, residue and remainder of my estate, of whatever kind and nature . . . I give devise and bequeath to my [sole] trustee (George Palmer Putnam) in trust. . . ." George was to administer the estate and, "during the lifetime of Amy Otis Earhart, to pay over and distribute to her in quarterly or monthly installments as she may elect, the net income therefrom. . . . Upon her death, or if she shall predecease me, then upon my death to transfer or pay over . . . the principal of the said trust to my husband George Palmer Putnam, outright." In the event of George predeceasing Amy, then the Estate would eventually be paid over to Muriel or her surviving issue.[67]

Eventually, receipts over the next few years would bring the actual gross value of the Estate to $59,108,[68] but authorized disbursements (every one meticulously receipted by George) for outstanding bills connected with the round-the-world flight, mortgage payments on the Valley Spring Lane property, Amy's upkeep and medical bills (more than seven thousand dollars),[69] and sundry other items such as taxes and property expenses amounted to $45,329, leaving a net balance of only $13,779.

What is not generally known is that George had to sell his Rye home at this point in order to remain solvent.[70] It is not generally known because George never talked of it. As he saw it, he had, along with Amelia, gambled and lost. However, the money was never important, considering the greater loss of his wife and friend.

Almost unfailingly, George wrote to Amy, often several times a month, telling her that she must keep her expenditure under control, that the Estate could not help her if she overspent, that anything in excess of $125 a month (a frequent occurrence) came from his pocket, which, though he didn't begrudge it, he couldn't afford indefinitely.

George's reward for this has been a spate of accusations by Amelia's biographers implying that he in some way defrauded Amy and the Estate. In fact, his behavior was exemplary in this respect, as can be seen by the Estate records and his letters to Amy. Far from defrauding her, he had been considerably more generous to her than the Estate's assets warranted.

Amy's distrust of George was continuously bolstered by her correspondents; she wrote up to fifty letters a day and was often uncomplimentary about him, claiming that he kept her short of money and that she was having to economize by going without food. Her monthly allowance was a reasonable sum in those Depression days and, as George told Amy, should be perfectly adequate if she would only plan her expenditure; "a great many older people are living very pleasantly indeed on $125 a month. . . . I cannot let you plunge blindly . . . just in the expectation that the Lord will provide. Because just now the Lord looks pretty poverty stricken!" Often these strictures ended with him sending some little item such as a trinket of Amelia's to soften his words, or a personal gift: "Because I don't doubt that you are having extra financial difficulties just now I am enclosing herewith an additional check for $50."[71]

George never managed to get through to Amy a realization of the facts and it seems she went to her grave (long after George's own death) feeling that he had taken advantage of her. An examination of the letters she received from her friends shows that they influenced her greatly in this regard and that friends often commiserated with and reflected back to Amy exactly what she wanted to hear. Their letters reinforced Amy's poor opinion of George, claiming, among other things, that he was badly brought up, spoiled, and ungracious in the way he carried out what would have been Amelia's wishes.

In this particular matter, one of the chief protagonists was Janet Mabie, who had now fallen out with George over the book *Soaring Wings,* and from whose pen dropped a ceaseless stream of vitriol aimed at him. It may be that she was justified to a greater or lesser extent, but the damage she did to the already tenuous relationship between George and Amy was enormous. She claimed that George had thrown her out of the house after a violent quarrel and had subsequently refused to pay her anything, stating that he had had to rewrite all her work.

This, she told Amy, was quite incorrect, for she had read the book and 85 percent of the finished work was exactly as she had written it. She also told Amy that she was "not surprised but . . . contemptuous" that George had removed an acknowledgment of her work from the book's foreword.[72]

Each letter to Amy suggested that Ms. Mabie should ghostwrite a book about Amelia in collaboration with Amy, but to do this, she needed Amelia's papers (those that had survived the fire at Rye), and the scrapbooks. Could Amy get them from George? she wondered. Or could Amy persuade George to donate them to a foundation such as Purdue, where Ms. Mabie could gain access without having to approach George?

It is more than probable that George treated Janet Mabie badly—a number of people such as Elinor Smith and Lady (Mary) Heath had similar tales to tell—and anyone unlucky enough to have George as an enemy was unfortunate indeed. The reverse is equally true, however, and there are many people who knew from George only generosity of spirit, although even his closest friends marveled at his ability to explode in a most spectacular manner. However, he remained impressive in the scope of his vision; "George dared," one friend said. "He had power, knew, used it and enjoyed it. If George had been on the bridge of the Titanic, the iceberg wouldn't have had the gall to collide with him. Or if it had, George would have sunk the iceberg!"[73]

By now, George had produced the first books under his own imprint, "G.P. Putnam."[74] He continued to place his own writing, however, through Harcourt, Brace and this now included plans for his autobiography. The offices on Hollywood Boulevard were too big for George and Cap Palmer (whom George employed on an ad hoc basis as ghostwriter/ editor/free-lance writer). He therefore sublet part of his offices, which were upstairs, over a tearoom that George promptly dubbed Menopause Manor. "He had a great flair for attracting gifted people," Cap Palmer recalled. "And he got young talent who later made it big."[75] Pereira and Luckman, leading California architects, were just starting and they took space; further space was let to two young writers, Jerome Lawrence[76] and Robert E. Lee,[77] who were collectively referred to by George as "the boys." Bob Lee recalls George during those days when he was trying to reestablish his life and career after losing Amelia:

> It must have been a strange marriage; [although Lee never met Amelia] the world's most famous aviatrix and the iconoclastic publisher-explorer who loved the entire planet but had a short-fused impatience about most of the people who lived on it. . . .
>
> Unquestionably, George was enormously attractive to women; a trim but husky hulk of a man, handsome, irascible, sly, opinionated, a total stranger to fear, gifted (or cursed) with a vinegar wit, the champion of raw charm. Though George and Amelia had exchanged some endearing letters I suspect it was something less than a marriage made in heaven, [but] . . . I know she was much in his mind.[78]

There was another reason, aside from the obvious need to regularize the administration of the Estate, why George now needed to have Amelia declared legally dead. In the autumn of 1938, he had met Jean-Marie Cosigny James and from the start was strongly drawn to her.

"GPP was never a loner," Bob Lee stated. "A wife was a lunar presence in his life. He could endure, temporarily, the dark of the moon, but he needed a feminine satellite to orbit his activity and tug at his emotional tides."[79]

Jean-Marie was in the process of divorcing her husband, William James, a Los Angeles attorney. She was extremely pretty, bright and amusing and good company. At that time, it was fashionable, among Beverly Hills housewives, to hold "rather smart parties, salons, which a guest speaker would attend. Often, it would be a movie star or sometimes a writer, but always someone well known."[80] Jean-Marie was on the salon circuit and always enjoyed them, but she particularly remembers one at which she arrived late. She had been working in her garden and had forgotten the time.

> When I arrived at my friend's house, I was greeted with the words "Hush! He's already started."
>
> I had no idea who the speaker was but as I walked in through the hall, there was George Putnam speaking. He looked up at me, and looked, and looked. I was very conscious of his gaze but I found a seat and sat down and later, after he'd finished speaking, he came over and said to me, without any preamble, "I'm going to marry you."
>
> He was so tall and so good-looking that I was devastated. I loved him at first sight . . . he was alert and sharp and full of ideas, and though he was twenty-four years older than I, he was always much *peppier.*
>
> On the next occasion that we met, over dinner, he suggested that I should go over to see his house. I was very reluctant, and said I really couldn't think of going to a man's house alone. He roared with laughter. "You must be kidding!" he said. "You ought to see how many people live with me!"[81]

She soon found out what George was talking about. Usually, he had his secretary, Jo Berger, and the Filipino houseboy, Fred, in residence. But the house was always filled with visitors, writers whom he was "encouraging, who were invited to come and stay while they worked on a book; friends from back east . . . he knew so many people."

It did not take George long to obtain a consent to his proposal, and Jeannie (as George quickly came to call her) broke the news to her disapproving family, while George told Amy and Muriel. Amy was incredulous; it was only a little over a year since Amelia had disappeared and she—at least—was convinced her daughter was still alive and would be found. Muriel was more sympathetic; she agreed with George that her sister had almost certainly perished within a very short time of her disappearance.[82]

At first, Amy was wary in her meetings with Jeannie, but this gradually became a tolerance of Jeannie and a condemnation of George. While never openly stating her feelings, Amy made it clear in many small ways that she held George indirectly responsible for Amelia's disappearance and, since his engagement, for his abandonment of Amelia. But Jeannie explained:

> His feelings were never shallow—not for any of his wives—there was nothing superficial about him at all. But he couldn't stand not being married, not having a companion; he needed that background in his very busy life.[83]

George and Jeannie had to wait for the various legal processes to formalize her divorce and to free him by declaring Amelia dead. Under normal circumstances, it took seven years before a missing person could be assumed legally dead. However, George's attorneys argued that this was a special case. The entire world had witnessed the massive search for Amelia and detailed, iron-clad testimony from senior naval officers was available to the court. Richard Black, Amelia's on-the-spot representative at Howland, ended his comprehensive statement on the entire flight and search with the somber statement, "It is my belief and opinion that Amelia Earhart died on or about July 2nd 1937."[84] The well-documented air-sea search, letters from inhabitants of island groups, and proof of George's own inquiries, subsequent to the official search, all led to an inevitable conclusion. On January 5, 1939, Amelia was declared legally dead.[85] Jeannie's divorce would not become final until May 18.

Amy's letters to her former son-in-law now took on a bitter tone, and it is probable that she never forgave George for abandoning hope of Amelia's survival. In April, she wrote from Berkeley, California, where she was living, as a temporary measure, in the Berkeley Women's City Club, telling him that she really *could not* live on the $125 a month that he allowed her. She needed an increase, she said, and this ought to be possible as the entire income from the Estate was legally hers. She gave details of a house she wished to rent, implying she felt it unfair that he should continue to live in Amelia's Valley Spring Lane property, and she enclosed a list of items left by Amelia that had special associations for her and that she would like to have.

George wrote a long, patient reply saying that Amy's letter had troubled him greatly:

I do want to impress upon you that you have had, in the last year and a half, a great deal more than the "income" from the Estate. Unfortunately I am not able to face more out of my own pocket. . . .[86]

George explained how much was owed against the principal sum and that he paid the Estate a fair rental for his occupancy of the property; he further went on to suggest how Amy should work out her monthly budget. Perhaps she should consider sharing a house with someone, he ventured. Amelia's papers, medals, and certain books were being presented to Purdue University and some to the Women's Archives in New York. He would send most of the things for which she asked, and though some of the hangings she had listed were "always my own," he would let her have a couple; but he intended to sell the rest to realize some money on them if he could.

Perhaps you have some notion that I am embarking upon personal extravagances and extra expenditure in connection with my forthcoming marriage. While that is an intimate situation which concerns only myself, the fact is that the new set-up should involve some decrease in my own costs. I will continue to live as simply as I have in the past. . . . Perhaps the comfort of companionship will not only make life more happily livable, but also enlarge my earning abilities.[87]

He finished with a note of cheerful news in a postscript—that he had been approached regarding a "possible sale of a motion picture based on the life of AE."

Despite the seemingly lavish lifestyle at the Hollywood house, with a full-time secretary, a houseboy, dinner parties for contacts whom George wished to influence, not to mention a constant stream of visitors and would-be writers, Cap Palmer remembers how financially tight things were for George at this time. To maintain credibility, George was using the capital from the sale of his Rye house to bolster his image of success. He needed to earn enough money to live on, however, and when George suggested a publicity stunt to promote a new book based on a success he'd had many years earlier, Cap was frankly skeptical. "No one will ever fall for that!" he told George.[88]

George had published a novel called *The Man Who Killed Hitler.* European politics in the spring of 1939 gave the book a big potential market and George felt that he could improve sales tremendously with the assistance of a little media attention. Therefore, in April he informed the Los Angeles district attorney's office that he had received an anonymous letter threatening his life unless he halted publication. A letter, written in German, appeared the following night in many newspapers:

> If you have any regard for your future safety, stop publication of this book at once. The arm of Greater Germany reaches far and we have no desire to continue warning you. If you are wise you will do what we tell you because something can happen to you and your future may be extinguished.[89]

George stated in interviews that the author of the novel, which had gone on sale a week earlier, wished to remain anonymous and that he (George) wasn't much worried about the threat.

Three weeks later (after several more letters, a threatening telephone call, and a bullet-riddled copy of the book had been received by George's publishing firm, and after George had fired two shots at a man climbing a tree outside his bedroom window), on Friday, May 13, George got—or almost got—what he wanted for headlines: PUTNAM KIDNAPPED. "Anti Hitler book seen as link." George had been discovered, bound and gagged but otherwise unharmed, in a partially built house near Bakersfield, California, some hours after his staff reported him missing.[90]

It was very similar to the "fascist plot" stunt George had pulled off in 1929, but this time it misfired. Few people believed it and some newspapers, scenting a ploy, openly insinuated their suspicion. Little action was taken by the authorities, although George may have been warned not to waste police time. No fool, George quickly realized that he hadn't quite pulled it off, but he had no option but to bluff his way out. In a letter to Amy two days later, he said sheepishly:

> As to myself, I look all right. It wasn't a pleasant experience and took a good deal out of me, but there was no physical harm done. I have had a pretty good rest over Sunday and am feeling nearly back to normal again. . . . Next weekend . . . it might not be a bad idea for you to be unavailable . . . on the offchance that newspapers should seek some comment from you. . . .[91]

The next weekend (on May 21, 1939), George married Jeannie in Boulder City, Nevada.

Chapter Twenty-two

1939-1950

I nitially, the marriage was a very happy one, and though George was concerned about his personal finances, especially the loss of income from some European investments due to the political situation there, he felt he had made a new start. Encouraged by Amy, though, Jeannie "was never really sure, in the early days, that Amelia was dead."

> I always thought there was a real possibility that she was still alive and might come walking in the door one morning. G.P. had no doubts, though he rarely talked about her—or Dorothy—but I knew he missed her very much.
>
> Fred, the houseboy, talked to me about A.E. a lot. I remember him telling me that just before she left on that final trip, she took him to one side and said to him very carefully, "Fred, I want you to take very good care of Mr. Putnam." Fred said he never forgot the manner in which she said this and he more or less regarded it as a sacred trust.
>
> We were very happy. George loved to give parties and Fred was marvelous, always knowing just what was needed. We always had lots of famous people there and it was very exciting. I remember Stokowski was a frequent visitor when he was dating Garbo—though she never came and of course we never mentioned her.
>
> Most of his income came from speaking tours and he was in great demand and away from home quite a lot. He used to have the audience in the palm of his hand and was sometimes so funny that they would be in stitches.[1]

It was not always easy, being married to George. He was still a great practical joker and Jeannie felt that some of his japes were "rather cruel on the subject." Jeannie, sweet-tempered and a little shy, was overawed by George's volatile disposition.

> I loved him very much but he had a terrible temper. It would just erupt and he would bellow at the top of his voice; not over big things, just some little incident that might irritate him. I remember we once had a new gardener and G.P. couldn't stand him from the moment we saw him, so whenever this man worked in the garden, G.P. was unhappy. Once when he was working outside G.P.'s study window, the poor man did something, pruned a twig or something. . . . G.P. was up like a shot, roaring at the top of his voice. "Stop that you son of a bitch . . .!" Afterward, it was all forgotten—it was all bluster and noise really—but he was very impatient.
> If his secretary wasn't around to organize him, he would just stuff all the papers he could find on his desk into a briefcase and rush off—of course he never had the correct papers when he got to where he was going. But he had an absolute knack of keeping people happy working for him. His staff loved him and were very loyal to him.[2]

George was still harassed by Amy's letters because the Estate still had not, at that time, been probated. In addition, the Amelia Earhart Foundation was causing him concern with a flush of publicity releases aimed at fund raising. Claiming that it had the support of President Roosevelt, Amelia's family, Paul Mantz, and other connections of Amelia's, the Foundation announced a two-year search of the Pacific by the crew of an oceangoing yacht, in whose crew would be Margot de Carrie, "Amelia Earhart's personal secretary."

Paul Mantz wrote immediately, disassociating himself, because although he "wished to see the mystery solved it would be embarrassing to be misunderstood."[3]

George, who had been questioned by reporters after the news releases, was more direct in his letter to the Foundation's principal, Elmer Dimity:

> . . . As you realize, I know nothing. I have never been informed what money has been raised, nor what accounting, if any, has been made. I do not know who is associated with the project (except as it comes to me indirectly) nor what the plans are. . . . I do find a great deal of publicity coming up hither and yon that Margot de Carrie was AE's secretary. You and AE's mother know that Margot, a very sweet and loyal girl, was never AE's secretary. She worked here at odd jobs and we graced her with that title to make things easier. . . .[4]

After warning Dimity to keep all transactions "within the bounds of careful business exactness," George wrote to Amy, telling her, too, to be extremely careful. The name Amelia Earhart Foundation was already in use by Purdue University, he reminded her. "Naturally I must protect those who did so much for AE from any embarrassment. I do suggest you discuss this matter with Mr. Dimity and see that I am equipped with a statement of facts. . . ."[5]

Amy's reply was unpleasant despite George's carefully worded return letter explaining why the Estate could not sanction the organization, "especially in view of Paul Mantz's involvement."[6] The Estate had a claim against Mantz for the value of half the business in which he and Amelia had been partners, but there was a signed contract,[7] which gave a surviving partner the entire business should one of them die, so the Estate lost its claim. George thought this very unfair and openly doubted that Amelia could have known what she was signing. George and Paul Mantz, never friends but tolerant of each other during Amelia's lifetime, now became enemies.

To George's other sins was now added the charge by Amy that he really didn't want Amelia found, and surviving correspondence reveals Amy busily recruiting champions to her cause—in the form of Paul Mantz and Dimity—by telling them how badly she was treated by George. Dimity wrote that he felt the Estate was left for Amy's benefit and that she should be given a sufficient amount to live decently and without worry."[8] Paul Mantz, on hearing that Amy was in dire straits, immediately offered to make her a loan but, after learning how much Amy was receiving from George, rescinded his offer.[9] Dimity sent small amounts to Amy to bail her out of various small financial embarassments; these were never repaid and it is clear that Amy was simply not able to manage money, which Amelia and George had always known.

But despite George's misgivings, the Foundation did organize a search of sorts. The skipper of the yacht *Yankee of Gloucester,* diverted from a world cruise, and at the Foundation's commission, spent four weeks sailing around the Gilbert and Ellice Islands (which, according to navy archives, had already been thoroughly searched). A letter from the yacht's captain to Elmer Dimity stated that the results of the expedition were negligible, with only one new point emerging: that Amelia's plane had been heard passing over the island of Tabiteuea during the night of July 2. This statement places the Electra almost directly on its great circle course from Lae to Howland. Captain Irving concluded, "It is my opinion and that of all those with whom I have talked in this area that the search be considered finished and that everything humanly possible has been done to find any trace of Miss Earhart."[10]

Unfortunately, the money raised by the Foundation had been spent on administration and publicity and Captain Irving's bill had to be paid by a member of the Foundation who loaned the sum of eighteen hundred dollars for the expedition, an amount that was never repaid.[11] George's caution about the organization was proven well founded, although it must be stressed that its failure to perform was due to nothing more sinister than poor management; possibly George's open opposition may have also had a direct bearing on its failure to attract donations. However, Dimity, who came to be known as "Dilly Dally Dimity" by his fellow members, was simply not capable of running the foundation that he had been instrumental in creating and that ended up owing some two thousand dollars.[12]

Since Amelia's disappearance, there had been much correspondence regarding the making of a film about her. George worked on proposals from film director Gabriel Pascal, and had set Cap Palmer to work drafting a screen treatment entitled *For Woman, the World.*

Amy, meanwhile, was approached by William C. Hollister, who proposed a film in which Amy and Muriel would play themselves. In a series of letters, he offered Amy various sums for screen rights to Amelia's story, but "not less than fifteen thousand dollars." Katharine Hepburn, he said, would play Amelia.[13]

This must have seemed a tempting proposition to Amy: fifteen thousand dollars *and* the opportunity to have Amelia portrayed as Amy felt she *ought* to be depicted.

> Please do not think me mercenary [Amy wrote naïvely to Hollister].
> . . . To make the fitting memorial that you plan for my beloved daughter, I would do everything in my power gladly and willingly without money and without price, but there [are] other considerations—plans my daughter had for others dear to her. . . . Because of the deep love and understanding between us I wish to do these things. The way the Estate has been managed leaves me with very little and utterly impossible to carry out her wishes without something outside my small income.
> . . . I have no specific information but believe we will find Mr. Putnam has reserved rights to everything he might consider worth while, for my younger daughter and myself have thought only of our great loss, not what profit could be made from her dear name. For the sake of all of us I have kept as close as I could to Mr. Putnam

and have tried to be as near as possible to what he still calls me—
Mother—though he is a difficult person to deal with. . . .
. . . If our negotiations prove fruitful I shall have to have my
attorney present . . . to protect me from Mr. Putnam's plans of
representing me which would mean his advantage would be first—he
doesn't seem able to do differently . . . though he is kind in many
ways.[14]

When George's discussions with Pascal came to nothing, he contacted
Hollister at Amy's request, only to find no substance to the proposals.

That spring, George was distressed and unsettled when Jo Berger, the
efficient and loyal secretary he had shared with Amelia for many years,
died of cancer.[15] George's financial situation had not greatly improved
and the income from his lecture tours and publishing business was hardly
keeping pace with his lifestyle, but he refused to reduce his standards.

Since Amelia's disappearance, George had paid rent to the Estate for
the Valley Spring Lane house. Now he decided it would be financially
advantageous to rent the house to a tenant and buy a home of his own,
somewhere out of town—preferably a cabin in the mountains, where he
would find the personal contentment he always felt in wild country but
also where they could live more economically than in Hollywood. His
business interests could be maintained by renting an apartment when he
needed to be in Los Angeles. In due course, the Valley Spring Lane house
was let to actor Eddie Albert, and George and Jeannie found their new
home in Lone Pine, California, high in the Sierra Nevada mountains.

The couple had made vacation trips out of their searches through
Tahoe, Oregon, San Jacinto, Carmel, Arizona, and Yosemite. At every
stop, they inquired at gas stations, motels, and coffee shops whether
anyone knew of a suitable cabin—or even an ideal place to build one. "We
. . . chased many rainbows, with disappointments at the end of them,"
George recorded, but at last in the small town of Lone Pine in the Owens
Valley, they heard about a unique stone lodge at Whitney Portal. It had
been built for a much-loved priest of the small community, but he had
been killed in an automobile accident before he could take up residence.[16]

Thirty days after seeing the lodge, George owned it. The Putnams' new
home nestled among huge boulders at an elevation of over eight thousand
feet with a stunning view of Mt. Whitney (highest peak in the continental
United States) from its huge windows. Totally isolated, it was twelve miles
and a four-thousand-foot climb from Lone Pine, the nearest township.
Hearing that Roosevelt had just named his house at Camp David *Shangri-
la*, George decided to call the lodge *Shangri-Putnam*. [17]

The time they were able to spend in Shangri-Putnam was idyllic, if short. George used it to write his autobiography, which he did "in a very slapdash way at first," Cap Palmer said. "Having sold the idea and taken an advance from Duell, Sloan & Pearce, he simply pulled out a load of letters, files, and articles and pasted them together. Then he gave them to me, saying, "I want you to tell me honestly how great this is."

> Well, it was awful; and I told him it was a collection of junk, not a piece of writing at all. He'd had it typed into a manuscript and that was all. He screamed at me that I was a Johnny-come-lately and what did I know about writing; then sent it off to Sam Sloan. When it was returned, he screamed again. "Damn it! What does Sam Sloan know about the book business?"
>
> Well, he had to do something because he'd spent the advance and he was a realist. Eventually, he calmed down and I got him to take a look at it as if it was an unsolicited manuscript that had been sent to him for evaluation. After he'd read it, he turned to me and said, "Damn it! It *is* junk!" and he got to work on it again.
>
> Occasionally, I'd wander in and remind him of some incident or anecdote that he'd told me about and he'd say, "Didn't I have that in the book?" Each day George would write and I would edit and so the book was finally completed. Of course, it was typical of him that it was mainly a collection of stories about other people—I've always said it ought to have been called *Autobiography About Other People*.
>
> He was a publicity hound but he never cared about publicity for *himself*—it was always for some project he was pushing, or some person he was promoting.[18]

George and Jeannie were staying in Los Angeles during the first week of December 1941. George had finished and delivered his manuscript that week and was concentrating on trying, yet again, to promote a movie film of Amelia. On Sunday the seventh they were to have lunch at Danny Kaye's house in Malibu. On the way there, they stopped at some friend's for a drink; "It was just a normal leisurely Sunday," said Jeannie.

> When we got there, our friend came rushing out with shaving foam still over half his face. "Have you heard?" he said.
>
> "Heard what?" We hadn't had the car radio on, but apparently news had just broken about Pearl Harbor.
>
> Later, we all walked on the beach and talked about what might happen and G.P. said to me, "I'll call Roosevelt tonight."[19]

As a result of his talk with Roosevelt, George was offered a job in the Pentagon with the rank of colonel, but that didn't suit his plans at all. "He didn't want a faceless job behind a desk," his son David told me. "He wanted to *do* something."[20] Cap Palmer agreed. "He didn't want to leave Jeannie but he just was constitutionally *not able* to stand by and not get involved."[21] It took George about two weeks to organize matters the way he wanted them and then he went home to Jeannie and told her he'd enlisted. Within a short time, he was wearing a captain's uniform.

George was still working at promoting a movie about Amelia. All his efforts, which revolved around Cap Palmer's screen treatment (based on a story by George called *Lady with Wings: The Life Story of My Wife, Amelia Earhart)*, failed to reach fruition.[22] At one point, Howard Hughes had been interested, in order to provide a vehicle for Katharine Hepburn, and there were various other syndicates interested, but one by one the proposals disintegrated.

In the spring of 1942, RKO accepted a screenplay from scriptwriter Horace McCoy entitled *Stand By to Die.*[23] He had written it after speaking to one of the amateur radio operators who claimed to have heard Amelia's radio signals after she had officially disappeared. Although essentially a piece of fiction, the story contained elements based on some of Amelia's experiences (even the plane used for round-the-world flight scenes was a Lockheed Electra, though a smaller and later model than Amelia's), and very sensibly the studio made an offer to the Earhart Estate for rights to certain parts of Amelia's story.

While George was unhappy that his own biographical treatment had been superseded by this highly fictionalized story, he was practical enough to realize that it was better for the Estate to accept a reasonable sum (seventy-five hundred dollars) than hold out indefinitely on the off chance that someday a film based on his work might be made. Besides, he reasoned, such a film might reawaken interest in Amelia and enable a biographical motion picture to be made at a later date.

George signed on behalf of the Estate, approving the original movie treatment but stipulating that any too-obvious resemblance to Amelia must be avoided. The movie was eventually released under the title *Flight for Freedom*, starring Rosalind Russell and Fred MacMurray, and was the story of a 1930's aviatrix whose ambition was to fly around the world at the equator.

The film's heroine, Toni Carter, having completed the first leg of her flight, was about to take off on the second leg of the trip from Hawaii to

Howland Island when she received a call from government officials in Washington, D.C., asking whether she would take part in a secret mission under cover of her much-publicized world flight. Accordingly, she deliberately crashed the plane on takeoff, thus allowing time for the necessary preparations.

Subsequently, the plot called for her to fly by the same reverse route as Amelia, land secretly on a small island in the Pacific and pretend to be lost, thereby enabling a huge air/sea search to take place that would allow Americans to fly over Japanese-mandated territory so they could ascertain what fortifications had been made.

The movie shocked George, for it showed the heroine madly in love with the man chosen by the navy to be her navigator. In view of the rumors that had circulated while Amelia had been on her last flight, George felt the film hinted that Amelia had been in love with Fred Noonan. He sued RKO but settled out of court for a sum of twenty-five hundred dollars. He made no public comment about the publicity for the movie, which included poster banners proclaiming, THE STORY THEY COULDN'T TELL BEFORE PEARL HARBOR, and DID WOMAN FLIER STRIKE FIRST BLOW AT JAPS?[24]

Preempting the movie's release, however, was an article written by George's friend and colleague Charles "Cap" Palmer that appeared in the magazine *Skyways* under the title "The War's First Casualty?" It referred to "rumors that Amelia may have been on a government mission and had been captured by the Japanese."[25] The article reached no conclusion but it is now clear that this article was the first of the genre that might be called "The Earhart Mystery," which is still very much alive and flourishing.

Recently it has been suggested that this was a publicity stunt organized by George to promote the film or a book or, alternatively—since "Cap" was George's house writer—that it proves George knew something he could not tell the world more openly. Cap Palmer refutes this, however. Questioned for this book, he stated that "it was definitely not a promotion ploy."

The suspicion that the Navy went to extraordinary effort and expense to "search" for AE as a cover for getting cameras over the forbidden area was *ours*—GP's and mine—we had not the slightest hard information pointing to it.

But the carrier *Lexington* left San Diego amazingly soon after the "down" message, which led to the logical *guess* that the planes were loaded with cameras rather than rubber boats, and the motives were practical rather than humanitarian—especially since the *Lexington* couldn't possibly reach the site until days after AE and Noonan were certainly dead—with the Japanese knowing that world opinion would clobber them if they interfered with the "rescue" attempt.

The success of our Navy bombers later on indicated success of the mission/gamble. It may be that AE served her country wonderfully well . . . but there was never the faintest doubt in GP's mind that AE died within a few miles of Howland and the *Itasca*. [26]

The film was released at a time when almost everyone attended the cinema at least once a week, and many people came to believe that the film was based on fact—hence the growth of the Earhart Legend and the general willingness to accept sensational and outrageous theories. It is also possible that Amy came to believe this myth too, for in 1949 she inferred as much at a press conference. Examination of her personal correspondence, however, makes it clear that she came to this conclusion only after the release of the film.[27]

It was some months before George was called to active duty, for the service chiefs had a problem deciding what to do with this mid-fifty-year-old "retread" (as he called himself), with his impressive connections. It was proposed that George, with his experience of arctic conditions, be posted to the North Atlantic, but eventually—after he reminded the army that he was still waiting for orders—he was instructed to report to the Army Air Force Officer Training School in Miami Beach, Florida.[28] After successfully completing the training courses, where he was "old enough to be the father of every man in his class,"[29] he was transferred to the Air Intelligence School in Harrisburg, Pennsylvania. When he left there, with a commendation, his commanding officer wrote:

> It is with much regret that I learn of your transfer from my command and it is desired to express officially and personally appreciation of your superior performance here at the Army Air Forces Air Intelligence School. Your work and accomplishments here . . . have been an inspiration to other officers working with you.[30]

The commendation earned George a promotion to major, a rank he treasured because of his boyhood affection for his uncle, who had been known simply as "the Major." George never sought further promotion.[31] In a letter to one of his many correspondents, he explained his role in the war:

468TH BOMBARDMENT GROUP
SMOKY HILL ARMY AIRFIELD
SALINA, KANSAS

Dear Joe [Joseph Henry Jackson],

. . . I have been with a combat unit here getting the big new secret bombers ready to take a hand in what goes on overseas. The time is getting fairly close I imagine, when we will be shoving off.

I'm intelligence officer for a group of four squadrons and enjoy my rugged job immensely. Indeed I'm tickled no end to be with a gang like this, with plenty of geography and, likely, of adventure before us. . . .[32]

At about the time of this letter, George went home to California on leave. During the time he had been in the army, his marriage to Jeannie suffered irreversibly and to his dismay, she told him she wanted a divorce. Jeannie, a dedicated Christian Scientist, was a gentle creature and felt she could no longer tolerate living in the eye of the hurricane with George, though she still professed to love him. "I always loved him . . . I've never stopped loving him," she said in June 1988. "I should never have divorced him."[33]

George returned to Salina confused and upset. Shortly afterward, Bob Lee telephoned him to ask whether there was any news on a book he had written that George was attempting to have published. George was simply told it was a call from Hollywood, Lee recalled:

> I don't think I merely imagined the sound of sinking disappointment when my voice came on the line. He thought it might be Jeannie calling him. I didn't realize that The Major and his wife were on the brink of marital bankruptcy. A few weeks later she began divorce proceedings. Grounds? Extreme cruelty. The inveterate fighter chose not to fight. . . .[34]

Several things happened before George was shipped out. The divorce went ahead smoothly, uncontested, and some months later at the home of mutual friends, he met Margaret Haviland.

Like Amelia, Miss Haviland was a small-town girl. Born and reared in Michigan City, Indiana, on the southernmost tip of Lake Michigan, she had a happy and secure childhood, attended good schools and eventually graduated from college with a Bachelor of Arts degree. In 1941, she was asked to return to her college to help in fund raising and this is what she was doing until December 7, 1941.

... as American men were being mobilized and trained in many parts of the country a dire need sprang up for servicemen's clubs—places where they could write letters home, make phone calls, eat light lunches and enjoy entertainment. One of the largest such clubs was in Salina where it was not unusual to have 2,000 to 3,000 men in each evening . . . and it was from Salina that they all went overseas.[35]

Anxious to help in the war effort, Margaret was drafted to Salina by the USO (which operated the clubs) as an executive. The relationship between Margaret and George, at that stage, was merely a friendship between two intelligent people who both enjoyed each other's company. Margaret remembers that George was lonely and sad about the breakup of his marriage.

Quite by chance, at this time George's son David was flying a B-17 on a delivery mission and passed through Salina air base. He, too, remembers his father's depression over the breakup of the marriage but recalled that it didn't stop them having a marvelous evening together singing around a piano.[36] George's younger son, George Palmer Putnam, Jr., was by this time an officer in the U.S. Navy.

A week after David saw his father, George was on his way to India, and later flew over "the Hump" (as he called the Himalayas) to China in the first B-29 bomber squadron to make that trip. His role was intelligence officer for the squadron and once again he found himself the "father of the unit"; his commanding officer was only twenty-three years old![37]

George's war service was "comprised in equal parts [of] boredom, discomfort, disillusion and adventure," and indeed there must have been plenty of each, but overall he felt "that curious satisfaction of being a part of such matters, a stimulation deep beyond that most of the ways of peace can offer."[38] The squadron's task was to make the first bombing raids on Japan, and it was George's responsibility to brief the young pilots before missions, to debrief them afterward, and generally update the intelligence-data files for the men who came after them. He spent more than a year in the Far East and as the unit moved around, they often lived in the most basic conditions, "off the land as the indigenous population did."[39] The army had managed to get weapons, ammunition, and spares—the logistics of war—through to their lines, but rations were sparse.

Rice became a staple. "If a peasant brought in a pig, they'd buy it and cook it. The pig may have been diseased but they had no choice; it was all there was. They used to have a thin gruel, porridge they called it, and even this had maggots in it. George told friends that he often had to pick out the grubs before he could eat."[40] Poor living conditions, polluted water, and bad food inevitably took their toll on George, who, despite appearances, had never been physically strong. He developed a parasitic infection in the kidneys and was eventually ordered home. He had plenty of time to think on the long Pacific voyage to America and decided that what he wanted more than anything now was to live full-time in his mountain home at Whitney Portal. There, he thought with affection, was "cold clear water, an open fire, and a woodpile."

> Round about stood high country clothed with pines, scented with sage; a region of brawling streams, meadows bright with lupins, penstemon, and paintbrush; and, below, deserts with silver holly and gay carpets of tiny flowers, rimmed by purple hills, granite peaks.
> In every way so very different from Bengal, wet, dirty, stifling and crowded; or the raw, tragic hinterlands of China.[41]

At some time during this period of service, George visited Saipan. By now, rumors that Amelia had been captured by the Japanese and taken to Saipan had started to circulate widely, fueled by reports that a white woman pilot had been seen there before the war and fanned by cinemagoers who had watched *Stand By to Die.* George drove all over the island making extensive inquiries about the white woman flier but he got no answers that gave him any hope that Amelia had ever been there.

In the spring of 1945, after his release from a military hospital, George went directly to Cap Palmer's house in Hollywood and stayed there until the divorce became final.[42] Physically, he bore the signs of his recent illness, but George's great personality was not affected and his presence filled the Palmers' home for the weeks he stayed with them.

Soon after his return, George "very purposefully" started dating women, Cap Palmer said, "but he wasn't looking for a woman, he was looking for a wife with whom to share his life."

> Women found him very attractive. One particular woman from Kansas, whom he had met when serving there, wrote to him every day for years; her letters filled up a large box in the kitchen and then we started putting them in another box on the porch. All his ladies were very glamorous. Greer Garson was one—she *was* lovely, much more beautiful than in pictures and a lovely person.
> One night he came home very shocked. The woman he had taken to dinner had, according to him, "made improper advances!"
> "What happened?" we asked. "She asked if I'd like to come in for the night!" he told us, appalled.
> He was a bit like that, tough in business but innocent in many

54. From left to right: Unidentified, George Putnam, Amelia, Gene Vidal, c. 1936.

55. Amelia looks aft through the Electra's fuselage after the massive fuel tanks have been fitted. Cabin windows on left have been used for fuel filler pipes, c. 1936.

56. Harry Manning and Amelia at the navigator's position in the rear of the Lockheed Electra's fuselage, 1936. The instrument mounted on the tripod is a pelorus (sighting device for the compass).

57. Left, Clarence Williams and Amelia plan the route of her round-the-world flight.
58. Above, commemorative stamp issued in 1964.

59. Left to right: Paul Mantz, Amelia, Harry Manning, and Fred Noonan, pictured prior to the takeoff from Oakland for Hawaii.

60. Amelia in the cockpit of her Electra. It measured 4'6" by 4'6" wide by 4'8" high—cramped quarters for long flights with no copilot to relieve her at the controls.

61. The Electra pictured over San Francisco's Golden Gate Bridge on Amelia's first attempt to fly around the world in 1937.

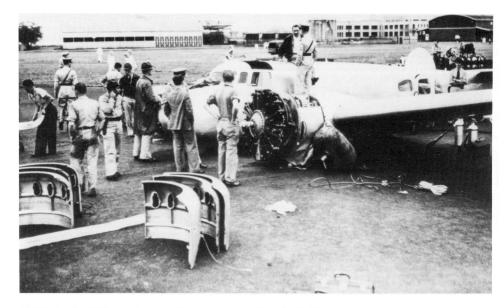

62. The Lockheed Electra after ground-looping on takeoff at Luke Field, Hawaii. Paul Mantz is in the hatchway. The occupants were lucky to escape without serious injury; that there was no fire was miraculous.

63. George and Amelia on May 31, 1937, the evening before her last flight.

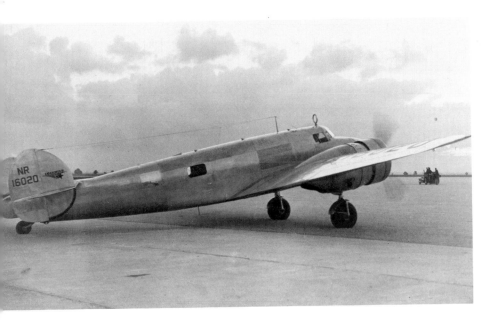

4. The Electra taxis for takeoff on Amelia's ill-fated round-the-world flight. Miami, Florida, June 1, 1937.

65. Left, breakfast en route. Note the crate containing spares for Amelia's Wasp engines.   66. Above, Africa. The refueling process was arduous, for all fuel had to be siphoned from large drums and strained through chamois leather—each step carefully supervised by either Amelia or Fred Noonan.

67. Left to right: Mr. and Mrs. Eric Chater, Amelia, and Fred Noonan. One of the last photos taken of Amelia and Noonan—prior to their departure on the fateful Lae–Howland leg of their round-the-world flight.

68. Toward the end of her flight, Amelia's face reveals signs of extreme physical exhaustion (insert shows Amelia before start of her round-the-world flight).

69. July 2, 1937: World headlines shrieked the news of Amelia's disappearance.

70. George married Jean-Marie Cosigny in Boulder City, Nevada, in May 1939.

71. Major George Putnam with his son David prior to being "shipped out" to the Far East.

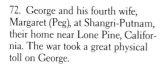

72. George and his fourth wife, Margaret (Peg), at Shangri-Putnam, their home near Lone Pine, California. The war took a great physical toll on George.

73. George Putnam, writer, pictured with his favorite dog, Baskerville, c. 1948.

ways. For example, he was always great friends with our daughter, Gay. The day after he met her, we found them sitting talking together in Latin. Before the war, she was a little girl and he would tell her bedtime stories. Well, the day he came home, after he'd greeted us, he asked, "Where's Gay?" "She's in the bath," I said, and before we could stop him, he marched straight into the bathroom to give her a hug.

The problem was she'd grown up by then and was very embarrassed. He hadn't and didn't give it a thought.[43]

Margaret and George had kept in touch during the time he'd been overseas and she was phoning to see how he was. The two met again and their friendship deepened into courtship. As usual, George wasted no time, and though Peg (as Margaret preferred to be called) was reluctant to make such an important decision so quickly, he swept her concerns aside. On June 10, 1945, they were married at a friend's home in Pasadena.

There were just a few friends present—and an army of pressmen. Bob Lee, the best man ("actually the worst," he recalled), and Jerry Lawrence, still collectively known as "the boys," kept them waiting for two hours because of a flat tire. "Was George annoyed or irritated?" Bob wrote. "Gross understatement. He was whopping MAD!" But the ceremony eventually got under way and when Peg went up to bed that night, she was greeted by the spectacle of the marriage certificate stapled firmly to the bedroom door.[44]

After a short honeymoon, George took Peg to the Whitney Portal lodge, high in the Sierras, where they spent that summer and winter. "I dislike the cold and believe me it *was* cold at close to nine thousand feet," Peg told the author. "But to keep me happy, George organized expeditions into the hot sun of Death Valley some eighty miles away. . . ." There, the couple used to stay at a small inn called Stove Pipe Wells. "We used to go down on snowshoes to Lone Pine, where the snowline ended and we had a car parked."[45]

During this time, George wrote prolifically. Always an early riser, he went straight to work at his typewriter. On the first morning of their residency at Whitney Portal, Peg awoke to find a note on her bedside table:

Madam,

Breakfast of canteloupe, cream of wheat, toast and possum-with-hot-milk will be served either in the bedroom or on the terrace, as desired. The time suggested is 10 A.M.

A simple luncheon is planned on the patio.

Dinner will be arranged at the Mt. Whitney Grill. There will be Owens Valley steak, broiled and embellished with Swiss Chard à la Shangri-Putnam, salad and chocolate pie. The Management wishes to know whether you desire Sautern or Tokay as a beverage.

The Management also loves you very much and finds he misses you greatly between the hours of six A.M. and ten A.M. (circa). Other times, too.

Ring, and service will appear. . . .

The Management*46

*Temporary

Peg was fascinated with George's fertile mind, his sense of fun, his raw energy, his need to "never waste a minute." An endless procession of houseguests came up the steep, winding, narrow road to the stone lodge. "The main house slept fourteen people and higher up the mountain we had a guest house for eight more. In addition, those who brought sleeping bags could use other little buildings. It was not unusual for us to sit down to breakfast with twenty-five at the table, or lunch for thirty-five or forty," Peg remembered.

> He wrote various books during this time, had a secretary living with us, sometimes two, and a houseman to do the chores. It was a mighty busy place. Streams of writers, mostly hopeful would-be writers, came for his advice and occasionally there came a good one.
>
> My life consisted of seeing that we had plenty of food in the house, trucked up from Lone Pine, and that there was always enough clean bed linen available. G.P. knew *everyone* of importance in America and they were all fascinated by what he was doing up there in the mountains and most came to see. No one ever wanted to leave. . . .[47]

From time to time, an echo of Amelia's legend would blow into their lives, but mainly it was a time of work and relaxation and a time of great personal happiness for both George and Peg. George found many ways to express his love, such as this note, which Peg found in her Christmas stocking that first Christmas with "a very large check":

Madam:

I am instructed to turn over to you this slight check with the understanding that it is to be spent exclusively on your cherished person.

S. Claus.[48]

These intimate letters and notes convey a different George from the one portrayed by his business associates, but according to his family and closest friends, he hadn't changed and had always been as loving and playful in his personal relationships. So although most of the letters between him and Amelia were destroyed in two house fires,⁴⁹ it is reasonably safe to assume that he was equally loving and protective in his personal life with Amelia. Was this the real secret of Amelia's ability to achieve—a secure home life coupled with the sheer driving force of a partner who was able to make *anything* happen?

Often Peg and George drove to Los Angeles, where he would conduct some piece of publishing business. Sometimes he would make a trip back east, or to his agent, George Bye, in New York.

AT BYE'S ON MONDAY MORNING

Wonderful,

Your letters are a delight. I love you and miss you ridiculously. . . . Saw Ham Nelson [Bette Davis's first husband] this morning; have red [sic] Helen's *Piney Bear* script, have letter and script from Karl; as a huckster I am prancing from one end of Manhattan to t'other.

Dined last night at the Copacabana with the fabulous parents of Mr. Leeds. Now Sock is back from lunch and I must vacate his typewrite. Love, love, love

P.S. A publishing fellow named Putnam
Discovered he couldn't quite butnam
What caused the hiatus
Was meat and potatoes
And eating whole pies without cutnam

Another letter said:

Miss you a lot. This is hard grind but I believe the results will please you. I love you a lot and miss you and wish I were with you. And nothing is so nice as being together on the hill in the coolth . . . including, of course, Basket [George's dog].

Kiss the boys [Bob and Jerry] for me . . . though I don't want to be misunderstood.⁵⁰

Well aware of Peg's dread of winters on the mountain, George decided to do something about it. "One day he came home with such a mischievous look on his face and eventually I got him to tell me what he'd been up to. 'I've bought the Stove Pipe Wells inn for you, Peg. Now you'll never be cold in the winter,' he said. It really tickled him to have a home in the highest possible position in America, and in the lowest, too. He thought that was fantastic!"[51]

Since his return from active war service, George had been troubled with periods of illness. The symptoms were continuous and often distressing, "but he would never say anything or complain; just every once in a while he'd say to me, 'Peg, I think we've got to see a doctor in Trona . . .' and then I knew it was bad. But he was no invalid."[52] "He loved to play tennis, hated to lose and rarely did," Bob Lee recalled.[53]

George still derived a great deal of enjoyment from his practical jokes. One day when he and Peg were staying at Stove Pipe Wells, he found there were some archaeological excavations not far away. Immediately, he phoned his son David. "Have you still got that old Eskimo skull?" he asked. "Well, I'd like to borrow it!" Shortly afterward, those involved in the dig were appalled to unearth from the floor of Death Valley a skull that was clearly that of an Eskimo.[54]

Owning the inn meant that someone had to be there constantly, so Peg had to spend time in Death Valley while George worked on the mountain at his latest book, *Up in Our Country*, a conversational essay of the inhabitants, flora, and fauna of the area.[55]

"I still think this is a lovely place," he wrote to Peg, mischievously, "and am thinking of trying a want ad in the *Times* to see who'd like to share it with me. . . ." The house was, as usual, full of guests and on this occasion there were several small children. "As soon as I breakfast them they are off fishing. Domestic, that's what I am!"[56]

George had a way with children; he made them feel adult. They were never left out at his cocktail parties and were served special fruit-juice drinks made to look identical to real cocktails. When the tray came around to a child, it was presented so that the nearest drink was a "special" and the child never knew he was being served anything different from anyone else.[57]

Many people who visited George and Peg at Whitney Portal recall their time there with affection. Typical is a letter from Helen Ogston, whom George encouraged to write the children's book *Piney Bear*.

I personally appreciated George for his love of the English language. His conversation was a delight, his choice of words exquisite—just the right word to drop into a slot in a sentence. He also loved to tell stories but anything amusingly off-color was told by suggestion.

Once, standing in front of the large window framing Mount Whitney I asked him, "Does it make the mountain any more beautiful because we know it is the highest?" George answered, "No, but it's like a beautiful woman. If you know she has a million dollars, she looks just a little bit better to you."

. . . Another time I rounded the corner of the guest house and banged my head on a low beam. It was a real bump that made me bite my lip. Because there were no tears George came over and gave me a gentle little kiss on the hurt spot.

A wonderful mind, nary a mean streak. . . . most of all I'm glad I knew him.[58]

In 1949, George was asked by Isaiah Bowman, an old friend and principal of Johns Hopkins University, to serve on the visiting committee of the mathematics department. George had many such requests from various places and he had served previously with the men on this committee. Now, he suggested that the college "try to find younger men, not with any thought of reducing the present incumbents, but by way of carrying the average age down a bit. Other than that I think the Committee is an excellent one and functions very well. I shall looking forward to meeting with you again. . . ."[59]

George was never able to serve on the mathematics committee, however, for as the winter of 1949 set in, he became too ill to travel. A few weeks later, just after Christmas, George was taken to Trona Hospital with kidney failure and internal hemorrhages, and he died there on January 4, 1950, at the age of sixty-three.

Peg received hundreds of letters after George's death, many of the writers testifying to the inspiration they had received from him. Lawrence M. Gould credited George with getting him started in exploration and on the first Byrd expedition. He said that George was a complex character who went out of his way to do many kind and thoughtful things for him.[60]

Rockwell Kent, George's boyhood friend—and once his "bridegroom"—wrote to Peg that he had never forgotten his time together with George and that if it hadn't been for George's faith in him, he never would have undertaken the writing of his first book, *Wilderness*, or his subsequent books, *Voyaging* and *N by E.*[61]

George Agnew Chamberlain wrote to Peg that his friendship with George never knew a setback of any kind. He stated that George was not an easy man to know and that his complex character led to "collisions" with those who didn't understand him. Above all things, he recalls George's "terrific courage" as something he constantly admired.[62]

These letters, and many others, define George's contribution to the lives of hundreds with whom he came into contact. His personal brand of dynamism, aggression, business acumen, and belief that nothing was impossible inspired many people to extend themselves into previously undreamed-of realms of achievement. Amelia Earhart was only one for whom this unusual and remarkable man made everything possible. That was his way. To inspire and, if necessary, to provide, or help to provide, the practical means to turn dreams into reality.

Sometimes George's enthusiasm for a project overrode moral principles. He could not tolerate fools or dissemblers, and despite the glittering array of famous personalities who regularly beat a path to his door, he was just as impressed by a mountain dweller living in total contentment and alive to his whole world than by the rich and famous who lived on their reputations.[63] He upset many people in his life and could not bear to be balked. He could be an implacable and unpleasant enemy, crushing and vindictive if his projects were threatened, terrifying in a temper, menacingly cold when cornered, and his active and fertile brain shot into overdrive at the merest hint of opposition.

But those who knew him well and who spent any time with him loved the sheer vibrancy of life in his shadow. Life with George was turbulent, tumultuous, often disturbing, but always exciting. "He was a very great man," one friend said simply.[64] It seems a fitting and apt epitaph, and one, I think, with which Amelia Earhart would have agreed.

George never knew of the fever that gripped the Western world in the early 1960s when several writers produced books about Amelia that seemed to offer proof that she had been on a government spy mission when she made her last flight. Public interest in the subject was enormous, especially since it coincided with the Gary Powers U-2 "spy-fly" affair.

The most famous of these books, Fred Goerner's *The Search for Amelia Earhart* (New York: Doubleday, 1966) proved to be a real blockbuster. Goerner was a CBS reporter who came across the story when a former Saipan islander gave a newspaper interview claiming she had seen Amelia Earhart and Fred Noonan being brought ashore there by Japanese soldiers before the war.

Amelia was back in the news again, and has really never left it since. From time to time, a newspaper will run a story about her disappearance, hinting that another clue has been found, and a flurry of correspondence usually results. A writer will produce a book that debunks the theories of previous authors and produces yet another new theory, insisting that this is what *really* happened to Amelia.

Even Fred Goerner now states that Amelia was not on a spy mission, though he does believe she fell into Japanese hands and died in captivity. The spy theory, at least, is almost put to rest and the mass of declassified official documents reveal that confidentiality was maintained due to the early requests from Amelia and George for secrecy about her flight plans. The mystery of what happened to Amelia and Fred Noonan after that last radio message, however, remains very much alive and there are several organizations, as well as individuals, planning further searches for the remains of the Electra.

Opinions vary as to where the plane might have ended up before running out of fuel, but based on what is known (that is, from Amelia's radio contacts), it was probably in the ocean somewhere in the vicinity of Howland Island. After much research into dozens of theories, I have concluded that Elgen and Marie Long (and Roy Nesbit, who recently wrote a series of magazine articles) are most likely to be correct in their hypothesis that the Electra ran out of fuel and was forced down about forty miles north-northwest of Howland Island. The Longs recently established a fund to finance a properly organized search, but in the meantime they have personally financed a survey of the ocean bed in the area in which they will commence their search. They needed to know whether the area consists of a flat sea bottom or whether it consists of chasms and deep gulleys. The reason is obvious: On a flat surface, any wreckage would stand out "like a basketball on a gym floor," Elgen says.

Elgen Long is a careful man by nature. A senior pilot with the Flying Tigers airline until his retirement a few years ago, he also made a record-breaking solo world flight of his own. He understands the stresses on a pilot involved in this type of venture and the technicalities of navigation and radio-to-radio direction finding. He is also well aware that in the fifty-odd years since the Electra disappeared, deterioration on a massive scale is likely to have taken place and that what he is searching for may be mere scraps of metal, but he is determined to resolve the mystery.

However, what is left of Amelia herself—of the free spirit that those who knew her well were fortunate enough to glimpse? Amelia's legacy is the legend of an ordinary girl growing into the extraordinary woman who dared to attempt seemingly unattainable goals in a man's world. It is impossible to evaluate the inspiration that Amelia handed down to the generations of women who came after her. Impossible, too, to evaluate the motivation that Amelia and her contemporaries, the pioneers of civil aviation, provided for designers and manufacturers; for always these record-breaking pilots demanded better, faster, and safer equipment, and they flew constantly at the outer limits of technology. Often, like Amelia, they paid the ultimate price, but the airplanes of today are a direct result.

I set out to research this book with only the faintest impressions of my subjects. I thought of Amelia, hazily, as a female Lindbergh and had a deeply unfavorable impression of George Palmer Putnam from my conversations with Paul Mantz so many years earlier. My work has involved interviewing family, friends, and business contacts of both, as well as reviewing their letters and writing. Research not only changed those initial impressions and created annoyance that George has been so misinterpreted but also left me with a genuine regret that I never met him. He must have been an exceptional man to have been the springboard for Amelia's abilities. A friend told me:

> ... AE had to conquer George almost as Lindbergh had to conquer the Atlantic, yet it was GPP's hell-fire determination that provided *design* for these adventures of hers, and pulled them off. I wonder if the slim, frail girl-in-slacks would have startled the world without the explosive, pragmatic apostle of the impossible to goad her on.
>
> When glory shone, it was *her* limelight—the evenings at the White House, weekends at Hyde Park, the invitations from Royalty, the confrontation with Il Duce, whom GPP had denounced in print. One night George told the details of that meeting; the coldness with which [Mussolini] had received him, while dancing fond attendance on his illustrious wife. "Mr. Earhart" undoubtedly chafed at this "stage-door Johnny" role, but both husband and wife knew they had a good thing going and I suspect Amelia needed George more than George needed her.[65]

What George and Amelia each brought to their relationship was exactly what was required to stimulate the unique talents of the other person. The combination of their individual abilities enhanced the regard they had for each other and deepened into love. It was an unusual love, at times, but a deep and genuine one, and it played an important part in the story of Amelia Earhart.

Epilogue

The following are notes on other principals in this book:

Amy Otis Earhart died on October 29, 1962, at the age of ninety-five.

Muriel Earhart Morrissey still lives in West Medford, Massachusetts. For many years, she gave lectures on the subject of her sister and has donated the family papers to the Schlesinger Library at Radcliffe College. This is now one of the primary sources of information on Amelia Earhart's life.

Her marriage to Albert Morrissey survived the difficulties they experienced in 1936–1937 and ended only with Albert's death many years later. Of George Putnam, Muriel said to this writer, "I ended up liking him. He was very kind to me after Amelia disappeared and helped me and mother a lot."

Jean-Marie, George's third wife, married George T. Asp. Now widowed, she lives in San Diego, California.

Margaret (Peg), George's fourth and last wife, continued to run the Stove Pipe Wells hotel after his death. His estate was not—contrary to speculation—enormous (some $18,000). As tourism increased, she built up the business, increasing the original tiny accommodation to take 265 persons, and achieved a first-class reputation for comfort and standards. In 1962, she met Willard Lewis and they were married. The hotel was sold four years later. Mr. Lewis died in 1981.

Peg lives an active life, in a quiet and very beautiful suburb of Los Angeles, "fund raising again," she says, "but as a volunteer this time. . . ."

Paul Mantz became one of the most famous of Hollywood's aviation movie stuntmen. If this conveys the impression of a daredevil flier, it is incorrect; he was meticulous and precise, devising and planning his every move. Almost inevitably, though, he was killed as a result of his profession—while making the movie *The Flight of the Phoenix* in 1965.

Appendix A: Radio Communications

Amelia's radio communications with Lae and subsequently with *Itasca* comprise the only documented evidence of the events leading up to her disappearance:

GMT and Time Elapsed	Local Time at Lae[1]	
00:00	10:00 A.M.	Takeoff from Lae
05:00	3:00 P.M.	Earhart to Lae: "AT 10,000 FT. BUT REDUCING ALTITUDE BECAUSE OF BANKS OF CUMULUS CLOUD"
07:00	5:00 P.M.	Earhart to Lae: "AT 7,000 FT. AND MAKING 150 MPH"
07:20	5:20 P.M.	Earhart to Lae: ". . . POSITION LATITUDE: 4 DEGREES 33.5′ SOUTH, LONGITUDE: 159 DEGREES 07′ EAST"
08:00	6:00 P.M.	Earhart to Lae: "ON COURSE FOR HOWLAND ISLAND AT 12,000 FT."

Note: All the above were received from Amelia by Harry Balfour. Balfour is on record as stating that he was in contact with Amelia every hour when position reports and height were received from her. Since her transmission times were at fifteen and forty-five minutes past each hour, it is probable that the times given are approximate, with the exception of the one contact at

5:20 (07:20 GMT), which was reported in full detail to *Itasca* on July 3. These snatched versions of her initial radio transmissions are all that have ever been recorded.

At the last contact, Amelia informed Balfour that she was changing from her daytime radio frequency (6210 kcs.) to her nighttime one (3105 kcs.).[2] "We requested her to remain on her present frequency but she told me she wished to contact the American Coast Guard Cutter *Itasca* so there was nothing to do about it but pass the terminal forecast to her and the upper air report from Ocean Island. . . ."

10:30	8:00 P.M.	*Earhart* overheard by Nauru radio ". . . A SHIP IN SIGHT AHEAD . . ."

This message also appeared in the log of the U.S.S. *Lexington.*[3]

In 1969, however, former Nauru resident T. H. Cude claimed he had heard her say "Lights in sight ahead," which led him to believe she had seen either the beam of the Nauru light, which was visible for 34 miles, or the lights of the phosphate workings, which had been left switched on purposely.

No two-way transmission was established, but Amelia's voice was heard by several people on Nauru on shortwave radio.[4]

The following extracts are taken from the official report of Commander Warner Thompson, *Itasca*'s captain, and the ship's two radio logs.

GMT and Time Elapsed	Local Time at Howland	
12:42	1:12 A.M.	*Itasca* to San Francisco: "Have not heard Earhart signals up to this time but see no cause for concern as plane is still 1000 miles away. . . ."
13:45	2:15 A.M.	*Itasca* log: "Nothing on 3105"
14:00	2:30 A.M.	*Itasca* log: "Itasca to Earhart on phone 3105"
14:15	2:45 A.M.	*Itasca* log: "Heard Earhart plane on 3105 but unreadable through static." Radio operator Leo

Bellarts however caught Amelia's low monotone voice and reported that she said ". . .
CLOUDY AND OVERCAST. . . ." Various people
were present, including two reporters familiar
with Amelia's voice. They agreed it was she but
could not decipher the message.

14:30	3:00 A.M.	*Itasca* log: "Sent weather to KHAQQ."

14:45	3:15 A.M.	*Itasca* log: "Nothing heard from Earhart."

15:00	3:30 A.M.	*Itasca* log: "Sent Weather. KHAQQ from *Itasca:* What is your position? When do you expect to reach Howland? Itasca has heard your phone go ahead on key. Acknowledge this broadcast next schedule." [Weather referred to is weather at Howland.]

15:15	3:45 A.M.	Earhart: "ITASCA FROM EARHART. OVERCAST . . . WILL LISTEN ON HOUR AND HALF HOUR ON 3105."

15:30	4:00 A.M.	*Itasca* log: "Broadcast weather on phone 3105 . . . and key 3105." Also transmitted: "What is your position? When do you expect to arrive Howland? We are receiving your signals please acknowledge this message on your next schedule."

15:45	4:15 A.M.	*Itasca* log: "Earhart unheard on 3105 this time."

16:00	4:30 A.M.	*Itasca* log: "Repeated previous transmission."

16:23	4:53 A.M.	*Itasca* log: "Sent weather/code/phone/3105 kcs."

16:24	4:54 A.M.	Earhart: ". . . PARTLY CLOUDY . . ."
		Itasca log: "Volume S-1"

16:25	4:55 A.M.	*Itasca* log: "Earhart broke in on phone—unreadable."

16:30	5:00 A.M.	*Itasca* log: "Sent weather. 'What is your position etc.' "

16:43	5:13 A.M.	*Itasca* log: "Earhart signals unheard on 3105."

17:00	5:30 A.M.	*Itasca* log: "Sent weather. 'What is your position.' "

17:15	5:45 A.M.	*Itasca* log: "No hear during [scheduled time]."
17:30	6:00 A.M.	*Itasca* log: "Sent weather data."
17:44	6:14 A.M.	Earhart: "[Want] BEARING ON 3105/ON HOUR/ WILL WHISTLE IN MIC."
17:45	6:15 A.M.	Earhart: "ABOUT TWO HUNDRED MILES OUT. APPROXIMATELY. WHISTLING NOW."
		Itasca log: "Volume S-3" [*Note: Sunrise was recorded in log at 6:15 A.M.*]
18:00	6:30 A.M.	*Itasca* log: "Sent weather and asked position."
18:12	6:42 A.M.	*Itasca* log: "KHAQQ came on air with fairly clear signals calling *Itasca.*"
18:15	6:45 A.M.	Earhart: "PLEASE TAKE BEARING ON US AND REPORT IN HALF HOUR I WILL MAKE NOISE IN MICROPHONE—ABOUT 100 MILES OUT."
		Itasca log: "Earhart signal strength 4 but on air so briefly bearings impossible."
18:30	7:00 A.M.	*Itasca* log: "Sent weather, maintained contact on 500 kcs. for 'homing.' "
18:48	7:18 A.M.	*Itasca* log: "Cannot take bearing on 3105 very good/please send on 500 or do you wish to take bearing on us/go ahead please."
		Itasca log: "No answer."
19:00	7:30 A.M.	*Itasca* log: "Please acknowledge our signals on key please."
		Itasca log: "unanswered."
19:12	7:42 A.M.	Earhart: "KHAQQ CALLING ITASCA WE MUST BE ON YOU BUT CANNOT SEE YOU BUT GAS IS RUNNING LOW BEEN UNABLE TO REACH YOU BY RADIO WE ARE FLYING AT ALTITUDE 1000 FEET."
		Itasca log: "Other log reads—Earhart says running out of gas only half hour left [verified as heard by other witnesses]/can't hear us at all/ we hear her and are sending on 3105 and 500 same time constantly and listening in for her frequently." [*Note: Itasca had two logs in radio room.*]

19:13	7:43 A.M.	*Itasca* log: "Received your message signal strength 5 (sent AAA's etc. on 500 and 3105). Go ahead."
		[Note that in consideration of the power of Amelia's transmitter—50 watts—the strength of these signals (strength 5 is the maximum possible) indicates that she must have been very close to *Itasca* at this point. According to the commanding officer, "It was also the time we expected her to arrive."]
19:17	7:47 A.M.	*Itasca* log: "Received your message signal strength 5.
		Itasca log: "Sent AAA's on 3105."
19:19	7:49 A.M.	*Itasca* log: "Your message okay please acknowledge with phone on 3105."
		Itasca log: "Keyed AAA's."
19:28	7:58 A.M.	Earhart: "WE ARE CIRCLING BUT CANNOT HEAR YOU GO AHEAD ON 7500 EITHER NOW OR ON THE SCHEDULE TIME ON HALF HOUR."
		Itasca log: "Volume S-5" [very loud, maximum strength on meter]
19:29	7:59 A.M.	*Itasca* log: "AAAAAAAAAAAA (on 7500). Go ahead on 3105."
19:30	8:00 A.M.	Earhart: "KHAQQ CALLING ITASCA WE RECEIVED YOUR SIGNALS BUT UNABLE TO GET A MINIMUM PLEASE TAKE BEARING ON US AND ANSWER 3105 WITH VOICE."
		[AE sent long dashes on 3105 for five seconds or so. This was the only direct reply that *Itasca* received from KHAQQ. It was later believed that she turned away at this point.]
19:35	8:05 A.M.	*Itasca* log: "Your signals received okay we are unable to hear you to take a bearing it is impractical to take a bearing on 3105 on your voice/how do you get that?/go ahead."
19:36	8:06 A.M.	*Itasca* log: "Go ahead on 3105 or 500 kilocycles."

		Itasca log: "Itasca sending on 7500 as her only acknowledgement was for signals on 7500."
19:37	8:07 A.M.	*Itasca* log: "Go ahead."
19:42	8:12 A.M.	*Itasca* log: "Itasca to Earhart. 'Did you get transmission on 7500 kcs/go ahead on 500 kcs so that we may take a bearing on you/it is impossible to take a bearing on 3105 kilocycles/please acknowledge.' "
19:43	8:13 A.M.	*Itasca* log: "repeated above message on 7500."
19:45	8:15 A.M.	*Itasca* log: "Do you hear my signals on 7500 kcs or 3105 please acknowledge receipt on 3105/go ahead."
		Itasca log: "sent on 3105 and repeated on 7500."
19:48	8:18 A.M.	*Itasca* log: "Will you please acknowledge our signals on 7500 or 3105/go ahead with 3105."
		Itasca log: "no answer."
20:03	8:33 A.M.	*Itasca* log: "Will you please come in and answer on 3105/we are transmitting constantly on 7500 kcs and we do not hear you on 3105/please answer on 3105/go ahead."
		Itasca log: "this unanswered."
20:04	8:34 A.M.	*Itasca* log: "Answer on 3105 kcs with phone/how are signals coming in/go ahead."
20:14	8:44 A.M.	Earhart: "WE ARE ON THE LINE OF POSITION 157–337, WILL REPEAT THIS MESSAGE ON 6210 KCS. WAIT, LISTENING ON 6210 KCS. WE ARE RUNNING NORTH AND SOUTH."
		Itasca log: 'On 3105—volume S-5."
20:17	8:47 A.M.	*Itasca* log: "We heard you okay on 3105 kcs. Please stay on 3105 do not hear you on 6210 maintain QSO on 3105."
		Itasca log: "This broadcast by voice on 3105 and by key on 7500. Nothing was heard on 3105 or 6210."

In addition to the above transmissions, *Itasca* transmitted other numerous voice and code messages to which there was no response. Those above are merely the more important ones, which show that the radio schedule requested by Amelia was maintained. In most cases, although a precise time was given, the transmission lasted several minutes or more.

Appendix B: Technical Aspects
of the Lae–Howland Flight

FUEL

The amount of fuel carried by the Electra determined its flying time and range, so it has been an important factor in plotting the most likely area of Amelia's forced landing; but it has kept countless researchers guessing. Amelia's decision on the amount of fuel she carried would have been made in the knowledge of the distance involved (Lae to Howland is 2,561 miles)[1] and the conditions affecting takeoff at Lae.

In her final telegram to the *Herald Tribune,* Amelia stated that the plane was "weighted to capacity." Did she mean, by this, that the plane was full to the capacity of the fuel tanks (1,150 gallons according to Lockheed's archives); or did she mean—mindful of her experience at Luke Field, Honolulu, in the previous March—to the maximum capacity she thought she could safely manage on the takeoff at Lae? There is conflicting evidence.

James Collopy, district superintendent of civil aviation in Papua New Guinea, reported after Amelia's disappearance that "according to Captain Noonan," the Electra was carrying 1,100 gallons of fuel, which included 50 gallons of 100-octane fuel. The high octane fuel was intended to be used during the takeoff to give extra power; the balance was 87-octane aviation gas, and there were 64 gallons of oil.[2] Earhart researchers Elgen and Marie Long recently interviewed Robert Ivedale, the mechanic who worked the Electra at Lae, who also claimed that the Electra had 1,100 gallons on board when Amelia took off from Lae.[3]

The airport at Lae used imperial measures. If 1,100 imperial gallons had been pumped aboard the Electra, this would have been the equivalent of 1,321 U.S. gallons—clearly impossible as there was not that capacity. So perhaps there is room for doubt in the statements made by Collopy and Ivedale because of the conversion factor.

Noonan told reporters on the eve of takeoff that they would be carrying "950 gallons of petrol—sufficient to give a still-air cruising range of 2,750 miles,"[4] and although one hesitates to believe newspaper reports over the firsthand evidence of Collopy and Ivedale, they are worth examining. One report by the aviation correspondent of the Sydney *Telegraph* quoted Noonan saying that with 950 gallons "the plane was overloaded by two tons." This is almost exactly what was said before the flight from Oakland to Honolulu, three months earlier, on the first attempt at the round-the-world flight. Was it an accurate report? Would Noonan, a responsible and experienced navigator, consider a theoretical margin of less than 10 percent adequate on a flight where there was no alternative landing site and the destination was potentially difficult to locate?

It seems improbable; and yet when Amelia flew from Oakland to Honolulu in company with Paul Mantz, Harry Manning, and Fred Noonan, the Electra carried only 947 gallons for the twenty-four-hundred-mile flight (which took fifteen hours and forty-seven minutes). Afterward, Amelia stated that of the 947 gallons "more than four hours fuel remained,"[5] but during that flight, Paul Mantz had monitored fuel consumption and throttle controls, for he was always unhappy at her tendency to fly with the throttle wide open. Fuel conservation was an important issue, hence the two instruments that Mantz had insisted on fitting aboard the Electra as an aid to economic use of fuel.

Amelia's disastrous attempted takeoff from Luke Field (which had a one-thousand-yard concrete runway) was made with nine hundred U.S. gallons of fuel on board. In a press interview on April 24 at Burbank, Amelia said she felt that the "Electra had ground looped because it was overloaded." If Amelia considered the Electra to be overloaded with 900 gallons for takeoff on a concrete runway, how could she possibly consider that she could take off with 1,100 gallons on Lae's *unpaved* runway of one thousand yards?

The Luke Field crash undoubtedly made a big impression on Amelia and there is no evidence that she had ever taken off in the Electra with a fuel load of more than one thousand gallons. A cable from George to Jacques de Sibour indicated that tests would be made with 850 and 1000 gallons, but it is not known whether this was ever carried out.[6] Furthermore, manufacturer's specifications indicate that the Electra was *not capable* of taking off with a fuel load of 1,100 gallons in one thousand yards, in still-air conditions.[7]

Even taking into account the fact that Amelia's plane had been stripped of all superfluous equipment/effects, and that magnesium alloys had been used for various parts of the plane in order to reduce weight, the minimum possible net weight of the airplane would have been 9,200 pounds.[8]

A U.S. gallon of aviation fuel (0.8327 of an imperial gallon) weighs six pounds (an imperial gallon of aviation fuel weighs 7.2 pounds); and 1,100 U.S. gallons of fuel weighs 6,600 pounds.

If Collopy and Ivedale were correct, the gross weight of the airplane with 1,100 U.S. gallons of fuel would have been a minimum 15,800 pounds. Lockheed figures show that with this gross weight, takeoff of the *standard* Model 10 under the prevailing conditions at Lae (hot, humid, still air) would have required more than twenty-five hundred yards (seventy-five hundred feet) of runway.[9]

Allowing for the additional power available because Amelia's 10E model was fitted with twin 550 hp Wasps, the maximum gross weight limit for a takeoff on Lae's one-thousand-yard runway would be 15,300 pounds. With a net weight of 9,200 the airplane could have carried only 1,000 (U.S.) gallons at the outside.

Firsthand information also exists that Amelia never intended to carry more than one thousand gallons (even before her Honolulu disaster). In order to obtain the necessary permission to fly over British territories during the round-the-world flight, Jacques de Sibour had approached Sir Francis Shelmerdine (director of civil aviation) on her behalf. Following his meeting, de Sibour suggested to Amelia that she should write a personal letter to allay Shelmerdine's concerns. In this letter, Amelia states:

> . . . Your interest is no doubt in its fuel tankage; i.e. 1150 gallons. Such amount provides a maximum cruising range of 4,000 miles. My longest hops over the Pacific are about 2,500 miles—at which time I shall carry probably 1,000 gallons of gasoline.[10]

Various researchers have highlighted pieces of circumstantial evidence in order to advance theories regarding the amount of fuel in the Electra's tanks when Amelia took off from Lae, but in fact no hard evidence has ever been discovered. A scrap of paper on which Amelia had scrawled some figures relates to fuel taken on board and totals 684 gallons. It was mailed to George from Lae, but as it was included with Amelia's notes of the journey from Bandoeng, there is no way of knowing whether it related to the fuel taken on board at Lae, or Darwin, or some other place.[11]

In the light of Lockheed's figures on the plane's performance, fuel consumption, the prevailing conditions, and the amount of time that Amelia was *known* to be in the air, it is unlikely that Amelia was carrying more than a thousand gallons, which would have given her between twenty and twenty-one hours range depending on how efficiently she flew the airplane. She expected the flight to take about eighteen and a half hours, but head winds of 10 mph greater than forecast, if encountered over the entire trip, would add an extra two hours to the flight.

Amelia's last message to *Itasca* was transmitted after twenty hours and fourteen minutes of flight.

FUEL CONSUMPTION

At Paul Mantz's suggestion, the Electra had been equipped with a fuel analyzer to measure the effect of the fuel and air mixture on the power output and to enable the pilot to select the most efficient and economic combination. In flight trials, Mantz worked out the most effective settings for various stages of flight and these had worked remarkably well on the Oakland–Honolulu flight in March. Records exist at Lockheed showing that Amelia was reasonably proficient at using this instrument, employing settings provided by Mantz.

From these and manufacturer's figures,[12] it can reasonably be assumed that during the takeoff and fight to gain airspeed and height, the fuel consumption may have been as high as one hundred gallons an hour; and the long slow climb of the heavily burdened plane to ten thousand feet would burn fuel at a rate of approximately seventy gallons an hour.[13] Once the fuel load reduced to within recommended levels, the fuel consumption could drop to thirty-eight gallons an hour while still maintaining an airspeed of 150 mph. Thus, a speculative (and very approximate) attempt can be made to calculate the amount of fuel used during the time Amelia was *known* to be in the air.

Takeoff and gain airspeed	.33 hours at 100 gph	33 gallons
Climb to 10,000 feet	5 hours at 70 gph	350 gallons
Descend to 7,000 and cruise (say)	5 hours at 50 gph	250 gallons
Remaining time at maximum efficiency	10 hours at 38 gph	380 gallons
	Total fuel consumption	1013 gallons

It should be remembered, however, that fuel consumption would take a gradual curve between these reference points and the application of a reasonable 5 percent contingency to cover this fact could put consumption as low as 956 U.S. gallons or as high as 1,070 U.S. gallons.

NAVIGATION

Amelia and Noonan had two navigational choices. They could either fly a great circle course (as set out by Clarence Williams), relying totally on frequent star sightings, or Noonan could have plotted a constant compass bearing (rhumb line)[14] course for Howland. In northern latitudes, the great circle route (while appearing to be longer on a map) is more direct since it follows the earth's curvature. The difference between the two alternatives at the equatorial latitudes between Lae and Howland would be only fifty miles or so, however.

Whichever system was chosen, Noonan would have frequently checked his position by shooting what he called "the heavenly bodies" (sun, moon, planets, and stars). He is on record as stating that fixes based on stellar observations at night were more reliable than those taken during the day because of the ability to cross-check.

During the day, cross-checks could be made "by crossing a line of position [derived by sun shots] with a radio direction finding (RDF) bearing;" but, he said, this was not totally reliable "due to the amount of error which would be introduced by even a small angular error in long range DF bearings." Noonan understood and had considerable experience working with direction finders, and he had used them successfully in his work in the Pacific with Pan American.

Knowing Noonan's navigational methods, which are a matter of record,[15] it is possible to ascertain his tactics on this occasion. At some point before the airplane reached Howland Island, having ascertained a position by celestial navigation, Noonan would have plotted a course that would take them either well to the north or well to the south of the island. It did not matter which; it was only necessary to be *sure* that the island was somewhere to the north, or somewhere to the south, when they arrived at a parallel position. This system of navigation was pioneered by Francis Chichester in 1931 (when he flew in his Gipsy Moth to the remote Lord Howe and Norfolk islands en route from New Zealand to Australia).

> I had worked out a fine system of navigation. I had found that I could follow an invisible curved path to the island by taking sextant shots of the sun every hour; this was based on the fact that measuring the height of the sun above the horizon with a sextant enabled one to calculate the distance of the [air]plane from the spot vertically below the sun on the surface of the earth.
>
> . . . I had to aim well to one side of the island in case error in the dead reckoning caused by a faulty compass reading, or undetected wind effect, should put me on the wrong side of the island. And the island being out of sight, I must be certain when I turned to the right I was turning towards it, and not away from it. This system was afterwards dubbed by one of my friends as "my theory of deliberate error. . . ."[16]

In Chichester's case, he introduced a deliberate error of two hundred miles; in other words, he flew to a position that he assumed was two hundred miles to the north of the island that was his destination. It is known from several contributions to *Weems* navigation manual, by Noonan, between 1931 and 1935, that he was an adherent of this "find the island" system and had used it successfully to navigate the Pan Am clippers to Pacific islands.

From what is known, it is most probable that Noonan chose to aim to the north of Howland. Radio transmissions from Amelia to *Itasca* during the early hours reported "cloudy and overcast" conditions. A little over an hour before her final radio contact, Amelia said they were flying at one thousand feet. The most probable reason for this was cloud, since they would have been able to see farther at a higher altitude; and had they been in clear weather, they would have obviously taken advantage of greater visibility.

Howland itself, and the area south and east of it, was in clear sunlight with occasional scattered small clouds. The crew of *Itasca,* however, reported thick cloud in an area estimated to be forty miles to the north and west of Howland. This cloud, said air corps observer Lt. Cooper, would have prevented the fliers seeing the island from a distance greater than ten miles unless the clouds were very high above them. However, the *Itasca,* which was lying northeastward of the island, was emitting thick black smoke that hung around for several hours and that Commander Thompson felt should have been visible up to thirty miles away.[17]

Had Noonan elected to aim south of Howland Island, the Electra would have been flying in clear and cloudless skies; if the line of position 157–337 was accurate, Amelia and Noonan could hardly have missed seeing Baker Island (a little under forty miles to the southeast).

Assuming, then, that when the Electra reached the point on the plotted course where Noonan could have been reasonably certain that Howland Island lay approximately due south of them (a position that could be confirmed by a sun shot), he would have advised Amelia to turn right and fly in a southerly direction until the island was reached. This sounds simple, but Sir Francis Chichester noted his own doubts when he first put his theory to the test:

> I had a feeling of despair. After flying in one direction for hour after hour over markless, signless sea, my instinct revolted at suddenly changing direction in mid-ocean. . . . I had been so long on the same heading that the island must lie ahead not to the right. I was attacked by panic. . . .[18]

It is tempting to wonder whether Amelia experienced these same feelings of doubt, for everything indicates that it was a reliance on her own similar instinct that led her to ignore Noonan's navigational instruction on the flight to Dakar when she turned north instead of south and put them 163 miles north of their destination.

In order to obtain an accurate line of position, Noonan would have used tables from the *Nautical Almanac for 1937*, which provided details of the sun's azimuth,[19] which for 17:55 GMT—sunrise—on July 2, 1937, was 067 degrees.

The fact that Amelia gave a line of position has led many researchers to suppose that Noonan achieved an actual sun shot because according to the relevant almanac it was an accurate one for that morning. However, using the information in the almanac, it was possible for him to have *precomputed* lines of position in advance, using sun-pointing angles, azimuths, and attitudes at (say) 6:15 A.M. (sunrise), 7:30 A.M., and 8:30 A.M., so that in the event of his not being able to see the sun due to cloud, he would at least have a theoretical north/south line at dawn.[20]

The problem in this case is, in simplistic terms, that although the Electra was flying south on the line of position that Amelia gave, the line would not necessarily intersect Howland Island unless Noonan's dead-reckoning position (which assumed they were due north of the island) was accurate. They may, for example, have been running north and south on a line that was thirty or forty miles short of the island (that is, parallel to Noonan's supposed position). Furthermore, even with a sextant shot at the sun, it was impossible for Noonan to know how far north of the island they were without a bearing on, for example, a radio signal.

Amelia reported that they were running north *and* south (N es S in the radio operator's shorthand code is north and south, and those present in the radio room agreed this is what she said, and repeated in correct radio transmission procedure), not north *to* south, which provides reason to believe that she may have turned—at least once—on this line and was hunting for Howland along a length that allowed for a reasonable error factor—perhaps of fifty or sixty miles.

Noonan clearly believed that they should have located the island at approximately 7:42 ship's time (19:12 GMT) and he was so sure, he instructed Amelia to circle, which she reported sixteen minutes later at 7:58 (19:28 GMT). Two minutes later, she reported that she had received *Itasca*'s signals but was "unable to get a minimum" on which to tune her direction finder. It was the only reply that indicated she ever received any signals from *Itasca* during that flight, and hence it is assumed that at that point she was closest to Howland Island.

One wonders why, if Amelia and Noonan were so certain that they must be in the vicinity of Howland Island ("must be on you but cannot see you"), they did not engage in a square search; that is, to fly in a square pattern that increases in size progressively by the distance visible to the naked eye. Theoretically, provided one has sufficient fuel, the target must be located sooner or later. Had Amelia been carrying 1,100 gallons when she took off, she would have almost certainly had sufficient fuel to have performed this maneuver. However, she had already reported that she was low on fuel. An hour and two minutes before her last radio contact, she had reported either that she was low on fuel or that she had only approximately half an hour's supply left. It may not have been possible for her to have been more precise—there was always a quantity of fuel that could not be used due to attitude of the plane/gravity, and so on, and it is unlikely that she would have known what that amount might have been.

There is one further navigational factor to take into consideration, which in itself is insufficient explanation for Amelia's disappearance, but it might have been part of the reason why Amelia and Noonan never located Howland Island.

The area of the Pacific around Howland was largely unknown and poorly charted. The reported positions (latitude and longitude) of the many uninhabited islands dated from the logs of sailing ships a century or more earlier. Clarence Williams, Amelia's navigational consultant, had used the coordinates of Howland given in *Lippincott's Geographical Dictionary of the World,* and used by the U.S. Navy Department's Hydrographer's office. On Amelia's charts, Williams clearly marked the island's position as "Latitude 0 deg 49′00 North; Longitude 176 deg 43′ 09 West," correct according to *Lippincott's* in the spring of 1937.

Ironically, in the survey conducted a year earlier, the *Itasca* had corrected this position to Latitude 0 deg 48′ 06 North; Longitude 176 deg 38′ 12 West, but the change had not found its way into print when Williams consulted the Hydrographer's office.[21]

The difference amounts to just under six miles. Howland Island was not where Amelia and Noonan expected it to be.

RADIO AND RDF

It is generally agreed that the overriding factor leading to Amelia's disappearance was her lack of expertise in radio communications. Commander Thompson stated, "Viewed from the fact that Miss Earhart's flight was largely dependent on radio communication, her attitude towards arrangements was casual to say the least."[22]

It seems certain that had Amelia ever been able to establish reasonable two-way communication with *Itasca,* the end result would have been very different and tragedy averted.

The radio aboard Electra has always been assumed to have been the Western Electric equipment fitted by Joe Gurr. Elgen Long's research, however, indicates that this may be incorrect. He interviewed a former Bendix employee, who stated that before Amelia left Miami she was persuaded by Bendix to discard the Western Electric equipment for the new Bendix RA–1 series. The Longs also have located photographs of the Electra's interior, taken at Miami, showing an RA–1 receiver fitted on top of the instrument panel directly in front of Amelia. "Bendix offered Amelia five thousand dollars to ditch the Western Electric gear," Elgen Long told me. The reason was obvious: The publicity surrounding a successful navigation of the world using *entirely* Bendix equipment would be very valuable. Furthermore, Bendix was one of the major original backers of the Purdue "Flying Laboratory" project.

Elgen Long also states that he has further proof of this via Stan Rose, the mechanic who checked Amelia's radio and DF equipment at Darwin and who replaced the blown fuse. Rose apparently stated that *all* the radio equipment was Bendix.

There is one further piece of evidence for this claim—a letter from Lockheed on the subject of "Radio Equipment of Earhart Electra," dated July 30, 1937, which states, ". . . we have good reason to believe that additional equipment was installed by Miss Earhart in Miami."[23] Perhaps this was one of the reasons for the confusion that has arisen over the years regarding what frequencies were available to Amelia.

The *Itasca*'s instructions were that Amelia's plane was "equipped with a 50 watt transmitter for operation on 500, 3105, and 6210 kilocycles, and with a receiver covering all frequencies. The direction finder covers 200 to 1500 kilocycles." A subsequent message corrected this cable, advising that the direction finder covered 200–1400 kcs. *Itasca* was also informed that "on the previous trip [Oakland to Honolulu] communications were handled by Pan American Airways with the Electra working on 3105 and Pan American on 2986 kilocycles.[24] However, George advised *Itasca*, "When Amelia Earhart took off from Miami she stated she would not try to communicate with any radio station but would broadcast her position every 15 and 45 minutes past each hour . . . her receiver will be used most of the time taking radio bearings."[25] (Records show that Amelia did not transmit her position on a regular basis at any stage of the trip.)

Itasca acknowledged this communication, requested information on the frequency best suited to Amelia's homing device, and asked her to designate "time and type of our signal. We will give smoke by day and searchlight by night."[26] However, Commander Black commented, "It will be noted in the event that the *Itasca* was to be used as a homing-in agency, and was to transmit on 3105, that it would be impossible for the plane to receive the above frequencies on its direction finder the range of which was 200–1400."

Subsequently, *Itasca* received the following messages from Amelia regarding communications:

HOMING DEVICE COVERS FROM 200–1500 AND 2400–4800 KILOCYCLES ANY FREQUENCIES NOT REPEAT NOT NEAR ENDS BANDS SUITABLE.[27]

SUGGEST ONTARIO STAND BY ON 400 KCS TO TRANSMIT LETTER N FIVE MINUTES ON REQUEST WITH STATION CALL LETTERS REPEATED TWICE END EVERY MINUTE. SWAN TRANSMIT VOICE 9 MEGACYCLES OR IF I UNABLE RECEIVE BE READY ON 900 KCS. ITASCA TRANSMIT LETTER A, POSITION, OWN CALL LETTERS AS ABOVE ON HALF HOUR 7.5 MEGACYCLES. POSITION SHIPS AND OUR LEAVING WILL DETERMINE BROADCAST TIMES SPECIFICALLY. IF FREQUENCIES MENTIONED UNSUITABLE NIGHT WORK INFORM ME LAE. I WILL GIVE LONG CALL BY VOICE 3105 KCS QUARTER AFTER HOUR POSSIBLY QUARTER TO.[28]

While a further cable instructed (after weather reports were transmitted to her in naval code):

REPORT IN ENGLISH NOT CODE ESPECIALLY WHILE FLYING WILL BROADCAST HOURLY QUARTER PAST HOUR GCT [GREENWICH CIVIL TIME].[29]

To which *Itasca* replied:

FOLLOWING FOR AMELIA EARHART PUTNAM LAE QUOTE ITASCA TRANSMITTERS CALIBRATED 7500 6210 3105 500 425 KCS CW AND EITHER CW OR MCW. ITASCA DIRECTION FINDER FREQUENCY RANGE 550 TO 270 KCS.[30]

It has been stated that Amelia was never informed that in addition to the direction finder on *Itasca*, another direction finder, an experimental high-frequency piece of equipment, had been installed on Howland Island. It was so experimental that it was still in the "breadboard" stage of development. Paul Mantz's biographer states that Paul had arranged to borrow this DF from the navy and, working for George as Amelia's formal representative at Howland, Richard Black had arranged the installation and operation of the unit. The equipment, however, was mentioned in a cable from George to Admiral Leahy dated April 29, 1937,[31] before Amelia left on the round-the-world flight, so it appears highly unlikely that Amelia would not have been aware of its existence. There was no evidence, however, that it was of any assistance in the project, though *Itasca* maintained contact with the operator, Frank Cipriani, constantly and a log was kept of the operation. At the time when Amelia was closest and the Howland Island shortwave DF might have been most useful, it was running low on power, the dry-cell battery arrangement rigged up by *Itasca's* engineers almost exhausted from the night's work, and in need of recharging. According to an official report by Lt. Daniel Cooper of the air corps, who was on Howland as an official observer, the equipment on Howland Island was capable of working on 3105 kcs., but Amelia never transmitted for a long enough period to enable Cipriani to obtain a bearing on her.[32]

In summing up the mission, Commander Thompson stated:

> . . . Ship's direction finder manned at 0725 [ship's time].

> *Itasca* transmitters were accurately calibrated.

> *Itasca* signals clearly received by other units.

> *Itasca* fully covered all Earhart schedules 7500, 3105 etc.

> Earhart never answered *Itasca* questions and never gave a position. Communications were never really established.

> Earhart acknowledged receiving *Itasca* signals at 0800 [ship's time]. This formed the only case and was apparently for signals sent by *Itasca* on 7500.

> Earhart could not secure null on *Itasca* signals.

> Earhart's last message was hurried, frantic, and apparently not complete. Earhart did not return to air on 6210.

> Earhart was on air very briefly and apparently over modulated. The attempts of the radioman on Howland to secure cut failed.

> Judging from signal strength Earhart was closest between 0730 and 0844–46, when her signal strength was 5 with a 50 watt transmitter.

> Earhart probably had receiver trouble.

> Earhart apparently did not know position.

> Earhart asked *Itasca* to take bearings on her. This was never planned. Earhart knew that *Itasca* could give her accurate bearings on 500 [kcs.] and yet never transmitted on 500 in order for *Itasca* to assist her. Earhart knew that she could use 500 when close in if necessary.

> The signals which Earhart acknowledged were transmitted on 7500. Her direction finder loop could not handle this frequency. It is possible she was referring to other signals.[33]

Commander Thompson did not know that Amelia almost certainly could not communicate on 500 kcs. because the 250-foot trailing antenna, necessary for operating on that frequency, had been left in the United States, along with the code keys. It was said that neither Amelia nor Noonan could use code at operational speeds, though both must surely have been capable of tapping out a call-sign letter. For some reason, Amelia had convinced herself that she did not need code and that voice communications were adequate. In respect of the direction finder, Elgen and Marie Long have conducted research using an antenna system identical to that used on Amelia's Electra. "The directional qualities were practically nil. It didn't have high points of nulls and voids on it. So the waves radiating from it would be very little, regardless of what direction the antenna or airplane was pointed at the time."[34]

AMELIA'S LOCKHEED ELECTRA 1OE: SUNDRY SPECIFICATIONS FOR THE ROUND-THE-WORLD FLIGHT:

Normally a ten-passenger plane, the Electra had been cleared of all seats and about half of the cabin was filled with additional fuel tanks with a capacity of 753 gallons. The wing tanks were capable of taking 398 gallons—its total capacity was 1,151 gallons.[35]

About 18 inches off the floor is a wide chart table. Beneath it, visible through a glass inset in the table top is a master aperodic compass. Special windows of flat glass have been installed on both sides of the aircraft, free from the distortion of standard cabin windows. Through them the navigator makes his celestial observations using a bubble sextant. A pelorus also is mounted for use at both windows.

An arrangement has been devised to open the cabin door about four inches, where it is held rigidly in place. A Pioneer Drift indicator is mounted for looking down through this aperture to check wind drift on the earth or sea below. For this work flares are used at night over water, smoke bombs in daylight. Beside the chart table are mounted three chronometers, altimeter, air speed indicator and temperature gauge. A Bendix Direction Finder was fitted, its loop mounted on the top of the cockpit is adjustable by Amelia from inside the cockpit.

Amelia's entire wardrobe all in matching shades of brown fits into one small suitcase. In the fuselage there will be a two-man rubber lifeboat, instantly inflatable from capsules of carbon dioxide. Likewise a Very pistol for firing distress signals, flares that ignite off the surface of the water and as Amelia says, "a very orange kite."[36]

Appendix C: The Earhart
Disappearance Theories

Probably it was the film *Flight for Freedom*, screened in 1943, that first planted the idea in many people's minds that Amelia's disappearance may not have been a straightforward "ditch" in the Pacific Ocean. Rumors eddied and swirled throughout the war that Amelia had, either deliberately or accidentally, flown over Japanese-mandated territory, been forced to land, and been taken prisoner. Some people believed that after the war, she would be found and liberated.

In March 1944 in the Marshall Islands, a native called Elieu Jibambam talked to U.S. Navy Lieutenant Eugene Bogan. Elieu said he had been told by a late friend, a Japanese trader called Ajima, that an American woman flier had come down on a reef near Jaluit Island and was picked up by a Japanese ship. Ajima told him the woman was a spy and had been taken away by soldiers to another island. Bogan reported this to his senior officer but no official report was filed, on the grounds that it might raise false hopes that Amelia Earhart was still alive.[1]

The *American Weekly* ran a story about Amelia on September 10, 1944 after the island of Saipan was taken by the U.S. Marines. The article told how marines had found a photograph album filled with "pictures of Amelia in her sports togs" in a captured barracks. Although Amelia had not carried such an album with her on her last flight, the finding of this item somehow bolstered belief that there was a connection between the album and Amelia's disappearance.[2]

It was probably as a result of this story together with talk that a Caucasian woman pilot had been seen there before the war that George Putnam made a point of visiting Saipan. With carte blanche to go anywhere and talk to anyone, George traveled all over the island and questioned numerous people. Later, he told his family that he never discovered a single piece of information that led him to believe Amelia had ever been there. George Putnam, the great publicist, would *never* have passed up an opportunity to write a sensational book and make a war heroine of Amelia had there been the slightest hint of a story. Accusations that he did not want Amelia found because he had remarried are patently without foundation; by then he was divorced from Jeannie and had not yet begun courting Peg.

George was always convinced that Amelia had run out of fuel somewhere near Howland Island and had died either during the emergency landing at sea or very shortly afterward. He did, however, strongly believe that the massive sea and air search for Amelia probably *also* had been used to gather information about a sensitive area in the Pacific.[3]

In 1944–45, Thomas E. Devine, a sergeant in the U.S. Army Postal Corps, was based at Saipan. Two incidents caused him to become involved in the Amelia Earhart mystery. In early July 1944, he heard rumors that Amelia Earhart's plane was locked in a hangar at Aslito Airfield. Devine went to the airfield and saw a twin-engine metal airplane in a hangar. He stated the plane bore the registration NR16020. Shortly afterward, he claimed, the airplane was destroyed by the U.S. Army. About a year later, at the Japanese cemetery of Garapan, he and a friend were shown a grass-covered spot by a native woman who, through an interpreter, told them it marked the grave of two white fliers, one of whom was a woman.[4]

Jackie Cochran, who also had a personal interest in Amelia's fate, had headed up the WASPS organization of women ferry pilots during the war. When hostilities ceased, she was directed by General "Hap" Arnold to make an official investigation into the role of women in the Imperial Japanese Air Force. In Jackie's autobiography, *Stars at Noon*, written in 1954, she related how, while engaged on this mission, she discovered "numerous clippings and photographs about Amelia Earhart, Jimmy Doolittle and other American pilots including myself. There were several files on Amelia Earhart," at the Dai-Ichi building in Tokyo.[5]

Jackie did not describe the contents of those files and some writers have implied that there is a sinister reason for this. However, had the files revealed anything contrary to Jackie's belief that Amelia had ditched and drowned, surely she would have commented on the fact, or else not repeated in the same book her *certainty*, because of her telepathic abilities, that her friend had died after drifting on the ocean for several days. It is likely that the files contained nothing more than a collection of cuttings and photographs (there were so many newspaper articles and stories on Amelia), and Jackie never mentioned them because she felt they were unimportant.[6]

After the war ended, the rumors remained so widespread that the U.S. Navy Department was compelled to take the unusual step of formally denying that Amelia had been involved in any military operation during her round-the-world flight. They also stated that no evidence had been found in captured documents or from interrogation of Japanese prisoners that Amelia had fallen into Japanese hands. In the meantime, however, thousands of American servicemen had liberated islands all over the Pacific. Undoubtedly, in view of the rapidly growing Amelia Earhart legend, many would have asked questions or talked about the subject to islanders.

In 1945, a dentist serving with the U.S. Navy on the island of Saipan in the Marianas was told by his young assistant Josephine Blanco that she recalled seeing a twin-engine plane land on the water in Saipan Harbor. She was able to fix the date as summer 1937 because she was eleven years old that year and about to start attending a new school. Her brother-in-law was Japanese and she was taking lunch to him in a restricted area, which she had a pass to enter. When the girl met her brother-in-law, he took her to see the American woman who had been taken off the plane. To the child's surprise, the woman was wearing what appeared to be men's clothing (slacks and shirt) and also wore her hair cut short like a man. The woman was accompanied by a tall man. The two captives were led away to a clearing in nearby woods by soldiers; Josephine heard shots and the soldiers returned alone.

Miss Blanco later married, became Josephine Akiyama and settled in California. Both she and her former employer told this story to Captain Paul L. Briand, Jr., an assistant professor of English at the USAF Academy in Colorado, who had been interested in Amelia's story. As a result Captain Briand wrote his book, *Daughter of the Sky*, published in 1960, in which he outlined Mrs. Akiyama's testimony and suggested that Amelia might have wandered off course during the night while Noonan slept.[7]

For Captain Briand's theory to be correct, Amelia's error would have had to have been more than 100 degrees from the point of her last reported position; instead of flying east, she would have had to fly northwest. But a simple glance at her compasses (she had more than one) would have told Amelia she was flying almost in the opposite direction.

What about the evidence of *Itasca*'s radio log and those who heard Amelia's transmissions at strength five toward the end of her flight? For *Itasca* to have received strength-five signals from Amelia's 50-watt transmitter from the Marianas Islands was most improbable, especially during daylight hours (the condition known as "skip," which can cause freak radio reception, is more common at night). What is more, the Marianas are a very large group of islands covering a huge area of the North Pacific Ocean. Amelia could hardly have been out of sight of land for the length of time reported had she been in the Marianas and flying the course she would have to have steered to get there from the Nukumanu islands. Captain Brian maintained his belief, however, that Amelia had finished her flight in Saipan, and in 1967 he wrote to Ann Pellegreno that he was convinced Amelia and Noonan had been captured and executed.

In 1960, just before the publication of Paul Briand's book, a San Francisco–based CBS journalist, Fred Goerner, came across Mrs. Akiyama's story in a local paper. Goerner spent more than five years investigating the matter, which included four trips to Saipan, during which he interviewed more than two hundred people, as well as investigation of the role played by U.S. military organizations in Amelia's flight.

Goerner concluded that Amelia had been on a mission for the U.S. government: that she had detoured to Truk for the purpose of taking photographs of

Japanese fortifications and subsequently became lost in a tropical storm during the night. Goerner's contention was that she landed in the lagoon at Mili Atoll in the southeastern Marshall Islands some seven hundred miles northwest of Howland Island. She waded ashore to get help for Noonan, who had hurt his head in the landing. Later, some eleven days after the Electra had landed, a Japanese fishing boat arrived at the island and took Amelia and Noonan aboard, transferring them either to the seaplane tender *Kamoi* or the survey ship *Koshu*. They were taken first to Jaluit, then to Kwajalein, and finally to Japanese military headquarters in Saipan for questioning.

"Death may have been a release they both desired," Goerner said on the final page of his best-selling *The Search for Amelia Earhart*. The frontispiece was a photograph of Amelia sitting on the running board of a car with a Japanese driver. The caption said pointedly that the photograph had been among the effects of a captured Japanese officer during the 1944 invasion. The photograph was later identified, however, as having been taken before Amelia's round-the-world flight; the driver was employed by Standard Oil and the bracelet Amelia is wearing in the photograph (the elephant-hoof bangle with silver insets) is part of the Ninety-Nines' collection.[8]

After the Goerner book came a whole crop of theories. Marines Everett Hansen and Billy Burks, who were on Saipan in 1944, claim that under the command of a Captain Griswold they excavated a grave. The remains of two bodies were taken away by Captain Griswold. When Burks and Hansen asked what it was all about, Griswold is said to have winked and said mysteriously, "Did you ever hear about Amelia Earhart?"[9]

Donald Kothera had seen a civilian plane without its engines in a canyon on Saipan in 1946. With a friend, Joe Davidson, he returned to the island in 1967 and interviewed islanders who claim that they remember seeing Amelia and Noonan there in 1937. The result was a book entitled *Amelia Earhart Returns from Saipan.*[10]

Many people who set out to prove that Amelia was captured and died in Japanese hands contacted Amy. For the old lady, the possibility that her daughter had died in the service of her country was a more palatable explanation to Amelia's disappearance than that Amelia had simply gotten lost and run out of fuel. Amy told newsmen in 1949 that she believed Amelia to have been on a mission for the U.S. government: "Amelia said there were things she couldn't tell me. . . ." There were always things Amy could not be told prior to one of Amelia's record-breaking flights, however, and the reason was that Amelia could not rely on her mother not to reveal her plans.

Perhaps one of the most bizarre episodes of all was based on genuinely detailed and well-assembled initial research by Joe Gervais, from which he produced a manuscript called *Operation Earhart.* Like Goerner, Gervais maintained that Amelia was a spy whose mission had been to fly over Truk and the Marshalls to photograph them, and was then to "get lost" on Canton Island. He had first tried to visit Saipan in 1960, but unlike Goerner (who was an accredited pressman), he could not get permission. Instead, he went to Guam and questioned natives who had formerly lived on Saipan. He continued his research for six years, but when Goerner's book was published, it was scornful of Gervais's work (surely a somewhat hostile act toward a fellow author and contemporary researcher), which temporarily hampered Gervais because he lost a great deal of credence. This did not deter him, however, but his research now deviated from its former sound basis.

In 1965 while lunching on Long Island, Gervais met a woman who was wearing an oak-leaf decoration that can only be worn by holders of the American Distinguished Flying Cross. Gervais thought that she looked exactly as Amelia Earhart would have looked had she survived. He spoke to the woman, Irene Bolam, and she told him in conversation that she belonged to the Ninety-Nines and Zonta. After a complicated calculative process, Gervais concluded that the woman *was* Amelia Earhart, who had survived the flight, having successfully accomplished her spy mission. However, Gervais claimed, she had wished to opt out of her former high-powered life, so the government had secretly brought her back to the United States and given her a new identity.

She (Amelia, according to Gervais) later married, and a key factor in Gervais's new theory was that the letters in her husband's name (Guy Bolam) could be made to represent each of the eight islands of the Phoenix Group. Furthermore, this produced a code that equated to the correct coordinates of Hull Island (Gull Island being the Pacific Island where Toni Carter, heroine of *Flight for Freedom*, was supposed to "get lost." The coincidence was too much for Mr. Gervais to accept). Despite evidence from Mrs. Bolam's friends, such as aviatrix Viola Gentry, who had known both Mrs. Bolam *and* Amelia Earhart in 1928, Gervais insisted that no records (pilot's license, etc.) of Mrs. Bolam existed prior to 1937.

Gervais was even more convinced when he found photographs of an Electra 10E bearing the registration number NR16020, which had crashed in the mountains in California. He maintained that Amelia had never taken the Electra 10E on her round-the-world flight, that she had actually flown a larger military version called the Lockheed XC–35, which had supercharged engines. This plane had a cruising range of forty hours and a speed in excess of 200 mph and was test flown in May 1937. This, Gervais maintained, was the real reason for Amelia's crash in Hawaii on the first attempt, so that the XC–35 could be substituted when the original Electra was being rebuilt at Lockheed.

After a book written by Joe Klaas (who had worked with Gervais for some years on the story) called *Amelia Earhart Lives* was published in 1970, Mrs. Bolam had to sue Gervais to stop his harassment of her in a multi-million dollar suit. One of the pictures in his book showed Amelia in Japanese dress being served with tea and it was hinted that this was evidence of her temporary capture; but the picture concerned was taken in Hawaii prior to her solo transpacific flight when she was staying in a house full of Japanese servants. The airplane with the same number as Amelia's Electra was a sister ship bought by Paul Mantz after the war; he had obtained permission to use Amelia's old registration. Only one Lockheed

XC–35 was ever built and it was in a museum in the United States when Gervais wrote his book, so it could not have been shot down over a Pacific Island as he claimed.[11]

And so it went on, the Earhart Legend. Subsequent books on the subject tended to use what was known and build on it, so they were less subject to the traps and pitfalls suffered by earlier writers. Among the more credible is one by Vincent Loomis, *Amelia Earhart—The Final Story;* and his theory about where the Electra landed is shared by Oliver Knaggs in *Amelia Earhart—Her Last Flight.* Both writers believe that after failing to locate Howland, Amelia turned and headed for the Gilbert Islands, but a navigational error put her over the Marshalls, where the Electra landed in a lagoon at Mili Atoll. From here, the fliers were taken by the Japanese to Saipan, where Fred was executed after throwing a bowl of food into the face of his guard and where Amelia died of dysentery.

Paul Mantz and Muriel Morrissey were each concerned enough by the crop of stories to write to Eleanor Roosevelt. Both received her personal assurance that Amelia was not involved in a government mission.[12] Senior Japanese officers who were stationed in the Marianas and the Marshalls, and who would have known if two American fliers had been captured, have been interviewed. Having served prison terms for their part in war crimes, they have nothing to fear from confession at this point and yet they still profess to know nothing. The Japanese have steadfastly denied all claims that Amelia was in their custody since the war ended. However, if they had captured her and suspected her of spying, would they not have used this as a propaganda weapon against the United States, leveling an accusation of espionage?

Yet there is such a wealth of evidence from islanders who claim to have seen two white fliers (many say one was a woman, but not all), both in the Marshall Islands and Saipan, before the war that it would be irresponsible to dismiss it out of hand. Serious discrepancies exist, however, between the verbal evidence of eyewitnesses in the various books where testimony has been presented, and sometimes even within the same narrative. The Electra has been "seen" crashing in the sea off several different islands, but turning up intact in another. It has also been witnessed in a series of different locations, sometimes as a wreck, sometimes only slightly damaged; and it has also been seen as it was destroyed by the U.S. Army. Amelia has been summarily executed on landing in some stories, and has been incarcerated in a jail according to other witnesses. Sometimes witnesses claimed that she was not jailed but lived in semicaptivity in a hotel, free to come and go within a limited area. Most witnesses, though, say that the woman flier died of dysentery. Many were shown photographs of Amelia with the question "Was this the woman?" The answer was invariably "Yes."

There were even claims that Amelia may have been Tokyo Rose, the wartime woman disc jockey who beguiled Pacific-based American troops. Tokyo Rose had a marked American (New York) accent and it is not impossible to imagine some Seabee remarking idly that it must be Amelia Earhart. Laughable as this may seem, George once made a special trip to the front lines to listen to a Tokyo Rose broadcast in order to confirm that the voice was *positively not* Amelia's.

With so many eyewitnesses (the number seems to grow each year despite the passing of time), it must be assumed that there probably were two white fliers on Saipan and/or the Marshalls before the war. Whether these two fliers were Amelia Earhart and Fred Noonan is open to serious doubt.

No *hard* evidence has ever been found or presented, in spite of countless thousands of research hours in American and Japanese military archives, and after millions of words have been written on the subject by scores of authors, to prove that Amelia and Noonan survived an emergency landing in the ocean in the vicinity of Howland Island.

As stated in a previous chapter, the theory that Amelia was a spy is now almost dead. The welter of documents released by the U.S. government and those available in the Roosevelt Library at Hyde Park must convince all but the most cynical researcher that there was no covert operation involved in Amelia's disappearance. Apart from anything else, Amelia's flight over the area concerned in these theories would have been at night, yet Amelia had no equipment available for nighttime photography. Much of the credit for exploding the spy theory must go to Dick Strippel for a highly readable and technically laudable book, *Amelia Earhart—The Myth and the Reality,* published in 1972. Even Fred Goerner now agrees that Amelia was not a spy, but like many others, he is convinced that Amelia ended up in the hands of the Japanese.[13]

Appendix D: Chronology of Important Events in Amelia Earhart's Life

Age on July 24	Year	
	1897	Amelia Mary Earhart, first child of Edwin and Amy Otis Earhart, is born (July 24) in Atchison, Kansas.
11	1908	Amelia sees her first airplane, at the Iowa State Fair.
21	1918	Amelia becomes a nurse at Spadina Military Convalescent Hospital in Toronto, Canada.
22	1919	Returns to the United States to live with her sister and mother in Massachusetts. Enrolls in fall as medical student at Columbia University.
23	1920	Leaves Columbia University after one semester. Joins parents who are living in Los Angeles. Meets Sam Chapman. Takes first flight with Frank Hawks.
24	1921	Takes flying lessons from Neta Snook and buys first airplane (Kinner Airster).
25	1922	Sets unofficial women's altitude record of 14,000 feet.
26	1923	Becomes engaged to Sam Chapman.
27	1924	Amy and Edwin Earhart separate and begin divorce proceedings. Amelia sells Kinner Airster and buys automobile in which she drives her mother from California to Massachusetts, where they settle with Muriel.
29	1926	Becomes social worker at Denison House.

Age on July 24	Year	
30	1927	Receives call from Captain H. H. Railey, who later asked if she would like to be the first woman to fly across the Atlantic. Writes Ruth Nichols regarding forming an organization for women who fly.
31	1928	Becomes first woman to cross Atlantic by air, as a passenger (June 17–18). Buys Avro Avian airplane. Writes *20 Hrs. 40 Min.* Announces that her engagement to Sam Chapman is ended. Makes first solo-return transcontinental flight by a woman (September–October).
32	1929	Acquires Lockheed Vega and competes in first Women's Air Derby (Santa Monica, California, to Cleveland, Ohio), taking third place. George Palmer Putnam and his wife, Dorothy, separate.
33	1930	Becomes first president of the Ninety-Nines, the first women pilots' organization. Joins Ludington Lines airline as vice-president. Edwin Earhart dies of cancer. George Putnam's divorce becomes final. Amelia sets women's speed record of 181.18 mph over a three-kilometer course (July). Acquires transport license (October).
34	1931	Amelia marries George Putnam (February 7). Acquires an autogiro and achieves altitude record for autogiro of 18,451 feet (April), then becomes first person to make solo-return transcontinental flight in an autogiro (May–June).
35	1932	Writes *The Fun of It.* Becomes first woman (and only the second person) to fly the Atlantic solo, and the first person to cross the Atlantic twice by air (May 20–21, the fifth anniversary of Charles Lindbergh's transatlantic flight). Sets women's record for fastest non-stop transcontinental flight (Los Angeles to Newark, New Jersey) in 19 hours and 5 minutes (August). Receives the following awards:

- Distinguished Flying Cross, given by the U.S. Congress;
- The Cross of Knight of the Legion of Honor, given by the French government;

Age on July 24	Year	

- Gold Medal of the National Geographic Society, presented to Amelia by President Herbert Hoover;
- Honorary membership in the National Aeronautic Association.

Wins the Harmon Trophy as America's Outstanding Airwoman.

36	1933	Visits the White House as guest of the Roosevelts. Participates in National Air Races in Cleveland, Ohio. Breaks own transcontinental record in time of 17 hours, 7 minutes, and 30 seconds. Wins the Harmon Trophy.
37	1934	Wins the Harmon Trophy for the third year in a row.
38	1935	Becomes first person to fly solo across the Pacific Ocean from Honolulu, Hawaii, to Oakland, California (2,408 miles), in 17 hours and 7 minutes (January 11–12). Becomes first person to fly solo from Los Angeles to Mexico (April), by official invitation of the Mexican government. After record-breaking return flight from Mexico City to Newark, New Jersey, Amelia is mobbed by welcoming crowds. Named America's Outstanding Airwoman by Harmon Trophy committee. Competes in National Air Race with Paul Mantz.
39	1936	Takes delivery of Lockheed twin-engined airplane termed the "Flying Laboratory," which was financed by Purdue University (July). Starts planning round-the-world flight.
39	1937	First leg of round-the-world flight (Oakland, California, to Honolulu, Hawaii) sets record for east-west crossing in 15 hours and 47 minutes (March 17). Amelia ground loops while taking off for Howland Island (March 20), and airplane is badly damaged. Airplane is repaired and a second attempt at world flight begins from Miami, Florida, on June 1, 1937. On July 2, after completing 22,000 miles of the flight, Amelia and her navigator, Fred Noonan, take off from Lae, New Guinea, for Howland Island. Several radio contacts are subsequently made but neither the airplane nor the fliers are ever seen again.

Glossary

Altimeter:	Instrument that indicates the altitude of an airplane in flight.
Azimuth:	An arc of the horizon, normally measured clockwise from the north.
Barnstorm:	Pioneer aviators used to travel around the country, carrying fare-paying passengers on local pleasure flights. Usually they operated out of farm fields. This was known as barnstorming.
Bubble sight:	A sextant observation in which a bubble floating in liquid is used instead of the horizon.
Dead-stick landing:	An airplane making a landing when the propeller has ceased turning (or when it is still turning but the engine has stopped) is said to be making a dead-stick landing.
Dolly:	A wheeled cart, placed under a tail skid (in the days before tail wheels) to assist in moving the airplane on the ground.
Dope:	A tautening agent used on fabric airplane surfaces, it is painted onto the fabric to make it drumskin tight and impenetrable by wind and weather.
Drift:	The sideways angle of movement of an airplane in relation to the ground, caused by crosswinds.
Drift indicator:	An instrument for determining drift. This was accomplished by sighting an object on the ground along the wires of a grid incorporated in the instrument.
Great circle:	The shortest distance between any two points on a hemisphere.

Glossary

Ground loop:	An uncontrollable turn by an aircraft while it is rolling over the ground at a speed too low for the rudder to be effective.
Ground speed:	The speed of an airplane relative to the ground. This will be affected by wind speed to give airspeed.
Line of position:	A straight line obtained by plotting on a chart a sextant observation of a celestial body. An accurate line of position passes through the point of observation. The intersection of two lines of position, with compensation for the time difference between the first and second sightings, establishes a position on the earth's surface.
Pancake:	To hit the ground too hard after leveling off too high for a proper landing.
Stall:	The condition of an airplane that has lost the airspeed necessary to maintain forward flight or control.
Sun line:	A line of position obtained from a sextant observation of the sun.
Variation:	The difference in angle in a compass reading between true north and magnetic north.

Notes

Abbreviations used in the Notes are as follows:

AE for Amelia Earhart
AOE for Amy Otis Earhart
BL for Butler Library, Columbia University, New York, New York
GPP for George Palmer Putnam
SL for Schlesinger Library, Radcliffe College, Cambridge, Massachusetts

PROLOGUE

1. Southampton *Daily Echo,* June 19, 1928.
2. Ibid.
3. Ibid.
4. Amelia Earhart, "Lucky Turning Point," in New York *Herald Tribune,* date unknown.
5. George Palmer Putnam, "Amelia's Career Described," in Providence *Sunday Journal,* Sept. 19, 1937.

ONE. 1897

1. History of Altman Family, Ref: A129, folder 2(d), SL.
2. Ibid.
3. A brief History of Earhart Ancestors, Ref: A129, folder 2(a), SL.
4. Ref: A129, folders 2(a) and 2(d), SL.
5. Ref: A129, folder 2(a), SL.
6. Ibid.
7. Genealogy of Isaac Otis, His Family and Descendants (29 sheets), Ref: A129, folder 1, SL.

Notes

8. Ref: Amy Otis Earhart, Oral History Collection, BL.
9. A. T. Andreas, *History of State of Kansas* (Chicago: privately published, 1883), p. 396.
10. Reference is specifically to settler George Million. Information from article entitled "Early Atchison," Atchison County Library, Local History Collection, Atchison, Kansas.
11. From "Early Atchison."
12. Information from "Happenings in 1858," Atchison County Library, Local History Collection.
13. Information is from general file, Atchison County Library, Local History Collection.
14. Ref: Amy Otis Earhart, Oral History Collection, BL.
15. A. T. Andreas, *History*, p. 396.
16. Atchison *Globe*, Apr. 27, 1905.
17. Ref: Amy Otis Earhart, Oral History Collection, BL.
18. Ibid. Family legend has it that each time another child arrived, the judge built on another room.
19. A. T. Andreas, *History*, p. 396.
20. Ref: Amy Otis Earhart, Oral History Collection, BL.
21. Ibid. In her second recorded interview, Amy states that she satisfied the entrance requirements for Wellesley College.
22. Ibid.
23. Muriel Earhart Morrissey, *Courage Is the Price* (Wichita, Kansas: McCormick-Armstrong, 1963). Hereafter referred to as *Courage*.
24. Ref: Amy Otis Earhart, Oral History Collection, BL.
25. Ibid.
26. Baptismal Register: Trinity Episcopal Church, Atchison, Kansas. Also, the Atchison *Globe*, July 27, 1897.
27. Ref: Amy Otis Earhart, Oral History Collection, BL.

TWO. 1897–1914

1. Jean L. Backus, *Letters from Amelia* (Boston: Beacon Press, 1982), p. 18; Muriel Earhart Morrissey, *Courage*, pp. 80–81.
2. Ibid.
3. Morrissey, *Courage*, p. 27. Letter dated May 12, 1903.
4. Author's interview with Mrs. Muriel Morrissey, West Medford, Massachusetts, June 1987.
5. Amelia Earhart, *The Fun of It* (New York: Brewer, Warren & Putnam, 1932), p. 11. Hereafter referred to as *Fun*.
6. Ibid, p. 12; see also Ref: Amy Otis Earhart, Oral History Collection, BL.
7. Atchison *Globe*, special edition, June 21, 1963.
8. Ref: Amy Otis Earhart, Oral History Collection, BL.

9. Backus, *Letters*, p. 15.
10. Ref: Amy Otis Earhart, Oral History Collection, BL.
11. Mrs. M. O. O'Keefe, Atchison *Globe*, July 21, 1963.
12. Morrissey, *Courage*, p. 52.
13. Mrs. M. O. O'Keefe, Atchison *Globe*, July 21, 1963.
14. Earhart Collection, Atchison Museum, Atchison, Kansas.
15. Backus, *Letters*, p. 18.
16. Ref: 83–M69, SL.
17. Letter from Helen Rogers to AE, June 30, 1932, Ref: 83–M69, SL.
18. Ref: Amy Otis Earhart, Oral History Collection, BL.
19. Morrissey, *Courage*, p. 78.
20. Ibid.
21. Backus, *Letters*, p. 20.
22. Letter from Mather, Rock Island Lines, dated Dec. 5, 1912, Ref: 83–M69, SL.
23. Ref: Amy Otis Earhart, Oral History Collection, BL.
24. Ibid.
25. Backus, *Letters*, p. 18.
26. Ref: 83–M69, SL.
27. Morrissey, *Courage*, p. 88.

THREE. 1914–1920

1. Los Angeles *Times*, June 19, 1928, "Dad Proud . . . ," p. 2.
2. Morrissey, *Courage*, p. 96.
3. Ibid.
4. Backus, *Letters*, p. 22.
5. Morrissey, *Courage*, p. 99.
6. AE to AOE, dated Saturday (March 1917), Ref: 83–M69, SL.
7. AE to AOE, dated Tuesday (July 31, 1917), Ref: 83–M69, SL.
8. AE to AOE, dated Aug. 14, 1917, Ref: 83–M69, SL.
9. AE to AOE, dated Aug. 8, 1917, Ref: 83–M69, SL.
10. AE to AOE, dated Aug. 14, 1917, Ref: 83–M69, SL.
11. Ref: Amy Otis Earhart, Oral History Collection, BL.
12. AE to AOE, Nov. (undated) 1917, Ref: 83–M69, SL.
13. Two letters from AE to AOE, dated Oct. 31 and Nov. (undated) 1917, Ref: 83–M69, SL.
14. AE to AOE, Nov. 1917, Ref: 83–M69, SL.
15. Bill for school fees from Ogontz School for Girls, dated June 11, 1917, Ref: 83–M69, SL.
16. Earhart, *Fun*, p. 19.
17. Ibid.
18. Ibid, p. 20.

19. Ibid.
20. Letter from AE to Kenneth Merrill, written from Northampton, Massachusetts, Dec. 26, 1918, Ref: 84–M21, SL.
21. Earhart, *Fun*, p. 21.
22. Letter from AE to Kenneth Merrill, March 13, 1919, Ref: 84–M21, SL.
23. Earhart, *Fun*, p. 21.
24. Ibid.
25. Pilots licenses; registration cards at BL and SL.
26. Letter from AE to AOE, no date, probably Sept. 1919, Ref: 83–M69, SL.
27. Earhart, *Fun*, p. 23.
28. Muriel Morrissey and Carole Osborne, *Amelia, My Courageous Sister* (Santa Clara, California: Osborne Publishers, 1988).
29. Neta Snook Southern, *I Taught Amelia to Fly* (New York: Vantage Press, 1974), p. 104. Hereafter referred to as *I Taught*.

FOUR. 1920–1921

1. These were not enacted until the administration of his successor, Franklin D. Roosevelt.
2. Morrissey, *Courage*, p. 119.
3. Earhart, *Fun*, p. 24.
4. Ibid.
5. Amelia Earhart, *20 Hrs. 40 Min.* (New York: G. P. Putnam's Sons, 1929), p. 46. Hereafter referred to as *20 Hrs.*
6. Operated by Emery Rogers, this was the first commercial field in Los Angeles. It was located west of Wilshire Blvd.
7. Earhart, *Fun*, p. 25.
8. Ibid.
9. Ibid.
10. Southern, *I Taught*, pp. 92–95.
11. Ibid, p. 92.
12. Ibid, p. 95.
13. George Putnam, *Soaring Wings* (New York: Harcourt, Brace and Company, 1939), p. 44. Hereafter referred to as *Soaring*.
14. Southern, *I Taught*, p. 1.
15. Morrissey, *Courage*, p. 102.
16. Southern, *I Taught*, pp. 105–106.
17. Earhart, *Fun*, pp. 25–26.
18. Southern, *I Taught*, p. 106.
19. Ibid, p. 110.
20. Ibid.
21. Ibid.
22. Ibid, p. 112.

23. Ibid, pp. 121–122.
24. Ibid, p. 122.
25. Earhart, *20 Hrs.*, p. 66.
26. Ibid, p. 67.
27. Earhart, *Fun*, p. 27.
28. According to Neta Snook Southern's logbook, she gave Amelia five hours of instruction in the Canuck and fifteen hours in the Kinner Canary. Further hours were required with John Montijo before Amelia went solo. A good average for students is reckoned to be (and was then) twelve hours.
29. This airplane was the first of the DC aircraft, had a fifty-six-foot wingspan, a twelve-cylinder Liberty engine, and was the first airplane to carry its own weight as a payload.
30. Southern, *I Taught*, p. 126.
31. Ibid.
32. Interview with Neta Snook Southern, *News Press*, St. Joseph, Missouri, Feb. 20, 1977.
33. Earhart, *20 Hrs.*, p. 76.
34. *American Magazine*, Aug. 1932, p. 72.
35. Earhart, *20 Hrs.*, p. 56.

FIVE. 1921–1927

1. *American Magazine* (no date but probably late 1928), p. 72; AE's scrapbooks at Purdue University, West Lafayette, Indiana.
2. Elgen and Marie Long's taped interview with Lloyd Royer, Los Angeles, California.
3. *American Magazine*, op. cit., p. 72.
4. *American Magazine*, August 1932, p. 15.
5. Long/Royer interview.
6. Letter from AE to Lloyd Royer, Oct. 5, 1921; and taped interview Long/Royer. Courtesy of Marie and Elgen Long.
7. Los Angeles *Examiner*, Aug. 8, 1922.
8. This record does not appear in official archives. Ruth Law had already reached fourteen thousand some years earlier, but as there were no separate classifications for women's records and they had not exceeded the altitude achieved by men, such attempts and achievements were regarded as unofficial.
    Many such unofficial women's records (recognized by the aviation fraternity) were set until the first officially recorded woman's altitude was set by Louise Thaden in December 1928 when she reached 20,260 feet.
9. Earhart, *20 Hrs.*, pp. 80–81.
10. Amelia was later to claim, incorrectly, that this was the first license issued to an American woman.

Notes

11. Letters to the author from AE's cousins Ann Cain Tibbetts and Doryce McKelvy.
12. Long/Royer interview.
13. John Underwood, *Madcaps, Millionaires and "Mose"* (Glendale, California: Heritage Press, 1984; reproduction of official program is on back cover).
14. Earhart, *20 Hrs.*, pp. 85–86.
15. Long/Royer interview.
16. Long/Royer interview.
17. Student registration card at Columbia University.
18. Earhart, *Fun*, p. 48.
19. Putnam, *Soaring*, p. 47.
20. Earhart, *20 Hrs.*, p. 86.
21. Letter from Waldo Waterman (first vice-president of the Early Birds), April 19, 1962. Mr. Waterman was the subsequent owner of but had little use from the plane, as it suffered a broken crankshaft shortly after his purchase of it. NA&SM Library, Smithsonian Institution, Washington, D.C. Amelia Earhart General file: F0171300.
22. Earhart, *20 Hrs.*, p. 88.
23. Long/Royer interview.
24. AE to Lloyd Royer. Letter is in possession of Elgen and Marie Long, by whose kind permission it is reproduced here.
25. Earhart, *Fun*, p. 52.
26. Ibid.
27. 76 Brook Street, West Medford, Massachusetts.
28. Job application form, Denison House records, SL.
29. Their company, Montijo and Royer, was formed to build a five-passenger cabin biplane called *The California Coupe;* information courtesy of John Underwood.
30. Letter from AE to Lloyd Royer. NA&SM Library, Amelia Earhart General file: F0171300.
31. Women's Union files, Radcliffe College, Cambridge, Massachusetts.
32. Backus, *Letters*, p. 62.
33. Putnam, *Soaring*, p. 54.
34. *Christian Science Monitor* clipping (undated, but in 1928 scrapbook), front page.
35. Unidentified news clipping in AE's scrapbook, circa 1928, Purdue.
36. From AE to Bernard Wiesman, May 6, 1928, Purdue.
37. Earhart, *Fun*, pp. 59–60.

SIX. 1887–1909

1. George P. Putnam, *Wide Margins* (New York: Harcourt, Brace and Company, 1942), p. 3. Hereafter referred to as *Wide*.
2. Ibid, p. 3.

3. Ibid, p. 25.
4. Ibid, pp. 23–24.
5. Ibid, p. 7.
6. Ibid, p. 30.
7. Ibid, pp. 34–35.
8. Ibid, pp. 41–42.
9. Ibid, pp. 38–39.
10. Ibid, p. 38.
11. Matthew Baigell, *Dictionary of American Art* (London: John Murray, 1979).
12. Putnam, *Wide*, pp. 43–47.
13. Ibid, p. 45.
14. Ibid, p. 47.
15. GP to Harvard College, note dated March 17, 1908, Harvard College Archives (students' records), Cambridge, Massachusetts.
16. Putnam, *Wide*, p. 49.
17. Ibid.
18. Wellesley College (archives), Wellesley, Massachusetts. Class of 1910 biographical records and reunion books.
19. Theodore John Winthrop, *The Canoe and the Saddle* (1862).
20. Putnam, *Wide*, pp. 48–49.
21. Ibid, p. 49.

SEVEN. 1909–1915[*]

1. James LeRoy Crowell, *Frontier Publisher* (thesis, June 1966, Bend, Oregon), pp. 21–22. Hereafter referred to as *Frontier*.
2. Putnam, *Wide*, p. 51.
3. Ibid, pp. 51–52.
4. Ibid, p. 53.
5. Ibid.
6. GP stated in *Wide Margins*, apparently incorrectly, that there were 1,200 people in Bend, but Crowell points out that the federal census of 1910 lists 536 living in Bend. "The discrepancy lies in the statistics of the precinct

[*]Apart from the various newspapers cited for Chapters Seven through Nine, there are two main sources of information. One is GPP's own autobiography *Wide Margins;* the other is a thesis written in June 1966 by James LeRoy Crowell of Bend, Oregon, entitled *Frontier Publisher: A Romantic View of George Palmer Putnam's Career at the Bend Bulletin 1910–1914.* Mr. Crowell has most generously allowed me to use the results of his college research, his excellent thesis, and his scholarship.

of Deschutes, which had 616 residents [which] had been annexed to Bend."
Frontier Publisher, p. 53.

7. Crowell, *Frontier,* p. 50. The author makes the interesting point that three hundred dollars, in the days when a wholesome meal could be purchased at the hotel for thirty-five cents, gave Putnam a great advantage over the average newcomer to Bend in 1909.

8. Ibid, p. 52.

9. Ibid, p. 3.

10. Ibid, p. 75.

11. Bend *Bulletin,* Aug. 18, 1909.

12. Crowell, *Frontier,* p. 82.

13. Palmer Bend (pseudonym of George Palmer Putnam), *The Smiting of the Rock* (New York: G. P. Putnam's Sons, 1919).

14. Crowell, *Frontier,* p. 88.

15. Bend *Bulletin,* Feb. 16, 1910.

16. Crowell, *Frontier,* p. 90.

17. Bend *Bulletin,* March 16, 1910. However, Mr. Crowell states on p. 2 of his thesis that GP merely obtained a half-interest.

18. Putnam, *Wide,* p. 62.

19. Ibid.

20. Crowell, *Frontier,* pp. 95–96.

21. Wellesley College (archives), Class of 1910 biographical records and reunion books.

22. Pinelyn, 606 Congress Street, Bend, Oregon.

23. George Palmer Putnam, *In the Southland of North America* (New York: G. P. Putnam's Sons, 1913).

24. Bend *Bulletin,* Nov. 15, 1911.

25. Crowell, *Frontier,* p. 141.

26. Putnam, *Wide,* p. 65.

27. Ibid.

28. Ibid, p. 67.

29. Crowell, *Frontier,* pp. 145–146.

30. Putnam, *Wide,* pp. 54–55.

31. Ibid.

32. Ibid.

33. Crowell, *Frontier,* p. 151.

34. Putnam, *Wide,* p. 64.

35. Wellesley College (archives), Class of 1910 biographical records and reunion books.

36. Crowell, *Frontier,* p. 61.

37. Crowell, *Frontier,* p. 135.

38. Putnam, *Wide,* p. 68.

39. Ibid, pp. 55–56.

40. Wellesley College (archives), Class of 1910 biographical records and reunion books.
41. Crowell, *Frontier*, p. 194.
42. The *Portland Oregonian*, Nov. 28, 1914.
43. Crowell, *Frontier*, pp. 139–140.
44. Ibid.

EIGHT. 1915–1922

1. Putnam, *Wide*, p. 79.
2. Ibid.
3. Ibid.
4. Crowell, *Frontier*, p. 213.
5. Ibid, p. 214.
6. Honourable Discharge Papers of G. P. Putnam, Oregon National Guard, December 30, 1916.
7. Bend *Bulletin*, Sept. 6, 1916.
8. Crowell, *Frontier*, p. 217.
9. Putnam, *Wide*, p. 79.
10. Ibid.
11. Ibid, pp. 4, 10.
12. Ibid, p. 79.
13. Honourable Discharge from army, document dated Dec. 20, 1918.
14. *Who Was Who 1951–1960;* also Putnam, *Wide*, p. 14.
15. Crowell, *Frontier*, p. 223.
16. Putnam, *Wide*, p. 80.
17. *Ladies' Home Journal*, May 1, 1920, p. 41; *Collier's* magazine, June 5, 1920, p. 54.
18. Putnam, *Wide*, p. 94.
19. Ibid, p. 91.
20. The friend was a neighbor in Rye—Mrs. Caroline O'Day.
21. Putnam, *Wide*, p. 94.
22. Ibid, p. 164.
23. Editorial, *Publishers Weekly*, edition date unknown, 1921.
24. William J. Robinson, *Married Love and Happiness* (New York: Critic and Guide, 1922).
25. *The New York Times*, Aug. 5, 1922, p. 20.
26. Corey Ford, *The Time of Laughter* (Boston: Little, Brown, 1967). pp. 203–205. Hereafter referred to as *Time*.
27. Ibid.
28. Crowell, *Frontier*, p. 235.
29. Putnam, *Wide*, pp. 109–110.
30. Ibid, p. 153, and Putnam family tradition.

Notes

NINE. 1926–1928

1. Author's interview with Charles "Cap" Palmer, Los Angeles, California, June 1988.
2. Putnam, *Wide*, p. 252.
3. Ibid, p. 217.
4. *The New York Times*, Feb. 21, 1926, section IX, p. 7.
5. Formerly named the *Effie Morrisey*.
6. *The New York Times*, June 21, 1926, p. 1.
7. *Geographical Review* (The American Geographical Society of New York), vol. XVIII, no. 1, Jan. 1928, p. 4; and *The New York Times*, Feb. 21, 1926.
8. Dan Streeter, *An Arctic Rodeo* (New York: G. P. Putnam's Sons, 1929).
9. David Binney Putnam, *David Goes Voyaging* (New York: G. P. Putnam's Sons, 1925).
10. David Binney Putnam, *David Goes to Greenland* (New York: G. P. Putnam's Sons, 1927); and *David Goes to Baffin Land* (New York: G. P. Putnam's, 1928).
11. Putnam, *Wide*, pp. 252–253.
12. *The New York Times*, June 21, 1926, p. 1.
13. *The New York Times*, May 11, 1926, p. 3.
14. Streeter, *Arctic*, p. 226.
15. *The New York Times*, Aug. 19, 1926, p. 1.
16. *The New York Times*, Aug. 25, 1926, p. 4.
17. *The New York Times*, Sept. 25, 1926, pp. 1–3.
18. Putnam, *Wide*, p. 373.
19. *The New York Times*, Oct. 3, 1926, p. 20.
20. Expedition sponsors were James B. Ford and Frederick C. Waltcott of the American Geographical Society Council; W. F. Kenny of New York; Gustavus D. Pope of Detroit; George Grey Barnard of New York; the Museum of the American Indian; Heye Foundation; and the Buffalo Society of Natural Sciences. George Palmer Putnam, director of the expedition, underwrote the balance.
21. *The New York Times*, Sept. 11, 1927, p. 1.
22. Edward Jablonski, *Atlantic Fever* (New York: Macmillan, 1972), p. 294.
23. Walter S. Ross, *The Last Hero* (New York: Harper & Row, Publishers, Inc., 1964), p. 139.
24. Charles A. Lindbergh, *The Spirit of St. Louis* (New York: Charles Scribner's Sons, 1953), p. 504. Hereafter referred to as *Spirit*.
25. Putnam, *Wide*, pp. 231–232.
26. Lindbergh, *Spirit*, p. 547.
27. Putnam, *Wide*, p. 232.
28. *Geographical Review*, op. cit., p. 4.
29. Putnam, *Wide*, p. 234.
30. Ibid.

31. *Geographical Review*, op. cit., p. 4.
32. Lindbergh, *Spirit*, p. 547.
33. Putnam, *Wide*, p. 235.
34. Lindbergh, *Spirit*, p. 547.
35. Putnam, *Wide*, p. 235.
36. Ibid, p. 236.
37. Ibid, p. 233. Lindbergh eventually received about two hundred thousand dollars in royalties on sales of *We*.
38. Ibid, p. 237.
39. *Geographical Review*, op. cit., p. 4.
40. Richard Evelyn Byrd, *Skyward* (New York: G. P. Putnam's Sons, 1928). In recognition of his flight over the South Pole on Nov. 29, 1929, Byrd was promoted to the rank of Rear Admiral U.S.N. (Rtd.) by an Act of Congress.
41. Putnam, *Wide*, pp. 301–303; also Paul O'Neil, *Barnstormers and Speedkings* (New York: Time-Life Books, 1981).
42. *Time* magazine, Aug. 25, 1930.
43. Putnam, *Wide*, p. 236.
44. Ibid.

TEN. 1928: AMELIA MEETS GEORGE

1. Putnam, *Wide*, p. 293.
2. Hilton H. Railey, *Touched with Madness* (New York: Carrick & Evans, 1938), p. 100. Hereafter referred to as *Touched*.
3. Ibid.
4. Putnam, *Wide*, p. 293.
5. Ibid.
6. Railey, *Touched*, p. 101.
7. Putnam, *Wide*, p. 171.
8. Railey, *Touched*, p. 101.
9. Putnam, *Wide*, p. 294.
10. Railey, *Touched*, p. 103.
11. Ibid.
12. Ibid, p. 104.
13. Earhart, *20 Hrs.*, p. 100.
14. Ibid, p. 101.
15. Jablonski, *Atlantic*, p. 190; also *The New York Times*, July 2, 1929, obit of Wilmer Stultz.
16. Letter to author from Richard K. Smith (air historian) Nov. 22, 1987; and article by Richard S. Allen, *Air Britain Digest*.
17. Ibid.
18. Peggy Phipps Boegner, *Halcyon Days* (New York: Old Westbury Gardens/ Harry N. Abrams, Inc., 1986), p. 192. Hereafter referred to as *Halcyon*.

19. Ibid.
20. Frederick Guest: Highly decorated for war service, Freddie—as he was universally known—served as assistant private secretary to his cousin Winston Churchill (as Parliamentary Under-Secretary of State for Colonies, President of the Board of Trade, and latterly as Home Secretary); he then served in various key positions in the Treasury before becoming Secretary of State for Air and president of the Air Council.
21. See various references in *Bror Blixen, The African Letters* (New York: St. Martin's Press, 1988).
22. Boegner, *Halcyon,* pp. 192–193.
23. Letter to the author from Mrs. Helen Ogston regarding her conversation with McCracken.
24. Amelia Earhart, "Lucky Turning Point," in New York *Herald Tribune,* undated clipping.
25. Miami *Herald,* May 22, 1937.
26. Amelia's career described by George Putnam in Providence *Sunday Journal,* Sept. 19, 1937.
27. *The Illustrated Love Magazine* interview with Amelia Earhart, Jan. 1932, pp. 25–27, courtesy of Special Collections Library, Purdue University, West Lafayette, Indiana, Ref: AE's scrapbooks.
28. Ibid.
29. Morrissey and Osborne, *Amelia,* p. 78.

ELEVEN. 1928: BEFORE THE FLIGHT

1. Ford, *Time,* pp. 101–103; and Earhart, *20 Hrs.,* pp. 96–101.
2. Earhart, *20 Hrs.,* p. 101.
3. Amelia's diary entry for June, 1928. Amelia Earhart Collection 1061, Seaver Center for Western History Research, Natural History Museum of Los Angeles County, California.
4. Amelia's will dated May 20, 1928, ibid.
5. Railey, *Touched,* p. 103.
6. Purdue, Ref: I A.2.
7. Letters to the author from Richard S. Allen and Richard K. Smith.
8. Earhart, *20 Hrs.,* p. 100.
9. Ibid.
10. Ibid, p. 109.
11. Ibid.
12. Amelia's will dated May 20, 1928. Amelia Earhart Collection 1061, Seaver Center for Western History Research.
13. Ibid.
14. George Palmer Putnam found these two letters some months after Amelia's

disappearance, held together with a perished rubber band. Clipped to them was a note, "Popping off letters."

15. Earhart, *20 Hrs.*, p. 121.
16. *Spur* magazine, July 15, 1928, p. 39.
17. Anne Morrow Lindbergh, *Hour of Gold, Hour of Lead* (New York: Harcourt Brace Jovanovich, 1973), p. 121.
18. Julia Houston Railey, "Amelia Earhart—Aviatrix," in Boston *Evening Post* (exact date unknown, 1928).
19. Putnam, *Soaring*, p. 58.
20. Author's interview with Charles "Cap" Palmer, Los Angeles, California, June 1988.
21. Letter to the author from Richard K. Smith.
22. Earhart, *20 Hrs.*, p. 131.
23. Amelia's diary entry for June 3, 1928. Amelia Earhart Collection 1061, Seaver Center for Western History Research.
24. *Lantern*, July–August 1928.
25. Amelia Earhart, "The Man Who Tells the Flyers: Go!" in Hearst's International *Cosmopolitan*, May 1929.
26. *Spur* magazine, July 15, 1928, p. 39.
27. Ibid.
28. Earhart, *20 Hrs.*, p. 165.
29. Amelia's diary. Amelia Earhart Collection 1061, Seaver Center for Western History Research.
30. Western Union Cable from GPP to Wilmer Stultz, June 12, 1928, Purdue, Ref: I.B.
31. Letter to the author from Richard K. Smith.
32. Jablonski, *Atlantic*, p. 206.
33. *Time* magazine, June 18, 1928.
34. Amelia's diary entry for June 11, 1928. Amelia Earhart Collection 1061, Seaver Center for Western History Research.
35. Earhart, *20 Hrs.*, pp. 165–166.
36. Cable dated June 12, 1928, Purdue, Ref: I.B.
37. Cable dated June 13, 1928, 1 P.M., Ibid.
38. Ibid.
39. Amelia's diary entry for June 13, 1928. Amelia Earhart Collection 1061, Seaver Center for Western History Research.
40. Earhart, *20 Hrs.*, pp. 1, 66.
41. Cable dated June 13, 1928, 5 P.M., Purdue, Ref: I.B (1928).
42. Cable dated June 13, 1928, 10:30 P.M., Purdue, Ref: I.A3 (1928).
43. Purdue, Ref: I.B13 (1928).
44. Letter to the author from Richard K. Smith.
45. Cable; Putnam/Earhart in Purdue archives, Ref: I.B (1928), Atlantic Flight file.
46. Putnam, *Soaring*, pp. 64–65.

Notes

47. Amelia's diary entry for June 16, 1928. Amelia Earhart Collection 1061, Seaver Center for Western History Research.
48. Putnam, *Soaring*, p. 65.
49. Earhart, *20 Hrs.*, p. 170; see also Amelia's diary entries for June 16 and 17, 1928. Amelia Earhart Collection 1061, Seaver Center for Western History Research.
50. Putnam, *Soaring*, p. 65.
51. Letter to the author from Richard K. Smith.
52. Earhart, *20 Hrs.*, p. 170.
53. Ibid, p. 171.

TWELVE. 1928: THE TRANSATLANTIC FLIGHT

1. Los Angeles *Times*, June 18, 1928, p. 2.
2. *The New York Times*, June 18, 1928, p. 1.
3. Earhart, *20 Hrs.*, pp. 171–176.
4. Ibid, p. 182.
5. Ibid, p. 187; see also unidentified newspaper cutting in NA&SM Library, Smithsonian Institution, Washington, D.C., Amelia Earhart General file: F0171300.
6. English daily papers, June 19 and 20, 1928.
7. Earhart, *20 Hrs.*, p. 199.
8. Cyril Jeffries, *I Was There* (commemorative booklet by Burry Port Chamber of Commerce, May 1978).
9. Report of Amelia Earhart interview in Los Angeles *Times*, June 19, 1928, p. 2.
10. Amelia had taken up fencing the previous winter.
11. New York *Sun*, June 20, 1928.
12. Mr. Williams, resident of Burry Port, in unidentified newspaper cutting dated 1987: AE's scrapbooks at Special Collections Library, Purdue University, West Lafayette, Illinois.
13. Part of AE's log was reproduced in the program of a reception given by the city of Medford.
14. *The New York Times*, June 19, 1928, p. 1.
15. Los Angeles *Times*, June 18, 1928, p. 2.
16. Copy of original cable at Purdue, file I E.1.
17. Putnam, *Soaring*, p. 66.
18. *Southern Daily Echo*, June 19, 1928, p. 1.
19. New York *Sun*, June 20, 1928, p. 1.
20. Not traced; probably among the papers destroyed by fire at Whitney Portal in 1953 (see Chapter Twenty-two). Amelia's reply is at Purdue, file I E.I.
21. *Flight* magazine, editorial, June 21, 1928.
22. Lady Heath to AE, June 20, 1928 at Purdue, file I D.17.

23. *Daily Express*, June 25, 1928.
24. Ibid.
25. Unidentified cutting in AE's scrapbooks at Purdue. This speech was repeated several times after she returned to the United States; see specifically *The New York Times*, July 29, 1928.
26. Earhart, *20 Hrs.*, p. 209. Beryl Markham, who flew the Atlantic from east to west in 1936, said much the same thing after sailing back to England. She later told a friend that if she had any comprehension of the amount of water, she would never have made the flight.
27. Earhart, *Fun*, p. 87.
28. Unidentified cine-clipping in the author's collection.
29. Los Angeles *Times*, June 19, 1928, p. 2.
30. George Putnam told this story several times in newspaper articles, many years afterward. See also Morrissey, *Courage*, p. 167.
31. Cable to Porter Adams, July 9, 1928; NA&SM Library, Amelia Earhart General file: F0171300.
32. Letter from Clarence Young, Assistant Secretary for Aeronautics, to Porter Adams, dated Aug. 3, 1928, NA&SM Library, file F0171300.
33. Letter to Clarence Young from Porter Adams, NA&SM Library, file F0171300.
34. AE to Richard Byrd, July 1928; also Byrd's reply dated July 30, 1928, NA&SM Library, file F0171300.
35. *The New York Times*, July 31, 1928, p. 8.

THIRTEEN. 1928–1929

1. Earhart, *20 Hrs.*, p. 280.
2. AE to AOE, Aug. 12, 1928, Ref: 83–M69, SL.
3. AE to AOE, Aug. 26, 1928, Ref: 83–M69, SL.
4. Elinor Smith, *Aviatrix* (New York: Harcourt Brace Jovanovich, 1981), p. 135.
5. Earhart, *20 Hrs.*, p. 280.
6. Author's interview with Mrs. Jean-Marie Asp, San Diego, California, June 1988.
7. *The New York Times*, Sept. 1, 1928, p. 1.
8. Amelia's second diary. July–November, 1928. Amelia Earhart Collection 1061, Seaver Center for Western History Research, Natural History Museum of Los Angeles County, California.
9. Ibid.
10. Earhart, *Fun*, p. 91.
11. Putnam, *Soaring*, p. 79.
12. *The New York Times*, Oct. 1, 1928, p. 14.
13. *The New York Times*, Oct. 5, 1928, p. 27.

14. Putnam, *Soaring,* p. 81.
15. *The New York Times,* Nov. 23, 1928, p. 22.
16. Smith, *Aviatrix,* p. 70.
17. Ibid, p. 71.
18. Author's interviews with Elinor Smith Sullivan, Santa Clara, California, June 1987 and July 1988.
19. Putnam, *Wide,* pp. 286–287.
20. Donna Veca and Skip Mazzio, *Just Plane Crazy* (Santa Clara, California: Osborne Publishers, Inc.), p. 106.
21. GPP to Stephen Mather, Berkeley College Library, University of California at Berkeley, Special Collections, Mather file.
22. *The New York Times,* Dec. 26, 1928.
23. Smith, *Aviatrix,* p. 102.
24. Ibid, p. 103.
25. Ibid, pp. 93–94; and author's interviews with Elinor Smith Sullivan.
26. Ibid.
27. Ibid.
28. *The New York Times,* March 29, 1929, p. 16.
29. Extract from Amelia's second logbook, which began on July 20, 1929 and ended March 2, 1932; courtesy of Richard Sanders Allen. The logbook is in the possession of a collector in Culver City, California.
30. *The New York Times,* March 29, 1929: "Amelia Earhart is fourth woman to whom transport license is granted. Others are 1: Ruth Nichols; 2: Phoebe Omlie; 3: Lady Mary Heath . . . although other women hold 'limited commercial' licenses."
31. Harry Bruno, *Wings Over America* (New York: Halcyon House, 1942), p. 222.
32. *The New York Times,* July 1, 1929, p. 1.
33. *The New York Times,* July 16, 1929.
34. Amelia Earhart, "Afraid to Fly?" in *Cosmopolitan* magazine, July 1929.
35. Ibid.
36. Earhart, "Fly America First," in *Cosmopolitan* magazine, Oct. 1929.
37. Earhart, "Adventures Beneath the Sea," in *Cosmopolitan* magazine, Aug. 1929.
38. Many letters and phone calls between the author and freelance aviation researcher Mr. Peter Stevenson were needed before the hyperbole was recognized as such. At one point, Mr. Stevenson dared the author to duplicate AE's exit from a submarine. The author declined.
39. Earhart, *Fun,* p. 153.
40. Smith, *Aviatrix,* p. 108.
41. Ibid. Note: This interview between Elinor Smith and GP obviously occurred before the rule change. Originally, applicants had to be accompanied by a mechanic. A flood of entries from Hollywood actresses in partnership with qualified male-pilot "mechanics" resulted, in a transparent attempt to

obtain free publicity. Accordingly, the rules were changed and entrants had to fly the course solo.

42. Author's interviews with Elinor Smith Sullivan.

43. Ibid.

44. Earhart, *Fun,* pp. 152–153.

45. Yuma *Morning Sun,* Aug. 20, 1929, p. 1; see also *The New York Times* and New York *Sun,* Aug. 20, 21, 1929.

46. Earhart, *Fun,* pp. 153–154; see also *AAHS* magazine, Fall 1963 issue, pp. 223–224.

47. Judy Lomax, *Women of the Air* (New York: Dodd, Mead, 1986), pp. 55–57; and Veca and Mazzio, *Just Plane Crazy,* pp. 114–127.

48. Ibid.

49. Lomax, *Women,* p. 56.

50. *AAHS* magazine, Fall 1963.

51. Putnam, *Wide,* p. 287.

52. Smith, *Aviatrix,* p. 133.

53. Ibid, p. 134.

54. Ninety-Nines newsletter from AE to members, dated Jan. 19, 1932; Ninety-Nines archives, Oklahoma City, Oklahoma; also Library of Congress reading room: TL 501. N5.

55. Letter to the author from Mrs. Elinor Smith Sullivan, Nov. 29, 1988.

56. Ford, *Time,* p. 205.

57. *The New York Times,* Sept. 27, 1929, p. 11.

58. Cutting in AE's scrapbook for 1932, Special Collections Library, Purdue University, West Lafayette, Illinois; believed to be from *The Illustrated Love Magazine,* January 1932, pp. 25–27.

59. Author's interview with David Binney Putnam, Fort Pierce, Florida, June 1988.

60. Author's interview with Elinor Smith Sullivan, June 1988.

FOURTEEN. 1929–1931

1. *The New York Times,* Dec. 19, 1929.

2. *The New York Times,* March 21, 1930.

3. Maddux was a close friend of Lindbergh's and president of Maddux Airlines.

4. AE to AOE, Ref: 83–M69, SL.

5. Luke Christopher, secretary FAI to J. Mikrent, Directing Official of Speed Trial held in Los Angeles on Nov. 22, 1929.

6. *The New York Times* and *The Times* (London) covered this event in most issues between Dec. 30, 1930 and Jan. 4, 1931.

7. Author's interview with Charles "Cap" Palmer, Los Angeles, June 1988.

8. *The New York Times*, Jan. 30, 1930. The marriage took place in the West Indies on Jan. 12.
9. Both Amelia's sister, Muriel Morrissey, and the writer Jean Backus stated that George proposed six times to Amelia. See: Backus, *Letters*, p. 87; and Morrissey and Osborne, *Amelia*. George is on record as saying she refused him "twice, at least"; see Putnam, *Soaring*, p. 76. I was unable to find any original source for this information, which is now often quoted. It is possible that George told Muriel, but unfortunately she has been too ill recently to be interviewed again.
10. Putnam, *Wide*, p. 300.
11. Ibid.
12. *Time* magazine, Aug. 25, 1930, p. 39.
13. Edwin Earhart to AOE, April 19, 1930, Ref: 83–M69, SL.
14. From transcript of unidentified radio interview with Eugene Vidal: Vidal papers, University of Wyoming. Courtesy of Mrs. Kit Smith.
15. Letter from AE's secretary to F. Neely at the NAA, Dec. 2—NA&SM Library, Smithsonian Institution, Washington, D.C., Amelia Earhart General file: F0171300.
16. Backus, *Letters*, p. 93.
17. Putnam, *Soaring*, p. 79.
18. Ibid, p. 93.
19. AE to AOE; undated; addressed from A.W.A. Club House, 353 West 57th St., N.Y., N.Y., Ref: 83–M69, SL.
20. Putnam, *Soaring*, p. 76.
21. AE to AOE, Feb. 1930, Ref: 83–M69, SL.
22. AE to AOE, Feb. 25, 1930, Ref: 83–M69, SL.
23. Information, courtesy of Mr. Richard Sanders Allen. Note that courses were measured, for reasons of international competition, in meters. Amelia's speed record was subsequently converted to miles per hour.
24. *Publishers Weekly*, Aug. 30, 1930, p. 757.
25. Syndicated article in unidentified newspaper: from AE's scrapbook at Purdue University. In the first thirty days, the line carried 5,000 passengers, according to a letter she wrote her mother in Oct., Ref: 83–M69, SL.
26. The *Virginia Pilot*, Sept. 25, 1930, p. 1.
27. Amelia's passenger was Mr. Carl Harper.
28. AE to AOE, Oct. 2, 1930, Ref: 83–M69, SL.
29. Letter to the author from Mr. Richard Sanders Allen.
30. *The New York Times*, Nov. 10, 1930, p. 11.
31. *The New York Times*, Nov. 11, 1930, p. 27.
32. George Palmer Putnam, *André: The Record of a Tragic Adventure* (New York: G. P. Putnam's Sons, 1930).
33. AE to AOE, letters dated Dec. 31 and Jan. 19, 1931, Ref: 83–M69, SL.
34. AE to AOE, Feb. 4, 1931, Ref: 83–M69, SL.

35. Putnam, *Wide,* p. 282.
36. Putnam, *Soaring,* p. 77.
37. Ibid, p. 78.
38. AE to GP. Undated (but known to have been written on Saturday, Feb. 7, 1931). Amelia Earhart Collection 1061, Seaver Center for Western History Research, Natural History Museum of Los Angeles County, California. The letter was reproduced in the museum's quarterly, vol. 8, no. 1 (Summer, 1969) in "Itasca calling KHAQQ" by Russell E. Belous, Curator of Western History at the museum. For many years it was supposed that this letter had been destroyed in the fire at Lone Pine after George's death.
39. Author's interview with Mr. and Mrs. Charles "Cap" Palmer, Los Angeles, California, June 1988. Mr. Palmer was a close friend and colleague of GP's and his relationship is mentioned in latter chapters of this book.
40. Putnam, *Soaring,* p. 77.
41. Author's telephone interview with Gore Vidal, January 21, 1988.
42. *The New York Times,* Feb. 9, 1931, p. 1; and many other newspapers.
43. Unidentified Boston newspaper, Feb. 7, 1931. News clipping in AE's 1031 scrapbook, Purdue.
44. AE to AOE, Feb. 22, 1931, Ref. 83–M69, SL.
45. AE to AOE: ". . . Mrs. Putman is here (can't spell my own name!)"; see letter dated Sept. 16, 1933. Ref: 83–M69, SL.

FIFTEEN. 1931–1932

1. Putnam, *Soaring,* p. 81.
2. Frank Kingston Smith, *Legacy of Wings* (Northvale, N.J.: Aronson, 1981), p. 176.
3. Ibid, p. 183.
4. Ibid, p. 188.
5. Author's interview with David Binney Putnam, Fort Pierce, Florida, June, 1988.
6. *The New York Times,* June 20, 1931; also letter from AE to AOE, July 1931, Ref: 83–M69, SL.
7. AE to AOE, April 27, 1931; June 27, 1931; and July 1931; Ref: 83–M69, SL.
8. Cable to AE from Hiram Bingham, dated April 24, 1931: NA&SM Library, Smithsonian Institution, Washington, D.C., Amelia Earhart General file: F0171300.
9. AE to Mr. and Mrs. Oldham of Abilene, July 17, 1931, NA&SM Library, Amelia Earhart General file: F0171300.
10. Putnam, *Soaring,* p. 194.
11. AE to AOE, Sept. 17, 1931, Ref: 83–M69, SL.
12. AE to AOE, envelope postmarked Nov. 1931, Ref: 83–M69, SL.

Notes

13. AE to AOE, Dec. 1, 1931, Ref: 83–M69, SL.
14. Author's interviews with David Binney Putnam and Margaret Putnam Lewis, Fort Pierce, Florida, June 1988.
15. Letter to the author from Elspeth Huxley, Jan. 1988.
16. Author's interview with George Palmer Putnam, Jr., Boynton Beach, Florida, June 1988.
17. Letter to the author from Elspeth Huxley, Jan. 1988.
18. Cutting in AE's scrapbook for 1932, Special Collections Library, Purdue University, West Lafayette, Indiana; believed to be from *The Illustrated Love Magazine*, January 1932, pp. 25–27.
19. Putnam, *Soaring*, p. 160.
20. Ibid, p. 105.
21. Earhart, *Fun*.
22. Putnam, *Soaring*, pp. 97–98.
23. Ibid.
24. Organized by the American Society for the Promotion of Aviation.
25. Putnam, *Soaring*, pp. 98–99.
26. Letter to the author from Richard K. Smith, Nov. 22, 1987.
27. Putnam, *Soaring*, p. 102.
28. Bert Hinkler had flown the South Atlantic solo, in November 1931.
29. Earhart, *Fun*, p. 210.
30. Mary Heath, "Why I Believe Women Pilots Can't Fly the Atlantic," in *Liberty Magazine*, May 21, 1932, pp. 46–51.
31. Father of Major Edwin Aldrin, astronaut in crew of *Apollo XI;* second man to walk on the moon, in July 1969.
32. Earhart, *Fun*, p. 212.
33. Heath, "Why I Believe," pp. 46–51.
34. Ibid.
35. AE to AOE, May 4, 1932, Ref: 83–M69, SL.
36. Putnam, *Soaring*, pp. 102–103.
37. Loretta Gragg, Resource Center of the Ninety-Nines, Inc., Will Rogers Airport, Oklahoma City, Oklahoma, June 1987.
38. Earhart, *Last Flight* (New York: Harcourt Brace and Company, 1937), p. 17.
39. Amelia Earhart, "Women and Courage," in *Cosmopolitan* magazine, Sept. 1932.
40. Cable from AE to GP, May 19, 1932, Purdue, file III A.1.
41. Ibid, file III A.2.
42. Valerie Moolman, *Women Aloft* (Alexandria, Virginia: Time-Life Books, 1981).
43. Earhart, *Last Flight*, p. 18.
44. Earhart, *Fun*, pp. 212–214.
45. To GPP from "Parkes," May 20, 1932, Purdue, file III A.3.
46. Barographs were instruments commonly used to record the variances in height during flight. They were often sealed to prevent tampering, and used

on altitude record attempts and on flying tests to give an indication of the pilot's ability to maintain straight and level flight.

47. *The Times* (London), May 23, 1932.
48. *Yorkshire Post,* May 23, 1932.
49. Putnam, *Soaring,* p. 106.
50. Earhart, *Fun,* p. 217.
51. "The Society's Special Medal Award to Amelia Earhart," *National Geographic Magazine,* July 1932, pp. 358–367.

SIXTEEN. 1932–1933

1. There is a great deal of confusion about the actual time of this flight. The National Geographic Society, in its award to her, stated that the time was sixteen hours, twelve minutes. On examination, this confusion appears to have been caused because of the time zones; a misunderstanding of how British Summer Time (BST) works; and a correction for the time Amelia claimed to have spent (some fifteen minutes) circling the pasture before landing.

   She left Newfoundland at 7:12 P.M. local time, which equates to 11:12 P.M. BST, and landed at Culmore shortly before 2 P.M. BST on the following day.
2. In various reports, Mr. Gallegher is named James and Robert, while his surname is sometimes spelled Galagher or Gallagher. I have used Amelia's version.
3. Janet Mabie, "Conversations," from unidentified magazine, circa 1932. In AE's scrapbooks, Special Collections Library, Purdue University, West Lafayette, Indiana.
4. The *Sunday Mail,* May 22, 1932, p. 1.
5. Putnam, *Soaring,* p. 112.
6. "Mrs. Putnam's Four Wreaths of Laurel," in *The Literary Digest,* June 4, 1932, p. 5.
7. The pilot of the charter plane, I. W. C. MacKenzie, expressed his admiration of Amelia's flying when he saw the field in which she had landed. "With the Vega's high landing speed, it was no mean feat to bring the big airplane into such a limited space," he said.
8. Acknowledgment letter from AE to Mrs. Franklin Roosevelt, June 15, 1932, Ref: 83–M69, SL.
9. Cable from Mother and Muriel to AE (c/o G. P. Putnam's Sons), May 22, 1932, Purdue, file III(c)42.
10. AE to AOE (written from 4 St. James Square—Lady Astor's London house), June 2, 1932, Ref: 83–M69, SL.
11. GPP to AOE May 26, 1932, Ref: 83–M69, SL.

Notes

12. "Miss Earhart Tells the Prince All About It," in *Daily Express,* May 29, 1932.
13. Putnam, *Soaring,* p. 112.
14. Ibid.
15. Violette de Sibour was the daughter of Gordon Selfridge (owner of the famous London department store). The de Sibours became firm friends of the Putnams.
16. George Putnam, "Interview" in *American Weekly, Inc.,* 1933.
17. "Amelia Denies Flying Atlantic Takes Courage," in *Daily Tribune,* June 4, 1932.
18. G. C. Grey, "The Atlantic Again," in *The Aeroplane,* May 25, 1932, p. 924.
19. NAA files, May 8, 1932, NA&SM Library, Smithsonian Institution, Washington, D.C., Amelia Earhart General file: F0171300.
20. Putnam, *Soaring,* p. 117.
21. To AE from the Abbassade de Belgique, Washington, D.C., July 11, 1932, Purdue, file III G.2.
22. *Boston Evening Transcript,* June 20, 1932.
23. *Congressional Record,* June 20, 1932.
24. "Lesser Halves of Famous Wives," in *New York World Telegram,* Feb. 8, 1932.
25. G. P. Putnam, "The Forgotten Husband," *Saturday Review,* Dec. 1932.
26. Earhart, *Fun.*
27. AE to Hiram Bingham, June 29, 1932, NA&SM Library, Amelia Earhart General file: F0171300.
28. AE to Hiram Bingham, July 19, 1932, NA&SM Library, Amelia Earhart General file: F0171300.
29. Amelia had to return east for the official launch of a new automobile, the Essex "Terraplane."
30. Ruth Nichols's flying time had been thirteen hours, twenty-one minutes, but due to a delay in Wichita, her elapsed time was twenty-nine hours, one minute, forty-nine seconds.
31. Air Racing champion and the man who had piloted Amelia on her first flight.
32. *The New York Times,* July 13 (probably), 1932.
33. Associated Press report, July 13, 1932.
34. *Philadelphia Inquirer,* Oct. 6, 1932, p. 1.
35. Author's interview with Muriel Morrissey, West Medford, Massachusetts, June 1987.
36. *Morning Journal* (Marquette, Michigan), Oct. 25, 1932.
37. AE to AOE, Dec. 24, 1932, Ref: 83–M69, SL.
38. AE to AOE, letters dated Jan. 27 and Feb. 14, 1933, Ref: 83–M69, SL.
39. Ibid.

40. AE to AOE, April 20, 1933, Ref: 83–M69, SL.
41. Putnam, *Soaring,* pp. 123–124.
42. Letter to the author from Mr. Robert E. Lee.
43. Transcript of the Amelia Earhart Symposium held at NA&SM Library, Smithsonian Institution, Washington, D.C., 1983, Amelia Earhart General file: F0171300.
44. AE to Hiram Bingham, NA&SM Library, Amelia Earhart General file: F0171300.

SEVENTEEN. 1933–1935

1. *Screenland,* June 1983, pp. 29–30.
2. Ibid.
3. AE to AOE, June 8, 1933, Ref: 83–M69, SL.
4. AE to AOE, June 14, 1933, Ref: 83–M69, SL.
5. AE to AOE, July 4 (probably), 1933, Ref: 83–M69, SL.
6. New York *Sunday Mirror,* July 9, 1933, p. 1.
7. Author's interview with David Binney Putnam, Fort Pierce, Florida, June 1988.
8. Atchison Library, Atchison, Kansas, Amelia Earhart collection.
9. Letter from John H. Leh to Frederick Goerner, dated March 6, 1967, NA&SM Library, Amelia Earhart General file: F0171300.
10. It was later transferred to the National Air and Space Museum at the Smithsonian Institution, where it may be seen on permanent display.
11. Amelia Earhart, "Flying and Fly-Fishing," in *Outdoors,* Dec. 1934, pp. 16 ff.
12. Carl Dunrud, "Amelia Earhart in Wyoming," in *In Wyoming,* date unknown, circa 1970, p. 31.
13. Putnam, *Soaring,* p. 235.
14. *Oakland Tribune,* Jan. 3, 1935.
15. Backus, *Letters,* p. 158.
16. From transcript notes of unidentified radio interview with Eugene Vidal; Vidal papers; University of Wyoming, Laramie, Wyoming. Courtesy of Mrs. Kit Smith.
17. AE to AOE, Dec. 26, 1934, Ref: 83–M69, SL.
18. Nothing was ever found of C. P. T. Ulm, his crew, or airplane. John Williams, "Earhart Plan for Solo Hop Opposed," in Los Angeles *Times,* undated news clipping, Special Collections Library, Purdue University, West Lafayette, Indiana.
19. AE to AOE, Jan. 6, 1935, SL.
20. Amelia Earhart, "My Flight from Hawaii," in *National Geographic Magazine,* May 1935, pp. 593, 609.
21. Ibid.

22. George Palmer Putnam, "A Flyer's Husband," in *The Forum*, June 1935, pp. 330–332.
23. Various newspaper reports: specifically *Oakland Tribune*, Jan. 12, 1935, pp. 330–332.
24. Earhart, "My Flight from Hawaii," p. 596.
25. Putnam, "A Flyer's Husband," p. 330.
26. Ibid., pp. 330–332.
27. Ibid.
28. President Roosevelt to AE, Jan. 18, 1935, Purdue, file V B.1.
29. GP to AOE, Feb. 11, 1935, Ref: 83–M69, SL.
30. Cable from AE to AOE, undated, Ref: 83–M69, SL.
31. . . . *World Herald* [full title unreadable], Feb. 19, 1935.
32. Putnam, "A Flyer's Husband," pp. 330–332.
33. It was during Lindbergh's flight to Mexico that he met his future wife, Anne Morrow Lindbergh, daughter of his hosts.
34. Stamp value: twenty centavos.
35. George Palmer Putnam, "A Husband's Farewell to his Wife," in *North American Newspaper Alliance*, Sept. 1937.
36. Ibid.
37. AE to AOE (written on White House paper), March 4, 1935, Ref: 83–M69, SL.
38. AE to Eleanor Roosevelt, March 14, 1935, Purdue, file V B.2.
39. Eleanor Roosevelt to AE, March 1935, Purdue, file V B.3.
40. Putnam, *Soaring*, p. 220.
41. Earhart, *Last Flight*, p. 4.
42. "Mexico–New York Record Set by Miss Earhart," in *Oakland Tribune*, May 9, 1935.
43. GPP to Gene Vidal, June 3, 1935, Vidal papers, University of Wyoming, by kind permission of Mr. Vidal's widow.
44. AE to AOE, July 5, 1935, Ref: 83–M69, SL.
45. AE to AOE, July 28, 1935, Ref: 83–M69, SL.
46. Ruth Freehafer, *R. B. Stewart and Purdue University* (West Lafayette, Indiana: Purdue University Press, 1983).

EIGHTEEN. 1935–1937

1. Earhart, *Last Flight*, p. 46. By 1975, there were over twelve thousand women students at Purdue University.
2. A personal recollection of Amelia Earhart written by Helen Schleman, April 13, 1975. Also letter from Ms. Schleman to the author, Oct. 1988.
3. Special Collections Library, Purdue University, West Lafayette, Indiana, Amelia Earhart file XII A.3.
4. Putnam, *Soaring*, p. 228.

5. GPP to AOE, Nov. 26, 1935, Ref: 83–M69, SL.
6. *Brockton Daily Enterprise*, Dec. 11, 1935.
7. Don Dwiggins, *Hollywood Pilot* (New York: Doubleday, 1967), p. 95.
8. AE to AOE, Dec. 17, 1935, Ref: 83–M69, SL.
9. AE to GP, April 18, 1936, Purdue, unnumbered file.
10. AE to GP, November 25 (probably), 1936, Purdue, unnumbered file.
11. *Christian Science Monitor* (Boston), Jan. 25, 1936.
12. Los Angeles *Times*, March 3, 1936, p. 1.
13. Ibid.
14. GPP to AOE, March 4, 1936, Ref: 83–M69, SL.
15. AE to AOE, March 23, 1936, Ref: 83–M69, SL.
16. Terry Gwynn-Jones, *Magnificent Gamblers* (London: Orbis, 1981), pp. 79–86.
17. Ibid.
18. Boston *Globe*, March 18, 1937.
19. Freehafer, *R. B. Stewart*.
20. Ibid.
21. Letter to the author from R. B. Stewart, dated Nov. 22, 1987.
22. Freehafer, *R. B. Stewart*.
23. Draft of Associated Press Release by Foster Hailey, April 19, 1936.
24. The engines supplied to Amelia were the *civilian equivalent* of the engines specified for the military version of the Electra model 10E. There was nothing "special or secret" about them according to Lockheed files.
25. Morrissey and Osborne, *Amelia*, p. 178.
26. "Miss Earhart Makes Detailed Preparations for World Flight" in *Oakland Tribune*, March 7, 1937.
27. AE to AOE, April 1, 1936, Ref: 83–M69, SL.
28. AE to AOE, May 5 (probably), 1936, Ref: 83–M69, SL.
29. AE to AOE, long letter written in pencil and undated but probably late May or early June 1936, headed "Suggestions and Comments," Ref: 83–M69, SL.
30. The letter *R* designates Restricted use. Amelia had applied for a license covering "Long distance flights and research." At a later date, the U.S. license registration letter *N* would be added, viz: NR 16020.
31. Dwiggins, *Hollywood Pilot*, pp. 101–102; also author's conversations with the late Paul Mantz, circa 1962.
32. GP to Eleanor Roosevelt, June 1936, Purdue.
33. Letter from Eleanor Roosevelt's secretary to Richard Southgate, June 29, 1936, U.S. Navy archives.
34. Ibid.
35. GPP to Gene Vidal, August 3, 1936, Vidal papers, University of Wyoming, Laramie, Wyoming.
36. Ibid., August 11, 1936.
37. AE to Eleanor Roosevelt, cable dated Sept. 15, 1936, NA&SM Library,

Smithsonian Institution, Washington, D.C., Amelia Earhart General file: F0171300.

38. Ibid., cable dated Sept. 17, 1936.
39. AE to F. D. Roosevelt, November 5, 1935. Ref: 83–M69, SL.
40. Author's telephone interview with Gore Vidal, January 21, 1988.
41. Sundry letters in following collections: University of Wyoming; Purdue University; SL, Ref: 83–M69; NA&SM Library.
42. AE and GPP provided a loan to try to alleviate the financial problems and save the marriage.
43. Letters Oct. 1–14, 1936 between GPP and Captain A. G. Reid, U.S.N., U.S. Navy archives.
44. Generally accepted spelling for Tokyo in 1937. The new version was not generally adopted in the West until after the Second World War.
45. AE to President Roosevelt, Nov. 10, 1936, Purdue, file VII A.1.
46. Paul Bastedo to Chief of Naval Operations, Internal Memorandum, Oct. 16, 1936, U.S. Navy archives.
47. Memorandum regarding discussion between Mr. Miller of Air Commerce and Commander Hill, dated Feb. 3, 1937, U.S. Navy archives.
48. Letter and article (unpublished) from Lt. J. G. Johnson (who served aboard the *Itasca* on the 1936 exploratory mission to Howland) to *New York Times* editor, March 18, 1937. NA&SM Library, Amelia Earhart General file F0171300.
49. Dick Strippel, *Amelia Earhart: The Myth and the Reality* (New York: Exposition Press, 1972), p. 40.
50. Dwiggins, *Hollywood Pilot,* pp. 97–98.
51. AE to President Roosevelt, Jan. 8, 1937: Purdue, file VII A.1.
52. Letter from Assistant Secretary to the President, dated Jan. 12, 1936. Purdue, file VII A.1.
53. Aviation tapes, Sound Archives collection, Columbia University, New York, New York.
54. Sundry cuttings in AE's scrapbooks at Purdue. Specifically: *Cleveland Press;* New York *Daily Mirror,* Feb. 16, 1937.
55. Ibid.
56. Ibid.
57. Jacqueline Cochran, *The Stars at Noon* (London: Robert Hale Ltd., 1955), pp. 87–91.
58. AE to Muriel Morrissey, Jan. 31, 1937, Ref: 83–M69, SL.
59. Strippel, *Amelia Earhart.*
60. Sundry letters and internal memorandum in National Archives, Room 400, Washington, D.C., Jan. to May 1937, file: M1067 (Roll 48).
61. *Airpost Journal,* vol. 8, Feb. 8, 1937.
62. Blackwell *Sunday Tribune* (Oklahoma), Feb. 21, 1937, p. 1.
63. Putnam, *Soaring,* p. 212 (this incident also repeated in another context in article by GPP, unidentified news cutting in AE's scrapbooks at Purdue).

64. *Time* magazine, July 19, 1937, pp. 45–46.
65. Oakland *Tribune,* March 7, 1937.
66. Letter from Lt. Cmr. P. V. H. Weems; *Popular Aviation Magazine* (USA), May 1938.
67. Author's interview with Elgen and Marie Long, San Mateo, California, July 2, 1988.
68. Conversation between the late Clarence L. Schildhauer and Richard K. Smith in the early 1970s. Courtesy Richard K. Smith in a letter to the author dated October 9, 1987.
69. Ibid.
70. Dwiggins, *Hollywood Pilot,* p. 99.
71. "Story of 'Dream' Come True Told by Miss Earhart, Starting Flight," in New York *Herald Tribune,* March 18, 1937.
72. Cable from C. B. Allen (in Oakland) to New York *Herald Tribune,* July 3, 1937, 3 P.M., Purdue, file VIII D.4.
73. Unidentified article, New York *Herald Tribune,* Purdue.
74. Cable from GP to *Herald Tribune,* Purdue, file VII C.3.
75. Earhart, *Last Flight,* pp. 57–58.
76. Earhart, *Last Flight,* p. 63.
77. Dwiggins, *Hollywood Pilot,* p. 100.
78. Ibid, pp. 100–101.
79. Ibid, p. 102.
80. Memorandum (date obscured, circa April 1937) from Lt. Arnold E. True to Chief of Naval Operations; Ref: SECNAV 1315–1544, U.S. Naval archives.
81. *Time* magazine, March 29, 1937, p. 36.
82. Dwiggins, *Hollywood Pilot,* pp. 99, 103.
83. Eyewitness report of George Miller (civilian employee at Luke Field) and others, to the official board of inquiry, March 23, 1937, U.S. Navy archives, Exhibits C–F.
84. Official report from cmdr. of Hawaiian Air Depot, Luke Field to the official navy inquiry, U.S. Navy archives, Exhibits C–F.
85. *Time* magazine, March 29, 1937, p. 36.
86. Fred Goerner's speech at Amelia Earhart Symposium held at NA&SM Library, Smithsonian Institution, Washington, D.C., 1983. A full transcript of the symposium appeared in *Aviation Journal* (California) in various issues from April 1983 to May 1984. Mr. Goerner's speech appears in the Feb. 1984 issue, p. 5.
87. Another eyewitness, Pan Am's Captain "Lodi," said it looked to him as though the accident had been caused because she had neglected to lock the tail wheel.
88. Earhart, *Last Flight,* p. 71.
89. Putnam, *Soaring,* p. 261.
90. Ibid, p. 260.

91. Ibid.
92. *Advertiser* (Hawaii), March 20, 1937.
93. New York *Herald Tribune,* March 20, 1937; Backus, *Letters,* p. 213.
94. Cleveland *Press,* March 31, 1937; also syndicated to other newspapers.
95. New York *Herald Tribune,* April 7, 1937.

NINETEEN. 1937: MIAMI–LAE

1. Earhart, *Last Flight,* p. 73.
2. Letter and invoice in amount $1,086.10, dated May 13, 1937, National Archives, Ref: Y197.
3. Lockheed's bill was fourteen thousand dollars.
4. Earhart, *Last Flight,* p. 78. Among the donations from generous friends was a check from Richard Byrd for fifteen hundred dollars, exactly the amount Amelia had given him for the Antarctic expedition in 1929.
5. Called United Air Services Ltd., the business included airplane charter and a flying school.
6. Author's interview with Elgen and Marie Long, San Mateo, California, July 2, 1988.
7. Frederick Goerner related Manning's remarks in a speech given at the Amelia Earhart Symposium held at NA&SM Library, Smithsonian Institution, Washington, D.C., 1983. A full transcript of the symposium appeared in *Aviation Journal* (California) in various issues from April 1983 to May 1984. Mr. Goerner's speech appears in the Feb. 1984 issue, p. 5.
8. *World Flight* was the proposed title for Amelia's book. However, it was published posthumously under the title *Last Flight.*
9. Interview with Harry Bruno, November 16, 1960, at the Adventurer's Club; on tape at the Oral History Collection, Butler Library at Columbia University, New York.
10. Denison House Records, SL.
11. Author's interview with Margaret Putnam Lewis (GP's fourth and last wife), Los Angeles, California, June 29, 1988.
12. Author's interview with Albert Bresnik, Los Angeles, California, June 28, 1988.
13. Ibid.
14. Dwiggins, *Hollywood Pilot,* p. 104.
15. Ibid.
16. GPP to Admiral Leahy, May 8, 1937, U.S. Navy archives.
17. Joseph Gurr to Fred Goerner. Letter on file at NA&SM Library, Amelia Earhart General file: F0171300.
18. Ibid.
19. C. B. Allen, aviation correspondent of the *Herald Tribune* from 1923 to 1953. A longtime friend of George's, he had written many articles about

Amelia from the time of her 1928 flight and had answered the damaging Williams article following the crash in Hawaii.

20. New York *Herald Tribune,* July 8, 1937.
21. Letter to the author from Mrs. William Lee Reed, January 22, 1989. Amelia spent a few days aboard the yacht *Brownie* deep-sea fishing and relaxing with Mrs. Reed's parents, the Bruce McIntoshes.
22. Unidentified newspaper article by GPP (probably Sept. 1937), Scrapbook no.: 18, Special Collections Library, Purdue University, West Lafayette, Indiana.
23. Putnam, *Wide,* pp. 297–298.
24. Earhart, *Last Flight,* pp. 97–98.
25. Ibid, p. 100.
26. Ibid, p. 102.
27. Ibid, p. 110. Author's note: In giving the names of cities where Amelia stopped on her last flight I have used the names and spellings as they appeared in her log.
28. New York *Herald Tribune,* June 8, 1937.
29. Earhart, *Last Flight,* p. 129.
30. Ibid, p. 130.
31. Inflight note from Fred Noonan to AE, Purdue.
32. New York *Herald Tribune,* June 8, 1937.
33. Earhart, *Last Flight,* p. 152.
34. de Sibour to GPP, April 29, 1937, Purdue, file: VIII A.1.
35. Earhart, *Last Flight,* p. 180.
36. GPP to AOE, June 16, 1937, Ref: 83–M69, SL.
37. Cable from AE to GPP, June 16, 1937, Purdue, file VIII B.3.
38. Ibid., Purdue, file IX A.1; and cable from GPP to AE, Purdue, file IX A.2.
39. Dwiggins, *Hollywood Pilot,* p. 108.
40. Transcript of author's conversation with Mr. Gore Vidal, January 21, 1988. See also Gore Vidal, *Armageddon* (London: Andre Deutsch, 1987), pp. 25–29.
41. The original pages of Amelia's informal log are held at Purdue, file VIII B.
42. Putnam, *Wide,* p. 292.
43. Cables from AE to GP, Purdue, file VIII B.
44. Earhart, *Last Flight,* p. 195.
45. Ibid, p. 197.
46. Ibid, pp. 211–212; see also Morrissey and Osborne, *Amelia,* pp. 220–224.
47. Earhart, *Last Flight,* pp. 212–213.
48. Author's interview with Elgen and Marie Long.
49. Ibid.
50. Earhart, *Last Flight,* p. 217.
51. Ibid, p. 222.
52. Amelia's bracelet was subsequently donated to the Ninety-Nines and is held

at their headquarters in Oklahoma City as part of their extensive Amelia Earhart collection.

53. Report by Francis X. Holbrook, NA&SM Library, Amelia Earhart General file: F0171300.
54. Cable from AE to *Herald Tribune* offices, New York, dated June 31, 1937, Purdue, file VIII B.2.
55. Earhart, *Last Flight*, pp. 225–226.
56. Ibid, p. 102.
57. Cable from AE to GPP, dated June 30, 1937, Purdue, file VIII B.4.
58. Transcript of author's conversation with Mr. Gore Vidal, January 21, 1988. See also Vidal, *Armageddon*, pp. 25–29.

    Because of the source, I have given this suggestion of an early menopause considerable attention in my researches. I have now discounted it for two reasons:

    1. Amelia was only thirty-nine years old; this is not only disagreeably early but most unlikely, and George would surely have known about it, yet he told no one, not even his family, subsequent wives, or closest friends.

    2. It is doubtful that Amelia, liberated as she was, given the mores of 1937, would have found it easy to discuss such a matter with a male friend.

59. Ann Holtgren Pellegreno, *World Flight* (Ames, Iowa: Iowa State University Press, 1971), p. 144.
60. Author's interview with Elgen and Marie Long.
61. *Itasca* report, p. 27, U.S. Navy archives, Washington, D.C.
62. Ibid, p. 29.
63. Ibid, p. 9.
64. Cable from de Rabaul to AE at Lae, undated, Purdue, file VIII I.6.
65. It was Noonan who specified the navigational equipment for the first *Pan American Clipper* services in 1935—a choice not made because he necessarily considered one instrument more superior to another but by the fact that the equipment he recommended, he "had used extensively . . . and [it] had been proven satisfactory." The following is an extract from a letter from Fred Noonan to Commander P. V. H. Weems (founder of the Weems School of Navigation in Maryland) May 11, 1938. I have quoted it at length because it reveals Noonan's working methods.

    . . . for instance parallel rulers versus protractors—and I suspect that plain prejudice which actuates so many of us, carried some weight. . . . parallel rulers, where room permits their use, are more satisfactory for rapid plotting of long range Direction Finding bearings . . . those carried were of the Captain Fields Improved type—graduated in degrees—and consequently the greatest objection to their use in aircraft, namely creeping when referring to compass roses, was removed.

    . . . Time pieces carried were a Longines Civil Time Chronometer and Longines second setting watch. The latter was set to correct GCT [Greenwich Civil Time. Same as Greenwich Mean Time (GMT), the base time at Greenwich, London, from which all other world times are taken], at all times by checking with the chronometer. Two sextants were carried, a pioneer bubble octant and a mariner's sextant. The former was used for all sights; the latter as a preventer. I also carried a Dalton Mark VII Navigational Computer, which I find a great convenience.

. . . fixes were determined entirely by stellar observations at night. These fixes were more reliable than would be possible by crossing a line of position with a Direction Finding bearing, due to the amount of error which would be introduced by even a small angular error in the long range Direction Finding bearings. By day, having only the single heavenly body for determining the lines of position, we did not cross the bearings, however during daylight hours we were nearer the radio stations and consequently the error introduced was considerably reduced.

The accuracy of fixes was very gratifying. By that an accuracy of approximately ten miles is implied. My experience is that such a degree of accuracy is about the average one might expect in aerial navigation. . . .

The greatest difficulty is, of course, the determination of drift angle. We carried smoke bombs and water flares for this purpose [these were not entirely satisfactory, due to cloud] and consequently the difference between "no wind" positions and fixes established by observation were utilized, entirely for determination of drift angle, and, of course, wind direction, and velocity for laying new courses. However [where sudden wind shifts could be expected] reliance would necessarily have to be placed on Direction Finding bearings despite their lack of extreme accuracy.

In addition to the actual navigation I maintained a very detailed log . . . in addition to recording courses, variation, deviation, track made good, indicated and true air speeds etc, a complete meteorological record was kept. As you may imagine, each hour represented 60 very busy minutes.

I consider the development of the Greenwich Hour Angle the greatest contribution to the science of Navigation . . . and have used it exclusively since first published in the Air Almanac. The second-setting watch runs it a close second as a time saver and an aid tending to minimize errors. . . . I suppose you wonder which method I use for computation of observations. I use Dreisonstok exclusively. Probably another prejudice but I have used it since it first became available in 1927 or 1928 and still prefer it.

66. New York *Herald Tribune,* July 3, 1937, p. 1.
67. Report by J. A. Collopy (District Superintendent of Civil Aviation at Lae), Aug. 28, 1937. File WF2 "Search" No: 9, SL.
68. Cable, File WF2 "Weather," SL.

Notes

1. The international date line referred to is the 180th meridian.

     The U.S. Navy and Coast Guard subdivide hourly time zones into half hours and it is this "ship's time" that is referred to as local time at Howland in all logs and reports used in this chapter; *Itasca* log: reel C, U.S. Navy archives, microfilm file on Amelia Earhart.

2. Pellegreno, *World Flight*, p. 144; also Vincent Loomis, *Amelia Earhart* (New York: Random House, 1985), p. 11.

3. Report by J. A. Collopy, dated Aug. 28, 1937, copies at Purdue, SL, and Smithsonian.

4. Balfour was later to claim to the writer Vincent Loomis that Amelia had asked him to go along with her as radio operator. This seems extraordinary when she had stripped the plane of every item of personal luggage, every slip of paper, and had even discarded safety equipment in order to carry a greater fuel load.

5. All distances quoted for this flight have been checked by computer at the Royal Geographic Society, London, using verified coordinates; they do not necessarily agree with contemporary assessments of distances between points, some of which have proved to be incorrect.

6. British Earhart researcher Roy Nesbit examined the meterological records for Nauru and the British Gilbert and Ellice Islands for July 2, 1937, which are held at the National Meteorological Archives, Bracknell, Berkshire; and he discovered that winds at a "medium height" were 25 mph from due east. This also equates to reports in the *Itasca* log that winds were in the first sector of the flight were "stronger than forecast."

7. Letter from Harry Balfour to Dr. Robert Townley, Dec. 31, 1969. However, a report by Paul Rafford states that Balfour told him he had been unable to pass the met report to AE, which gave 25 mph head winds. Both reports are in NA&SM Library archives at the Smithsonian Institution, Washington, D.C.

8. *Itasca* radio transcripts report, June 30, 1937, p. 32, National Archives, Washington, D.C. Ref: 8018–2200.

9. Note from Captain Blakeslee to Peter Stevenson, May 24, 1988, given to the author by Mr. Stevenson.

10. Official report by the Commander of *Itasca*, page 2 "Known Facts" (number 17). U.S. Navy archives; also, similar report by captain of the U.S.S. *Lexington*, p. 2, National Archives, Washington, D.C.

11. Letter from T. H. Cude (director of police at Nauru in 1937) to Francis X. Holbrook, NA&SM Library, Amelia Earhart General file: 0171300.

12. Figures provided by computer at the Royal Geographical Society, London.

13. Note from Captain Blakeslee to Mr. Pete Stevenson, May 24, 1988, given to the author by Mr. Stevenson.

14. *Itasca's* log.
15. Vincent E. Loomis with Jeffrey Ethell, *Amelia Earhart: The Final Story* (New York: Random House, 1985).
16. Ibid—see also Appendix A.
17. All radio communications between Amelia Earhart and *Itasca* are taken directly from the *Itasca's* radio log and from the official report of the incident made by *Itasca's* captain, Commander Warner Thompson. Detailed extracts from this log will be found in Appendix C. The original documents are freely available for researchers at the National Archives Bldg., and on Microfilm Reels 1–5 of the U.S.N. file on Amelia Earhart, and at the office of U.S. Coast Guard—all in Washington, D.C.
18. *Itasca* report on Earhart search, p. 36.
19. *Itasca* radio log, p. 42.
20. *Itasca* report, p. 35.
21. That final message, interpreted in the *Itasca* report appears in the log as follows:

> KHAQQ TO ITASCA WE ARE ON LINE 157 337 WL REPT MSG WE WILL REPT N ES S THIS ON 6210 KCS WAIT 3105/A3 AS (?) KHAQQ TSMISION "WE ARE RUNNING ON LINE LSNIN 6210 KCS."

22. Pellegreno, *World Flight.*
23. In June/July 1967 on the thirtieth anniversary of Amelia's last flight, a commemorative round-the-world flight was made in a standard Lockheed Electra—model 10. It was piloted by Ann Holtgren Pellegreno, copiloted by Bill Payne, and navigated by Bill Polhemus. They found difficulty in locating Howland even with the vastly superior communication technology available to them. In ideal conditions they got their first glimpse of the island at "ten or twelve miles away" and reported that it looked like a small cloud or shadow. Ms. Pellegreno recorded the story of this flight in her book *World Flight* (p. 162).
24. *Itasca* report, pp. 43, 49.
25. Elgen and Marie Long have already conducted several impressive underwater studies in conjunction with Hawaiian-based oceanographic laboratories. It is their intention to launch a massive underwater search/survey for the Electra, using submarines of the type used to locate the *Titanic.* Author interview with Elgen and Marie Long, San Mateo, California, July 2, 1987.
26. Based on the Longs' theory, the Electra lies at a depth of 16,800 feet.
27. Roy Nesbit, "What Did Happen to Amelia Earhart?" in *Aeroplane Monthly*, London, Jan. and Feb. 1989.
28. Pellegreno, *World Flight.*
29. *Itasca* radio log, p. 45.
30. August 1967; air accident reports FAA archives. None of the ten Lockheed Electra aircraft involved in the reported sea landings broke up as a result

of the landing. This incident reported in Pellegreno, *World Flight* (see "The Earhart Controversy").

TWENTY-ONE. 1937–1939

1. New York *Herald Tribune,* July 4, 1937, p. 1.
2. *Itasca* report, National Archives, Washington, D.C., p. 48.
3. New York *Herald Tribune,* July 3, 1937.
4. Although both men were using radios from home, as amateurs, both were in fact skilled professional radio operators.
5. *Itasca* report, p. 104. Other messages, Thompson maintained, were "criminally false transmissions."
6. San Francisco *Chronicle,* July 6, 1937, p. 1.
7. Letter from Joseph H. Gurr to author Fred Goerner, dated May 3, 1982, NA&SM Library, Smithsonian Institution, Washington, D.C., Amelia Earhart General file: F0171300. Note that Mantz was not aware of all the work Gurr had carried out. Mantz assumed that the only aerial available for transmissions on 500 kcs. was the trailing one that Amelia had "left behind because she felt it 'a nuisance.'" In fact, it seems possible that because Gurr "had fitted a loading coil and resonated the top antenna system" with wire antennae to the two tail surfaces that Amelia, at least, believed this new arrangement worked equally well and therefore left the trailing antennae because it seemed surplus to requirements.
8. The U.S.S. *Swan* was two hundred miles from Howland, waiting to act as plane guard on the Howland–Honolulu leg. See the Washington *Post,* July 3, 1937.
9. San Francisco *Chronicle* July 5, 1937, p. 1.
10. *Itasca* report, p. 57.
11. New York *Herald Tribune,* July 3, 1937, p. 1.
12. *Time* magazine, July 12, 1937.
13. *The New York Times,* July 8, 1937.
14. Letter to Secretary of Navy Department from W. A. Levett, acting officer in-charge, Beru, Gilbert Islands, U.S. Navy archives: 361030.
15. New York *Herald Tribune* July 7, 1937, p. 1.
16. *Itasca* report, p. 76.
17. Ibid.
18. San Francisco *Chronicle,* July 9, 1937, p. 1.
19. Cable from Admiral Leahy to GP, undated, Special Collections Library, Purdue University, West Lafayette, Indiana, file X B.3.
20. *Itasca* report, p. 88.
21. Eleanor Roosevelt, "My Day," in New York *Telegraph,* July 7, 1937.
22. Memo from FDR to Marvin McIntyre, July 20, 1937, Franklin D. Roosevelt Library, Hyde Park, New York.

23. GP to Marvin McIntyre, July 31, 1937, Franklin D. Roosevelt Library, and Purdue, file: X B.7.

24. Letter from Joseph H. Gurr to author Fred Goerner, May 3, 1982, NA&SM Library, Amelia Earhart General file: F1071300. Belief in the theory of the buoyancy of metal airplanes was dispelled during World War II when a great number of all-metal airplanes ditched and sank almost immediately.

25. Cochran, *The Stars*, pp. 90–91.

26. Ibid.

27. This episode reported in *The Stars at Noon* differs from Miss Cochran's verbal statements to an interviewer in tapes held in Columbia University's Sound Archive library. There she states that she was "on a ship on the way to Europe when Amelia went missing."

Her claims that she had never heard the name *Itasca* are also surprising since it had been publicized that the *Itasca* would stand by for radio contact during the first planned attempt on world flight and that for three weeks the newspapers had been carrying reports that *Itasca* was standing by at Howland to meet Amelia. It seems highly unlikely that she could have missed all these reports of her friend's flight, in which she surely must have been interested.

28. Cable from GP to Daniel Roper, dated July 23, 1937, U.S. Navy Archives.

29. Telegram from Gray to American Embassy, July 30, 1937, Franklin D. Roosevelt Library, Hyde Park, New York.

30. *The New York Times*, July 25, 1937.

31. National Archives, Washington, D.C., file A4-5 (5).

32. Ibid.

33. Welles to McIntyre, Aug. 5, 1937, Franklin D. Roosevelt Library.

34. Memo sent from National Geographic Society to GP, dated Sept. 7, 1937, SL.

35. Ibid.

36. Letter from GP to AOE, July 29, 1937, Ref: 83–M64, SL.

37. Cable signed "Gray" to American Embassy, London, Aug. 2, 1937, Purdue.

38. National Archives, file A4-5(5) 361030-3.

39. Ibid.

40. National Archives, file A4-5(5) 361030-5.

41. GP to AOE, May 9, 1939, Ref: 83–M69, SL.

42. GP to AOE, Dec. 3, 1940, Ref: 83–M69, SL.

43. GP to AOE, May 9, 1939, Ref: 83–M69, SL.

44. Author's interview with Mr. Albert Bresnik, Los Angeles, California, July 1988.

45. Original page of manuscript, received from Amelia by George after her disappearance, Purdue.

46. Earhart, *Last Flight*, p. 108.

47. Janet Mabie to AOE, Aug. 19, 1939; Janet Mabie to AOE, July 28, 1941, Ref: 83–M69, Box 2, File 61, SL.
48. *The New York Times*, Oct. 8, 9, 1937, p. 21.
49. *The New York Times*, Aug. 27, 1937.
50. *The New York Times*, Aug. 5, 1937, p. 25; Aug. 6, 1937, p. 18.
51. GP to Benigua Green, Oct. 28, 1937, Ref: 83–M69, SL.
52. "Amelia Earhart Putnam," Superior Court, Los Angeles, California, probate file 181709.
53. Note that after this first sentence, the document had been cut and pasted together, obviously to edit material that was either irrelevant to this trip or perhaps contained material too personal to be included. In an article written by GP in an unidentified newspaper (clipping in Purdue scrapbook "Amelia Always Held Self Responsible for Flights"), he did include part of the missing message: "However, I believe my equipment is the best available."
54. Special Collections Library, Purdue.
55. GP to AOE, Dec. 24, 1937, Ref: 83–M69, SL.
56. Letter to the author from Robert E. Lee, Dec. 1987.
57. Janet Mabie to AOE, July 28, 1941, Ref: 83–M69, Box 2, File 61, SL.
58. Records of the Amelia Earhart Foundation, Ref: 83–M69, file "Dimity," SL.
59. GP to AOE, May 20, 1939, Ref: 83–M69, SL.
60. "The Bronco That Would Not Be Broken," Putnam, *Soaring*, p. 23.
61. GP to Muriel Morrissey, Sept. 15, 1938, Ref: 78/M147, SL.
62. Putnam, *Soaring*, p. 63.
63. GP to AOE, Sept. 28, 1938, Ref: 83–M69, SL.
64. GP to Admiral William D. Leahy, National Archive, file A4–5(5).
65. National Archives, file A4–5(5).
66. GP to AOE, Dec. 1, 1938, Ref: 83–M69, SL.
67. Last will and testament of Amelia Earhart Putnam; made in New York, April 5, 1932, and originally filed with Superior Court, Los Angeles, California, Jan. 5, 1939; probate file 181709.
68. Ibid.

At the first appraisal the Estate was valued as follows:

	$
Cash in Fifth Ave. Bank, NY	8,190
Property at Valley Spring Lane	21,000
Tract of land and property inhabited by Helen Earhart	1,500
2 Terraplane automobiles	1,190
1 Cord automobile	900
1 Electric Power Company bond	962
Promissory note from Paul Mantz	4,973

Furniture and effects	350
Contract regarding sale of name	
Amelia Earhart for promotional purposes	850
Outstanding amount due from publishers	
for *The Fun of It*	1,000
50% interest in *Last Flight*	
appraised at	5,000
Clothing including two fur coats	900
Jewelry	75
Total	46,890
Additions at later date:	$ 2,790
Film rights, etc.	9,429
Total	59,109

69. Amy had been injured in a car accident in the previous year.
70. The house at Rye was actually sold in December 1938. Reported in *The New York Times,* Jan. 6, 1939, p. 37.
71. GP to AOE, May 9, 1939, Ref: 83–M69, SL.
72. Janet Mabie to AOE, Aug. 4, 1939, Ref: 83–M69, Box 2, File 61, SL.
73. Letter to the author from Robert E. Lee, Dec. 1987.
74. *Stunt Girl* and *Hollywood Doctor.*
75. Author's interview with Charles "Cap" Palmer, Los Angeles, California, June 1988.
76. Jerome Lawrence: playwright/director, who in collaboration with Robert E. Lee created outstanding American theater productions: *Inherit the Wind, The Night Thoreau Spent in Jail, Auntie Mame,* etc.
77. Robert E. Lee: see previous citation. Mr. Lee was also cofounder of the Armed Forces Radio Service and the American Playwrights Theatre.
78. Letter to the author from Robert E. Lee, Dec. 1987.
79. Ibid.
80. Author's interview with Jean-Marie Asp, San Diego, California, June 27, 1988.
81. Ibid.
82. Author's interview with Muriel E. Morrissey, West Medford, Massachusetts, June 1987.
83. Author's interview with Jean-Marie Asp.
84. "Amelia Earhart Putnam," Superior Court, Los Angeles, California, probate file 181709.
85. *The New York Times,* January 6, 1939, p. 4; author's interviews with Jean-Marie Asp and Muriel Morrissey; Superior Court, Los Angeles, California, probate file 181709.
86. GP to AOE, May 4, 1939, Ref: 83–M69, SL.
87. Ibid.
88. Author's interview with Charles "Cap" Palmer.

Notes

89. Los Angeles *Times,* also Los Angeles *Examiner,* April 20, 1939.
90. *The New York Times,* April 21, 1939.
91. GP to AOE, May 15, 1939, Ref: 83–M69, SL.

TWENTY-TWO. 1939–1950

1. Author's interview with Jean-Marie Asp, San Diego, California, June 27, 1988.
2. Ibid.
3. Paul Mantz to AOE, March 22, 1940, Ref: 83–M69, SL.
4. GP to Elmer Dimity, April 6, 1940, Ref: 83–M69, SL.
5. GPP to AOE, April 19, 1940, Ref: 83–M69, SL.
6. Ibid.
7. Paul Mantz file, Ref: 83–M69, SL.
8. Elmer Dimity to AOE, May 20, 1940, Ref: 83–M69, SL.
9. Paul Mantz to AOE, May 20, 1940, Ref: 83–M69, SL.
10. Captain Irving to Elmer Dimity, June 4, 1940, Ref: 83–M69, file "Dimity," SL.
11. Letter from Bessie M. Young to E. H. Dimity, Aug. 4, 1940, Ref: 83–M69, SL.
12. Letters to AOE from Bessie Young, March 29, 1940, Ref: 83–M69, SL.
13. Letters to AOE from William C. Hollister, March 1941, Ref: 83–M69, SL.
14. AOE to William C. Hollister, March 23, 1941, Ref: 83–M69, SL.
15. Josephine Berger died of cancer in New York, March 1941.
16. Author's interview with Margaret "Peg" Putnam Lewis, Los Angeles, California, June 29, 1988.
17. Author's interview with Jean-Marie Asp.
18. Author's interview with Charles "Cap" Palmer, Los Angeles, California, June 1988.
19. Author's interview with Jean-Marie Asp.
20. Author's interview with David Binney Putnam, Fort Pierce, Florida, June 24, 1988.
21. Author's interview with Charles "Cap" Palmer.
22. Elizabeth Hyatt Gregory Collection, University of California at Los Angeles, Special Collections Library, Box 6101, L615.
23. McCoy was the writer of many screenplays. He also wrote the novel *They Shoot Horses, Don't They?*
24. The Academy of Motion Picture Arts and Sciences; RKO; and motion picture subject files.
25. Letter to the author from Charles "Cap" Palmer, Feb. 15, 1989.
26. Ibid.
27. AOE told reporters: "Amelia told me many things, but there were some

things she said she could not tell me. I am convinced she was on some sort of government mission . . . and died in Japan." *The New York Times,* July 25, 1949, p. 17.

George was astonished at Amy's statement, dismissing it as "nonsense." Muriel also disassociated herself from Amy's line of thinking, having received personal assurances from Eleanor Roosevelt that Amelia had not been involved in any clandestine arrangement to spy.

28. U.S. Army diploma, dated Oct. 17, 1942, in possession of Mrs. Margaret Putnam Lewis.
29. Author's interview with David Binney Putnam.
30. Colonel Harvey H. Holland (Air Corps) to GPP, March 9, 1943, letter in possession of Mrs. Margaret Putnam Lewis.
31. Author's interview with Charles "Cap" Palmer.
32. GPP to Joseph Henry Jackson, undated, University of California at Berkeley, Special Collections Library.
33. Author's interview with Jean-Marie Asp. She also stated, "I always hoped, indeed thought, that we *would* get together again. . . . I never remarried until after I heard that GP had remarried. . . ."
34. Letter to the author and enclosure entitled "Reminiscences of GP," from Robert E. Lee, dated Aug. 6, 1988.
35. Author's interview with Margaret Putnam Lewis and subsequent letters from her to the author.
36. Author's interview with David Binney Putnam.
37. Author's interview with Margaret Putnam Lewis.
38. George Palmer Putnam, *Up in Our Country* (New York: Duell, Sloan & Pearce, 1950), pp. 17–18. This was George Putnam's last book and was published, posthumously, in 1950. Hereafter referred to as *Up.*
39. Author's interview with Charles "Cap" Palmer.
40. Ibid.
41. Putnam, *Up,* p. 19.
42. Divorce decree, March 2, 1945. Courtesy of Jean-Marie Asp.
43. Author's interview with Charles "Cap" Palmer.
44. Author's interview with Margaret Putnam Lewis.
45. Ibid.
46. GPP to Margaret "Peg" Putnam, undated. Courtesy of Margaret Putnam Lewis.
47. Author's interview with Margaret Putnam Lewis.
48. GPP to Margaret "Peg" Putnam, undated. Courtesy of Margaret Putnam Lewis.
49. The fire at Rye in November 1934; also fire at the Whitney Portal lodge the year after George's death, which destroyed the bulk of his own and Amelia's private papers.
50. Courtesy of Margaret Putnam Lewis.
51. Author's interview with Margaret Putnam Lewis.

52. Ibid.
53. Letter to the author and enclosure entitled "Reminiscences of GP," from Robert E. Lee, dated Aug. 6, 1988.
54. Author's interview with David Binney Putnam.
55. Putnam, *Up*.
56. GPP to Margaret "Peg" Putnam. Courtesy of Margaret Putnam Lewis.
57. Author's interview with Charles "Cap" Palmer.
58. Letter to the author from Helen Ogston, Oct. 1988.
59. GPP to Isaiah Bowman, Johns Hopkins University Library, Baltimore, Maryland, Bowman files.
60. Lawrence M. Gould to Margaret Putnam. Courtesy of Margaret Putnam Lewis.
61. Rockwell Kent to Margaret Putnam. Courtesy of Margaret Putnam Lewis.
62. George Agnew Chamberlain to Margaret Putnam. Courtesy of Margaret Putnam Lewis.
63. Author's interview with Charles "Cap" Palmer.
64. Letter to the author and enclosure entitled "Reminiscences of GP," from Robert E. Lee, dated Aug. 6, 1988.
65. Ibid.

APPENDIX A

1. Considerable confusion has arisen in reports of Amelia's last flight because so many time factors were involved. Greenwich Mean Time has been used as the definitive time for Amelia's flight from Lae to Howland, with a conversion to local time at Lae, where appropriate, and to ship's time at Howland Island. The U.S. Navy and Coast Guard subdivide hourly time zones into half hours and it is this "ship's time" that is referred to as local time in all ship's logs and reports used as source material for Chapter Twenty and in the appendices to this book.
2. J. Collopy report.
3. *Itasca* report, page 2 "Known Facts," No: 17; confirmation of this also appeared in the log of the U.S.S. *Lexington*.
4. Cable from Alfred M. Doyle (U.S. consul in Sydney, Australia, to U.S. State Department, National Archives).

APPENDIX B

1. On Amelia's charts, the distance between Lae and Howland was given as 2,556. This was correct information if using the coordinates used by Clarence Williams. These, however, were found to be incorrect, as explained later in this appendix.

2. Unless otherwise stated, all fuel measurements are U.S. gallons. See Collopy report *Amelia Earhart*, dated Aug. 28, 1937, to Secretary Civil Aviation Board: "One tank contained only 50 gallons of its total capacity of 100 gallons. . . ." Note: There was no 100-gallon tank on the Electra but there were two wing tanks, each of which held 102 gallons; Special Collections Library, Purdue University, West Lafayette, Illinois, file X B.9.

3. Author's interview with Elgen and Marie Long, San Mateo, California, July 2, 1987.

4. *Daily Telegraph*, Sydney, Australia, July 6, 1937, p. 1; also see similar reports in other papers published in Australia, New Zealand, and New Guinea.

5. Unidentified news cutting, believed to be *Herald Tribune*, March 20, 1937.

6. Cable from GP to Jacques de Sibour, Feb. 13, 1937, Public Record Office, Kew, England, Ref: AVIA2/1082.

7. Author Dick Strippel's examination of the so-called Earhart Mystery *Amelia Earhart: The Myth and the Reality* (hereafter referred to as *Amelia Earhart*) used calculations from Lockheed, statements by Paul Mantz, and the expertise of Bill Polhemus (who flew as navigator on a duplicated commemorative flight to Howland in a standard Lockheed 10 in 1967) to make these points. My own research bears out his statements.
   See also Pellegreno, *World Flight*.

8. Strippel, *Amelia Earhart*, p. 116.

9. Ibid.

10. Letter from Amelia Earhart to Sir Francis Shelmerdine, dated Feb. 13, 1937, Public Record Office, Kew, London, Ref: AVIA2/1082.

11. Fuel notes and other unidentified notes, Purdue.

12. Figures taken from information contained in Dick Strippel's article in Lockheed house magazine *Horizons* by Roy Blay, May 1988 issue, pp. 23–36; research notes from SL and Purdue.

13. All fuel measures quoted here are U.S. gallons.

14. On a Mercator projection chart, a compass bearing (rhumb line) plots as a straight line, intersecting each meridian at the same angle. A great circle arc intersects each meridian at a different angle and appears longer but is actually the shortest distance around the earth's spere. The great circle is the route followed by any radio signal or electromagnetic propagation, and the visual line of sight is also a great circle arc.

15. Fred Noonan wrote several articles on navigation; see also his letter to Weems, quoted at length in the notes to Chapter Nineteen, note 64.

16. Sir Francis Chichester pioneered this system of "find the island." It is described fully in his book *The Lonely Sea and the Sky* (London: Hodder and Stoughton, 1964). The extract used here appears on pp. 119–121.

17. Ibid, pp. 108–141.

18. Ibid.

19. An arc from zenith in sky to horizon: An angle is measured to this from a meridian.

20. Line of position: 157–337 ran from north, northwest to south, southeast (through Howland), assuming Noonan's dead-reckoning position north of the island was accurate.

21. I am indebted to the staff (especially Mr. Tom De Clare) in the U.S. Hydrographer's Archives office, Madison Building, Library of Congress, Washington, D.C., for this information. Correct coordinates for Howland first appeared in *Lippincott's* in the 1941 edition.

22. *Itasca* report, National Archives, Washington, D.C., p. 106.

23. Morrissey and Osborne, *Amelia*.

24. *Itasca* radio log, June 19, 1937, National Archives, p. 3.

25. *Itasca* radio log, June 12, 1937, p. 3.

26. *Itasca* radio log, June 23, 1937, pp. 10, 17.

27. *Itasca* radio log, June 25, 1937, p. 21.

28. Cable from Amelia Earhart in Lae, to Richard Black aboard *Itasca*, via Radio Manila, June 27, 1937, *Itasca* log, p. 23.

29. *Itasca* radio log, June 29, 1937, p. 29.

30. *Itasca* report, p. 25.

31. U.S. Navy archives, Earhart Files, Microfilm reel B SC A21–5(25) Nav 327.

32. Report by Lt. D. Cooper of army air corps, dated July 27, 1937. This report was declassified in 1977.

33. *Itasca* report, pp. 104–106.

34. Transcript of Earhart Symposium held at NA&SM Library, Smithsonian Institution, Washington, D.C., in 1983.

35. Department of Commerce Aircraft Inspection Report—FAA.

36. Oakland *Herald Tribune*, March 17, 1937.

APPENDIX C

1. There are various sources for this, but specifically see books by Goerner; Loomis; and Pellegreno in Selected Reading. Original statements by Elieu stated only that a woman flyer landed, but later the woman seems to have acquired a male companion.

2. *American Weekly*, Sept. 10, 1944, p. 9, as well as other sources. The album seems to have been lost after this story was released, probably taken by a souvenir hunter, but many early researchers claimed that the album was confiscated by the government as part of their cover-up of the *real* story.

3. Author's interview with Charles "Cap" Palmer and Jean-Marie Asp, California, June 1988.

4. Thomas E. Devine has now written a book, *Eyewitness: The Amelia Earhart*

Incident (Frederick, Colorado: Renaissance House, 1988). I have not had the opportunity to read *Eyewitness* before finishing *Sound of Wings*.

5. Cochran, *The Stars*, p. 160.

6. Ibid, pp. 90–91.

7. Paul Briand, *Daughter of the Sky* (New York: Duell, Sloan & Pearce, 1960), p. 214.

8. This paragraph is not, however, intended to denigrate a fine book. It remains one of the most readable on the subject.

9. Letter from Billy Burks to Col. John Miller, U.S. Marine Corps, March 27, 1983, NA&SM Library, Smithsonian Institution, Washington, D.C.

10. Joe Davidson, *Amelia Earhart Returns from Saipan* (Canton, Ohio: Davidson Publishing Company, 1969). See also letter from Florence Kothera, NA&SM Library.

11. Joe Klaas, *Amelia Earhart Lives* (New York: McGraw Hill, 1970), pp. 133–149.

12. Eleanor Roosevelt to Muriel Morrissey, July 14, 1961, SL. Letter to Mantz is published in *Hollywood Pilot* by Don Dwiggins.

13. Fred Goerner's speech during Amelia Earhart Symposium in 1983 at the Smithsonian Institution, Washington, D.C., and his article "In Search of Amelia Earhart," in *Unsolved*, Vol. 2, Issue 18, 1984 (London: Orbis).

Selected Reading

Adams, Jean, and Kimball, Margaret. *Heroines of the Sky.* New York: Doubleday, 1942.

Allen, Frederick Lewis. *Only Yesterday.* New York: Harper & Brothers, 1931.

Babington-Smith, Constance. *Amy Johnson.* London: Collins, 1967.

Backus, Jean. *Letters from Amelia.* Boston: Beacon Press, 1982.

Balchen, Bernt. *Come North with Me.* New York: E. P. Dutton, 1958.

Batten, Jean. *My Life.* London: Harrap, 1938.

Beaty, D. *The Water Jump.* London: Secker & Warburg, 1976.

Bilstein, Roger E. *Flight in America 1900–1983.* Baltimore: Johns Hopkins University Press, 1983.

Boase, Wendy. *The Sky's the Limit.* London: Macmillan, 1979.

Bostok, Peter. *The Great Atlantic Air Race.* London: Dent, 1970.

Briand, Paul, Jr. *Daughter of the Sky.* New York: Duell, Sloan & Pearce, 1960.

Brooks-Pazmany, Kathleen. *United States Women in Aviation 1919–1929.* Washington, D.C.: Smithsonian, 1983.

Bruno, Harry. *Wings Over America.* New York: Robert McBride & Co., 1944.

Burke, John. *Winged Legend—The Story of Amelia Earhart.* London: Arthur Barker, 1970.

Byrd, Richard E. *Skyward.* New York: G. P. Putnam's Sons, 1928.

Cadin, Martin. *Barnstorming.* New York: Duell, Sloan & Pearce, 1965.

Chadwick, Roxane. *Amelia Earhart—Aviation Pioneer.* Minneapolis: Lerner, 1987.

Chichester, Sir Francis. *The Lonely Sea and the Sky.* London: Hodder and Stoughton, 1964.

Cochran, Jacqueline. *The Stars at Noon.* London: Robert Hale, 1955.

Collins, Paul F. *Tales of an Old Air-Faring Man.* Stevens Point, Wisconsin: UWSP Foundation Press 1983.

Davidson, Joe. *Amelia Earhart Returns from Saipan.* Canton, Ohio: Davidson Publishing Company, 1972.

Davis, Burke. *Amelia Earhart.* New York: G. P. Putnam's Sons, 1972.

Davis, Kenneth. *The Hero: Charles A. Lindbergh and the American Dream.* New York: Doubleday, 1959.

De La Croiz, Robert. *They Flew the Atlantic.* New York: Muller, 1967.

De Leeuw, Adele Louise. *Story of Amelia Earhart.* New York: Grosset & Dunlap, 1955.

Dixon, Charles. *Conquest of the Atlantic by Air.* Philadelphia: Lippincott, 1931.

Dwiggins, Don. *Barnstormers.* Summit, Pennsylvania: Tab, 1986.

————. *Hollywood Pilot.* New York: Doubleday, 1967.

————. *Flying Daredevils of the Roaring Twenties.* London: Arthur Barker, 1969.

Earhart, Amelia. *20 Hrs. 40 Min.* New York: G. P. Putnam's Sons, 1929.

————. *The Fun of It.* New York: Brewer, Warren and Putnam, 1932.

————. *Last Flight.* New York: Harcourt Brace and Company, 1937; London: Harrap, 1938.

Farmer, James H. *Celluloid Wings.* Summit, Pennsylvania: Tab, 1986.

Ferris, Helen J. *Five Girls Who Dared.* New York: Macmillan, 1931.

Ford, Corey. *The Time of Laughter.* Boston: Little, Brown, 1967.

Frazer, Chelsea. *Famous American Flyers.* New York: T. Y. Crowell, 1942.

Gallagher, Desmond. *Shooting Suns and Things.* Dublin, Ireland: Kingford Press, 1986.

Garst, Doris Shannon. *Amelia Earhart: Heroine of the Skies.* New York: Messner, 1950.

Gentry, Viola. *Hangar Flying.* Privately published in Chelmsford, Massachusetts, 1975.

Gilroy, Shirley Dobson. *Pilot in Pearls.* McLean, Virginia: Link Press, 1985.

Goerner, Fred. *The Search for Amelia Earhart.* New York: Doubleday, 1966.

Gower, Pauline. *Women with Wings.* London: John Long, 1938.

Gywynn-Jones, Terry. *Aviation's Magnificent Gamblers.* London: Orbis, 1986.

————. *The Air Racers.* London: Pelham Books, 1984.

Hawks, Frank M. *Once to Every Pilot.* New York: Stackpole, 1936.

————. *Speed.* New York: Brewer, Warren and Putnam, 1931.

Heath, Lady, and Murray, Stella Wolfe. *Women and Flying.* London: John Long, 1929.

Howe, Edward. *The Story of a Country Town.* New York: Holt, Rinehart & Winston, 1928.

Howe, James Moore. *Amelia Earhart: Kansas Girl.* New York: Bobbs Merrill, 1950.

Huxley, Gervase. *Both Hands.* London: Chatto & Windus, 1970.

Ireland, Norma Olin. *Index to Women of the World.* Westwood, Massachusetts: Faxon Company, 1970.

Jablonski, Edward. *Atlantic Fever.* New York: Macmillan, 1972.

————. *Ladybirds: Women in Aviation.* Los Angeles: Hawthorne Books, 1968.

Selected Reading

Jenkinson, Sir Anthony. *America Comes My Way.* New York: Publisher unknown, 1941.

Johnson, Amy. *Skyroads of the World.* London: Chambers, 1939.

———. *Myself When Young.* London: Muller, 1963.

Klaas, Joe. *Amelia Earhart Lives.* New York: McGraw-Hill, 1970.

Knaggs, Oliver. *Amelia Earhart: Her Last Flight.* Cape Town, South Africa: Timmins Publishers, 1983.

Lauwick, Herve. *Heroines of the Sky.* London: Muller, 1963.

Lindbergh, Anne Morrow. *North to the Orient.* New York: Harcourt Brace and Company, 1963.

———. *Bring Me a Unicorn.* London: Chatto & Windus, 1972.

———. *Hour of Gold—Hour of Lead.* London: Chatto & Windus, 1973.

———. *Locked Rooms and Open Doors.* London: Chatto & Windus, 1974.

———. *The Flower and the Nettle.* London: Chatto & Windus, 1976.

Lindbergh, Charles. *The Spirit of St. Louis.* New York: Charles Scribner's Sons, 1953.

Lomax, Judy. *Women of the Air.* New York: Dodd Mead, 1986.

Loomis, Vincent. *Amelia Earhart.* New York: Random House, 1985.

Mollison, Jim. *Playboy of the Air.* London: Michael Joseph, 1937.

———. *Death Cometh Soon or Late.* London: Hutchinson, 1932.

Mondley, David. *Women of the Air.* Houe, Sussex, England: Wayland Publisher, 1981.

Moolman, Valerie. *Women Aloft.* New York: Time-Life Books, 1981.

Morrissey, Muriel. *Courage Is the Price.* Wichita, Kansas: McCormick-Armstrong, 1963.

———. *Amelia Earhart.* Santa Barbara, California: Bellerophon, 1985.

———, and Osborne, Carol. *Amelia, My Courageous Sister.* Santa Clara, California: Osborne Publishers, 1988.

Mosley, Leonard. *Lindbergh: A Biography.* New York: Doubleday, 1976.

Nichols, Ruth. *Wings for Life.* Philadelphia: Lippincott, 1958.

Oakes, Claudia. *United States Women in Aviation 1929–39.* Washington, D.C.: Smithsonian Studies in Air and Space, 1978.

O'Neil, Paul. *Barnstormers and Speedkings.* New York: Time-Life Books, 1981.

Pellegreno, Ann Holtgren. *World Flight.* Ames, Iowa: Iowa University Press, 1971.

Plank, C. *Women with Wings.* Publishing details unknown.

Putnam, David Binney. *David Goes to Greenland.* New York: G. P. Putnam's Sons, 1922.

Putnam, George. *Soaring Wings.* New York: Harcourt Brace and Company; London: Harrap, 1939

———. *Wide Margins.* New York: Harcourt Brace and Company; London: Harrap, 1942.

———. *Up in Our Country.* New York: Duell, Sloan & Pearce, 1950.

Railey, Hilton Howell. *Touched with Madness*. New York: Carrick & Evans, 1938.

Rickenbacker, Eddie. *Rickenbacker*. London: Hutchinson, 1968.

Roseberry, C. R. *The Challenging Skies*. New York: Doubleday, 1966.

Ross, Walter. *The Last Hero*. New York: Manor Books, 1974.

Rowe, Percy. *The Great Atlantic Air Race*. London: Angus & Robertson, 1977.

Schoneberger, William A., and Sonnenburg, Paul. *California Wings*. Los Angeles: Windsor Publications, 1984.

Smith, Elinor. *Aviatrix*. New York: Harcourt Brace Jovanovich, 1981.

Southern, Neta Snook. *I Taught Amelia to Fly*. New York: Vantage Press, 1974.

St. John, Adela Rogers. *Some Are Born Great*. New York: Doubleday, 1974.

Strippel, Dick. *Amelia Earhart: The Myth and the Reality*. New York: Exposition Press, 1972.

Tate, Grover Ted. *The Lady Who Tamed Pegasus: The Story of Pancho Barnes*. Los Angeles: Maverick, 1984.

Thaden, Louise. *High Wide and Frightened*. New York: Stackpole Sons, 1938.

Underwood, John. *Madcaps, Millionaires and "Mose."* Glendale, California: Heritage Press, 1984.

Veca, Donna and Mazzio, Skip. *Just Plane Crazy*. Santa Clara, California: Osborne Publishers, 1988.

Vidal, Gore. *Armageddon*. London: Andre Deutsch, 1987.

Voisin, Gabriel. *Men, Women and 10,000 Kites*. London: G. P. Putnam's Sons, 1960.

Wykes, Alan. *Air Atlantic*. New York: David White, date unknown.

Index

A

Achilles, 294, 295
Acosta, Bert, 143
Across the World (Johnson), 90
Adams, Porter, 131
Aeronautic Airway, 49
Aero-News and Mechanics, 160
Aeroplane, The, 190
Albert, Eddie, 319
Alcock, John, 123, 185
Aldrin, Edwin, 178
Allen, C. B., 252, 260
Alstulund, Nora, 157, 160–161, 164, 168, 172
Altman, Anthony, 3
Altman, Catherine, 4
Altman, Louisa, 3–4
Altman, Philip, 3–4
Amelia Earhart Foundation, 304, 316–318
America, 86, 120, 125
American Girl, 94
Anderson, Judge, 165
André: The Record of a Tragic Adventure (G. P. Putnam), 163
Andrews, Roy Chapman, 205
Argles, Arthur, 112
Asosemena, Pablo, 66
Astor, Lady, 126, 128, 186
Atchison, David, 6
Autogiro. *See* Pitcairn PAC-a autogiro
Aviatrix (Smith), 139–140

Avro Avian, 127–128, 131, 135–137, 142, 148

B

Bailey, Lady, 186
Baker, Lee, 281
Balboa, General, 191
Balch, Earle, 159
Balchen, Bernt, 92–93, 96, 176–177, 179–182, 205
Balfour, Harry, 267, 277–280
Balis, Nancy, 232
Barnes, Peter, 45–46
Barnes, Ralph, 46
Bartlett, Bob, 81–85
Batten, Jean, 215
Beebe, William, 81–83, 205
Beech-Nut Packing Company, 170, 214
Believe It or Not (Ripley), 76
Belknap, Reginald K., 95
Bellanca, 140, 143
Bellarts, Leo G., 281–286
Bendix, Vincent, 229, 255
Bendix receiver, 288
Bennett, Floyd, 90, 96
Berger, Jo, 167, 256, 311, 319
Bingham, Hiram, 193, 200
Binney, Dorothy. *See* Putnam, Dorothy Binney
Birchall, Fred, 87
Black, Richard, 281, 284, 307, 312
Blakeslee, H. W., 279–280
Blixen, Bror Von, 98
Bobbed Hair (Twenty Authors), 78

Index

Index